Righteous Dopefiend

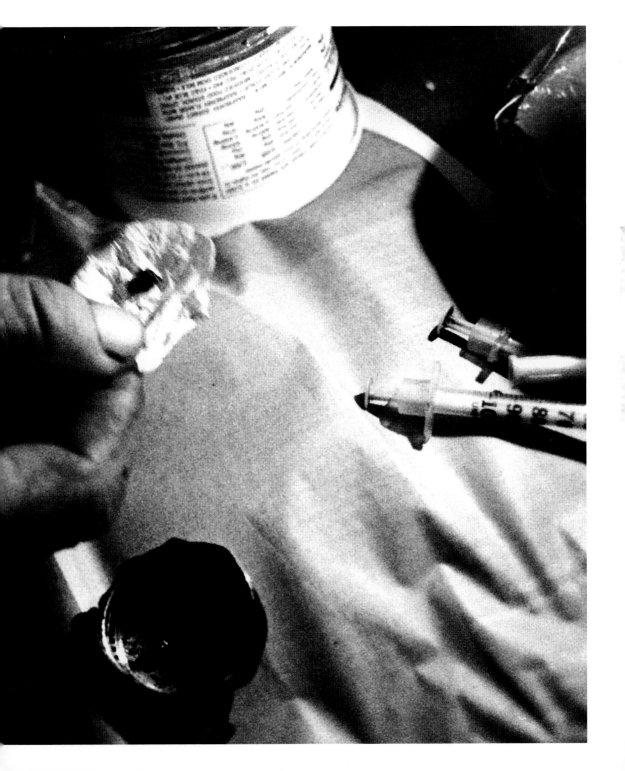

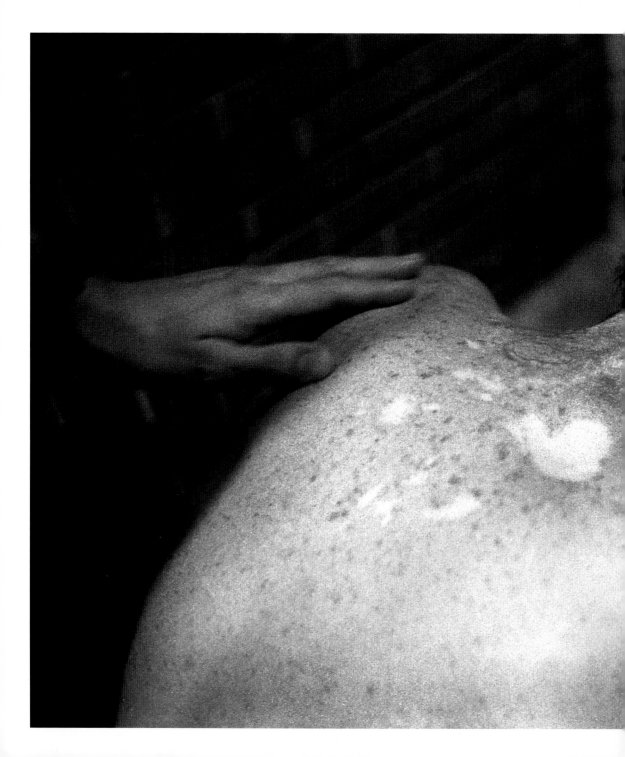

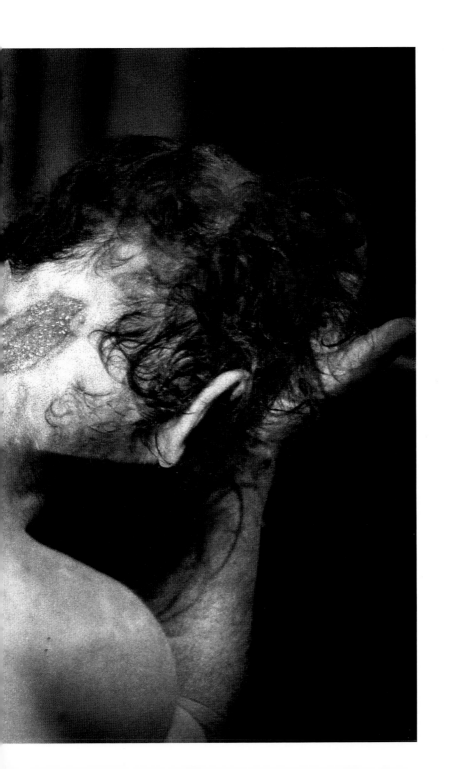

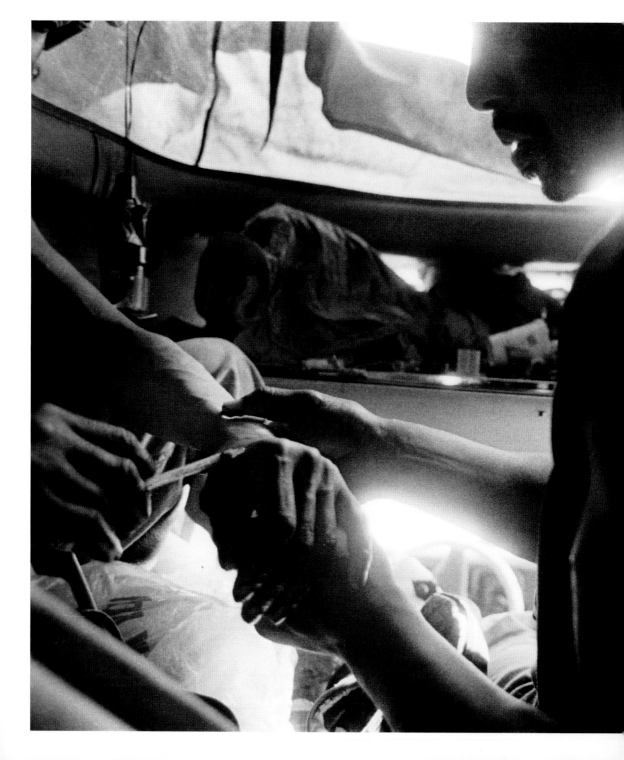

California Series in Public Anthropology

The California Series in Public Anthropology emphasizes the anthropologist's role as an engaged intellectual. It continues anthropology's commitment to being an ethnographic witness, to describing, in human terms, how life is lived beyond the borders of many readers' experiences. But it also adds a commitment, through ethnography, to reframing the terms of public debate—transforming received, accepted understandings of social issues with new insights, new framings.

Series Editor: Robert Borofsky (Hawaii Pacific University)

Righteous Dopefiend

Philippe Bourgois | Jeff Schonberg

University of California Press

Berkeley

Los Angeles

London

The publisher gratefully acknowledges the
generous support of the General Endowment
Fund of the University of California Press Foundation.

University of California Press, one of the most distinguished university
presses in the United States, enriches lives around the world by advancing
scholarship in the humanities, social sciences, and natural sciences. Its
activities are supported by the UC Press Foundation and by philanthropic
contributions from individuals and institutions. For more information, visit
www.ucpress.edu.

University of California Press
Berkeley and Los Angeles, California
University of California Press, Ltd.
London, England

Text: 9.25/14 Scala
Display: Akzidenz Grotesk
Designer: Nola Burger
Compositor: Integrated Composition Systems
Indexer: Sharon Sweeney
Printer and Binder: Friesens Corporation

Library of Congress Cataloging-in-Publication Data

Bourgois, Philippe I., 1956–.
    Righteous dopefiend / Philippe Bourgois, Jeff Schonberg.
        p.   cm.
    Includes bibliographical references and index.
    ISBN 978-0-520-23088-0 (cloth : alk. paper)
    ISBN 978-0-520-25498-5 (pbk. : alk. paper)
    1. Drug addicts—United States—Social conditions.   2. Drug addicts—
United States—Economic conditions.   3. Homeless persons—Drug use—
United States.   4. Marginality, Social—United States.   I. Schonberg,
Jeff, 1967–.   II. Title.
HV5825.B677   2009
305.9'0874—dc22   2007050924

Manufactured in Canada
18   17   16   15   14   13   12   11   10   09
10   9   8   7   6   5   4   3   2   1

The paper used in this publication meets the minimum requirements
of ANSI/NISO Z39.48–1992 (R 1997) (*Permanence of Paper*).

For Philippe's mother, Ann,
and for Jeff's family, Julie, Zane, and Sebastian

Contents

There is nothing righteous about dopefiends. They're assholes; they'll screw you. There is nothing enjoyable about this life. —*Max*

A Theory of Abuse

Jeff's Fieldnotes

Cars shoot one by one around the blind curve of the exit ramp as they descend from the freeway without reducing their speed. Frank is the first to cross. He strains to listen, but the background roar of rush hour traffic above us drowns out the sound of oncoming cars. He takes a deep breath, jumps off the curb, and sprints safely past the DO NOT ENTER *sign onto the median. Felix follows, crossing carefully but more confidently. Now it is my turn. I timidly stick out one foot as though testing the temperature of water, hold my breath, and dash to the other side. I have driven past this spot weekly for the last ten years, but when I feel it for the first time below the rubber sole of my shoe, and when I grab the iron guardrail to hoist myself onto the median, I feel as if I am stepping onto foreign soil.*

We are approaching a shooting gallery known as "the hole," a recessed V-shaped space beneath the juncture of two major San Francisco freeways. To enter it, we have to sidestep along a six-inch-wide cement beam for another ten yards, with cars rushing by on either side.

A discarded metal generator sits at the far end of the space. Three catty-corner, earthquake-reinforced concrete pylons support the double-decker freeways high above us and also shield us from the view of passing cars. My foot sinks into something soft just as Felix warns, "Careful where you step." I move more cautiously now to avoid the other piles of human feces fertilizing the sturdy plants that were selected by freeway planners to withstand a lifetime of car exhaust. The ground is also littered with empty plastic water bottles, candy wrappers, brown paper bags twisted at the stem containing empty bottles of fortified wine, the rusted shards of a metal bed frame, and a torn suitcase brimming with discarded clothing. Behind the generator, a sheet of warped plywood rests on a milk crate; on top of the plywood, a Styrofoam cup half full of water and the bottom half of a crushed Coke can sit ready for use.

Frank and Felix eagerly hunch over the plywood table and prepare to "fix" a quarter-gram "bag" of Mexican black tar heroin. They are running partners, which means they share all their resources, including this twenty-dollar sticky pellet of heroin the size of a pencil eraser that has been carefully wrapped and knotted in an uninflated red balloon. Felix earned this bag as payment from his supplier. He gets one for free for every ten that he sells. Frank makes his money

1

painting signs for local businesses, and it will be his turn to pay for the next bag that they will need to share five to eight hours from now to stave off heroin withdrawal symptoms.

Frank holds his syringe up to the light so that Felix can see exactly how much water he has drawn into its chamber from the Styrofoam cup. Frank nods, and Felix drops the heroin pellet into the crushed Coke can that is about to serve as their "cooker." Frank squirts the water into the cooker and lifts it above the flame of a lit match cupped in the palm of his right hand to shield it from the wind. He moves the cooker back and forth over the flame to make sure it is evenly heated. A ribbon of smoke with the slightly sweet smell of burnt milk rises between us as the mixture erupts into a quick boil, prompting Frank to jerk the cooker out of the flame.

He stirs the sludge in the cooker with the flat top handle of the syringe, scraping the sides and bottom of the cooker until all the lumps have fully liquefied into a smooth broth. Satisfied, he licks the plastic handle so as not to waste a precious drop. The plunger has twisted slightly and turned black in the heat of the heroin concoction.

Frank calls out for "a cotton," and Felix tears at a cigarette filter with his teeth. The white fiberglass strands splay with static. He rolls a clump of fibers into a tight ball between his thumb and forefinger and drops it into the cooker. Frank gently nudges the ball into the center of the puddle of heroin with the tip of his needle. It immediately absorbs the precious liquid, expanding and matting. Frank pierces the center of the swollen cotton with his needle and pulls back on the plunger to fill the syringe chamber with a bubbly rush of heroin solution. The cotton goes from a chocolate brown to an ashen gray.

"Hey, man! That's more than half!" Felix shouts.

"Bullshit!" Frank retorts, but he obligingly squirts some of the heroin solution back into the cooker on top of the cotton, swelling it slightly. Satisfied, Felix eagerly draws the remaining heroin solution into his own syringe.

Frank pinches the back of his hand to search for a functional vein and then begins poking with the needle. Each time he punctures his skin, he pulls back gently on the plunger to see if blood is drawn into the syringe chamber, confirming that the tip of the needle is safely inside the tiny walls of a vein. On his third attempt, Frank finally registers blood and flushes all the heroin solution into his body at once. Flooded by an instant rush of heroin pleasure, he sits back and lets his chin drop onto his chest, sighing and bobbing in the euphoric state of relaxation called "nodding."

Felix "muscles" his heroin without trying to probe for a vein. He jabs the needle up to its hilt directly into his biceps and slowly pushes the heroin into his fatty tissue. It takes him a couple of minutes to feel the effects, but soon he too is in a deep nod.

They are awakened from their nods by Max, who enters sweating and panting, his nose dripping. He has spent the day carrying furniture on a moving job, but he will not receive payment until tomorrow, when the job is finished, and he has no money to cover this evening's injection. From several blocks away he must have spied us entering the hole because he has run over, hoping to receive a "taste" of heroin. Max expects Felix and Frank to treat him to the residue from their cotton filters at least once a day as "rent," because they have moved into his encampment a quarter mile down the freeway embankment after being evicted from their camp by the police last week.

Felix obligingly pushes the crushed Coke can with the cotton sitting in the bottom toward Max. "Take the cotton; it's a wet one." Max eagerly pulls a syringe from his sock, squirts some extra water onto the cotton, and proceeds to "pound" it by squashing it repeatedly with his plunger handle, hoping to wring out every last drop of heroin residue. He is relieved because this will stave off full-blown heroin withdrawal symptoms until morning, when he anticipates being able to scrounge another cotton. In real dollar terms, a wet cotton like this can be purchased for two dollars or less, and two dollars can normally be panhandled in a couple of hours, even on a bad day.

The Edgewater Homeless

From November 1994 through December 2006, we became part of the daily lives of several dozen homeless heroin injectors who sought shelter in the dead-end alleyways, storage lots, vacant factories, broken-down cars, and overgrown highway embankments surrounding Edgewater Boulevard (not its real name), the main thoroughfare serving San Francisco's sprawling, semi-derelict warehouse and shipyard district.

The maze of on-ramps and off-ramps surrounding the shooting gallery nicknamed the hole is part of the commuter backbone servicing the dot-com and biotech economies of Silicon Valley and downtown San Francisco. These freeways connect some of the highest-paying jobs in the United States to some of the nation's most expensive residential real estate. By building freeways all across the nation since the 1950s, granting generous mortgage tax breaks, and pursuing monetarist policies to stem inflation and lower interest rates, the U.S. government has effectively subsidized wealthy, segregated suburban communities, draining wealthy and middle-class residents from inner cities (Davis 1990; Self 2005). The hole was merely one of the many accidentally remaining nooks and crannies at the margins of this publicly funded freeway infrastructure where the homeless regularly sought refuge in the 1990s and 2000s. It was a classic inner-city no-man's-land of invisible public space, out of the eye of law enforcement.

Frank and Felix chose to inject in a filthy, difficult-to-access spot like the hole rather than in Max's nearby camp, where they were sleeping, not only out of fear of the police but also to avoid having to share a portion of their bag of heroin with Hogan, another one of their campmates, who had been complaining all day of being "dopesick." They did not mind treating Max to a "wet cotton shot" because they knew he would be receiving money from his moving job the next day and he was likely to reciprocate their gift should they need it some time in the future. Hogan, in contrast, had a reputation for being lazy and perennially broke.

At any given moment, the core social network we befriended usually consisted of some twenty individuals, of whom fewer than a half dozen were women. They usually divided themselves up into four or five encampments, which frequently shifted locations to escape the police. All but two of these injectors were over forty years old when we began our fieldwork, and several were pushing fifty. All but the youngest had begun injecting heroin on a daily basis during the late 1960s or early 1970s. In addition to the heroin they injected every day, several times a day, they also smoked crack and drank large quantities of alcohol—primarily inexpensive, twelve-ounce bottles of Cisco Berry fortified wine (each one equivalent, according to a denunciation by the surgeon general of the United States, to five shots of vodka [*Dallas Observer* 1994, November 17]). According to national epidemiological statistics, the age and gender profile of our social network of homeless men and women was roughly representative of the majority of street-based heroin injectors in the United States during the late 1990s and early 2000s (Gfroerer et al. 2003; Golub and Johnson 2001; Hahn et al. 2006).

A separate generational cohort of younger heroin or speed injectors also existed in most major U.S. cities, but they maintained themselves in entirely separate spaces from older heroin addicts. Most of these youthful injectors were whites fleeing distressed and impoverished families, and they represented a smaller proportion of their generation than those who had been attracted to heroin in the 1960s and 1970s (Bourgois, Prince, and Moss 2004). Hip-hop youth culture in the 2000s actively discouraged injection drug use or crack smoking despite its celebration of drug selling. Consequently, those African-American and Latino youth who used drugs primarily smoked marijuana and drank alcohol, even when they sold heroin or crack on the street (Bourgois 2008).

Addiction is a slippery and problematic concept (Keane 2002). The American Psychiatric Association's diagnostic manual does not have an entry under the word *addiction,* and its criteria for identifying substance abuse refer primarily to maladaptive social behaviors caused by "recurrent substance use," including, among others, the political-institutional category of "recurrent legal problems" (American Psychiatric Association 1994:182–183). Nevertheless, there is no doubt that within a couple of weeks of daily use, heroin creates a strong physiological dependence operating at the level of basic cellular processes.

The Edgewater homeless embrace the popular terminology of addiction and, with ambivalent pride, refer to themselves as "righteous dopefiends." They have subordinated everything in their lives—shelter, sustenance, and family—to injecting heroin. They endure the chronic pain and anxiety of hunger, exposure, infectious disease, and social ostracism because of their commitment to heroin. Abscesses, skin rashes, cuts, bruises, broken bones, flus, colds, opiate withdrawal symptoms, and the potential for violent assault are constant features of their lives. But exhilaration is also just around the corner. Virtually every day on at least two or three occasions, and sometimes up to six or seven times, depending on the success of their income-generating strategies, they are able to flood their bloodstreams and jolt their synapses with instant relief, relaxation, and pleasure.

The central goal of this photo-ethnography of indigent poverty, social exclusion, and drug use is to clarify the relationships between large-scale power forces and intimate ways of being in order to explain why the United States, the wealthiest nation in the world, has emerged as a pressure cooker for producing destitute addicts embroiled in everyday violence. Our challenge is to portray the full details of the agony and the ecstasy of surviving on the street as a heroin injector without beatifying or making a spectacle of the individuals involved, and without reifying the larger forces enveloping them.

Hustled in the Moral Economy

Begging, working, scavenging, and stealing, the Edgewater homeless balance on a tightrope of mutual solidarity and betrayal as they scramble for their next shot of heroin, their next meal, their next place to sleep, and their sense of dignity—all the while keeping a wary eye out for the police. Following the insights of the early twentieth-century anthropologist Marcel Mauss on the way reciprocal gift-giving distributes prestige and scarce goods and services among people living in nonmarket economies (Mauss [1924] 1990), we can understand the Edgewater homeless as forming a community of addicted bodies that is held together by a moral economy of sharing (Bourgois 1998b). Most homeless heroin injectors cannot survive as solo operators on the street. They are constantly seeking one another out to exchange tastes of heroin, sips of fortified wine, and loans of spare change. This gift-giving envelops them in a web of mutual obligations and also establishes the boundaries of their community. Sharing enables their survival and allows for expressions of individual generosity, but gifts often go hand in hand with rip-offs.

At first, we felt overwhelmed, irritated, and even betrayed by the frequent and often manipulative requests for favors, spare change, and loans of money. We worried about distorting our relationships by becoming patrons and buying friendship to obtain our research data. At the same time, we had to participate in the moral economy to avoid being ostracized from the network for being stingy and antisocial.

Homeless heroin users hustle everyone with whom they interact, fooling even themselves and betraying even their own bodies and desires. They are amazingly effective hustlers; if they were not, they could not continue to survive on the street. We had to learn, therefore, not to take their petty financial manipulations personally, and to refrain from judging them morally. Otherwise, we could not have entered their lives respectfully and empathetically. With time, we realized that there was nothing substantially different between how they extracted money from us and how they hustled everyone else in their network who had more resources than they at any particular moment. Gifts of money, blankets, and food were the primary means—aside from sharing drugs—they used to define and express friendships, organize interpersonal hierarchies, and exclude undesirable outsiders.

Participating in the moral economy allowed us to understand its importance on an embodied and intuitive level and revealed its social structural and public health implications. We had to become sufficiently immersed in the logics of hustling to be able to recognize, through an acquired common sense, when to give, when to help, when to say no, and when to be angry. We had to learn when to be spontaneously generous and when simply to walk away despite cries for help or curses of rage. Dogmatic rules for researchers with respect to giving money or doing favors for research subjects are out of touch with practical realities on the street. We, like the Edgewater Boulevard homeless, found ourselves more generous to those who reciprocated. The brute fact of the matter, however, is that homeless addicts are desperate for money, and, comparatively, we were rich. Nevertheless, they never took serious advantage of our generosity and our lack of "street smarts"; nor did they steal from us. Jeff occasionally left camera equipment in their camps. They had our phone numbers and addresses, and although Philippe lived only a few blocks from Edgewater Boulevard, they rarely contacted him or Jeff at home to ask for money or help.

Cultural Relativism, Confidentiality, and Respect

Our approach to scenes such as the one presented in the fieldnotes and the photographs that follow is premised on anthropology's tenet of cultural relativism, which strategically suspends moral judgment in order to understand and appreciate the diverse logics of social and cultural practices that, at first sight, often evoke righteous responses and prevent analytical self-reflection. Historically, cultural relativism has been anthropology's foundation for combating ethnocentrism. For us, it has also been a practical way to gain access to the difficult or shocking realities of drugs, sex, crime, and violence. Unfortunately, public opinion on the subject of illegal drugs is so polarized in the United States that applying cultural relativism as a heuristic device to document the lives of drug users is often misconstrued as celebrating drug use. As will be evident, this is not the case in the pages that follow. Nevertheless, learning about life on the street in the United States requires the reader to keep an open mind and, at least provisionally, to suspend judgment.

Jeff and Philippe's Fieldnotes

It is sunrise, and Sonny comes by Hank's camp to ask him for a favor: "Hit me in the neck." Hank has a good reputation for administering jugular shots painlessly. On cold mornings like today, Sonny is unable to inject into the scarred, shrunken veins of his arms, hands, and legs. He refuses to inject into fatty or muscle tissue for fear of causing an abscess, so he seeks help. Although Sonny has woken him up, Hank agrees to fix him because he anticipates that Sonny will give him a taste of his heroin, and he has no money set aside for his own "morning wake-up shot." Hank's nose is already running, indicating that full-blown withdrawal symptoms are on their way.

Hank, consequently, eagerly takes out two syringes, teasing Sonny for being "up to no good" because Sonny has no needle, no cooker, no water, and no cotton filter in his possession. Hank is right. Sonny never carries injection paraphernalia for fear of police frisks when he goes out scavenging at night to burgle and/or recycle.

Sonny places his thumb in his mouth as if to suck it, but he blows on it instead in order to swell up his jugular vein. He puffs up like a blowfish, eyes bulging from their sockets, with his entire body shivering from the pressure on his thumb. Hank tells Sonny to stay still and probes the needle slowly into his neck. He has to be careful not to spear through the jugular into the artery located just behind it. Sonny whispers nervously: "Steady now; that's right; you're in. Go ahead! Come on!" Hank pulls back gently on the plunger, wiggling the syringe between attempts, causing Sonny to wince. Finally, on the third try, a plume of blood registers into the syringe chamber. Hank chuckles, "Moby Dick!" Sonny cautiously pulls his thumb out of his mouth, keeping it safely poised in front of his lips, and whispers, "Thar she blows!" But he does not smile. If Hank's needle starts to slip while flushing the syringe into his jugular, Sonny will need to puff back up instantly.

The injection completed, Sonny massages his neck and rasps a soft thanks. His voice is already husky from the effects of the initial rush of heroin and he closes his eyes to appreciate it more fully. He points in slow motion toward the blackened bottle cap that served as their cooker. "The cotton is all yours, Hank."

The liquid residue left over in the cotton filter from Sonny's jugular injection fills only a tiny corner of Hank's syringe chamber—less than ten of the units marked on the barrel of the syringe. Determined to suck out every last drop, Hank pinches the cotton between his nicotine- and dirt-stained fingers onto the tip of his needle as he gently pulls back on the plunger. This gives him five extra units.

Hank does not probe for a vein. Instead, he unbuckles his belt, lowers his pants, and jams his needle into the scarred cheek of his left buttock.

A police siren wails from two blocks away. We sit up nervously and Hank stashes the needles behind a bush, kicking the cooker into the dirt. But the siren passes and we relax. Sonny gives Hank two hugs.

Viewed on their own and out of context, jarring photographs of a jugular injection or of a cotton being pinched by filthy fingers on the tip of a syringe might confirm a negative stereotype or fuel a voyeuristic pornography of suffering that obscures the fuller context and meaning of what is occurring between Hank and Sonny. An analysis of the photograph together with the fieldnotes enables us to understand the pragmatic rationality for what at first sight may appear to be entirely self-destructive or immoral. More important, embedding the photograph in text allows an appreciation of the effects of social structural forces on individuals (Schonberg and Bourgois 2002). For example, the event can be interpreted as a moment of cross-ethnic solidarity in the moral economy. Hank is doing Sonny the favor of injecting him in the neck so that he can benefit from the more intense pleasure of the initial rush of a heroin high. Sonny is reciprocating Hank's favor by treating him to the residue of his cotton, saving him from the pain of early-morning heroin withdrawal symptoms. In its opening and closing paragraphs, the preceding fieldnote excerpt also highlights the larger, systemic effect of law enforcement, revealing how fear of arrest exacerbates risky injection practices: discouraging possession of syringes, encouraging injectors to hide paraphernalia in unsanitary locations, and relegating the injection process to filthy hidden locales without running water. The note also documents preferences for injecting heroin either directly into a vein or into fatty tissue—an often-racialized phenomenon that we explore in chapter 3.

If our approach to the homeless is relativistic in the anthropological sense, we are nonetheless acutely aware of coercive forces and recognize the practical impossibility of cultural relativism in the "real world." From a political perspective, law enforcement was our most immediate ethical concern. Initially, we feared that our mere presence might inadvertently draw police attention to our social network. In all our years on Edgewater Boulevard, however, this never occurred. We would have stopped the project immediately and desisted from publishing Jeff's photographs had we thought we might significantly augment anyone's risk of arrest or harassment.

The question of the personal privacy of our research subjects is more complicated than the immediate practical risk of legal sanctions against them, however. It involves the imperative to respect personal dignity and to avoid essentializing difference. The major characters in this book wanted to be part of our photo-ethnographic project. They gave Jeff permission to photograph and encouraged us to use their real names when they signed the bureaucratic informed consent documents required by our university's internal review board overseeing research ethics. Arguably, however, this official "protection of human subjects" paperwork safeguards institutions from lawsuits rather than safeguarding the dignity and interests of socially vulnerable research subjects. Most important, the Edgewater homeless do not want to be treated as public secrets or hidden objects of shame. They struggle for self-respect and feel that their stories are worth telling.

We ultimately decided to use pseudonyms but to reveal faces in our publications. Nickie provided the most succinct and eloquent argument for showing faces. We asked her how

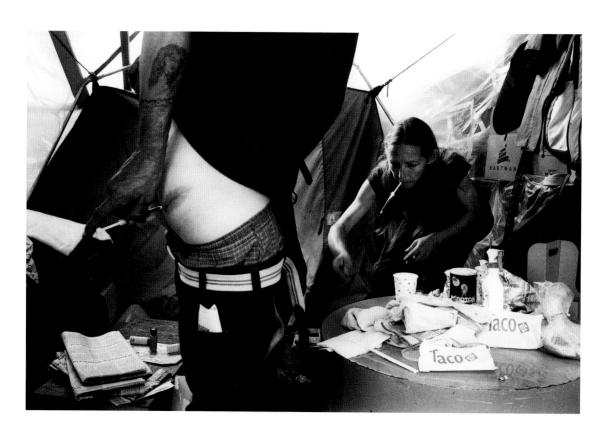

she felt about our displaying a photograph of her preparing an injection, with Petey in the foreground skin-popping into an abscess scar on his rear. She responded without hesitation: "If you can't see the face, you can't see the misery."

Collaborative Photo-Ethnography

There are surprisingly few examples of co-authored collaborative ethnographies in the history of anthropology, with the notable exception of works by married couples that too frequently have not acknowledged the intellectual contribution of the wife (for a critical review, see Ariëns and Strijp 1989; see also Mead 1970:326). The experience of the solo fieldworker in an exotic hamlet emerged as a rite of passage for anthropologists in the 1930s and 1940s (Gupta and Ferguson 1997; Stocking 1992). Collaborative fieldwork, however, can greatly improve ethnographic technique and analysis. Participant-observation is by definition an intensely subjective process requiring systematic self-reflection. Collaborators have the advantage of being able to scrutinize one another's contrasting interpretations and insights.

In our case, we often purposefully conducted fieldwork together and wrote fieldnotes side by side in order to compare what we had seen, heard, and felt. Working together was also more fun and safer. We each developed a range of different kinds of relationships with the Edgewater homeless, allowing broader access to more people and generating distinct perspectives on the same individuals and events. Over the years, seven additional ethnographers (named in the acknowledgments) also assisted us for more limited periods, further diversifying our access to individuals and interpretations of events.

With the exception of the final half dozen drafts of text editing and tightening, we wrote the book sitting side by side. To maintain the intimacy of first-person ethnography and to communicate the significance of the effects of personalities and positionalities on social dynamics, we present several distinct voices throughout our text. In addition to our jointly written narrative and analysis, we identify our fieldnote excerpts in the first person (with occasional references to members of the "ethnographic team"). We also, of course, include the words and extended conversations of the homeless themselves. Conveying these distinct voices required a range of different grammatical and punctuation styles.

The photographs were all taken by Jeff. The composition of the images recognizes the politics within aesthetics; they are closely linked to contextual and theoretical analysis. Some photographs provide detailed documentation of material life and the environment. Others were selected primarily to convey mood or to evoke the pains and pleasures of life on the street. Most refer to specific moments described in the surrounding pages, but at times they stand in tension with the text to reveal the messiness of real life and the complexity of analytical generalizations. On occasion, the pictures themselves prompted the writing. Jeff never deliberately staged the actions portrayed in the photographs.

Jeff's photography further integrated both of us into the scene. Many of the Edgewater homeless decorated their encampments with his pictures, and they often introduced Jeff to outsiders as "my photographer." They usually introduced Philippe as "my professor" and would often comment to Philippe when he was alone with them, "Too bad Jeff isn't here to take a picture of this." When they viewed pictures of themselves, they were often shocked by their appearance—unhealthy, skinny, old, wrinkled, dirty, tired. This usually precipitated self-reflective conversations about the state of their lives (cf. Collier and Collier 1990). When Jeff showed Hank the photo of him standing with his American flag, Hank responded, "Ain't that a shame! A goddamned Vietnam vet. Damn, look at how skinny I am. I look like Viet Cong. Y'know, when I put myself back together, I'm gonna help the homeless."

Ethnography is an artisanal practice that involves interpretive and political choices. On the one hand, the researcher merges into the environment, relaxing into conversations, friendships, and interactions and participating in everyday activities. On the other hand, the observer is mentally racing to register the significance of what is occurring and to conceptualize strategies to deepen that understanding. We steered our conversations with the Edgewater homeless toward specific themes. When a particular topic or story appeared significant, we returned to it several times over the course of the years to obtain more substantive content and poetic depth.

"Truth" is, of course, socially constructed and experientially subjective; nevertheless, we did our best to seek it out. We reexplored important stories, statements, and topics, varying the surrounding conditions and the interviewers, using different members of the ethnographic team to triangulate for meaning and contextual or personal biases. We also controlled for differing states of intoxication and mood. Our fieldnotes and transcripts came to several thousand pages. Some of the dialogues presented in the text are, consequently, combinations of excerpts from multiple conversations with more than one ethnographer spread out over time. Whenever possible, we fact-checked official records for births, deaths, marriages, military service, employment, and incarceration; we also consulted newspaper articles and public archives to confirm the veracity of accounts of past events. When we documented notable discrepancies, we discuss their significance.

The Politics of Representation

Editing street-based tape recordings is a literary and practical challenge with political and scientific implications. Oral discourse is a performative art, and written transcriptions lose the inflections and body language that punctuate speech (Gates 1988). The full meaning of colloquial language is lost when it is written down, and poetic passages often appear inarticulate when transcribed verbatim. Transcribing accents and pronunciation is especially problematic because a phonetic representation of language can distance readers from "cultural others." Accents, however, convey important sociostructural differences with respect to class, ethnicity, education level, and segregation. In order to communicate patterns of cultural/symbolic capital without turning individuals into caricatures, we maintained some of the significant grammatical distinctions verbatim in our transcription, but we only selectively documented accents. To retain original meaning, clarity, and intensity of expression, we sometimes deleted redundancies and clarified syntax (see discussion of editing in Bourgois 2003b:354n.20). We were careful, however, to maintain what we believe was the original sense as well as the emotion of what was spoken and performed. (We did not use ellipses in quoted speech to indicate deleted words. Rather, ellipses indicate that the speaker is struggling to find the right word or is pausing to make a point or change the subject. We did, of course, use ellipses conventionally when quoting selectively from publications and archives.)

Our fieldnotes contain descriptions of more than two hundred core and peripheral individuals, and our understanding of the street scene draws from this larger array of relationships. However, to keep the text to a manageable length and to avoid a confusing array of names, we excluded most of the peripheral characters. Similarly, to preserve the flow of a conversation or a narrative and to avoid redundancy, we have sometimes moved characters around in time and space and abbreviated sequences of events. We have on occasion separated incidents and passages from long conversations or extended episodes into different thematic chapters when they illustrate distinct analytical points. Once again, we made these changes carefully (and hesitantly) to respect the integrity of human character and to maintain the full contextual meaning.

Ethnographers and photographers are conduits for power because they carry messages through different worlds and across class and cultural divides, but they also develop relationships of trust with individuals who generously let them into their everyday lives. Published accounts of those relationships inevitably risk objectifying and betraying this intimacy. Understandably, ethnographers generally desire to present positive images of the people they study. The stakes around negative images are especially charged when one explores the subject of drugs, crime, race, sexuality, poverty, and suffering in the United States; and we paid attention to those stakes when making our editorial choices, but we did not sanitize or distort (see Bourgois 2003b:355n.24). For example, comic aggressive teasing, role-playing, and posturing are performances in street settings that can translate into negative or mocking portrayals when they are converted verbatim into written text. Consequently, we have omitted some interactions that appeared excessively cruel or outrageously shocking and would have distracted from the analysis or misrepresented the fuller character of an individual. Most commonly, we deleted interpersonal insults and sexually explicit bravado. Harsh curses and racist and sexist epithets abound in the language of the Edgewater homeless. We omitted repetitive curses and epithets, but we included enough brutal material to convey the strong, and sometimes abusive, emotions surrounding the hierarchical power categories that organize interpersonal interactions on the street, most notably ethnicity, gender, sexuality, and physical appearance. We hope readers will not be distracted from analytical points when they are documented by graphic text, and we hope they will appreciate the acerbic, often comic, poetry of streetwise dialogues.

The camera, the tape recorder, and the written word are technologies that have historically lent themselves to surveillance and social engineering as well as to art and projects of solidarity. Documentary photography has an especially long and mixed record. It emerged out of social activism, journalism, fine arts, science, and pseudoscience—including phrenology, physiognomy, and eugenics—as well as out of public health and criminology (Sekula 1989; Tagg 1988).

Photography's strength comes from the visceral, emotional responses it evokes. But the capacity to spark Rorschach reactions gives photography both its power and its problems (Harper 2002). Interpretation, judgment, and imagination move to the eyes of the beholder. The personality, cultural values, and ideologies of the viewer, as well as the context in which the images are presented, all shape the meaning of pictures (Berger 1972). The multitude of meanings in a photograph makes it risky, arguably even irresponsible, to trust raw images of marginalization, suffering, and addiction to an often judgmental public. Letting a picture speak its thousand words can result in a thousand deceptions (see Sandweiss 2002:326–333; Schonberg and Bourgois 2002). For this reason, we insist that without our text much of the meaning of the photographs we present could be lost or distorted. (For the classic critical portrayal of U.S. poverty combining photographs and text without captions, see Agee and Evans [1941] 1988; for different strategies of combining photographs and text depicting the U.S. inner city, see Duneier 1999; Goldberg 1995; Maharidge 1996; Richards 1994; Vergara n.d.; for a review of visual anthropology and "race," see Poole 2005; see Barthes 1981 and Mitchell 1994:ch. 9 on the productive tension between denotation and connotation in photography and text.)

Like photography, ethnography has a mixed record of uses and abuses. It is saddled with cultural anthropology's foundational predilection for community-based studies of exotic and dehistoricized others in a vacuum of external power relations (for a critique, see Wolf 1982). The discipline came of age in the twentieth century as a stepchild of colonialism and world wars and matured under the Cold War (Asad 1973; Nader 1997; Price 2004; Said 1989; Wolf and Jorgensen 1970). Participant-observation, however, has an inherently anti-institutional transgressive potential because, by definition, it forces academics out of their ivory tower and compels them to violate the boundaries of class and cultural segregation. Although it is framed by the unequal relationship of "investigator" and "informant," ethnography renders its practitioners vulnerable to the blood, sweat, tears, and violence of the people being studied and requires ethical reflection and solidary engagement. At the same time, the all-encompassing vagueness of anthropology's culture concept tends to essentialize difference and to obscure causal forces and negative consequences. The term *culture* is often applied sloppily across power gradients, inadvertently masking structures of inequality (Bourgois 2001a; Said 1989; Wolf 1982) and politically imposed physical suffering (Farmer 1992).

By arguing that social truth is an artifact of power, postmodern theory has humbled the totalizing enlightenment discourses that claim the moral authority to know what is best for others in the name of progress, science, and civilization. Our terms and categories of analysis and even our conceptions of reality are historical constructs. Consequently, there can be no transcendental solution to the contradictory tensions at the heart of both photography and ethnography. As representational practices they are torn between objectifying and humanizing; exploiting and giving voice; propagandizing and documenting injustice; stigmatizing and revealing; fomenting voyeurism and promoting empathy; stereotyping and analyzing. This book is especially vulnerable to ideological projections, because it confronts the social suffering of cultural pariahs through explicit text accompanied by images that expose socially taboo behaviors (drugs, sex, crime, and violence) and because it documents the politically and emotionally charged themes of race, gender, and indigent drug use (Schonberg and Bourgois 2002; see critique of the "bourgeois gaze" on the slums of Victorian England in Stallybrass and White 1986:ch. 3).

Silencing, censoring, and sanitizing photo-ethnographic critiques of suffering and inequality are not productive alternatives. Representing the Edgewater homeless solely as worthy victims for the sake of a positive politics of representation misrepresents the painful effects of marginalization, poverty, oppression, addiction, and violence. Following anthropologist Nancy Scheper-Hughes's call for a "good-enough ethnography" (Scheper-Hughes 1989) that critically engages the violence of everyday life despite a concern with the politics of representation, we advocate a "good-enough photo-ethnography" (Bourgois 1999). Photo-ethnography has the potential to effectively portray unacceptable social phenomena because it is more than the sum of its parts. It draws emotion, aesthetics, and documentation into social science analysis and theory and strives to link intellect with politics. Nonetheless, it is important to remain critically reflexive: What are we imposing? What are we missing? What are the stakes of exposure to a wider audience? Most important, however, there is urgency to documenting the lives of the Edgewater homeless. They survive in perpetual crisis. Their everyday physical and psychic pain should not be allowed to remain invisible.

Theoretical Approaches to Social Suffering

The destructive manner in which the Edgewater homeless administer drugs to themselves and the central role of violence and manipulation in their interpersonal relationships raise the question of individual responsibility. On a practical level, we had to pay close attention to individual character traits while conducting fieldwork because we depended on the goodwill and cooperation of the homeless for protection. We had to figure out who to trust and who to avoid (as well as when to run). The homeless were also constantly evaluating one another's personality traits in order to take advantage of individual weaknesses and to protect themselves from victimization. In short, interactions in everyday life operate on the basis of what academics call "agency." The conventional theoretical distinction between structure and agency, however, is too binary a conception to explain why people do what they do.

It equates incommensurable units of analysis in a moral calculus that reflects ideological debates rather than offering insight into complex historical and contemporary outcomes. To avoid the theoretical impasse of conventional structure-versus-agency debates, we have framed this book around a concept that we call "lumpen abuse."

In popular parlance, the term *abuse* generally refers to interpersonal relations or actions that contravene the norms of social interaction and violate an individual's human rights. The word *abuse* implies outrageous suffering—emotional, psychological, and/or physical. The definition in the *Oxford English Dictionary* includes, among other historical synonyms, "wronged," "worn out, consumed by use . . . obsolete," "chronic corrupt practice," "deceit, delusion," "violation." The entry also makes reference to "drug abuse." Finally, the dictionary definition specifies that, in modern use, the term refers "esp[ecially to] sexual or other mal-treatment." The index of the American Psychiatric Association's diagnostic manual (1994: 875) lists two primary sets of entries for abuse: one is grouped around substance abuse, and the other is divided into several subheadings that include neglect as well as physical and sexual mistreatment of children and adults.

The medical and popular resonances of the word *abuse* are useful analytically because they call attention to the misuse of power in intimate relations that conjugates victims with perpetrators in a trauma of betrayal over an extended time period. Our theorization of abuse sets the individual experience of intolerable levels of suffering among the socially vulnera-ble (which often manifests itself in the form of interpersonal violence and self-destruction) in the context of structural forces (political, economic, institutional, cultural) and embod-ied manifestations of distress (morbidity, physical pain, and emotional craving). Close ethno-graphic explorations of suffering must address its social distribution (Kleinman, Das, and Lock 1997; Kleinman and Kleinman 1991). The suffering of homeless heroin injectors is chronic and cumulative and is best understood as a politically structured phenomenon that encompasses multiple abusive relationships, both structural and personal. Our exploration of drug consumption, domestic violence, sexual predation, interpersonal betrayals, and in-terpersonal hierarchies examines these abusive phenomena in their relationship to politi-cal-economic, cultural-ideological, and institutional forces, such as the restructuring of the labor market, the "War on Drugs," the gentrification of San Francisco's housing market, the gutting of social services, the administration of bureaucracies, racism, sexuality, gender power relations, and stigma.

Linking suffering to power through a theory that analyzes the multiple levels of lumpen abuse coincides with redefining violence as something more than a directly assaultive phys-ical and visible phenomenon with bounded limits. Violence operates along a continuum that spans structural, symbolic, everyday, and intimate dimensions (Bourgois 2001b; Scheper-Hughes and Bourgois 2004). Structural violence refers to how the political-eco-nomic organization of society wreaks havoc on vulnerable categories of people (Farmer 2003). Scheper-Hughes began using the term *everyday violence* to call attention to the social production of indifference in the face of institutionalized brutalities. She reveals, for example, how the "invisible genocide" of infants dying of hunger in the Brazilian shantytown where she was living was routinized and legitimized by the rituals of bureaucracies, the banal procedures of medicine, and the religious consolation of the mothers who were her neighbors and friends (Scheper-Hughes 1996). We extend her concept to call attention to the effects of violence in interpersonal interactions and routine daily life. Recognizing the phenomenon of everyday violence and documenting how intimate violence interfaces with structural violence counteracts the marxist tendency toward linear economic determinism. But participant-observation of everyday interpersonal violence presents a theoretical problem. Ethnography is attuned to fine-grained observations of individuals in action; it tends to miss the implications of structures of power and of historical context because these forces have no immediate visibility in the heat of the moment.

Sociologist Pierre Bourdieu's concept of symbolic violence links immediate practices and feelings to social domination (Bourdieu 2000). It refers specifically to the mechanisms that lead those who are subordinated to "misrecognize" inequality as the natural order of things and to blame themselves for their location in their society's hierarchies. Through symbolic violence, inequalities are made to appear commonsensical, and they reproduce themselves preconsciously in the ontological categories shared within classes and within social groups in any given society. Symbolic violence is an especially useful concept for critiquing homelessness in the United States because most people (including the Edgewater homeless themselves) consider drug use and poverty to be caused by personal character flaws or sinful behavior. We hope to deconstruct the generalized misrecognition of the ways everyday, intimate, and structural violence generate (and are legitimized by) symbolic violence. In summary, we are combining and reshaping the approaches to power of Marx, Bourdieu, and Foucault in order to weave the concepts of politically structured suffering and the continuum of violence into a theory of lumpen abuse.

As a political economist critiquing capitalism, Karl Marx considers the economic relations that organize social classes to be key to explaining power relations, and he identifies class struggle as the motor force of history (Marx and Engels [1848] 2002). Accordingly, he would have summarily dismissed the Edgewater homeless as members of the lumpen proletariat. Marx defines the lumpen as a residual class: the historical fall-out of large-scale, long-term transformations in the organization of the economy. Members of the lumpen have no productive raison d'être. Expelled from engagement with the means of production, they become drop-outs from history. They are too marginal to be part of what Marx calls "the reserve army of the unemployed" that factory owners draw upon to undermine unions and lower wages. In one of his more polemical passages, Marx refers to the lumpen as the "scum, offal, refuse of all classes" (Marx [1852] 1963:75). (For discussions of Marx's attitude toward the lumpen, see Bovenkerk 1984; Bussard 1987; Draper 1972; Parker 1993; see Stallybrass 1990 on bourgeois representations and fantasies of the lumpen.) To understand the human cost of neoliberalism in the twentieth century, we are resurrecting Marx's structural sense of the lumpen as a vulnerable population that is produced at the interstices of transitioning modes of production. We do not, however, retain his dismissive and moralizing use of the term *lumpen*.

Bourdieu considers social class and the economic field of power to be of paramount importance, but he is most concerned with the way hidden forms of symbolic power maintain and legitimize hierarchy and oppression through everyday "practice." He develops the concept of "habitus" to show how social structural power translates into intimate ways of being and everyday practices that legitimize social inequalities. Habitus refers to our deepest likes, dislikes, and personal dispositions, including those of our preconscious bodies. It is grounded historically in the collective frameworks of culture and society, misrecognized as "instinct," "common sense," or "character," which becomes the basis for how we feel things and why we act. Most important, although every individual's habitus is unique, modulated by serendipity and individual charisma and constantly changing over the course of a lifetime, it also contains biographical and historical sediments filtered through past generations (Bourdieu 1977, 2000; Wacquant 2005).

We draw on Michel Foucault's understanding of power and normativity in order to better understand how the structural phenomenon of lumpenization is enmeshed in symbolic violence. According to Foucault, the locus of state power in the eighteenth and nineteenth centuries shifted from a logic of "sovereignty," which exacts obedience through bloody repression, to one of "biopower," which promotes the health and well-being of citizens (Foucault 1978:140–144). The mechanisms of control shifted from coercive terror and torture to an internalized self-disciplinary gaze that responsible individuals impose on their bodies and psyches as a moral responsibility. In Foucault's conception, power is not wielded overtly, but rather "flows" through the very foundations of what we recognize as reason, civilization, and scientific progress. It operates through processes of governmentality that may continue to include physical repression but are primarily organized around monitoring and regulating large population groups through broad interventions such as vaccination campaigns and censuses. Individuals are disciplined purposefully and explicitly through institutions, but also subtly and unconsciously through the "knowledge/power" nexus. The applied academic, medical, and juridical scientific disciplines (such as public health, criminology, social work, and psychiatry) emerged in the eighteenth and nineteenth centuries to define modernity, progress, truth, and ultimately self-worth: the docile bodies of healthy and "normal" citizens are shaped through responsible scientific knowledge and progress.

Nothing can escape the effects of power as conceived by Foucault. Capillary-like, these effects infuse our bodies and minds to set the agendas of our lives and to shape even our most oppositional thoughts. Distinct "subjectivities" emerge as patterns of historically situated ways of perceiving and engaging with the world. Unlike the term *identity*, the concept of subjectivity does not imply individual agency or self-ascription. It treats taken-for-granted characteristics such as demographic profile or psychological temperament as discursive products of modernity rather than innate categories. The French terms for subjectivity, *assu-jetissement* and *subjectification,* carry the clear implication of the "process of becoming subjected to a power" (see Deleuze 1995:81–118 on "subjectification"; see also Butler 1997:83 on "subjectivation"). For Foucault, subjectivity is a "soul that imprisons the body" (Butler 1997:86, citing Foucault 1995; see also Pine 2008:12–14, 17). It emerges through the knowledge/power nexus and is part of the disciplinary and security processes of governmentality (Foucault 1978, 1981a, 1995). Foucault did not examine illegal drug use, but the topic of "substance abuse" is ideal terrain for a critical application of biopower, governmentality, and the deconstruction of knowledge/power discourses.

Our theory of lumpen abuse highlights the way structurally imposed everyday suffering generates violent and destructive subjectivities. The version of punitive, corporate neoliberalism that has been spreading unevenly across the globe in the late twentieth and early twenty-first centuries as the dominant mode of production is producing growing numbers of lumpenized populations (see Ferguson 2006:39–40 on "*Afrique inutile*"). Biopower as a form of governmentality that is productively internalized by citizens may have characterized social democracy and capitalist fordism, but violent coercion (including state and parastate terrorism and war) increasingly characterizes neoliberal forms of governmentality. Bringing Foucault to bear on Marx, we are redefining the class category of lumpen as a subjectivity that emerges among population groups upon whom the effects of biopower have become destructive (Bourgois 2005a). The term *lumpen,* consequently, is best understood as an adjective or modifier rather than as a bounded class category. The lumpen subjectivity of righteous dopefiend that is shared by all the Edgewater homeless embodies the abusive dynamics that permeate all their relationships, including their interactions with individuals, families, institutions, economic forces, labor markets, cultural-ideological values, and ultimately their own selves.

Fieldwork in a Gray Zone

The autobiographical literature created by Holocaust survivors provides exceptional insight into how state coercion can make monsters of the meek. Auschwitz survivor Primo Levi developed the concept of the "Gray Zone" to capture the ethical wasteland imposed by the Nazis on concentration camp inmates struggling to stay alive under genocidal conditions (Levi 1988). In the Gray Zone, survival imperatives overcome human decency as inmates jockey desperately for a shred of advantage within camp hierarchies, striving to live just a little bit longer. The Nazis purposefully engineered the Gray Zone of the death camps to force inmates to self-administer to one another, with excruciating cruelty, the logistics of everyday life in the camps. As a contemporary ethical imperative, Levi urges readers to recognize the less extreme gray zones that operate in daily life, "even if we only want to understand what takes place in a big, industrial factory" (1988:40).

As with the concept of violence, we find it useful to think of gray zones in contemporary society as operating along a continuum of insupportable, structurally imposed settings. This perspective renders more visible the complex interaction between intimate behavior and larger coercive constraints. The homeless encampments along Edgewater Boulevard are obviously not equivalent to Nazi death camps. The Edgewater homeless sometimes quip, "No one put a gun to my head and made me shoot heroin." Their lives also often contain camaraderie, humor, and the joy of living. Nevertheless, addiction under conditions of extreme poverty and concerted police repression creates a morally ambiguous space that blurs the lines between victims and perpetrators. By extending the boundaries of the Holocaust's Gray Zone to the everyday world around us, we can understand the Edgewater homeless as surviving along an especially coercive and desperate swath of the gray zone continuum.

Levi and other survivors assert that we do not have the right to judge the actions of inmates in the concentration camps because the Gray Zone was omnipotent (Levi 1988; Steinberg 2000). He implicitly contradicts himself, however, by devoting much of his writing to eloquently dissecting the moral dilemmas of human agency at Auschwitz through detailed descriptions of individual behaviors, decisions, and interpersonal betrayals (see discussion in Bourgois 2005b). Following Levi, we explore the agency and moral responsibility of the homeless addicts we befriended without obscuring the structural forces that impose a gray zone. We examine in detail the micro-level mechanisms through which externally imposed forces operate on vulnerable individuals and communities.

Levi's insistence that we learn from the Holocaust in order to recognize the structural in-justices that pass for business as usual in normal times is consistent with anthropologist Michael Taussig's reading of Walter Benjamin's theory of history. Benjamin was also a vic-tim of Nazi repression for being a Jew (and a marxist). Shortly before committing suicide while trapped on the French border with Spain at the outbreak of World War II, he warned that most people fail to see the everyday "state of emergency" in which the socially vulner-able are forced to live (Benjamin [1940] 1968:257; see also detailed analysis by Taussig [1984, 1992] of the "space of death" and the "culture of terror" created by the Argentinean and Colombian states in the 1970s and 1990s and by the international rubber trade in the Ama-zon in the late nineteenth century).

Significantly, Benjamin was also excited about the potential of photography to foster a "politically educated eye" by provoking a "salutary estrangement" from one's surroundings. He distrusted the "free-floating contemplation" of pictures, however, and was worried by the capacity of a sentimental use of photography and film in fascist Europe to seduce view-ers with pretty pictures of a modernity that was increasingly brutal (Benjamin [1931] 1979:251). He admired Eugene Atget's photographs of everyday Paris—deserted, hard, and ordinary, nothing like the city's "exotic romantically sonorous" name. Consistent with his awareness of living in a perpetually misrecognized state of emergency, he noted, "Not for nothing have Atget's photographs been likened to those of the scene of a crime. But is not every square inch of our cities the scene of a crime? Every passer-by a culprit?" (Benjamin [1931] 1979:257; see also [1936] 1968:226). Ultimately, he argued, the way a photograph is "inscribed" in text and context or circulated as an object determines whether it will function as a reactionary "journalistic tool" or as a means to expose social relations: "Won't inscrip-tion become the most important part of the photograph?" (Benjamin [1931] 1999:527; see also discussions in Edwards and Hart 2004).

Outline of the Book

The book is written as a chronological narrative of the everyday lives of a dozen main char-acters (and another half dozen additional peripheral individuals) whom we followed for over a decade. We have organized the chapters around analytical themes related to the power re-lations and historical and institutional forces that shape their lives. Chapter 1, "Intimate Apartheid," addresses ethnic polarization and introduces most of the core members of our social network on the street. It also documents the ambiguous process of becoming home-less. We use the concept of "intimate apartheid" as a way to understand the enforcement of a racialized micro-geography of homeless encampments. Hostile social boundaries arise through intense interpersonal multiethnic proximity and forced mutual dependence rather than through the neighborhood-wide patterns of segregation that predominate in most of the urban United States.

The second chapter, "Falling in Love," explores gender relations on the street and the con-tinuum between romantic love and sex work. It features the life of a charismatic woman,

Tina, who grew up in poverty and violence with an unstable mother and no support from her father. In her middle age on Edgewater Boulevard, Tina attempts to carve out autonomy in her outlaw partnerships with Carter, but instead reproduces patriarchal arrangements through her search for romance, trust, and dignity.

The next five chapters address the body, childhood socialization, the legal labor market, experiences of parenthood, and male sexuality. Chapter 3, "A Community of Addicted Bodies," traces how physical and emotional dependence on heroin creates a morally bounded social network that allows clearly demarcated interpersonal hierarchies and personal agency in the construction of self-respect. From a social structural perspective, we examine how race and social marginalization become painfully inscribed on the bodies of homeless drug users and alcoholics. We critique public health and emergency hospital services and present explicit details of the painful and gruesome experience of everyday filth and infection among indigent heroin injectors. Most important, we emphasize the many ways in which the government's War on Drugs has exacerbated the physical and psychological harms of drug use and the overarching pain of the pariah homeless status. The chapter concludes with a close look at the routine experience of chronic physical and emotional suffering, ranging from hunger, cold, and filth to everyday interpersonal and institutional violence.

Chapter 4, "Childhoods," explores the ongoing kinship relations and diverse childhood experiences of the members of our social network, from violent and/or sexually predatory to neglectful or nurturing. The families of the African-American, Latino, and white men and women we befriended have dealt with addiction and homelessness in very different ways. We also set the Edgewater homeless in their historical epoch: they came of age in a working-class San Francisco neighborhood of single-family homes in the late 1960s and early 1970s, the epicenter for a youth culture that revolved around drugs, sex, rock 'n' roll, opposition to the Vietnam War, and rejection of middle-class values.

Chapter 5, "Making Money," examines income-generating strategies. We begin by analyzing the disappearance of industrial jobs in San Francisco and document the impact of this economic restructuring on men and women who did not adapt to the new service-based and high-tech economy that has made the San Francisco Bay Area one of the richest and most expensive regions in the United States. We show how the homeless survive in this wealthy environment through constantly shifting combinations of manual labor, panhandling, scavenging, welfare, and petty crime.

Chapter 6, "Parenting," describes the relationships of the Edgewater homeless with their children and explores the limits of identifying moral responsibility for long-term patterns of traumatic transgenerational relationships. The notion of a continuum between victim and perpetrator permeates much of the book (especially chapters 2 and 4), but it is portrayed most vividly here, along with an understanding of the patriarchal channeling of psycho-affective trauma around domestic violence.

Chapter 7, "Male Love," follows a long-term male running partnership to explore the phenomenon of homosocial love relationships among resolutely homophobic men. This chapter further documents the harmful effects of law enforcement on bodies and psyches and offers a detailed critique of the dysfunctional U.S. medical system, driven by market forces and retrenchment of public services. We revisit the painful topic of decaying bodies (explored in chapter 3) and raise the ante by confronting the large-scale phenomenon of premature aging among the homeless in the United States as a result of lifetimes of poverty and chronic drug, alcohol, and cigarette consumption. In this case, the county hospital in San Francisco provides excellent, expensive, high-tech medical services and has a dedicated, politically progressive medical staff. Unfortunately, the medical care is delivered in the glaring absence of community-based, low-tech social support services for the chronically infirm.

The last two chapters continue the narrative of the outlaw romantic couple described in the opening two chapters, Tina and Carter. Chapter 8, "Everyday Addicts," is written in an experimental style as a series of extended fieldnotes and conversations in order to convey, with greater texture and intimacy, the serendipity of daily life on the street. We evoke the passage of real time, showing how anxiety, excitement, fun, violence, and banality are interwoven. We also provide a glimpse of the wider range of peripheral characters in the Edgewater scene. The Bonnie-and-Clyde love affair between Tina and Carter ends in chapter 9, "Treatment," with an account of their attempts to quit heroin. This final chapter also describes experiences of treatment and recovery by other core members of our social network.

In our conclusion, "Critically Applied Public Anthropology," we propose short-term pragmatic policy recommendations and discuss the structural political and economic changes necessary for the longer-term improvement of the lives of the indigent poor in the United States. We end with a theoretical discussion of our current moment in history, at the turn of the twenty-first century, when people like the Edgewater homeless represent the all-American tip of an iceberg, overshadowing an ever-larger proportion of the world's population who, beginning in the early 1980s, have been politically and economically excluded by the imposition of U.S.-style neoliberal policies across the globe (Harvey 2005). In a nutshell, services for vulnerable populations have been dismantled in favor of a punitive model of government that has expanded investment in prisons, police forces, and armies while promoting income inequality and corporate subsidies.

Abuse in all its inevitably intertwined forms—institutional, political, structural, psychological, and interpersonal—is ugly. We present the full controversial range of behaviors and beliefs of the Edgewater homeless in these pages in order to convey the urgency of addressing their suffering pragmatically and humanely. Most important, we provide a critical means for theorizing the effects of power in our neoliberal era. The intellectual debates addressing poverty, addiction, and individual responsibility in the United States need to break out of the confines of moral judgment. The Edgewater homeless deserve to be taken seriously for who they are and not for who we want them to be. We believe that they tell us a great deal about the United States, and they alert us to the challenges the world faces in the early twenty-first century.

Chapter 1

Intimate Apartheid

If you notice, it's real racial. Whites in one camp, blacks in another camp. And I live right in the middle, by myself. They're all a bunch of racist motherfuckers—both the niggers and the whites.

The whites ain't no better than the blacks. They will rip you off too. I don't trust either group. So I'm alone. The only Latino . . . I don't have nothin' here. —*Felix*

Toward the middle of the first year of our fieldwork, a lull in law enforcement allowed a central camp to emerge that was larger and somewhat drier than the other, more precarious encampments we had been visiting in the alleys behind Edgewater Boulevard. This new camp was protected from the rain by a supersize I-beam retrofitted in the decade following the 1989 Loma Prieta earthquake to support a double-decker, eight-lane freeway. The site was also camouflaged by garbage and a canopy of scrub oaks and eucalyptus branches. A tangle of access and exit ramps further isolated the spot, which became its own mini-universe, despite the thousands of commuters speeding by on the freeway above and the steady flow of pedestrians on the boulevard a half dozen yards away. At rush hour, the dull white noise of traffic made the camp feel almost safe, although it reeked of urine and rotting detritus and was wet and cold. One of the freeway's cement panels also thumped unnervingly when SUVs or trucks passed overhead.

Max was the first to settle the spot, followed by running partners Felix and Frank, who moved there after they were evicted from a more exposed site at the foot of the freeway embankment. Petey and Scotty, two inseparable running partners newly arrived from Southern California, were the next to move in. They slept together on a twin-size mattress laid out on the bare ground. At night they spooned for warmth under a thin blanket given to them by a church soup kitchen in the residential neighborhood up the hill from the boulevard. Felix nicknamed Scotty and Petey "the Island Boys" because they spent most of their daylight hours panhandling and selling heroin on the surrounding traffic islands. Felix maintained the more profitable and safer sales spot in front of the A&C corner store. The heavy flow of anonymous pedestrian traffic heading to the three catty-corner bus stops surrounding the corner store allowed Felix to camouflage his dealing as panhandling.

Al, a toothless, forty-year-old man, moved into the encampment soon after the Island Boys. He built a shack out of loading pallets that was just wide enough to fit a full-size double bed, which he shared with his "girlfriend," Rosie. She visited once a month, on the day he received his Social Security Insurance (SSI) disability payments for alcoholism, and stayed only long enough to help him spend his entire check on crack, leaving him, dopesick, within forty-eight hours. Felix and Frank resented Rosie's exclusive access to Al's crack and eventually persuaded him to kick her out. Al's only comment was, "She never even let me fuck her! She's got something against sex. Seems like her stepfather raped her when she was a kid." Al was exceptionally easy-going, and after Rosie left, he allowed "no-hustle" Hogan to sleep at the entrance to his shack under a makeshift tarp.

Hank, an old-timer in his mid-fifties, was the last to establish himself as a regular inhabitant of the camp. He slept in a bright red pup tent, having just been thrown out of a housing project apartment in the residential neighborhood up the hill, where he had been living for the past year. According to Felix, the apartment belonged to "an old dopefiend lesbian bitch" whom they had all known since adolescence. The night he first arrived, Hank had a fresh "stab wound" under his right armpit, but Felix dismissed it: "Probably just an abscess they cut out of him at the county hospital. Don't ever believe a word Hank says." Nevertheless, Felix and everyone else treated Hank well because he was exceptionally generous, sharing heroin and fortified wine. Like Al, Hank was also energetic, constantly building and cleaning when high. On weekends, he would scavenge overripe vegetables from the dumpsters at the farmers market half a mile down the boulevard and cook stew for everyone in the camp.

Hank was the first person we actually saw "become homeless." Transitions to homelessness are often ambiguous, as individuals bounce in and out of single-room occupancy (SRO) hotels and the homes of ever-dwindling networks of family, friends, and acquaintances (Hopper 2003:77–85). Hank, for example, cycled through precarious housing arrangements for twenty-five years before he became homeless full time. Initially, he thought of it as "a temporary arrangement" on his way to "something better." When we asked Hank why he did not go to a public shelter instead of sleeping under the freeway in the cold, he replied without hesitating: "Shelters aren't safe. They got like gangs, like cliques, you know, running the show, and the staff doesn't know what's going on. Would you go to a shelter?" All of the Edgewater homeless referred to shelters with a similar disdain, if not with fear (see Marcus 2005:68–77 for a critique of a New York City shelter).

Besides Al's crack-smoking ex-girlfriend, Rosie, only two other women occasionally stayed overnight in the camp during our first year on Edgewater Boulevard. One, an acquaintance of Felix, worked at San Francisco's lowest-budget, sex-for-crack prostitute stroll on Capp Street, some twenty blocks away. The other woman was Nickie, who lived with her eight-year-old son in a project apartment a half mile down the boulevard, near the farmers market. Welfare paid her rent directly to the Housing Authority through the Aid to Families with Dependent Children program. Nickie supported her heroin habit by combining odd jobs cleaning houses with panhandling and shoplifting from liquor stores. She also let some of the Edgewater homeless use her apartment to shower, wash their laundry, and inject in return for shares of their heroin and alcohol. Life on the street was more dangerous for women than for men (Bourgois, Prince, and Moss 2004). Our fieldwork notes, for example, contain several references to the rape and murder of two women on the periphery of our social network as well as to a serial killer's rampage against Capp Street sex workers (*San Francisco Chronicle* 2004, March 21).

Ethnic Hierarchies on the Street

During our first year, all the homeless in the central encampment were white, except Felix, whose parents were from Central America. We rarely saw African-Americans, Asians, or Latinos visit the encampments. In the immediate neighborhood, however, the daytime and early evening population was a kaleidoscope of San Francisco's ethnic diversity. The bus stops abutting the A&C corner store served five major bus lines linking three adjoining neighborhoods with distinct ethnic compositions. One route led to unlicensed garment and light manufacturing sweatshops in the warehouse district, where the labor force consisted primarily of Pacific Islanders, Southeast Asians, Chinese, Latinos, and a dwindling number of African-Americans. This same bus line continued on to Third Street, through Hunters Point–Bayview, the city's poorest African-American neighborhood. This area, surrounding defunct navy shipyards, had San Francisco's highest gang murder rates throughout most of the 1990s and 2000s (*San Francisco Chronicle* 2008, January 15; see also Kevin Epps's 2003 documentary *Straight Outta Hunters Point*).

During World War II, an unprecedented employment boom in the San Francisco shipyards spawned the large-scale migration of rural African-Americans from Louisiana and East Texas. The majority of these immigrants settled in the swampy flatland immediately surrounding their workplaces, and Hunters Point became San Francisco's largest segregated black community. Some of the newcomers managed to buy single-family homes on the steep hill overlooking Edgewater Boulevard, and that neighborhood became the city's most ethnically diverse census tract (Latino, white, African-American, Filipino, and Pacific Islander). This was the residential neighborhood where most of the Edgewater homeless had grown up, and it was where Philippe lived (a few blocks up from the A&C corner store). Like most of San Francisco, the neighborhood gentrified rapidly during our fieldwork years and began losing many of its working-class Latino and African-American residents (Thorne-Lyman and Treuhaft 2003). According to census data, between 1990 and 2000, the city of San Francisco as a whole lost almost a quarter (23.4 percent) of its African-American population (U.S. Bureau of the Census 1991, 2002).

A second bus line headed north to the county hospital and continued through the heart of the poorer, but also gentrifying, predominantly Latino neighborhood known as the Mission District. A third bus line led to an underfunded local high school, home to several competing Latino gangs. Finally, three additional bus lines served San Francisco's southern suburbs, which were whiter and wealthier but retained scattered dwindling pockets of working-class communities.

On a typical warm summer evening, the main corner where the homeless spent a great deal of their time, in front of the A&C convenience store, attracted a half dozen very distinct groups of people. Most visible were the middle-aged African-American men who, on their way home from work, congregated and drank beer by a barbecue at the entrance to the alley behind the store. By nightfall, younger African-American crack dealers arrived. They camouflaged their sales by mingling with the barbecue crowd and by circulating among the Latino and Asian commuters around the corner who were waiting at the bus stops. Cars pulled up to the sidewalk, pausing just long enough for a subtle exchange of dollar bills through the passenger-side window. In the doorway of the A&C, two or three Yemeni men chatted in Arabic with the cashiers. Sometimes they chewed qat, a psychoactive stimulant imported from Eritrea. On rare occasions, the wife of the store's owner, fully veiled in a black chador that revealed only her eyes, walked out from the back of the premises carrying a shopping bag and a baby. Young, new-immigrant Latino men crisscrossed the sidewalk running late errands for the primarily white- and Arab-owned construction-related businesses along the boulevard.

In this mix, two or three of the white homeless leaned against a wall at the edge of the African-American barbecue scene or inside one of the bus shelters nodding in deep heroin sedation. Latino and Filipino youths, mostly high school age, in the latest hip-hop outfits, passed by to ask the Edgewater homeless to buy beer, cigarettes, and cigars for them. They would hollow out the cigars to prepare "blunts" of marijuana, but they rarely stopped to smoke on the corner.

The homeless, middle-aged, white heroin injectors we befriended were at the bottom of the corner's social hierarchy and often displayed their low status by begging in tattered clothing. An early set of fieldnotes reveals how rapidly we had to learn the meaning of our skin color in this scene. Even though we looked healthy and dressed in clean clothes, we were lumped by default with the low-status "stanky white dopefiends."

Philippe's Fieldnotes

While accompanying Al and Hogan back to the main encampment, I slow down as we pass the barbecue scene in the alley, hoping to initiate a passing conversation with one of the younger African-American crack dealers. My attempt at friendly eye contact is dismissed with a wave of the arm and a gruff "Keep moving, keep moving." When I smile and nod hello, the young man shouts, "I said keep moving!" I overhear him telling his partner in a lower voice, "Damn! Do those motherfuckers smell bad!" Embarrassed, I hurry to catch up with Al and Hogan, noticing that Hogan has brown stains in the rear of his pants, presumably from having lost control of his bowels this morning as a result of dopesickness.

The ethnic hierarchies of street culture in San Francisco are not exclusive to drug culture and homelessness. The hegemony of African-American style extends throughout the United States and through much of global popular culture. It is historically inscribed in slang (from jive to hip-hop), in music (from blues and jazz to rap), in clothing (from zoot suits to sagging jeans), and in body posture (from handshakes to gait and facial expressions).

But the "coolness" of African-American street culture does not translate into economic and political power in the United States. On the contrary, blackness and expressions of hip-hop or working-class street culture exclude individuals from access to upward mobility in the corporate economy. Despite their clear subordination within the local street-hustler hierarchy and their exclusion from mainstream white society, the durability of racism in the United States allowed the homeless whites on Edgewater Boulevard to hold on to an ideology of white supremacy. Among themselves, for example, they used the word *nigger* routinely. When African-Americans were in earshot, however, they practiced deference, fearing violence or humiliation. At first, it did not occur to the whites that we might not share their racism. They treated racialized distinctions as self-evident common sense and often used the clichés of middle-class society when we asked them about race relations.

Philippe: Why is this scene so white?

Hank: I've never really thought about it. We keep amongst ourselves. The black with the black and the white with the white. That's about it, you know. Basically, blacks stay to themselves.

Philippe: But where are the black dopefiends? I never see any here.

Hank: Well, they're around, but they don't hang out. Everybody buys from everybody, but for actually sitting there and actually using together? They don't do that. I've got a lot of black connections, but if I was to sit there and use with them. . . . I won't use with them.

Matter of fact, you'll see very few black people homeless . . . because they're knocking out kids on welfare.

Philippe: [surprised] 'Cause what?

Hank: You know, having kids. Every one of those black guys over there [pointing toward the barbecue grill in the alley] has three or four kids, and an old lady at home. They're all collecting welfare.

Have you ever seen a black guy really walk?

Philippe: [confused] Really what?

Hank: Walk. Just about every black guy I know owns a car, either a Cadillac or something new.

Yeah, they pretty much stay to themselves. I've never really got in to find out where they go or what they do, you know. Hell, they don't bother me, I don't bother them, you know. Keep the peace that way.

But when you start mixing the races, especially the blacks down there [pointing to the alley and rolling his eyes], everybody's kind of semi-prejudiced. So we don't really exchange information. We say hello—just general things.

Felix: [interrupting] Blacks are into crack . . . scandalous crack monsters. You can't trust niggers.

Hank: Yeah.

Felix: They'll rob you. They'll steal from their own mother. None of the blacks want to work. All they want to do is smoke crack all night.

Hank: Can't trust niggers.

Felix: I hate selling to them. They'll come back and mug you.

The irony of the assertion by the whites that they were the victims of black violence and theft emerged years later when we coded our fieldnotes and transcripts. We discovered that during our first year none of the whites in our Edgewater homeless scene had been robbed by an African-American. In fact, their most generous patron was an elderly African-American man who was an evangelical Christian. When it rained heavily, he allowed several of them to sleep under an old camper shell in a storage lot he owned on the boulevard. Furthermore, the only case of black-on-white violence we recorded that first year occurred when one of the whites peripheral to our social network stole thirty dollars' worth of crack from an African-American dealer for whom he was supposed to be selling on consignment. He was beaten "as a warning" for "smoking up the product," and when he "came up short" again the next week, he fled from the boulevard and never returned.

Irrespective of ethnicity, the United States has consistently had the highest levels of interpersonal violence of all industrialized nations, and that violence is disproportionately concentrated in poor urban communities. Handguns were cheap and easily available on Edgewater Boulevard. No one who spends long hours on streets where drug sellers congregate can escape the background threat of violence. Early in our fieldwork, one of the young crack sellers in the alley was stabbed in the neck while Jeff was photographing a couple of yards away. On one of Jeff's first visits to the corner, a crack seller, seeing Jeff with his camera for the first time, threatened him in a low voice, "You are not getting out of here alive." Overhearing the interaction, Hank confirmed, "He isn't joking. We have to go," and they hurried away. That particular crack seller, who flew into unpredictable rages when he drank too much, never came to like us, but on one occasion he shared a bologna sandwich, prepared by his wife, with a member of the ethnographic team.

The tendency to sensationalize the imminence of violence against outsiders by inner-city residents further isolates microneighborhoods (Bourgois 2003b:32–33). After dark, residents from the neighborhood up the hill avoided the corner where we spent most of our time. At night, bus drivers warned Philippe not to get off when he requested the local stop. Some drivers routinely refused to continue their official route through the nearby housing projects. Despite our early impressions of potential risk, and the occasional spectacular incidents of aggression we did witness in our periphery, violence was never, in fact, a significant problem for us. The men in our homeless network were middle-aged survivors who were physically weakened by long-term daily drug and alcohol consumption. Most of them, consequently, purposefully avoided engaging in physical aggression, and we felt safe among them.

The Arrival of African-Americans

During the second year of our fieldwork, an African-American heroin injector named Carter James became a regular in our homeless scene. He had grown up on the same block as Felix, in the neighborhood up the hill, and Hank also knew him, having used heroin with Carter's older brother during his adolescence. Directly contradicting everything Hank had previously told us about "never mingling with blacks," all the white heroin injectors welcomed Carter onto Edgewater Boulevard, referring to him by his nickname, C. J. He worked as a parking attendant for a Jaguar auto dealership and contributed generously in the moral economy of sharing. Every day, he came directly from work to the A&C corner store to buy heroin from Felix with the money he earned from tips.

As Carter spent more and more of his free time on the corner after work, his heroin habit and alcohol consumption escalated. At the time, he was living with his eldest sister, Beverly, in Hunters Point, sleeping on her living room couch. His trajectory into full-time homelessness took only six weeks. It began when he stopped contributing his share of rent and food to his sister's household. He would come to Edgewater Boulevard to inject early in the morning, complaining that everyone was "against" him. His sister, he said, was "always on my case" over "trivial" matters, and his boss was "riding me" for arriving late to work.

When Carter was finally thrown out of his sister's home, he presented it as a voluntary decision on his part, made to protect his patriarchal self-respect from a family that no longer acknowledged the authority of the older male:

> I came this close to strangling my niece. I'll never forget what she said to me. "I'm not going to let you kill my mother like you did your mother." That disrespectful bitch! I couldn't allow her to keep talking to me that way. But she can call the cops and say I hit her, and I'd go to jail. So I walked. I left, with Beverly, my oldest sister, standing there crying.

Carter was more afraid of losing his job than of becoming homeless: "I'll keep my job even if I have to sleep out here." For about a week, he managed to make daily payments for a single-room occupancy hotel room in the nearby Mission District. Finally, early one morning, Carter arrived with his army duffle bag full of clothes. He was not on his way to work, and he no longer had money to rent a room. Felix and his running partner, Frank, the sign painter, made room for Carter next to them under the I-beam, and he laid out a mattress of scavenged carpet remnants.

It rained the first night Carter slept on Edgewater Boulevard. Everyone had already settled to sleep as the drizzle began. Philippe was hurrying home when he heard Carter calling after him. He was dragging his bulging duffle bag, looking confused. He was scared to leave his possessions unattended in the camp, but he desperately wanted to talk. He had been injecting speedballs, a heroin/cocaine mixture, all evening and was shivering from the cold as well as from his overstimulated emotions. He spoke with the friendly intensity that coke rushes sometimes trigger. Philippe was eager to head home up the hill before the drizzle became a drenching rain. He also anticipated that Carter was going to make a pitch for a loan of money, so he tried to shake Carter's hand goodbye and politely cut the conversation short. Instead, Carter burst into tears, hugging Philippe repeatedly. "I'm to'e [torn] up, Philippe. Don't forget me. I lost my job . . . my home . . . everything. I'm to'e up."

Racial Disequilibrium

Within a week, Carter went from being an employed, housed, and high-status giver in the moral economy to a quarrelsome taker. Having suddenly lost his steady source of legal income, he had not yet established an effective street hustle. He considered begging from strangers demeaning. Instead, he coerced money out of friends and acquaintances and intimidated campmates to give him the leftover cottons from their injections. He gave up buying vodka and began bumming slugs of Cisco Berry. The whites now dismissed him as "nothin' but a fuckin' nigger peon."

Carter's full-time presence in the main encampment and in front of the corner store attracted three additional African-Americans into the core group of regulars on Edgewater Boulevard: Stretch, Sonny, and Tina. Stretch, in his mid-thirties, was the youngest, and he was only beginning to use heroin. He had recently left an aunt's house, evicted by the renovation and retrenchment of the housing project where she lived, in the gentrifying Fillmore neighborhood bordering Haight-Ashbury, a wealthy district and a magnet for tourists. Stretch still did not know how to inject himself, and he exchanged puffs from his glass crack pipe with Felix and Carter in return for assistance with administering shots of heroin. They were happy to help him, since his physical tolerance for opiates was still low, and they did not have to give him much heroin in exchange for his shares of crack. Tina, a woman in her early forties, never injected heroin. She drank large quantities of whatever sixteen-ounce can of malt liquor was on sale at the corner store and smoked crack. Sonny, in his late forties, had just "left" his girlfriend's apartment in the housing project on the far side of the residential neighborhood up the hill, following a stint in county jail for selling crack.

Stretch and Sonny placed their mattresses next to Carter's in the dry corner of the camp where Felix and Frank slept. Tina did not sleep in the camp because she still had access to a couch in a cousin's project apartment down the boulevard. Sometimes, however, she stayed up all night in the main encampment binging on crack with Carter, Sonny, and Stretch. Several additional African-American men, who had more stable housing, began visiting the encampment regularly to inject heroin, smoke crack, and hang out. They included A. J., Carter's older brother, who lived with his wife and children in Oakland; Vernon, who lived in a housing project apartment with his wife, a nurse; and Reggie, a fifty-year-old man, buff from lifting weights in the San Quentin prison yard. Reggie stayed at his sister's apartment in the same housing project where Tina lived. He drank and smoked crack avidly but dismissed heroin as a "loser drug."

The ethnic transformation of the main hang-out scene in front of the A&C corner store was most dramatic. Reggie, dressed in a black leather suit, would call out loudly to passersby,

"I need ya!" His smile would turn into a curse if no money was forthcoming. When white pedestrians failed to acknowledge eye contact, he accused them of racism. No one dared to cross Reggie except for Felix, who resented losing control of this optimal panhandling and heroin selling spot.

Philippe's Fieldnotes

Felix accuses Reggie of being "a racist motherfucker" and "bad for business" because of his intimidating panhandling style. Reggie responds with a howl of mirth and urinates into the gutter, facing out toward the passing traffic. While relieving himself, he pounds on the metal top of the trashcan on the corner, chanting, "Fuck you, Felix!" Reggie shakes his fist at a white driver who slows down to stare in disapproval. He blows a kiss at an African-American woman in a Volvo who has stopped at the red light and is frowning at his display. He makes a squishy baby face at her young child in the back seat, prompting the toddler to drop her imitation of her mother's frown and instead giggle and wave back at him, playing peek-a-boo.

Outraged, Felix slams his open hands onto Reggie's chest and shouts, "Pig!" Reggie shoves him back even harder, and their roughhousing escalates into solid punches aimed at the chest and the shoulders. Their blows to the face, however, are noticeably softer. Twice, Reggie loses his balance on his patent leather shoes, sliding off the curb into honking traffic. After one particularly energetic round, they de-escalate by hugging and take turns kissing one another on both cheeks, laughing.

There are a half dozen of us watching this choreographed fighting, including one of the "youngster rock stars [teenage crack sellers]" from around the corner. The youngster walks slowly over to the garbage can and urinates in the same spot as Reggie did, daring anyone to call him a pig, too.

Sonny notices that the roughhousing has unnerved me, and he gently steers me a few yards down the sidewalk with his arm around my shoulder. He whispers in a tone that is meant to reassure, "Reggie thinks I'll be on his side. Like, he thinks I don't love Felix—but I'm not about skin color."

From thirty feet away, Reggie notices Sonny by my side and yells, "You sucking up to the white boy!" Sneering, Reggie slaps hands in a high-five with two additional young African-American crack sellers who have run over from the barbecue and crack alley to check out the commotion.

Sonny immediately breaks away from me, mumbling, "See how they're talking shit about me for talking to you?"

To my relief, Felix refocuses the spotlight on his fight with Reggie and it becomes a racialized contest of masculinity:

Felix: "Pig!"

Reggie: "Miserable dopefiend! You sit in your shit and vomit! [imitating the heroin nod] You sleep in dirt. No one needs to live in the dirt."

Felix: "The pioneers lived in the dirt. At least I'm decent enough to go around the corner when I shit."

Reggie: [doubling over with laughter] "You have to take your panties off to shit, you modern-day pioneer. [grabbing his crotch] You wanna play with it? Suck my black dick."

Felix: [screaming in a falsetto voice and slapping Reggie's left cheek with an open hand] "Bitch!"

Once again, this successfully defuses the escalating tension, causing everyone, including Reggie, to laugh. Reggie ends the confrontation by hugging Felix. "Okay, man, I'm enjoying my high. You're enjoying your high. Leave me alone. Let's enjoy our highs."

Immediately after hugging Felix, however, Reggie walks over to me, grabs me by the shoulder, and drags me to the entrance of the store: "White boy! How about a bottle?" When I shrug my shoulders and try to change the topic, Reggie shouts, "What's the matter? You never look out for us brothers! You only throw shit down to the whites!" The Yemeni cashier walks out of the store to berate Reggie for the commotion. Reggie responds with a big smile, "What's the matter, cousin? I'm only hassling a white boy!" This elicits a laugh from the cashier and they exchange a high-five of solidarity over their heads.

Successfully intimidating a dollar out of me, Reggie follows the cashier into the store and buys a pint of vodka. Perhaps energized by his sexualized display of masculine domination over Felix, Reggie accuses the cashier of "never having touched any pussy." This prompts the young Yemeni to call out angrily in Arabic. A little boy about seven years old walks sheepishly out of a storage room in the back of the store that serves as living quarters. In broken English, the cashier shouts, "Who is your father?" Bewildered and embarrassed, the boy points back to the cashier and says in flawless, California-accented English, "He is my father." Laughing, Reggie reaches across the counter to give the cashier another high-five.

The cashier then calls Reggie a name, presumably an insult, but none of us can understand it because of his accent. He repeats the word several times to no avail. It sounds somewhat like the word never, but when he pronounces it more slowly, it approximates something like nehger. Finally, Reggie bursts out laughing, shouting for everyone out on the corner to hear, "The A-rab is calling me a nigger, and he's just an A-rab. And they all came from our nuts!"

White Flight

Ethnic tensions also mounted during these weeks in the main shooting encampment. The three new African-American residents, Carter, Sonny, and Stretch, appropriated the driest area in the camp by the central fire pit, and their spot became the center of late-night activity. Despite the early arrival of the heavy winter rains, the whites moved their mattresses away from the protection of the I-beam and slung up tarps for shelter on the edge of the camp. They expressed their racist response to losing control of the camp as moral outrage. As Hank complained, "They keep us up all night, bringing their other nigger crack friends by and making noise. Don't they realize that other people live here?"

Hogan was the first to move out of the encampment "to escape from the niggers." Carter had repeatedly threatened to beat him up unless he took a shower, changed his clothes, and cleaned out his half dozen abscesses. Hogan exemplified the low status of the whites in the scene, and everyone scorned him. Felix was especially dismissive: "Hogan's a wannabe dopefiend. He's only got a cotton habit. I've seen him bang a cotton that's already been banged. He's an animal! Dirty!" On several occasions, members of the ethnographic team found Hogan rummaging through other people's paraphernalia to harvest heroin residue from the sides of their used syringes, cookers, and discarded cottons. His especially unhygienic injection practices resulted in multiple foul-smelling chronic abscesses. Furthermore, in contrast to the other homeless, who were skinny to the point of emaciation, Hogan was obese, straining from the weight of his oversized body and constantly sweating as he hobbled with an uncoordinated gait on swollen feet.

Hogan set up camp three blocks away in a gully along the freeway embankment behind an all-night diner and bar, the Dockside Bar & Grill. The bar's flashing red neon sign, WE NEVER CLOSE, threw shadows over his camp twenty-four hours a day. The low-lying spot he selected in order to decrease his visibility flooded as the winter rains escalated. To stay above the rising water level, he piled three mattresses on top of one another, but this did not help him much because his only other protection was a plastic tarp that he pulled over his blankets when he was not too drunk. When the owner of the Dockside complained, the police attempted a raid. They did not want to get their feet wet, however, and they were too repulsed by the smell to enter and ticket Hogan for possession of injection paraphernalia. Homelessness was not technically illegal in San Francisco, but when an individual failed to appear in court to pay a misdemeanor ticket, a bench warrant was automatically issued, enabling the police to arrest that person.

Isolated in his new camp, Hogan tearfully told anyone who would listen that his festering multiple abscesses were the result of AIDS. His formerly scornful companions expressed sympathy and stopped by to give him wet cottons. Even the hardened storekeepers along the boulevard started giving him money and food. We too brought him clothes, food, blankets, and petty cash and began tape-recording his life story. There was not yet any effective treatment for HIV at this time, and Hogan said that he was talking to us "for posterity's sake."

Meanwhile, back at the main camp, ethnic tensions were deepening with complaints by the whites that the "scandalous niggers" were attracting too much attention from the police. Scotty and Petey, the Island Boys, who had emerged as the steadiest retail heroin sellers on the boulevard, moved to Hogan's camp but placed their mattress on drier ground, slightly higher up the embankment. Hank was the next white to leave. He obtained a beat-up motor home and parked it up the hill, on the same block where he had lived as a teenager. Al also left, but not out of antipathy to the African-Americans; he was simply taking advantage of an invitation from his parents to help renovate their garage in San Francisco's southern suburbs. Max, meanwhile, was hospitalized for several weeks for an abscess on his upper arm that required complicated muscle transfer surgery. Upon his release, he took "one look at the nigger camp" and joined Hogan in the gully behind the Dockside Bar & Grill.

Running partners Felix and Frank were the only two remaining original members of what had been the mostly white encampment. Frank stayed in the camp but moved his possessions ten meters farther up the embankment, claiming, "Those goddamn niggers thieve you blind." He jammed his mattress right up against the bottom of the freeway overpass so that he had to bend over double to avoid scraping his head on the cement panels. The roar of traffic speeding by just inches overhead made it impossible to hold a conversation, and the entire spot shook when trucks passed. Following heavy rains, highway runoff turned the steep climb to his mattress into a waterfall.

A Latino Interlude

Felix was the only member of our original social network to maintain friendly relations with Carter and the newly arrived African-Americans, sharing crack and heroin with them regularly. Frank, who had been Felix's running partner for years, was furious about this. He blamed Felix for having "turned our camp into a niggers' shooting gallery." Formerly, Felix had been the only Latino in the scene and had been treated as an "honorary white." The arrival of the African-Americans allowed him to establish a new ethnic space for himself, and he began referring to his former companions as "lame whites."

Felix asserted his Latino identity by befriending a Puerto Rican injector named Victor, who drove a forklift at a corrugated cardboard factory in South San Francisco. A barrel of glue had fallen on Victor at work, fracturing two disks in his lower back, and he was placed on disability payments for three months to recover. During those months, he spent most of his time with Felix. Shortly after returning to work, Victor was arrested while purchasing a ten-dollar bag of heroin during his lunch break. He claimed he needed the heroin to treat his ongoing lower back pain, but he spent three days dopesick in the county jail before the charges were dismissed. His supervisor immediately fired him for absenteeism, and he began hanging out full time on Edgewater Boulevard.

A few weeks later, Victor's twenty-four-year-old son, Little Vic, just released from two years in San Quentin prison for crack selling, drove up to the corner in a brand-new Mitsubishi Montero SUV looking for his father. Little Vic stayed with his grandmother in the housing project up the hill. He forced his girlfriend, whose parents owned the SUV he was driving, to sleep alone in the vehicle, which he parked in the alley behind the corner store because his grandmother did not approve of premarital sex.

Like most of the under-thirty-year-olds who passed through our scene, Little Vic spurned heroin and needle use, but he wanted to spend time with his father and treated him to a prolonged crack binge. Felix joined them, and soon Little Vic was calling him "uncle." Little Vic's mother was white, but he presented himself proudly as "Puerto Rican one hundred percent, just like my father." Maintaining a perennially angry expression on his face, he began harassing the whites. He referred to Felix's running partner, Frank, as "that white trash motherfucker." In contrast, he curried favor with the African-Americans and spent most of his time hanging out with the younger crack sellers by the barbecue grill and at the bus stops.

In the court deposition given by Little Vic's mother requesting that her son be remanded to drug treatment rather than sent to prison, the roots of Little Vic's polarized ethnic identity become clear. His mother begins by describing herself as "a third generation San Franciscan [from] a solid middle-class family . . . [of] Irish, Scottish and Italian descent" and pointedly notes that Victor Senior is "unfortunately . . . [from] quite a different background. He is a man of Puerto Rican descent from New York City."

> Victor would constantly awaken the children at all hours of the night, e.g., 3 A.M. and insist that they speak Spanish to him, although they did not know the language. He would argue with the young children as if they were his equal. . . .
>
> . . . My children and I . . . would barricade the front door to try to avoid Victor's drunken rages. He would come home and break down the barricades and my children and I would have to flee through the back door and over the fence to my parents' house 2 doors away. I kept a complete change of clothes for the children and myself packed so we could run away at a moment's notice. . . .
>
> Victor would steal money from Little Vic and the other children to buy drugs. He sold their television to buy drugs. He would take the welfare checks that would arrive, cash them, and spend the money for drugs. We'd be left with nothing for food. There were times when our family had literally nothing, furniture had to be repossessed, all went involuntarily . . . to support Victor's drug habit.

The details of her account illustrate how domestic violence is often channeled along patriarchal fault lines. In this case, a failed father figure was lashing out at the children he could no longer control (see Bourgois 1995:213–222, 301–307). In an incident reminiscent of Carter's outrage against his niece, "disrespect" from a young girl in the household elicits especially abusive behavior by the unemployed, drug-using, alcoholic father striving to hold onto his waning male privilege:

> Once while Little Vic was present his twin sister Nina made a "smart" remark to her father. Victor picked her up by her 2 ponytails up to his shoulder height. Victor would also stand by the corner of our children's school and yell obscenities at them as they were exiting the school . . . and spit on [them].

Little Vic's mother specifies that her son was socialized into male violence well before adolescence. Her account evokes a standard tragic/heroic oedipal scenario: the son valiantly protecting his long-suffering mother from a violent father.

> Once Little Vic happened to walk through the door with his cousin when Victor was beating me severely on the living room floor. . . . That night he told me, "Mom, if dad touches you one

more time I'm going to kill him." I told Little Vic that if he were to do such a thing he would be taken to jail and I would never see him again. Little Vic replied, "Mom, but if dad killed you I won't ever see you again." Little Vic was 8 years old at the time.

The judge was not sympathetic to the pleas of Little Vic's mother and sentenced him to two years in San Quentin instead of mandating drug treatment.

Victor Senior's memories of himself as a family man are remarkably different from those of his wife. He clings to a discourse of responsible patriarchy, buttressed by romance and evangelical faith.

I respected my wife and my children and my home. I never used [heroin] in my house or got them involved. I didn't fix [inject] in my house. I had a family that I cared about. I went through the Victory Ministry Christian program after prison, and my morals got stronger. I did love my wife.

Back on Edgewater Boulevard, Little Vic, now grown up, bonded with his father through crack smoking and aggression against the whites. He "beat down" Jim, a newly arrived heroin injector from San Francisco's white, formerly working-class suburb of Brisbane, chasing him permanently out of the scene. Little Vic also regularly bullied Hogan, the weakest man in the group, taxing his panhandling earnings. He also mugged Frank, and, to our surprise, Felix helped him:

Frank: Little Vic walks up the hill here at night with his father when I'm by myself. Felix is comin' up behind them. "Hey, Frank! Come here." They act all friendly.

Then the kid grabs me. [in a gruff voice] "Hey, man. Where's that twenty dollars you owe me from last year before I went to the pen?"

I don't know the kid from Adam. I just met the guy, and he starts this "I'm gonna mother-fuckin' kick your ass."

The kid is bigger than me, younger than me, and I'm thinking, "I got a problem here." He takes a swing at me and grabs me, but I break loose. But where am I gonna go? Through the trees and across the fuckin' freeway and get killed?

I'm backed up against the freeway, lookin' around. I call, "Hey, Felix! Come here." I'm figuring Felix would back me up, but instead Felix—he pushes me, grabs me around the back, and puts me in a bear hug. *Felix* does!

I twist around and Felix punches me in the stomach. When I flinch, the kid snatches the money from my pocket and runs down the hill. And Felix runs right after him. That mother-fucking lying sack of shit!

Scared and depressed after this betrayal by his long-term running partner, Frank entered a twenty-one-day methadone detox facility. He abandoned his mattress and all his posses-sions under the overpass, declaring, "Felix didn't stab me in the back. He stabbed me right here [patting his heart]." Frank lasted for a week in detox before dropping out and settling into the new encampment of whites behind the Dockside Bar & Grill. He became Max's running partner. Felix, meanwhile, felt guilty: "I wish Frank knew what really happened. I was trying to help him. I was just trying to push him aside, and now he blames me for beating him up. Oh, man! Frank has left me forever."

Shortly after mugging Frank, Little Vic drove off in his girlfriend's SUV with another woman and disappeared on an extended crack binge across town. Before leaving, Little Vic ordered his girlfriend to stay with Felix under the I-beam. To enforce his mandate, he took her shoes, leaving her barefoot in the mud. Little Vic's girlfriend remained semi-catatonic next to Felix's mattress, ignoring our offers to help. At first, she did not touch any alcohol or drugs, but Tina reached out to her and, in a gesture of feminine solidarity, shared food with her. Soon they were smoking crack together and drinking malt liquor. Reactions to Little Vic's girlfriend highlight the misogyny of street scenes. Felix bolstered his masculinity at her expense by jousting with Reggie in front of the A&C corner store:

> *Felix:* Little Vic ran off with some other ho', and now his bitch is cryin' all the time. Women can't live on the streets like a man. Why is she out here living in the dirt when she's got an apartment in the East Bay? She's got to wash her pussy, wash her ass. Women have more needs than men and I'm not going to change my style. I'm going to shit and piss where I have to and I don't give a shit about her.
>
> *Reggie:* Aw, shut up, Felix! That fat hairy bitch gives you good head.
>
> *Felix:* I wouldn't fuck her with your dick!

Little Vic's binge ended with his arrest for bashing a man over the head with a forty-ounce bottle of malt liquor while stealing his wallet. According to Little Vic's attorney, the woman accompanying him stabbed the robbery victim in the neck during the mugging, and they were both facing twenty-to-twenty-five-year potential sentences. Despite the violence of the assault, however, Little Vic was not prosecuted. Instead, because of overcrowding in California's courts—one of the effects of the War on Drugs—he was administratively sanctioned with a "parole violation" and received an automatic four-to-six-month sentence. This short sentence represents one of the many unintended bureaucratic consequences of the dysfunctional institutional dynamic that prevailed in the California courts following the state's "parole reform" initiative in the 1980s, which turned California's parole system into the most draconian in the nation (State of California, Little Hoover Commission 2003). Judges with overbooked dockets preferred to rely on streamlined administrative procedures for parole violators rather than preside over costly new trials, even for violent crimes.

Victor Senior reduced his presence on the boulevard following his son's reincarceration. He persuaded his mother to pay for him to enter a methadone maintenance program, and she invited him to move into her housing project apartment. We occasionally saw him in the neighborhood up the hill, carrying his mother's grocery bags in the supermarket or walking her to the Senior Services Center.

Victor's exit from Edgewater Boulevard left Felix isolated. He claimed that Victor refused to recognize him when he chanced upon him up the hill, where Felix scavenged for aluminum cans with his shopping cart. Felix now had no running partner and was sandwiched between the African-Americans and the whites. The one other Latino in the scene, Sal, a Chicano, was a successful heroin dealer who had moved his operations to the neighborhood several months earlier to escape a law enforcement offensive in the Mission District. He snubbed Felix as "a knucklehead." Sal gloated when Felix's heroin supplier eventually cut him off for failing to pay for a round of "fronted" bags.

At the time, Sal lived with his girlfriend, Carmen, a Chicana, in a metal shipping container parked on a vacant lot in the alley behind the A&C corner store. Carmen had just been released from jail. The couple adopted two pit bull puppies named My Girl and My Boy. Carmen smoked crack and maintained her habit by selling crack in the back alley. She carried a gun in her right pocket, and when a coke rush made her paranoid, she would pull it out to bolster her credibility as a woman dealer. Carmen eventually disappeared. It was rumored that she had been killed "turning tricks on Capp Street," but we did not dare verify the details with Sal.

Unable to compete with Reggie and Tina (who now maintained a full-time presence on the boulevard) for space in front of the store, Felix stopped panhandling at the corner. "You can't make money out there when there's five blacks in front of the store. It scares away the customers!" Instead, he scavenged full time for cans and bottles to recycle and began selling clean syringes for two dollars each. Syringe selling proved to be an excellent business. He would exchange "one clean one for two dirties" and was able to double his supply of clean syringes by regularly visiting the once-a-week needle exchange across town. He was also able to increase his heroin consumption because, in lieu of payment, he let customers come back to his camp to inject so long as they gave him a taste.

Felix began accusing his African-American campmates of stealing from his supply of used needles. He started carrying the syringes with him at all times in an overflowing fanny pack, sometimes confusing the clean ones with the dirty. This increased his risk of arrest for "possession of controlled paraphernalia with intent to sell." The epithet "nigger" returned to his everyday lexicon and he reduced his crack smoking. Soon he was routinely referring to the African-Americans as "crack monster motherfuckers" and blaming them for attracting the police. He responded defensively when we asked him about his change in attitude:

I might be racist, but hell! It's the niggers that are making me this way. They're power tripping. . . . Trying to take over the entire show. They didn't used to be like that with me, but once a nigger, always a nigger.

That Carter is the fuckin' ringleader. He's the biggest nigger of them all. The big, black nigger. I'm gonna move down with Frank and the whites. I gotta get away from the niggers.

As a first step toward rapprochement with the whites, Felix began parking his shopping cart at their camp overnight, to keep his cans and bottles "safe from the niggers." A week later, he moved into the white camp full time and slid back into his former honorary white status.

Ethnicity and Habitus

In everyday interaction, the Edgewater homeless were forced to commingle intensely across ethnic lines. African-Americans, whites, and Latinos shared and competed for the same limited resources—public space, income, and drugs. It might seem reasonable to suppose that physical addiction to drugs to the point of indigence would override the social distinctions that drive ordinary life and reduce people to a common human denominator. But the homeless on Edgewater Boulevard were deeply divided along racialized lines, and their hostility was exacerbated by their physical proximity.

In the 1990s and 2000s, San Francisco was an ethnically diverse city by U.S. standards. Its visible multiculturalism, however, was shallow. We developed the term *intimate apartheid* to convey the involuntary and predictable manner in which sharply delineated segregation and conflict impose themselves at the level of the everyday practices driven by habitus (Bourgois and Schonberg 2007). Intimate apartheid manifests itself explicitly in the special demarcations the Edgewater homeless drew between blacks and whites in their encampments. It also operates at the preconscious level, expressing itself as embodied emotions, attitudes, and ways of acting that reinforce distinctions, which in turn become misrecognized as natural racial attributes.

On one level, cultural difference and ethnic style are expressions of creative diversity. They frequently express resistance to subordination and assert dignity and self-respect (see Bourgois 2003b:8–11, 17; see also MacLeod 1987; Willis 1981). In the United States, however, cultural symbols carry a double-edged power valence that can have devastating implications for the socially vulnerable, especially the poor. What we call the ethnic components to habitus have emerged in the United States out of a history of slavery, racism, and socioeconomic inequality. They manifest themselves through everyday practices that enforce social hierarchies and constrain the life choices of large categories of vulnerable people, who become identified in an essentialized manner as "races" or "cultural groups." Ethnic components to habitus thereby become a strategic cog in the logic of symbolic violence that legitimizes and administers ethnic hierarchy, fuels racism, and obscures economic inequality.

Ethnographic and especially photographic documentation of ethnic habitus risks inadvertently reifying the racist stereotypes that we aim to critique through the lens of fieldwork. To expose and analyze coercive cultural distinctions in the United States, one needs to examine misrecognition in action among individuals because these routine interactions create the "common sense" that justifies conflict and subordination as if it were inherent in the essence of "race" or "culture."

In everyday practice, as Jeff's photographs document, individuals do not consistently behave in racially dichotomous ways. Segregation is frequently violated, and many individuals purposefully transgress ethnic practices. Al, for example, did not move into the white camp when he returned to Edgewater Boulevard after renovating his parents' house in the suburbs. Instead, he slept under the I-beam, curled up between Sonny, Carter, Tina, and

Stretch, a conspicuous white body in a now all-black scene. He also traveled regularly to Third Street, the main thoroughfare in the African-American neighborhood of Hunters Point, where crack was cheaper. His behavior was considered unusual by the African-Americans, but, for the most part, they welcomed him. He was dismissed by all the whites as a bizarre and embarrassing person. Nickie, for example, was genuinely befuddled: "I just don't know. . . . Al just likes to be with blacks." Felix was more aggressive: "Al likes the crack, and crack's around niggers." Felix conveniently ignored the inconsistency that he often binged on crack. Al referred to himself as having "black friends" but continued to treat racism against African-Americans as self-evident and acceptable. On one occasion, he used the epithet "nigger" in front of Sonny, provoking an awkward silence rather than the violent response we expected.

Early childhood socialization processes tend to generate many of the most durable dimensions of habitus. Al had grown up in the Potrero housing projects, a dozen blocks east of Edgewater Boulevard. "We were the only white family in the whole place, surrounded by niggers. I ran with the Medallions [a local African-American gang]." This background may have been the reason why he violated intimate apartheid with such ease. Sonny had belonged to another teenage gang, which fought with the Medallions. He would reminisce with Al about their famous childhood acquaintance in the Potrero projects, retired football star O. J. Simpson, whose prolonged televised trial for the murder of his ex-wife and her friend took place during the early months of our fieldwork. The reactions of the Edgewater homeless to Simpson's acquittal underlined the racialized divisions that existed all across the United States. National surveys revealed that whites were convinced that O. J. was guilty, whereas most African-Americans declared him innocent (CNN 1995). Significantly, Al defended O. J., claiming that "he was framed." This assertion did not stop Al from quipping, however, that Simpson's murdered ex-wife deserved her fate: "She's nothin' but white trash! After all, she married a nigger, didn't she?"

Al purchased a dilapidated 1979 Volvo station wagon with the money he earned renovating his parents' garage and invited Sonny to "move in" with him. They slept side by side on the folded-down bucket seats and became inseparable running partners. They eventually upgraded to a late 1970s Ford pickup truck outfitted with a camper shell, which was given to Al by a racist white construction worker, who told him, "I been watching you because I been wanting to give this camper to a good, hardworking white man. We white guys gotta stick together out here." At the time Al had been alone, pushing a shopping cart full of aluminum cans in front of the tool rental outlet on Edgewater Boulevard where he and Sonny sometimes stole tools from the backs of customers' pickup trucks. When recounting the story in front of Sonny, Al joked that he had responded, "Thanks. That's mighty white of you."

The cross-ethnic running partnership of Sonny and Al was the subject of hostile gossip on the boulevard. On one occasion, Sal engineered a confrontation between the two men, as if to prove the impossibility of companionship between blacks and whites. Sal, who was Chicano, portrayed Al as a feminized loser for partnering with an African-American:

> Why does Al stay with such a nigger's nigger like Sonny? He must like that dick in his ass. He needs to get that big black dick out of his mouth, because whenever I see Al, he complains and complains about Sonny. And Sonny is one punk-ass typical nigger.
>
> When I first started dealing, Sonny would let me fix in the camper in the morning and I was giving him a taste each time. He told me it was his camper, and that Al was only sleeping in it. He told me to be quiet because he didn't want me to wake Al up. He didn't want to have to turn Al on to a taste of my dope.
>
> Then one day I bumped into Al, and he told me that it wasn't Sonny's camper, but his camper. He asked me what time I would be coming by the next morning and told me, "I'll pretend I'm asleep, like the other mornings. Then you can ask him whose camper it is."
>
> So I come over the next morning. And I ask Sonny, "Whose camper is this?"
>
> And Sonny says, "Shhh, don't wake Al."
>
> And I ask him again.
>
> And he says, "It's my camper."
>
> And then Al gets up and says, "You fuckin' nigger. It ain't your camper."
>
> And Sonny says, "It's Al's and mine."
>
> And Al says, "No, nigger. It's my camper."
>
> And I tell Al, "I'm going to turn on the owner of this camper." And I give Al a big taste and tell him, "Don't give Sonny none of this. If you do, I'll never give you a taste again."
>
> And so Al did it. A big hit, while Sonny just sat there.

Like all running partners in the gray zone of Edgewater Boulevard, Al and Sonny frequently traded accusations of injecting heroin "on the sneak-tip [secretly]." Sonny, for example, complained:

> I don't wanna hurt Al's feelings and shit. But goddamn! He don't seem to care about nobody else's. Yesterday he come back and bring me some dope already mixed and in an outfit [syringe]. And tell me, "That's half of the bag."
>
> I tell him, "That's a sign of greed. Because when I get a bag, I bring it to the house [patting the seat of the camper]. I mix it on up in front of you. I even it up in front of you. And here you are bringing me shit that's already in the rig and I don't know what the fuck it is. It's probably just a cotton."
>
> He got a spot right here [patting the seat again]. He should mix the shit up in his own little house.

Al saw things differently:

> I give half of everything to Sonny. But Sonny just sits around and begs for dope. This morning I gave Sonny forty units. And he just sat around and watched me load up my buggy [supermarket shopping cart].
>
> And Sonny doesn't work. Only goes around looking for what he can steal. That's why the cops are around here all the time now.

Sonny reversed the moral valence on theft:

> I bust my ass late at night—three, four o'clock in the morning—and take a chance on a bur-glary to make sure we have dope in the morning. And all he has got is a little cardboard to re-cycle. He go and cash it in and don't come back to fix with me. Playing his fuckin' games.
>
> He wanna tell people that "Yeah, me and Sonny, we cool. We always split our shit. We ain't like the rest of them. We don't go behind each other's back. Doin' this and doin' that." But all the time that's what he's doing. He's not really lying to me—he's lyin' to his self.

Despite their bickering, Al and Sonny enjoyed one another's company and were often publicly affectionate. Sonny took great pleasure in his heroin highs and was prone to over-dosing. Immediately after injecting, he often fell into a heavy nod of euphoric relaxation or else became hyperenergized and "tweaked" in eccentric ways, such as shadowboxing furi-ously until collapsing, or twirling himself around a signpost, oblivious to the world around him. Al indulged Sonny's ecstatic displays by watching over him carefully to prevent Sonny from injuring himself:

Al: [his arm over Sonny's shoulder] I had to take care of my pal Sonny yesterday. He was in a different world. I called him back to our world a couple of times, you know.

Sonny: [nodding and hugging Al] I could have hurt myself bad, man.

Al: I go like this [pounding his chest]. Then, boom! He comes back from a different world, man.

Sonny: I'm tellin' you, man. I nodded straight off into the fire [pointing to the candle on the camper's Formica counter]. My hair was burning and shit.

Al: That's why I stay with him. I don't go nowhere.

Sonny: Yeah. Lord have mercy! We a close-knit thing, man. We watching out for each other and shit. When I get a bag, I bring it to the house, and I mix it on up in front of you [patting Al on the shoulder]. And Al too. If we divided, then we ain't caring nothing about each other.

> This morning, when Al went to pick up his welfare check, he went sicker than a mother-fucker. But I didn't go, you know, because I had to make sure we had some dope.
>
> And I got it, and I finished mixing it up and everything, and I ride down there to bring it to him, you know, at the welfare building. And I said, "You ain't got to worry about being dopesick no more." And I handed him the rig right then and there.

Al: I was happy to see Sonny! I went straight to the McDonald's [bathroom] and fixed.

Al and Sonny could not, of course, escape the logic of the gray zone and frequently be-trayed one another. Nevertheless, by Edgewater Boulevard standards, they maintained a friendship of exceptional solidarity that violated the patterns of intimate apartheid, to every-one's discomfort and surprise.

I'm a woman and I'm gonna have my damn way because I'm gonna demand it. I've been in these damn streets all by myself a long time. Don't nobody wanna treat me like the way I wanna be treated. I've turned the other cheek so many fuckin' times that I'm sick and tired. And it hurt, and it ain't easy, and I don't strut—but there ain't nobody no better than this person.

I'll let y'all know why I'm like this. Let me tell my story. —*Tina*

Carrying a sixteen-ounce can of discount malt liquor bearing the imprint of her always freshly applied lipstick, Tina projected a persona of defiant lumpen femininity. She dressed to the hilt in color-coordinated silk, satin, and leather outfits and identified herself publicly as an alcoholic. She spent most of her time and energy, however, in pursuit of crack, shoplifting from the stores on Edgewater Boulevard and throughout the Mission District. She also demanded money aggressively or seductively from friends, acquaintances, and strangers.

Her preference for crack and alcohol and her aggressive style of panhandling initially brought her into Reggie's orbit in front of the A&C corner store. He cultivated a hyper-virile persona—"I've got fourteen kids; you know I love that pussy"—and he fantasized about "pimping" Tina:

> I'd sell a bitch's pussy in a minute. I'll make Tina sell hers. "Hey, Tina, get him! [pointing to an imaginary customer] Get that money, girl!" She go around the corner, come back, and she got the money for me.

Tina, for her part, accepted Reggie's treats of vodka and crack but responded to his sexual advances with vehement curses.

Carving Out a Woman's Space on the Street

To counter her obvious physical frailty, Tina regularly erupted into rages when disrespected. These outbursts sometimes attracted the police. For example, she spent four days in the county jail for smashing windshields in a McDonald's parking lot, after a security guard ordered her to stop panhandling. She was soon in trouble again when the security guard in the neighboring parking lot of the Discount Grocery Outlet prevented her from helping customers unload their shopping carts into their cars. He claimed, with some justification, that her primary goal was not to earn tips but to run off with the groceries. Tina responded by scratching the side of a brand-new SUV with the shards of a crushed Coke can on her way out of the lot.

Tina's all-night crack binges with Carter, Sonny, and Stretch increased in frequency in the now all African-American I-beam camp. She returned less often to her cousin's apartment to rest and bathe. She derived a visible joy of living from the company of her new homeless friends and disliked getting high alone. When we stayed overnight in the encampment, she often proposed group activities. In the intimate glow of a spluttering candle, her face would light up with pleasure as she pulled out a set of dominoes or clapped the opening lines to her favorite parlor game, Slow Boat to China. She was fun to be with, so long as she was well stocked with crack and alcohol.

Despite the chronic level of violence against women on the street, Tina celebrated her femininity. Whenever she lit up her crack pipe, she draped her arms around whatever man was closest to her in a spontaneous expression of affection. She often pulled out a little compact, even in the candlelight, to apply lipstick, lip liner, mascara, and concealer.

Tina enjoyed being the center of attention, and, at first, all the men were energized by her presence. She began focusing her attention on Carter, who was openly courting her. He increased his crack consumption in order to spend more time with her and became jealous whenever she talked for too long with another man. He would call out threateningly from a few yards away, in the voice of an ambiguously playful/abusive parent, "Tina! Come over here. . . . Don't make me come over there and get you." At night by the campfire, he would sneak kisses on her cheek in between shouts and threats over who had smoked too much

of whose crack. On one occasion, in a pique of feigned rage, he grabbed the patent leather purse strap wrapped around Tina's shoulder and dangled her in the air until the purse strap snapped.

Reggie was jealous of Carter and increased his offers of alcohol and crack, which Tina continued to accept. It appeared that she was setting the two men on a collision course. She eventually resolved the ambiguity by smashing a portable radio over Reggie's head inside the corner store amid a shower of curses. Reggie responded by punching her squarely in the jaw, yelling, "Bitch! Nobody does me like that!" Tina sprawled backward over a display rack of potato chips, bringing several shelves of canned goods and fast-food boxes crashing to the floor with her. Shouting in Arabic, the Yemeni storekeeper ran from behind the cash register, striking at both Reggie and Tina with a broom. Dazed, Tina struggled to her feet, bags of Doritos crunching beneath her. Her lower lip swollen and bleeding, she staggered out of the store and ran, limping, to her cousin in the projects.

In the back alley afterward, Reggie rubbed the side of his face, also bleeding from the fight. He said he was worried that Tina might have given him HIV with her scratches. Tucking in his ripped shirt and straightening his jacket, now torn at the shoulder, Reggie returned to insulting her femininity in classically lumpen patriarchal terms:

> Sorry-assed bitch had it coming. She's lucky we weren't outside, because I would have pounded her. Bitch is crazy! That's her way of showin' love. Nobody ever looked at her as a woman. They look at her as a bitch.
>
> Spread her legs to have nine fuckin' kids, and they all got took. She don't have none of them.
>
> I got fourteen kids, and I'm separated from all the women, but it doesn't mean I'm gonna neglect the kids. My family have all the kids. Each and every one of my sisters took a kid.

Tina was furious at the Yemeni storekeeper, who, she claimed, "kicked me in the head when I was down." She was careful, however, not to involve Carter in the conflict and instead invoked the protection of her own close male family members, "to go take care of Reggie." Her eldest brother, a bank robber turned Christian minister, lived several hours away in Modesto, a mid-sized town in California's Central Valley. Her youngest brother, affectionately nicknamed Dee-Dee, had been released from prison recently; he was married to a drug treatment counselor and lived with her in the suburbs. Tina's eldest son, Ricky, was about to be released from prison.

No follow-up violence occurred, however, and within a few days, Reggie and Tina were once again panhandling at the entrance to the corner store from which they had both been "86'ed [banned from entering]." There was no longer a flirtatious undertone between them. By lashing out at Reggie, Tina had asserted her commitment to her budding relationship with Carter, but she had accomplished this on her own terms, without becoming dependent on Carter by demanding that he confront Reggie. When talking about the fight, Tina referred to her capacity for rage as an uncontrollable character trait: "I blacked out. I go off. I do that. I did wrong." This was her way of carving out a safer space for herself, in reaction to the misogyny and sexual objectification of women on Edgewater Boulevard.

Two weeks later, Reggie was arrested for brandishing a broken handgun during an argument over a crack purchase in the alley behind the corner. Everyone referred to the arrest as his "third strike" and anticipated that he would receive a life sentence under California's new mandatory sentencing laws. His mother and four of his eleven brothers and sisters came to his hearing to plead leniency from the judge. He eventually received an eight-year sentence on a plea bargain and disappeared from the Edgewater Boulevard scene.

Soon after the fight with Reggie, Tina began accompanying Carter on his nighttime scavenges, pushing his shopping cart and helping him fill it with anything that had potential resale value, primarily aluminum cans and copper metal. On one of their sorties, they recovered two Victorian mahogany chairs, upholstered in white with elaborately carved armrests. Carter referred to them as "the loveseats I got for Tina." They became the centerpiece of the I-beam camp, which, under the influence of Tina's scavenging skills, became an obstacle course overflowing with things for sale: coffee tables, settees, slabs of plywood, rolled-up rugs, assorted lampshades, ceramic figurines. For privacy from Sonny, Stretch, Al, and temporary overnight guests, Tina and Carter divided their section of the camp into two (roofless) "bedrooms," each about ten feet square, bounded by a double-decked perimeter of couches in various states of decay. At the center of their bedroom, Tina placed a shiny, red 1960s rotary dial telephone. It sat on an upturned Pampers box covered by a white lace antimacassar. Sitting in their loveseats smoking crack late into the night, the affectionate couple would gently clink their glass pipes together in a formal toast before each inhalation. Tina would drape her legs over Carter's lap, cuddling his head into the nape of her neck.

Tina had been living as an independent woman on and off the street for almost five years since her last serious love relationship, with the father of her youngest daughter, Jewel. One of her survival strategies was to cultivate a diverse set of male "friends" willing to give her money, drugs, food, and other resources in exchange for sex. Carter's version of masculine control and romance, however, required her sexual fidelity. He did not share Reggie's pimp fantasy. He began insisting that Tina stop "partying" with her "men friends." Tina seesawed between exhilaration over falling in love with Carter and fear of becoming subservient to a man and losing her core income-generating strategy:

> We fight because Carter's very jealous. He think everybody want me. But then, shit! They know that I'm his woman. And they known that I ain't gonna suck they dick for no fuckin' crack or for no money. Fuck that!
>
> If I do it, he 'a never know. It's gonna be somebody. . . . It ain't gonna be [somebody] black. Unless they a black rich man. Shit! I got white friends. They pick me up. I got a black friend in a Cadillac that picks me up. And he's not cheap at all.
>
> And I'm gonna keep my friends. I mean, he'd never know. I never tell him. Because I have to always look out for my damn self. Never let a person—a man—know every damn thing about you. Shit! I'd never succeed in life.

Tina knew she could not depend on Carter, because, as she put it, "He ain't nothing but a righteous dopefiend."

The men around Carter were outraged by Tina's insistence on autonomy. Stretch was especially misogynistic:

> She's got the mentality of a man. Carter's being scandalous with her. He doesn't keep her in check. We're doing her wrong. If she acts like this out there [pointing to the boulevard], she could get her ass whooped.
>
> It ain't right for her to be around men like this. She doesn't have no female friends. She told me that she hates bitches. And she's just a skinny ugly bitch herself who puts her twat out, but still wants to stick her tongue down a man's throat.
>
> That twat gotta be good for Carter to put up with her shit.

Stretch also engaged in sex work with men, but he did it secretly in San Francisco's skid row neighborhood, the Tenderloin. Eventually, Stretch left the I-beam camp, preferring to hustle full time downtown.

The Common Sense of Sex Work

Tina's instrumental relationships with men, even with those for whom she felt affection, illustrates the complex continuum between altruism and instrumentality that haunts all male-female sexual relations and intimate feelings but becomes more visible under conditions of urban poverty and masculine domination. Many social scientists have argued against the possibility of altruistic relations in sex and love (Zelizer 2005). The debate over the moral economy of intimate relations entered the mainstream of anthropology as early as the 1920s, when Marcel Mauss, the founder of gift exchange theory, criticized Bronislaw Malinowski, the pioneer of participant-observation methods in anthropology, for categorizing the presents that husbands offer to their wives in the Trobriand Islands as "pure gifts." Mauss reinterpreted these intimate, private exchanges "as a kind of salary for sexual services rendered" and asserted that they "throw a brilliant light upon all sexual relationships throughout humanity" (Mauss [1924] 1990). Tina's mode of interacting with men openly merged affection with money. She had grown up surrounded by sex workers and pimps. As a precocious child, disobeying her mother, she empathized with friendly neighbors in distress:

> *Tina:* When I was a kid, we stayed on Hayes and Fillmore; that's where the ho's used to walk up and down on our street.
>
> I used to let them in through our door, right at the bottom of the stairs. 'Cause they used to be runnin' from the police and stuff, and I likeded them. I felt sorry for them 'cause they pimps kick them and all that . . . beat them with clothes hangers and shit, kick them in they ass. Uh-huh!
>
> There was three favorite ones that I liked. I used to see them with they miniskirts on, and they pimps. They start giving me money for candy and shit. I look out the window for them. And if I didn't see them, I be very scared. One would be coming out of the car, you know, runnin'. And when they rang the doorbell, you know, to hide from the pimp or the police, I come and let them in.
>
> I was about eight. My mother used to be [angry voice], "Don't answer that door!"
>
> I'm like, "That's my friend, Ma."

Jeff: Did you understand what they were doing?

Tina: I knew they was whoring. I'm not stupid at eight. At eight, I knew! I seen them every night. And my brother, he was a player [pimp], my oldest brother and my first cousin too. They both dead now.

That was when the Black Panthers and all that shit was out. I knew about all that too.

Tina needed to be emotionally prepared to talk about her past. When references to her childhood surfaced in casual conversation, she would usually stop in mid-sentence, swallow hard, apologize, and stare through the windshield in awkward silence. She often broke these flashbacks of childhood trauma by exhaling from her cigarette, swigging on a beer, and reversing the focus of the conversation by asking us questions about our own intimate lives. Sometimes she would simply say, "I'm not ready to talk about that now . . . some other time." Tape recordings of Tina's life story had to be planned days in advance. She would dress up for the occasion, asking us to drive her to a private location. Months or years later, she would sometimes recollect affectionately the special occasions "when I shared my story with you."

Jeff's fieldnotes describing the events on the afternoon just before we tape-recorded her life story for the first time convey the banality of sex, sex work, violence against women, and interpersonal abuse. His notes also make reference to a diverse range of routine survival imperatives, joys, and everyday violences that the homeless encounter on any given day: fleeing law enforcement, losing shelter and all their possessions, exchanging and demanding favors, scavenging from the garbage, encountering bonanzas of useful junk, negotiating hostile social service bureaucracies, dismissing public stigma, ignoring sexual and scatological displays, anticipating potential assaultive violence, seeking legal employment, and getting high repeatedly.

Later in the day, speaking into the tape recorder, Tina revealed the deeper childhood foundations of her habitus. Sex, affection, and income were logically intertwined in the gray zone of poverty and abandonment that had engulfed her early years. She learned to mobilize her sexuality and femininity with personal charisma. Her account of coming of age in the segregated inner city during the 1960s clarifies more than just a psychological understanding of how her personality was affected by intimate violence. It reveals the limits of disciplinary biopower in shaping lumpen female subjectivity on the street. Gender power relations, household instability, poverty, racism, and abusive violence are foregrounded; and seeking material compensation from men for sex emerges as the commonsense adaptation of a vulnerable child struggling to decipher the turmoil among the men and women around her. In her search for adult love and affection, Tina learned the practical value of sex. Three decades later, she reflexively defined the worth of all relationships with males, whether sexual or not, through the gifts they generated—money, food, drugs, trinkets, or clothes.

Tina is waiting for me, as promised, for our life history "tape recording date." She jumps into the car and starts telling me that Caltrans [the California Transit Authority] evicted them from the I-beam camp yesterday at 2:00 P.M., true to the NOTICE TO VACATE *sign that had been posted last week on the chain-link fence. She, along with Carter and Sonny, lost all her possessions except for a few blankets they had managed to hide behind the ice machine at the Pizza Hut down the boulevard.*

Tina asks me to sign a welfare job search form because yesterday a social worker rejected her application, citing "lack of proof" that she had sought work from twenty different employers in the past month. "Shit! I asked everyone I know. What else they want me to do?"

She wants me to stay overnight in the camp because she lost her alarm clock in the eviction and does not want "to have to stay up all night" for fear of "not making it to the welfare office on time." I agree, and she gratefully hands me a strand of pooka beads, wrapped in clean tissue paper: "Jeff, give these to your girlfriend, from me, Tina."

Today happens to be the day when homeowners in the neighborhood are supposed to dispose of bulky items that do not fit in garbage cans. Mattresses, chairs, rugs, carpets, computer monitors fill the sidewalks. Seeing this, Tina orders me to stop the car, exclaiming gleefully, "Let's go shopping, Jeff!"

"You know I'm a pack-rat," she giggles, grabbing a garbage bag full of clothes, a broom with a Christmas wreath attached to its handle, and an orange porcelain horse. I enthusiastically load a sleeping bag and two blankets into my trunk for her, and she sings, "Jeff is shopping with me." After forty-five more minutes of "shopping," my car is stuffed.

We settle back into the crammed front seat, and Tina loads her crack pipe, a tiny Grand Marnier airplane-sized cocktail bottle with the bottom drilled out. Before lighting up, she asks if I see any police. Peering into my driver-side mirror, I see the reflection of a homeless man, dressed in rags, sprawled on his back. His body is twisted awkwardly with his head turned to the side. "Is he dead?" I ask, alarmed. Tina squints in the man's direction and exclaims, "That's horrible! Get your camera, Jeff. He's masturbating."

Instead I drive off and we park by a baseball diamond. Hyper from the crack, Tina immediately jumps out, squats right behind the open car door, and urinates into the gutter. Embarrassed, I avert my eyes and quickly adjust my rearview mirror to give her privacy.

A middle-aged woman Tina recognizes approaches us. She talks extremely slowly as though heavily medicated and asks me a series of precise questions—my name, my address, and where we are going. After she leaves, Tina explains, "She was looking out for me. She think you a trick [prostitute's customer] and want to make sure where I be if something bad happens."

Before letting me turn on the tape recorder, Tina announces that she wants me to buy beer for both of us and cigarettes for her. The woman behind the counter in the store is dreadful to us, curling her upper lip and spitting out the answer when we ask for prices.

Back in the car, Tina comments that once again I was mistaken for a trick, this time by the hostile cashier. These incidents prompt Tina to begin her childhood story on precisely this theme, so central to her survival strategies in life:

"I learned about pullin' tricks when we was living with my auntie. She was babysitting us. I was about twelve.

"A man would come by and she say to me and my sister, 'I gotta use the bathroom' and he'd go in with her. She would do whatever and come out with money; but before she went in she didn't have no money.

"My auntie make good money from her mens. And so I learned, like if we didn't have no money or nothin', I be [meek voice], 'Auntie, why don't you call that man that came over last week and gave you some money?'

[gruff voice] "'Girl! You shut up. What you talkin' about?'

"I'm like [meek voice again], 'You know … that man. When we didn't have nothin' and he came over and he gave you some money and borrowed somethin' to drink and had some cigarettes? Won't you call him, auntie? He a nice man.' 'Cause my auntie's men friends would come in the house and like, touch my booty. You know, like [deep voice], 'Hey, girl' and be pattin' my ass. All the time they was getting a free one. But I wasn't knowin' it.

"But I didn't start dating till I was sixteen. It was at the Presidio army base. My girlfriend Darlene from school, she turned me on to the army mens and I just went wild. 'Cause it was different— and they had money and I could drink all I wanted and go to the officers' club and just have a ball, right? Like I'm a grown lady. I was sixteen and I was hangin' at the Presidio with the army mens.

"That's when I first fucked, at the barracks with Darryl Dexter. I was just drunk and havin' fun. But I didn't even know if he bust my cherry 'cause I was drunk. But then afterwards I start feelin' it, right?

"And he brought me home with a wet pussy and I went straight to the bathtub. And my mother said, 'You don't come home and wash your nasty ass. You wash your ass where you lay it at.' And when I asked my mother for some bus fare and cigarettes, she say, 'Don't you never come beggin' round here when you stay out all night and come home with no money. You call that man right now. What's his number?'

"I called him, and my mother told him, 'Don't you ever keep my daughter out and not give her nothin'. She goes to school and blah, blah, blah.'

"He came over and he brought me some money and my mother some money. He say, 'Here, this is your bus fare for school for next week, and here is your lunch money.' It was probably about twenty dollars for me and probably twenty dollars for my mother."

Jeff: "So when you lost your virginity you got paid for it?"

Tina: "Not right then, but my mother made sure I did afterwards. That's when I felt that she gave me the okay to prostitute. I didn't know it was prostitutin'. I just knew that she gave me the okay to sell my body. That I could fuck."

Jeff: "When did you start pulling tricks?"

Tina: "Every time I go see Darryl Dexter. He had to give me some money because I couldn't go home. I stayed in the barracks. I was a wanderin' Jew. A child that didn't know shit and learnt it all by herself. [sirens passing]

   "My mother got me smoothed on birth control pills. I was going to the clinic down there. Right over there on Edgewater and Palmer.

   "And my doctor used to say, 'Your mother, she is so worried about you, about somebody abruisin' your body.' I'm like, 'Don't nobody abruise my body.' 'Cause I didn't let him just fuck me hard and shit. I'm like, you have to be nice and soft to me. And gentle.

   "Yeah, he wasn't rough and all that shit like a hound dog. No, uh-uh! No."

A generational disconnect between Tina and her mother, Persia, over interpretations of romance exacerbated Tina's sense of maternal betrayal. As a single woman overwhelmed by poverty, with a house full of children and no male breadwinner to help her, Persia was desperate to find income and stability for her vulnerable daughter. She also sought to redeem Tina's honor by having her fulfill the romantic patriarchal dream of marrying the man to whom one loses one's virginity. Instead, Persia further confirmed her daughter's common-sense understanding that sex and affection require remuneration, because Persia tried to pay Tina to marry Darryl Dexter. This violated Tina's late-1960s ideas about romantic free choice and played on her sense of suffering from maternal neglect and rejection:

> She pay me to call Darryl Dexter. He stay in Philadelphia, and he wanted to marry me. He beg her, and she was gonna make me marry him, but I wasn't in love with him.
>
> I was just a teenager, and she was going to sign papers for me to marry him. And I say, "You just tryin' to get rid of me. I ain't goin' nowhere!" She was gonna marry me off.

Childhood Violence and Sexual Abuse

Tina described growing up as a bored, lonely girl seeking adult attention and pocket change for treats in front of the local corner store after school let out. This was long before she began purposely selling her body, when "I was still a virgin but I was just used to standing with my hand on my hip. I didn't know shit." Tina did not describe her childhood years in a linear narrative. Her tape recordings are a confessional outpouring of vulnerability that triggered repeated flashbacks and sudden changes in affect. In mid-sentence one account of sexual assault and molestation often interrupted another. We had to edit her text more than most for clarity, and it was difficult to punctuate because of its stream-of-consciousness leaps occasionally interspersed with rapid-fire irony.

   Careful attention to Tina's vocabulary also reveals how the standard distinctions between rape, sex work, and consensual sex are inadequate to understand sex on the streets and in homes that are dominated by unstable and often predatory men and women. Jeff repeatedly interrupted Tina to ask her to explain the terms she was using interchangeably to describe a range of socially taboo and often violent or nonconsensual sexual activities that she had experienced by the time she was a teenager: "date," "ho'," "trick," "walk the stroll," "walk the street," "mess with," "be with," "have some fun," "fast-fuck," "manhandle," "molest," "abuse," and "abruise." Her account also reveals that long before she understood what was happening to her sexually, she had already learned the effectiveness of violence and rage as a means of self-defense. Furthermore, she was taking a wide range of legal and illegal psychoactive drugs during these early adolescent years.

Tina: I was kidnapped on Haight Street by this man that looks like Isaac Hayes. He had a bald haircut.

We had went together inside the store. But after a while his conversation wasn't about shit. He grabbed me like on the Flintstones, how Fred put the dog out the window, and threw me in the car and I was like, resistant. And I couldn't get out of his car 'cause he had those locks up in front—the electric locks. [long pause]

But he manhandled me till I was in his house. He was a big ol' guy and I was skinny. [long pause] I probably still know where that house is.

Jeff: How did you meet this guy?

Tina: I was on the corner at the store. I had came from school and I was lookin' for a date.

Jeff: A date? Does that mean you were selling your body?

Tina: Not then. I was only fourteen. This time I was just talking and sharin' words and shit, like we was on a date. I didn't start trickin' till I was sixteen—I just told you, with Darryl Dexter.

So he says, "Wait, I'm not gonna hurt you." So I calmed down. He said, "I just wanna have a little fun with you, and you can be on your way. . . . I just need me a woman right now. . . . And you look like a nice lady."

I'm like, "Yeah?" But he got out a bag of weed and some truinals, them blue ones. Them worser than the reds, right? And I was droppin' pills at that time, stealin' them from my mother. . . . And heaven knows I know how to take them.

He said he had been watchin' me for the longest time. Going to school, catchin' a bus, and shit. I don't know if he knew where I lived. But at that time I had ran away from home. I was living with this army mans and his wife.

Jeff: You mean, Darryl Dexter?

Tina: No, this was another army man. He was married and he was a trip! He molested me in my sleep. I woke up. He was suckin' my pussy.

Jeff: Wait. I don't understand, but first finish the kidnap story about the bald guy. Did he abuse you?

Tina: He didn't fuck me, if that's what you mean. He didn't get nothin'. He didn't molest me. He beat me. 'Cause I snap, Jeff. Just like my mother. I went crazy. He really wanted my body. I was scared but I tried to play along. But I kept prolonging it and not comin' out of my clothes . . . saying [meek voice], "I'm a virgin, I'm not even fifteen."

So he kept slapping me—[speaking faster] slappin' me slappin' me and slappin' me. And he had a waterbed and there was some scissors, and I took them scissors and I just punched a hole in that waterbed. And I start tearing his house up—everything! I kicked his floor model TV with some tennis shoes and glass is splattered. I even cut my feet, Jeff. And I was electric-shocked.

He said, "That tiny bitch! My TV!"

I tried to jump through the big picture window in his room but I just bounced right back off of it 'cause it was plastic. I was tearing his house up and finally he just opened his door and I ran to the police and told the police everything. They came back to investigate. But I let it go because I didn't want my mother to know because I had ran away from home. I was stayin' in the Haight with this lady and her husband from the Presidio. We used to take acid. They called it "window pane."

My girlfriend Darlene from school stayed there too. All the time I wasn't knowin' that she liked ladies. But she always would greet me with a kiss and a hug and that's how I normally greet because I'm raised up in church and that's how we do each other. We hug and kiss. Not for the sex, you know.

Jeff: So Darlene was having an affair with the woman?

Tina: And also with the man.

Jeff: Who? The husband who was molesting you in your sleep?

Tina: Yeah. This was after I got kidnapped and they had sent me to the psych ward. They was giving me pills, Thorazines, and I was sleepy from them. But I woke up . . . but I act like I was asleep, right. But I ain't goin' to lie, it was good, too, though. But I was scared 'cause his wife threw this other fuckin' bitch through the window.

Jeff: What!

Tina: Mmm-hmmm. . . . All the time he was molesting me in my sleep he was also fuckin' around with the neighbor, the lady who lived upstairs who had a little girl and a boy. And after his wife found out that her husband was sleeping with that lady she plotted and plotted. And we always in cahoots together, right? So we all set it up and she caught them one night together. And it was it! Right through the window. That bitch's arm was hangin' off. Her skin was just hangin' down bleeding.

Jeff: How terrible!

Tina: Yeah! I got emotional. Hell, I think I had a nervous breakdown and I went home after that. I told my mother what I wanted to tell her and then I went to bed. But then she put me in juvenile detention for two weeks during Easter vacation 'cause I started to be just a little bad-ass girl, right? And she thought I was fit to give up my pussy. She thought that I was out there fast-fuckin'. But I wasn't.

I was only fourteen and I was just . . . I was so stingy. I would just kiss. Ain't nobody gettin' in my pants so I was just kissin', Jeff. 'Cause I was thinkin' that if a man get in my pants, I'm 'a have a baby.

Because my grandmother and my mother, they used to say that if you be with a man, they roll on you, you gonna end up pregnant. That was what they told me. And shit, I'm stupid. I'm believing them.

My mother didn't take out time with explaining me all that. So I was a virgin up until I was sixteen because I was afraid to get pregnant. And I didn't get pregnant till I was twenty and I got married then.

I didn't want no damn baby 'cause I babysitted . . . [long pause] and my cousin who would molest me as a kid . . .

Jeff: Your cousin also molested you?

Tina: Mmm-hmmm. My first cousin. My mother raised him. It was my aunt's only child. My dead aunt that tricked in the bathroom and shit. She dead now—cirrhosis of the liver. It was her son and he died of cirrhosis too. He molested me.

He used to press my hair and all that. Get me ready for school and wash me up. He used to take good care of us because my mother always worked and went to school. She was always lookin' for a better job, you know, to take care of us. Even on welfare she still had to work.

He would put me in the bathtub and everything. I had to take a bath every morning because I peed the bed. Every time! I was a little girl, seven or eight.

I didn't never really know what was going on till I got older, but I wake up one time and he was gettin' up off me and I was soaking wet. I remember that he was pumpin' on me. And I remember that his dick was in me. And I was peeing and I would wake up when I start peeing. And I be scared and he was getting up off of me.

Then I started bein' so bad that he start shyin' away from me because I realize what he done. 'Cause I caught him that morning but he probably had been doing it all the time.

I didn't say nothin' until I was twenty-seven. I said, "I remember when you used to fuck me and I pussy wet. I was a kid."

And then I told him, "I loved you so much I didn't want you to get married." I hated his wife. But I loved her twins, right. They had twin girls, Jeanine and Jeanette.

I told him and he cried and cried and cried. If my cousin wasn't dead I'd introduce you to him.

And I told him everything. "That was the reason why I used to lie to your girlfriends when they called on the phone 'cause I want you to stay home with me. I didn't know why, but now I'm old enough to know why. You better be glad you didn't get me pregnant. Mother woulda' killed you."

But I wasn't on my menstruation or nothin' like that. I was, you know, only seven or eight, but he was about fifteen.

He kept saying, "Please forgive me, please forgive me."

I'm like, "I do. That's why I'm lettin' you know. But *don't* you *never* do it again."

They do that to girls, Jeff. Black mens . . . white mens too. Because white drunk mens always been on my body. Shit! You gotta pay me if you wanna do that.

Tina's mother, meanwhile, cycled in and out of Northern California's state psychiatric hospitals throughout Tina's childhood. Sex for remuneration became Tina's means to fulfill immediate practical survival needs and to seek minimal stability:

I used to sell my body just because I needed it and I was the type of person that was, you know, would give it up for money. If I didn't say it I showed it. "You gonna do somethin' for me?"

You wasn't gettin' my body if I wasn't gettin' nothing. You would have to buy me something to eat, and my cigarettes, my alcohol, my bus fare. Everything! Whatever I want I'm going to get. Everything. That's when I had my sugar daddies . . . different mens that I would, you know, be with, you know, on their payday and stuff like that. They come pick me up. They would give me money—twenty or thirty dollars.

But . . . and then sometimes I mess with people that I didn't know. But I ain't never walked the street. Well . . . I walked the streets but not the whole stroll, you know. And then I would see people and, you know, they adored me. They wanted me. They would proposition me. Then. . . . "Yeah."

Tina rejected the sex worker identity. She distinguished herself from "ho's," whom she defined as dependent on pimps. "I didn't know that I was a prostitute. But then I knew I wasn't no ho' 'cause I wasn't paying no man—no pimp."

The child psychology literature documents a strong relationship between early sexual abuse and sex work in later life, implying that the logic for prostitution is based on violent disempowerment generated at the level of the individual within the traumatized psyche (Herman 1992). A theory of abuse, however, that engages the interface of psycho-affective turmoil with structural and institutional forces such as historically engrained inequalities around gender, class, ethnicity, family arrangements, and the provision of social services to vulnerable children is useful for understanding why it might feel empowering to Tina to make men pay for her body. "My body's precious to me. I'm not going to give it up to nobody. And I a beautiful lady." Arguably, by selling her body, Tina obtained a sense of control over the multiple sexual exploitations she was subjected to as a child (and continued to suffer later in her life).

Feminist anthropologists and philosophers have debated whether sex work can be considered a form of resistance to masculine domination in coercive contexts rather than being solely self-oppressive and objectifying (Pateman 1999; Wardlow 2004). Classical marxism and early Western feminism provocatively accused "bourgeois marriage" of being a legalized form of prostitution (Engels [1884] 1942; Goldman [1911] 1969; Wollstonecraft 1790). This interpretation is consistent with anthropological work on intimate sexual relationships in both nonmarket societies and industrializing urban settings that argues that sex work is not categorically distinguished from gift-giving or from marital economic dependence (see, for example, Mauss [1924] 1990:73; Tabet 1987; Wojcicki 2002; Zelizer 2005; see also *Africa Today* 2000).

Domestic Outlaws

After several months of ambivalence, Tina suddenly stopped "seeing" all her other "men friends" and declared her love for Carter. During their honeymoon weeks, they established a separate new camp all to themselves under another freeway overpass farther down the boulevard. Pursuing domestic stability despite their homelessness, they adopted a large black and brown dog and named him Freeway.

Carter is banging hard on a sheet of metal with a hammer, looking every bit the honorable laborer. Sweat stains his otherwise clean white t-shirt and brown denim overalls. He has a plaid lumberjack shirt tied around his waist and his baseball cap is turned backward. A half dozen brand-new metal street signs are piled next to him. He is banging at the center of a large NO PEDESTRIANS highway sign to form a crease in the metal. He presses his knee with the full weight of his body into the weakened spot and successfully bends the four-foot aluminum sheet in half.

Tina is sitting in a wicker chair in the middle of the camp looking like a pioneer farmer's wife: cut-off jeans and a paisley cowgirl blouse tied in a knot at the belly button. She is peeling a potato; her feet are raised on a milk crate that she has covered with blue and gold chintz fabric.

She greets me warmly, springing up to give me a hug. "Stay for dinner, Jeff, with me and Carter," she asks as she points to a bag of groceries provided by a Baptist Church food pantry. She explains that a friend she had treated to a beer on the corner yesterday brought it over this afternoon. I can see a quartered chicken, an onion, potatoes, frozen spinach (rapidly thawing), a stick of vegetable lard, and butter. Carter walks over, wiping his brow. "Yeah, Jeff, stay for dinner. I'll cook up this chicken like you never had before. Just relax and take your pictures, we got it goin' on." He bends down and pecks Tina's cheek.

Carter starts a fire in a large metal garbage can and jams several squashed street signs into the flames. He explains that he sells the aluminum signs to the recycling center as scrap. He has to blacken them first to hide the fact that he stole them from the Caltrans service yard ten blocks away. When the flames settle, Carter places a grill on top and throws on a skillet, adding lard and then the chicken, which he seasons with salt and pepper from a white porcelain coffee mug.

Tina washes the potatoes in a tin basin and dices the onions. "I love to chop, Jeff. Yeah, I love them knives. I went to culinary arts school to get me my A-1 chef license. My drug rehab program got me the job. I could use those knives! And never cut myself but I hated that cheese cutter. I loved to fix the salad bar. I never graduated because my instructor he act like he had a crush on me. He would give me a hug and shit and then his hands would … he'd try to feel on my butt." Tina brings a large pan of water to boil on the fire and throws in the now fully thawed spinach. Carter asks Tina, as if he were proposing a cocktail, "Want a hit before dinner? Where's the pipe?"

Tina energetically pulls apart piles of clothing before finally locating the crack pipe in the chest pocket of Carter's blue jean jacket. Wagging her finger, she playfully scolds him for forgetting. She then jumps up and gives him a puff, pausing first to embrace him: stealing a kiss in the kitchen.

After the sun goes down, the flow of headlights on Edgewater Boulevard provides us with our only light for cooking. This does not faze Carter, however: "You can't see in this darkness if the juices are clear, so instead I just listen for the sizzle. You don't need to see to cook chicken; you can hear when it's just right."

Tina is back relaxing in her favorite chair, lighting a second hit of crack, her sandals kicked off and her feet up. She points to the freeway roaring above us and sighs, "Jeff, I'm tired. The cars are always going. The freeway never stops."

Finally Carter announces, "Dinner is ready." Tina grabs a jug of water for us to wash up. We take turns holding up a bathroom soap dispenser with Taco Bell stamped on the side. We are careful not to waste any of the water to avoid having to fetch more from the spigot at the farmers market half a mile away.

Tina sets the food out on a warped sheet of plywood balanced on top of a grocery store display case. Without fail, Carter always prays before eating, and after we sit down, he asks us to bow our heads in prayer. Once I saw Carter scold Tina for biting into her food without saying grace.

The chicken is delicious, and when I compliment Carter, he explains proudly that when he was in the army stationed in West Germany, he was appointed "number two chef." He elaborately describes the ice carvings of swans he used to prepare "with a seafood bisque in the center, and fresh shrimp laid out around it. I'd put my all into that."

For dessert, he announces, "Surprise!" and, smiling, pulls out an Entenmann's cherry pie from under his chair. "I'm just sorry it's not homemade."

Carter's older brother, Lionel, walks in unexpectedly. Carter offers him some food and introduces me, but Lionel is not interested. He is in need of a quick fix of heroin. Carter scrambles to find a syringe in the dark, and Lionel chides, "Hurry, the kids and my wife are in the car at the corner. I don't have much time."

As a special treat for his brother, Carter prepares a "speedball" by adding a pinch of crack to the heroin in the cooker along with a couple of drops of lemon juice to make the crack dissolve.

Tina warns, "Don't use up all the crack."

Carter snaps back, "Can't we just enjoy this without your complaining?" The brothers proceed with their injections, and Lionel runs off immediately afterward.

I rise to leave and Tina hugs me. Carter accompanies me to my car out on the boulevard, struggling to find words to describe our pleasant evening: "Y'know, it was ... it was ... normal."

During these early months of their relationship, Carter pursued the patriarchal fantasy of maintaining Tina "at home" while he went out to "hit licks [steal]." When we would run into him rushing around alone on the street, he would say affectionately and proudly, "I got to get my Tina well" or "I'm takin' penitentiary chances for my girl." Tina embraced this gendered division of labor and eagerly domesticated herself so long as her needs for crack and alcohol were fulfilled. She basked in the romantic outlaw masculinity of her "man." On one occasion, Jeff visited their camp to find Tina affectionately admiring Carter, who was sound asleep with his head on her lap. She explained, "I got me some crack, but I don't want to wake him up. No! I'm going to let him get his rest and smoke it all by myself because he do be tired. He and Sonny hit a lick last night. He was working hard."

On another visit, Jeff found Tina watching television alone in the encampment, saddened by the overdose death of a friend named Long John. He had been an occasional burglary and scavenging partner of Carter, specializing in stripping recyclable metal and wooden beams from abandoned buildings and unguarded warehouses. Tina recalled:

> They wouldn't let me in the buildings, because Carter says, "This work is not for a woman." So I just stand there as a lookout while the mens did all the heavy lifting. I don't like that. So instead I stay here and watch TV. I make sure Carter get me the batteries for the TV and everything before he goes out to work.
>
> Sometimes they be coming back with big old beams that need to be cleaned. 'Cause clean shit cost more. But I ain't cleaning that old nasty wood. I'm like, "I want my crack, Daddy." Besides, I be asleep when they come back with the wood. So they pay Al to take out the nails and scrape the beams. Al like to clean. And Long John, he likeded to sell it clean.

This particular conversation was interrupted by Carter running into the camp to ask Tina for a screwdriver. While she rummaged through the mounds of junk stacked around the camp, Carter grabbed a rusted trowel from the ground and ran off. He returned a few minutes later brandishing the broken-off corner of a license plate with a valid California registration sticker affixed.

> *Carter:* I'm gonna get ten or fifteen dollars for this. I took it from this Chinese or Mexican dude or something. He's the motherfucker I was telling you about, parked outside the McDonald's. He had a big ol' soda sitting on the roof of his car, and I seen that he wasn't drinking it no more. So I ask him if I can have the rest of it.
>
> But he picks up the fuckin' soda, takes a sip out of it, and throws the whole fucking thing down on the ground. Then he jumps in the truck, right, looks at me, laughs, and drives by. Pointing at me and shit, like I'm a fuckin' sideshow or clown or something.
>
> So I peeled his ass for the sticker on his plate when he happened to park in just the right spot. [holding up the trowel] This worked perfectly, steady, strong, and flat on one end. It fits in the groove of both a flat screw and a Phillips screw. How long was I gone, less than a minute? Thirty seconds for one screw, twenty-eight for the other.
>
> *Tina:* [hugging Carter] My man's a tiptoe burglar. . . . He so bold!
>
> *Carter:* Plus DMV [Department of Motor Vehicles] is closed now until Monday. That man going to have to take off a whole day of work to go get him another plate.
>
> *Tina:* [sighing] I gotta go back out to get me some more bottles and cans, get a few dollars and pick up some crack.
>
> *Carter:* [kissing Tina on the forehead] No you don't, Momma. We'll get by. I'll handle it. I know you tired and want to rest.
>
> *Tina:* [resting her head on his shoulder] Mmm-hmmm.

Tina's homeless version of the homebound bourgeois housewife did not endure. She increasingly took on the active role of outlaw running partner, joining Carter on his burglaries and in his instrumental bullying of the whites. This deepened their romance and was more consistent with Tina's habitus forged in a childhood of intermittent nurture and abuse by outlaw kin and neighbors. Carter and Tina publicly celebrated their commitment to one another as a couple through public displays of aggression against anyone who wronged them. They enjoyed, for example, telling the story of "whooping Frank's motherfuckin' white ass" after he double-crossed them on what they called "our cobblestone lick." On one of their nighttime forays Carter had "cased out" the city of San Francisco's underground storage site for cobblestones.

Carter: I'm talking about thousands and thousands of cultured cobblestones. The fabricated kind that they use to beautify houses, right, for false fronts that increase the value about twenty, twenty-five thousand dollars just on that look alone.

Frank, who was painting a sign for Sammy, the owner of the Crow's Nest liquor store, brokered a deal. Sammy was renovating his home and offered to buy one hundred cobblestones at fifty cents each. When Carter and Tina delivered the heavy shipment, however, Sammy insisted on dropping the price by half because Frank had explained to him the difference between "cultured concrete cobblestones" and genuine, old-fashioned ones.

Carter: We carried a hundred motherfucking stones up a fifty-foot-high hill from where the city stores them.

Tina: And had to take them over a chain fence, too, that got barbed wire on it. [inhaling crack and handing Carter the pipe]

Carter: At first I thought, I can't use Tina for this job, 'cause she short-winded, and I can't have her going over that high fence. The stones are heavy and her arms are just gonna turn to mush. [inhaling crack]

But Tina did great. That skinny frame of Tina's could work faster than any man's . . . better than Sonny and Al put together.

Tina: [grabbing the crack pipe from Carter] And one of them cobblestones fell on my damn leg. So when we saw Frank this morning, I was like *bam!* [throwing a slow-motion punch] Carter tells me, "I didn't know you was good with your left."

I said, "Shit! I'm good with both of 'em." And Frank said he wasn't gonna hit no girl. But I said, "Motherfucker! I ain't *no girl!* I'm a damn woman. Hit me." [laughing and swinging another punch] *Bam!*

Even Carter don't like to fight me. [inhaling crack]

Philippe: How did you learn to fight?

Tina: My sister made me fight when I was a kid going to school 'cause people used to pick on me and I didn't hit back. And she told me, "If you don't hit back, I'm gonna kick your ass."

She said [raising her voice], "Now hit her! Hit her in the jaw! [shouting] Hit her in the mouth!"

But I tell her [meek voice], "I don't like hurting people."

[threatening voice] "You better! Because ah'm'a whoop your ass my own damn self if you don't."

Philippe: How old were you?

Tina: I was eight years, and I didn't want my sister to kick my ass.

She said [angry voice], "Now stomp that bitch! Stomp that bitch! She tryin' to hurt you. *Stomp her, I said!*" [inhaling more crack and going silent]

Carter and Tina's next victim was an acquaintance nicknamed Bugs, who occasionally parlayed drug sales for Carter. On one of their deals Bugs ran off with two hundred dollars in cash that a contact had fronted Carter to buy powder cocaine, a high-end product that was difficult to find on the street in the 1990s and 2000s, in contrast to crack, which was easily accessible in homeless venues.

Carter: Bugs was sick this particular day, which I can understand that. When a dopefiend is sick, a dopefiend is sick! He do what he gotta do. But I had told him that I was gonna fix him that day, and I'm a man of my word. And there's certain things that you do, and certain shit that you don't do. And that was definitely a no-no on something that he shouldn't of did. He was the goddamn perpetrator instead of the dopesick victim.

Tina: [handing Carter a half-full bottle of Cisco] So when we saw him the next day, Carter knocked him out on the first punch. . . . Knocked him smooth out.

Carter: Well, yeah, but he woke up, and was attempting to try to stand up, but he was taking too long, so I snatched him up and knocked him down again.

Tina: After Carter knocked him down I was just stompin' him in his chest.

Carter: And we commenced to moppin' the concrete with his ass.

Tina: But the lady at the florist shop came running out talkin' about [shrill voice], "Just take that mess somewhere else." I was stompin' him in his chest. I had on them loafers with the two-inch heels and they leather ones, you know, the old-fashioned ones. The ones that tie up.

Carter: Tina had on some hard-toed shoes. Kickin' him in the back, and then the head and then the neck.

Tina: Stompin' him! His face was bloody red. And Sonny came tellin' us, "No! No! Stop that!"
I pushed Sonny back, "Sonny, you stay out of it. This motherfucker almost got us killed." But anyway we took off 'cause the police, the ambulance, and the fire truck came. [inhaling crack]

Carter: It was a spectacle . . . like a parachuter landing in the middle of Market Street at lunch time on a Wednesday.

Tina: [handing Carter the crack pipe and putting her two hands gently on both his cheeks] Thank you, Lord, for bringing us together. I'm Carter's partner his friend his lover his woman his fiancée—everything!

Carter: Tell it! [inhaling crack]

Tina: We don't need nobody in our way 'cause they ain't gonna do for us like we do for each other.

As an ironic closure to this expression of affection, Tina suddenly pulled back from Carter's embrace with a pained expression. She patted his jacket pocket and exclaimed, "You been carrying another Cisco on you all this time? Gimme some of it!" Sheepishly, Carter unzipped his down parka and handed her a brown paper bag. She yanked the bottle of Cisco out of the bag, held it up to the sunlight to reveal only a half inch of the pink fortified wine, and shook her head.

Tina: Ain't that a shame! Didn't even save me none. I *never* do you like that.

Carter: Don't be yelling at me. *Muscle mouth!*

Tina: [waving the empty bottle at Carter] I'm not your motherfuckin' fool, *ignorant son of a bitch!*

The outburst ended with Carter backing down: "Okay! *Excuse me,* I ain't saying nothin' else. I apologize if I said anything wrong. . . . I apologize. . . . [yelling and raising his hand threateningly] *I said I apologize!*" Tina smashed the bottle on the ground and clucked mockingly, "Tsk, tsk, tsk." Interpersonal flare-ups like this one between otherwise affectionate running partners and lovers reminded us that in gray zones, aggression is the most effective means of asserting rights. Violence is normalized as ethical. In Tina and Carter's case, violence also deepened their romantic bond. Following the same interpersonal gray zone logic, within a few months of his brutal beatdown, Bugs once again was periodically hitting licks with Carter and Tina and he sometimes slept over in their camp.

One evening, Jeff ran into Tina and Carter in a laundromat in the residential neighborhood up the hill from Edgewater Boulevard and offered them a ride to their camp. While Jeff was helping them load three garbage bags full of still warm laundry into the trunk of his car, a young bohemian-style white man dressed only in an undershirt and shorts (clearly down to his last set of clean clothes) began asking everyone in the laundromat, exasperated, if they had seen what happened to his clothing: "All of my laundry is gone. Everything I own. I can't believe this! I don't have any more clothes."

Jeff turned to Carter and whispered out of earshot, "Did you guys take 'em?" Tina responded so indignantly to the accusation that Jeff felt a little embarrassed at having suspected them: "C'mon, Jeff! We don't want his clothing."

Ten minutes later in a back alley off Edgewater Boulevard where they were unloading the overflowing laundry bags into Tina and Carter's shopping cart, a set of headlights on high beam blinded them. The same young man from the laundromat, still in his shorts, jumped out of his car pleading earnestly, "Please! I don't want any trouble." Shivering in the damp fog, he placed his hands on Carter's shoulders and pleaded again, "I just want my clothes back."

Carter pushed him away, shouting, "We don't have your damn clothing!"

The young man did not back down. He yanked a blanket out of the shopping cart, exclaiming, "This is my comforter!"

Carter protested loudly, "No it's not; it's mine."

The young man continued: "And this is my t-shirt; my girlfriend gave it to me. I can tell you the history of every piece of clothing in this pile!" He turned to Jeff, who was taking pictures: "What's going on here? Is this art?"

Carter suddenly slapped his forehead and changed his tone of voice: "Oh, wow, we must've grabbed your stuff by accident."

Also suddenly shifting to a friendly tone of voice, Tina chimed in: "Oh, my! How ridiculous! Isn't that funny? . . ." Then she whispered angrily to Jeff, "Motherfuckin' Carter stealin' other people's shit like that!"

Surprised at having been so blatantly double-crossed by Tina and Carter, Jeff stopped offering them rides for several months and began visiting the scene only on foot. Several years later Tina recalled the lick and apologized for it belatedly but sincerely. She and Jeff shared a laugh, remembering this awkward early incident when he and Philippe were still learning the limits of trust and the serendipities of petty crime among the homeless.

Stabilizing into Homelessness

A few weeks after the "laundry lick," Carter, sitting despondently, refused to acknowledge Jeff's greeting when he arrived early one morning. Tina pulled Jeff aside and whispered, "His little sister, Priscilla. She died." Carter sullenly prepared a large injection and immediately collapsed forward after hitting a large vein in his triceps. Panicking at this full-blown overdose, Jeff shouted in Carter's face while Tina slapped Carter's cheeks repeatedly. It took a full thirty seconds for Carter to flutter his eyes slowly. He then immediately jumped to his feet and stomped out of the camp without saying a word, leaving Tina calling after him, "You motherfucker! You scared us to death." On several other occasions when Carter was upset, he overdosed in a similar manner. Each time we were unsure whether it was a histrionic display for our benefit or an accidental near-death.

Carter was arrested at the Discount Grocery Outlet two hours after this particular overdose. He had slipped two five-pound sticks of salami down his pant legs, intending to bring the dried meat to his sister's wake. He punched the security guards when they stopped him. Tina, who had been waiting outside the store, cursed the police officers as they pushed Carter into the squad car. A member of the ethnographic team restrained her, and she strategically calmed herself down just in time. "I love Carter, but I'm not gettin' busted for no man, and Carter is on a tear. He don't give a fuck if he gets busted. I need to take care of myself."

Despite the assault and theft charge, Carter was released from jail "on his own recognizance" to attend his sister's funeral. Tina accompanied him. It was their first public appearance among Carter's extended family as a couple, and they were welcomed warmly. They began to go regularly to Carter's family reunions on holidays. Sometimes they stayed overnight at an "auntie's" home. They invariably returned from these events refreshed, with newly laundered clothes and overflowing containers of leftover food to share.

That Christmas, Carter and Tina spent a full week in the home of Carter's eldest sister, Beverly, the same household from which Carter had been evicted when we first met him. Tina was thrilled. "We had our own room . . . the guest room, all to ourselves."

Integration into Carter's kinship network, however, did not alter their outlaw lifestyle.

Tina: Our Christmas was beautiful. We gave everybody the same thing. Socks, ten pair in each bag. They were so happy.

Carter: See, Jeff, they was stacking, boxes and boxes and boxes, outside a store on Mission Street. And they got a person walking back and forth to watch the stuff. But a customer came up asking him something so he turned his back to the street for a moment. So I just picked up the biggest box. Walked to the corner and waited for the green light and just walked on.

Tina: Like it was the thing to do!

Carter: We had a hundred fifty pair. White thick socks. Ten pair in each bag.

Tina: And we didn't know what we was going to do for Christmas without no presents.

Carter's deceased sister, Priscilla, had been sick with AIDS for several years, and her family had allowed her to spend her final years in the home where she had grown up along with Carter and her seven other siblings. It was located exactly eight blocks up the hill from Edgewater Boulevard on the same block where Felix's aging mother still lived. Carter took Jeff to photograph the house before its sale shortly after Priscilla's death. Carter climbed onto the balcony, pointing out the city's pro football stadium, and reminisced about how everyone on the block would run out of their houses to celebrate touchdowns during Super Bowls, "with the roar of the crowd booming from the stadium."

Carter's share of the profits from the sale of his childhood home amounted to six thousand dollars, once the lawyers, liens, and outstanding taxes were paid. Carter and Tina's lives immediately improved, but strictly within the limits of their existence on the street.

Tina: Carter got money in the bank. Six in cash! He haven't messed with it. He been turnin' it over and turnin' it over. Keep it goin', buying dope and selling it and shit. But you can only go for so long when you're dippin' in it. Carter, he gonna get us a camper, and he say that he need clean clothes to get a start on that to go pick it out. So now we is washing up these clothes [pointing to a lime green polyester pantsuit drying on a clothesline stretched between their shopping cart and the chain-link fence].

Yesterday Al came with us van shopping in South San Francisco. That's where his parents live. But the man selling, he act like he was prejudice' and we didn't buy nothin'. We made a couple more stops, but where Al took us, it was very very very expensive. Like rich black people, you know. When Carter told them we had two thousand dollars to spend and that he got cashier's checks with him and everything, they just go like [frowning and looking down her nose] . . .

A week later, Tina and Carter were the proud owners of a fifteen-year-old orange and white Chinook camper. They christened it Betsy and embarked on a second honeymoon, unabashedly hugging, kissing, and crooning their pet names—"Momma" and "Daddy"—to one another during our visits. They remained "in pocket" without having to scavenge or steal for another entire month.

Tina: I haven't been wanting for nothin'. He been giving me money every day. I don't be broke and I don't have to ask. He automatically know his woman ain't got no money in her pocket and he know how much better I feel with money in my pocket. Even if it is only a couple dollars.

They parked their camper in an alley behind the McDonald's in order to use the restrooms more conveniently, and they began bathing every morning in the sinks. After their second ticket from the police, Carter and Tina moved their camper five blocks deeper into the warehouse district to a less conspicuous side street amid disabled big-rig trucks and garbage-strewn empty lots. Al and Sonny parked their pickup and camper-shell next to them. Sal, the dealer, also moved his sales spot onto this same side street using the Chinook to block his visibility. Carter was outraged, relishing the opportunity to display a "not-in-my-backyard" homeowner role, complete with the patriarchal detail of protecting his woman from scum:

> They be ten motherfuckers back there buyin' dope, and I got to be hollering, "*Ex-cu-use me!* Wait, wait, wait, wait. This ain't gonna work. You all gotta motherfuckin' disperse."
>
> I know they didn't feel good, and they is just trying to cop [buy heroin], but I had asked them before nicely, and they transact right on that little bench that Sal done set up behind my camper. And I got too much to lose. I got my woman in here [patting the side of the camper].
>
> Plus, half of them come on bikes or pushin' a buggy. They ain't got no vehicle that's registered or no license or nothin' to lose like me. And this here is my roof, my home, my transportation, and everything else. Everything I own is here, and I ain't gonna let these motherfuckers jeopardize me or get me my shit took. Who is gonna help me get it out of impound? Not a damn one of them.

Tina basked in the stability offered by the Chinook. On Mother's Day, she asked Jeff to take a portrait of her at Twin Peaks, San Francisco's most spectacular tourist vista point. She missed her mother and wanted to send her the picture as a gift. In preparation for posing, Tina washed her hair, pouring water from an empty Cisco bottle while leaning out the passenger side of the camper. She then dressed up for the occasion, putting a denim vest over a long-sleeve, décolleté silk blouse tucked into an ankle-length batik print skirt. She also wore her favorite black patent leather lace-up shoes with black stockings and applied black eyeliner along with her usual cherry red lipstick. Before hopping into Jeff's car she grabbed a purple chiffon scarf, a brightly patterned silk jacket, and crystal earrings. Al was washing his dishes off the back of his pickup, using a Chinese wok as a wash basin, and Tina offered him a ride. He had a box of records to sell and there was a vintage vinyl store in the upscale Castro neighborhood located on the way to Twin Peaks. In his dirty t-shirt, paint-splattered blue jeans, work boots, and battered baseball cap, Al offered a dramatic contrast to Tina, but he eagerly jumped into the car.

While waiting for Al to come out of the record store, Tina grabbed a few grapes from the display of a boutique-style produce market. The owner burst out the door, yelling in English with a strong Arabic accent, "This is the second time I've caught you stealing my grapes! If you do it again, I will call the police. Don't touch my goddamn grapes." Tina snapped back, "I'm only tasting your goddamn grapes. And I've never even been here before."

Al, still in possession of his heavy box of records, came out of the used record shop disappointed. He caught the end of the conversation and ran up behind the fruit seller, threatening, "You need to be careful who you're talking to like that. We've never been here before."

The storeowner was not intimidated and irately raised the ante: "What are you going to do about it?" Al retorted, "No! what are *you* going to do about it, you goddamn foreigner?" At the time, AM talk radio hosts in California were promoting a right-wing ballot initiative to deny health care, education, and welfare benefits to undocumented immigrants, and Al had fully imbibed their xenophobic arguments. The two men shouted heatedly at one another for a good two minutes, leaving Tina standing silently to the side. Sticking their fingers into one another's faces, it appeared they were about to escalate to punches. Finally the store-owner spun around and retreated inside his store with a dismissive, "I'm sick of you fucking homeless. Fuck you, homeless!"

"Can you believe that!" Al fumed. "He called us homeless. How did he know we were homeless?"

"I didn't hear him say that," Tina giggled innocently, barely holding back an outburst of hilarity. She then draped her arm over Al's shoulder and doubled over, gasping between outbursts of laughter, "Al, your teeth slipped out."

Al frowned, trying to remain angry. "And it's a good thing he didn't laugh at me losing my teeth or I would have decked him." He smiled, however, despite himself and snapped out of his rage: "Come on! Let's go try and sell these records somewhere else."

Back in Jeff's car, Tina looked into the rearview mirror and took out her makeup kit. No longer smiling, she whispered to no one in particular, "Homeless?" and then sighed resignedly, "Oh, well, homeless."

Outlaw Love

The Chinook camper allowed Tina and Carter to expand the reach of their burglaries. Formerly, they had been limited by their reliance on shopping carts to transport their scavenged and stolen goods. With the mobility, storage capacity, and camouflage of the camper, hitting licks became more profitable than recycling. With their home conveniently omnipresent and mobile, they seamlessly wove drugs, alcohol, and income generation into the cadence of their romantic domesticity. They no longer had to leave one another's side.

Carter considered himself to be a skilled entrepreneur who carefully weighed cost, benefit, and risk. For that reason he began specializing in "hitting" what he called "wood licks." Opportunities were plentiful during these years because of the spike in San Francisco housing values, fueled by the dot-com boom. In the 1990s, the median price of a three-bedroom home in San Francisco rose an unprecedented 80 percent, and rents more than doubled (San Francisco Board of Supervisors 2002:66, 68).

Carter: They got a lot of brand-new full six-unit complexes going up all over the city. The further west you go out toward the beach, the more stuff they leave out. You'll see stacks of this 'n' that laid out on the sidewalk. Ain't nobody figure it's gonna be took in those neighborhoods. And you pull up, dim your lights, load up ten or fifteen sheets of plywood, and go on about your business. [snapping his fingers] That quick. You know, be quiet be quick and be gone.

Some of them are one-time licks, but then it depends on how you leave it, you know. If you don't be real greedy, right, and only get a few at a time then you're all right. That's what I been doing. I get four from this stack, six from that stack, and four from that one, right, and then go on about my business.

But puttin' the wood up here [patting the roof of the camper] makes the camper top-heavy, and the clutch is winding out. I gotta get me a little pickup truck. Last week, we had two twenty-foot four-by-sixes . . . motherfuckin' whole house foundations! We was on full carryin' them. I couldn't believe it!

I found a client. Got paid. And fixed real goddamn good. Wasn't feelin' no pain. No pain. No pain. [pointing to a passing BMW] Oh that's nice, boy! Shiny!

I'm so proud of my girl. You should have seen how fast she worked last night. The cops had pulled around right when we were loading Betsy. We froze with the plywood sheets in our hands, and as soon as they passed we jammed them fast!

A few weeks after this conversation, Carter purchased a badly dented, orange 1970s Chevy Luv public works truck that had been retired from service by the city at a public auction. Tina named it Suzie-Q. They used it exclusively for hitting licks and maintained Betsy, the Chinook camper, inconspicuously parked in the back alley near the salvage yards. It looked like merely one more abandoned vehicle waiting to be stripped.

Jeff's Fieldnotes

Tina apologizes for the condition of the camper. "I was planning on cleaning it last night, but we were out on a lick and you know how it goes." Carter, dressed in a black sweatsuit made of parachute material also apologizes, but not for his role in the disarray. He is referring solely to Tina's negligence as the female homemaker. I push aside a pile of clothes and squeeze inside. Carter jokes that they have accumulated so much stuff for resale that they no longer have enough room to sleep side by side.

Carter finishes fixing and falls into one of his deep, post-injection nods, emitting periodic moans of pleasure to reassure us he has not overdosed.

A faint sound of buzzing snaps Carter to attention. He pulls out a vibrating beeper clipped to his waist and squints to read the message, announcing, "Awright, we gotta go!"

Smiling at my surprise, he explains: "My client, the contractor I was tellin' you about, gave me this beeper so's to contact me for special orders. He goes window shoppin' at the used lumberyard to get the prices, and I give him at least forty percent off on anything and everything that he orders. He ends up savin' a bundle."

Tina: "Yeah! How long you been working for him now? A couple months?"

Carter: "No! I never work for him. I been dealin' with him. I ain't working for the bastard. I work for myself. So, it's just like ..."

Tina: "... a job. He always comes to you."

Carter: "Everybody's always wanting to run their own business. Basically that's what I'm doing. Workin' my ass off, believe it or not, but that's enjoyable 'cause it's on my own time—talking to people; goin' to companies; sayin' hey, man …

All three of us squeeze into the front seat of Suzie-Q and Carter drives rapidly to the lumberyard. Moments later, a brand-new white pickup truck parks in front of us. An older Latino man wearing a baseball cap, a down vest, and a tape measure on his belt exits from the driver side. Carter jumps out to greet him, returning moments later with a big smile. He winks at Tina, "It's the lick I was telling you about."

We drive twenty minutes to a residential neighborhood and park under a shady tree across from a middle school. Carter and Tina each don road crew reflector vests, slipping them slowly over their clothing. I have never seen them move so slowly and deliberately on a lick and am confused. It is five o'clock and broad daylight. What can they be planning? There are no stacks of construction supplies in sight, nor any shipping containers or warehouses in the vicinity. They walk over to a series of traffic cones signaling a road repair trench, which is temporarily covered by thick sheets of plywood to accommodate the rush hour traffic.

Nonchalantly, they rearrange the barricades and cones, waving the commuter traffic to pass. Still moving slowly, they lift the large sheets of plywood one by one into the back of Suzie-Q. Tina flashes me a quick smile before lapsing into the bored, disengaged expression of a public works employee earning overtime pay.

They rearrange the cones to block the now-exposed trench and calmly climb back into the pickup, where they seal the success of the lick with a kiss before driving slowly back to Edgewater Boulevard.

Morality and the Public Secret of Addiction

We began hearing rumors that Tina had started injecting heroin. Both Carter and Tina denied it, but everyone suspected it. Sonny, who was Al's running partner during this period but who also occasionally burgled with Carter and Tina, was especially worried. He considered heroin injection inappropriate behavior "for a lady." Sonny expressed his concern for Tina's welfare in an old-fashioned patriarchal trope, but he also had a self-interest. Currently, Tina shared crack with both Carter and him without requiring reciprocal gifts of heroin. If she developed a physical dependence on heroin, resources would be drained from this microbalance in the local moral economy of sharing that currently favored both him and Carter. The subtle mechanisms of symbolic violence around appropriate gender roles probably made Sonny oblivious to his manipulative self-interest. He thought of himself as someone who genuinely cared for both Tina and Carter and celebrated their romantic dream. He was only too familiar with the interpersonal betrayals that accompany heroin addiction in extreme poverty:

> Bof' of them hooked, that's a fucked-up thing! It's hard enough tryin' to do this here [rubbing the injection scars on his arm] by yourself, but it's gonna be doubly hard if they doin' it together. Trying to take care of two people. [shaking his head] It don't work. Every time he have something, she got to have some of it too. Even a wake-up in the morning and shit. 'Cause now when he's sick, she's sick.
>
> If he goes out while she asleep or something to do a sack [bag of heroin] by hisself and get well while she stay back at the camper and wake up sick . . . [shaking his head] He'll come back without tryin' to let her know that he had made a hustle and got some money and heroin. And then she gonna get some and she ain't gonna wanna split it either. "Oh, you motherfucker, why you didn't save me none!"
>
> Or they be tryin' to do each other like how you add a little water on the sneak-tip to the cooker to make your partner think he's gettin' his fair share.
>
> It leaves her goin' out there in the streets to find someone who might have some dope. And whatever else it might lead a woman to do. . . . She a lot weaker than a man. Damn! Lay on your back just to get some dope. You know what I'm sayin'? Lay on your back to get ten dollars to get one fix. Then you gotta think about tomorrow, the next day, or even just later on that day.
>
> And the thing is, Carter care about the girl a whole lot, too, you know, and I think she probably genuinely cares about him a lot, too, but their relationship is a odd-couple thing.

I warned them they gotta try to find some kinda common ground and come to some kinda conclusion or solution. If she gets hooked on heroin it's gonna take bof' of them to hustle. I don't want to see a girl out there, turnin' no dates and stuff like this here man. Because she put herself in danger. You don't know who might pick her up—some wacko or somethin'. Then you goin' to the hospital because they done beat you up, took your money, and shit. It's sad. Really sad.

Man! I sure am glad I don't have no girl.

Tina chose a Thanksgiving cookout at the white encampment, organized by members of the ethnographic team, to confess her public secret. Guiding Jeff aside gently by the crux of his elbow, she whispered, "I have something I need to tell you. I've started shooting. I can't talk now, but I didn't want to hide it from you no longer. We'll talk later."

Y'know how when you're walkin' and you look up across the street and you see someone you think you know? And then you walk closer, and it turns out to be an old friend, someone you used to kick it with as a kid. And you walk up to each other, and you each ask how the other's doing. And you talk for a while. And then you leave, saying to yourself, "Wow! It was really good to see him." That's what heroin feels like to me. —*Hank*

Felix jolted awake at 1:00 A.M. with "migraines and the sweats." It was going to be a long night: dopesickness was coming on, and Sal the dealer was not going to open until 7:00 A.M. Felix tried to urinate into the plastic water bottle that he kept next to his blankets, but his body was shaking too hard. He stood up, but his leg muscles spasmed and he fell down the highway embankment. He had to drag himself on his hands and knees to get back up to his mattress, pausing twice to retch.

The next morning when we visited Felix, we found him in the corner of the bus shelter trying to escape the drizzling rain. He described what he had endured that winter night (while we were sleeping in our well-heated homes):

First I'm cold; then poof! Heat flashes, and I'm ripping the covers off. But it's cold out here, so I get like freezing, 'cause I'm covered with wet sweat. I try to spit, and all this green stuff comes out. Then I'm just squirtin' out my guts. My heart feels like it's going to stop. I can't pick up my bones. My knees hurt; my legs are locked; I can't breathe; I can't even think; I feel every nerve in my fingertips, every single one. I can't stand still. I can't lie down.

One simple act can instantly solve Felix's problems. Shooting heroin into his bloodstream will turn his physical pain and psychic distress into relaxed comfort—even bliss—for a few hours. Heroin addiction is not simply a psychological dependency or an emotional craving. It is physiological, deeply embodied at the cellular level of functioning. Ecstasy and agony play leap frog with chronic high-dose opiate use. Every five to eight hours, organs run amok: the nose drips, bowels burst, eyes burn, skin itches, and bones ache. Cell membranes scream out for the opiate proteins they require to function normally, and the psyche overflows with anguish.

All of the Edgewater homeless know exactly which foot to put in front of the other as soon as they wake up every day. Their needs and priorities are unambiguous: they must solve their most urgent physiological problem before worrying about anything else. Finding employment, acquiring food, obtaining shelter, appearing in court, applying for public assistance, or treating an abscess become inconsequential. Society's opprobrium and personal public failure are the least of their worries. Similarly, childhood psychological wounds of abuse or abandonment have long since been subordinated to the demands of daily heroin consumption.

The pain of heroin withdrawal was one of the few commonalities capable of transcending personal enmities and ethnic divisions on Edgewater Boulevard. For example, Frank, the sign painter, who normally minimized his interactions with African-Americans, spontaneously bonded warmly with Carter when he overheard Carter describing heroin withdrawal symptoms to us.

> *Carter:* You throwing up and fartin' and shittin' at the same time. It's like you don't have no control over your ol' muscles in your rectum whatsoever.
>
> *Frank:* But I can deal with that part. The worst part is the heebie-jeebies. . . .
>
> *Carter:* [patting him on the back] Yeah! That's what gets me, too. The anxiety part just makes me wanna scream. . . .
>
> *Frank:* Makes me want to climb the fuckin' wall. [doubling over and shaking with disgust]
>
> *Carter: Oh, man!* Frank, you so right! A million ants crawling through your skin and you just want to peel it right off. And there ain't no sense in bein', right—
>
> *Frank:* [the two talk simultaneously] —and you can't explain it. It's something you have to go through to know what we're talking about.

Carter: Oh, man! Yeah—

Frank: It's like someone is scraping your bones . . . for like a week straight, twenty-four hours a day. . . .

Carter: It's scary even thinkin' about it. . . .

Frank: It's like spider webs. . . . Scratch that. It's like spiders crawling all through your bones.

Carter: Oh, man! You so right!

Frank: It's like going in and out of death. Living and dying . . .

Carter: And the worst is when you in jail. Because they don't give a shit if you die. You be in there, curled up in a corner, right—

Frank: Yep! Yep!

Carter: And there are youngsters there in the cell with you, talkin' [in a deprecating voice], "Oh, you dopefiend." So you just try to sit there and grab your knees and rock.

Frank: Yep, yep! Back and forth, back and forth . . .

Carter: Side to side. That's all you can do for like three days. . . .

Frank: Yeah! They're all crackheads, so they don't go through that.

Carter: Yeah! Stoppin' crack ain't nothin' like being dopesick. [slapping high-five with Frank]

Frank: Yeah, well, maybe they got a mental thing—and crack is a very strong mental thing—but you ain't physically—

Carter: Yeah! That's the difference.

The Moral Economy

Protection from full-blown heroin withdrawal symptoms drives the moral economy of heroin sharing. It is considered unethical to leave a person stranded when he or she is dopesick unless one is openly feuding with that person. The best protection from withdrawal symptoms is to maintain a generous reputation, because everyone is eager to help someone who will reciprocate in the future.

Mexican black tar was the only kind of heroin available on the streets of San Francisco during the years of our fieldwork (Ciccarone and Bourgois 2003). Black tar heroin is brittle when cold and gooey when warm, making it difficult to partition accurately with a knife or razor blade. The only precise way to divide a chunk of black tar is to dissolve it into a measured quantity of water and draw it up into a calibrated syringe. When two or more people pool money to buy a bag of heroin, they carefully prepare the solution to ensure that all participants receive an amount proportional to the money they contributed. If someone is given more than his or her fair share, everyone understands that the favor must be reciprocated in the future. The process of preparing heroin, consequently, becomes an anxiety-filled, ritualized site for interpersonal conflict as well as for displays of generosity. It elicits emphatic displays of aggressive posturing to prevent victimization and to stake claims to future obligations of repayment.

Philippe's Fieldnotes

The sun is setting and Max is anxious. He has been able to panhandle only eight dollars over the past four hours and the Island Boys, Scotty and Petey, stop selling after dark. He cannot count on his running partner, Hogan, for help because, yet again, Hogan drank too much Cisco in the morning and never left the camp. Max approaches the Island Boys nervously. Their bags sell for twenty dollars. To Max's relief, they agree to "go in on one" with him. Better yet, because he has offered to pay eight dollars, almost two dollars more than a third of the cost, they agree to give him the rights to the cotton.

I follow them back to their camp, trotting to keep up. Their brisk, eager walk makes it clear that they are dopefiends on their way to fix. As we enter the camp, Hank runs over with a Styrofoam cup full of water. Hogan, who is splayed over his wet mattress, props himself up alertly to watch the reaction as Hank attempts to ingratiate himself for the rights to the cotton.

Scotty cuts Hank short without making eye contact. "Got any money? The cotton belongs to Max and I can't loan you anything." Hank throws down the water, shouting for everyone to hear, "And to think that yesterday I took all their fuckin' clothes to the laundromat! Paid for the soap and everything!" Hogan drops back onto his mattress, moaning softly to make sure Max knows he also needs help.

Hank grabs a crowbar and smashes a wooden pallet that he brought to the camp for firewood, sending chips flying. Scotty whispers to Petey, grinning, "Serves that asshole right." Scotty dislikes Hank, suspecting him of trying to edge in on his partnership with Petey by offering to do special favors (such as yesterday's laundry).

Scotty prepares the heroin, but as he fills the three syringes, one for each injector, Max launches into an argumentative tirade. He insists on holding each syringe up to the firelight to reverify that they all contain the exact same amount of heroin solution. Max has to be vigilant because, as running partners, Scotty and Petey might collude to rip him off in the sharing process. In fact, Scotty's syringe is slightly overfilled and Max forces Scotty to squirt some of his heroin back into the communal bottle cap cooker.

While injecting, Max tells Hogan, who is still whimpering, that he can "have the cotton." Suddenly agile, Hogan hops over, grabs the bottle cap with the leftover cotton at the bottom, and waits eagerly for Max to finish injecting so that he can borrow his syringe.

Initially we thought that the homeless constantly pooled money and shared ancillary paraphernalia out of economic necessity when injecting heroin. They were generally unable to raise enough money to pay for a bag of heroin alone before beginning to feel withdrawal symptoms. When the price of bags dropped threefold, however, from twenty dollars to seven dollars during the second year of our fieldwork, sharing did not decrease. We realized that cooperating to purchase bags is not simply a pragmatic, economic, or logistical necessity; it is the basis for sociality and establishes the boundaries of networks that provide companionship and also facilitate material survival. The sense of community and mutual obligation among network members offers some insurance against dopesickness. When members of the Edgewater Boulevard scene began injecting alone too frequently and refused offers to pool money to buy heroin, they were accused of being "selfish" and risked becoming socially isolated.

The moral economy generates frequent expressions of solidarity, but the logic of the gray zone imposes greed, deceit, and opportunism onto generosity. Every day is "a state of emergency" (Benjamin [1940] 1968:257), and aid to others must be meted out selectively as a zero-sum calculation. Inevitably, under conditions of scarcity, the help given to one person is at the expense of another who is also in desperate need. Furthermore, no plea for help can be taken at face value, because hustling for heroin by any means necessary is the defining attribute of a righteous dopefiend.

Carter, for example, was notorious for feigning dopesickness, and he often preyed on Vernon's generosity. Vernon qualified for a monthly disability check as a clinically diagnosed "victim of violence," the result of a beating he had received twenty years earlier. He also supplemented his income with off-the-books jobs as a part-time house painter, and his wife was a registered nurse who occasionally gave him extra pocket change. On one occasion, Vernon walked into Carter's encampment to inject, and Carter whispered to Philippe, "Watch this. I'm 'a get something from him!" He grabbed his stomach, moaned, and doubled over. Vernon fixed his heroin hurriedly, but left a "taste" in the bottom of the cooker for Carter. Winking at Philippe, Carter complained angrily to Vernon that the cotton he left was not "wet enough." His ploy backfired, however, and Vernon shouted angrily:

> I ain't gonna give you no more dope. I just gave you ten ccs. [turning to Philippe] He owes me money already. He's always behaving like a little bitch and getting mad. Last night I bought forty dollars' worth of goddamn dope and cocaine. And gave him some. And I didn't ask that motherfucker for one goddamn penny.

Nevertheless, the possibility of genuine withdrawal symptoms is an omnipresent reality, and abandoning someone when they are legitimately "sick"—especially a running partner—can destroy a friendship. Recriminations are often voiced in front of witnesses as a strategy to damage someone's reputation, but they can also precipitate destructive counteraccusations. Felix, for example, was eager to redeem himself in Frank's eyes following the breakup of their running partnership during the white flight episode (described in chapter 1). He eventually moved into Frank's camp, intent on disparaging Max, who had replaced him as Frank's running partner.

> *Felix:* [shouting for all to hear] Fuck you, Max! I was sick as a fuckin' dog this morning, asked you for a fuckin' cotton and you ain't give me shit. You was spent. You wouldn't even talk to me.
>
> *Max:* I didn't have a cotton. I had given it to him [pointing to Frank].
>
> *Felix:* I motherfuckin' live right here, and when you are motherfuckin' sick in the morning, I wake your ass up. You ain't did shit for me.

Max: That's a lie. [turning to Philippe] The other day, I took Felix back here and looked out for him and got him well.

Felix: Bullshit! That was my birthday. That's natural. And that was a motherfuckin' week and a half ago. I owe you nothing, motherfucker. I'm gonna motherfuckin' move.

Max: Bullshit! You only count yourself. Just Felix! Just Felix! Just Felix! I give you thirds of bags more than you ever give me.

Felix: Don't ever ask me for help again. Get the fuck outta here. [turning to Frank] What goes around, comes around. [announcing to everyone around] Just wait till that motherfucker is sick. I ain't gonna help him one fuckin' bit.

He's just like the niggers. He don't pay nobody back. He'll see, it's gonna rain sooner than he thinks. Next time he gets sick he ain't gettin' shit from me. Everybody else gets something. They'll never be sick in front of me, but Max! He can stay sick. I don't care.

Drug Consumption as Racialized Habitus

Heroin injectors often brag about the size of their habit, exaggerating how many "grams of dope" they inject per day. Like many of the identity and micropower relations along Edgewater Boulevard, competition over who had the biggest heroin habit often became racialized:

Felix: Man, none of these niggers is real dopefiends. They're crackheads. These guys can't shoot dope like I do. I don't have their kind of habit. They ain't even in my league. Give 'em a half a gram . . . and they'll die. Carter would die for sure.

Polydrug preferences also followed ethnic patterns. The whites, for example, referred to crack as "a nigger drug," even though most of them also smoked crack themselves. With the notable exception of Al, however, they were ashamed to admit it. Even those whites who smoked large quantities of crack would pretend shamefacedly, as they lit their pipes, that they only smoked opportunistically: "I never buy it. But if someone has it—sure, I'll take a hit." A few of the whites, such as Nickie and Max, never smoked crack, even when it was offered to them, claiming that it ruined their heroin highs. Everyone on Edgewater Boulevard, black and white, agreed that "crack makes you sicker quicker."

Virtually all the African-Americans devoted significant effort to raising money to buy crack once they had satisfied their daily physical need for heroin. When successful, they often stayed up all night on binges. The whites generally hustled less money than the African-Americans, and when they did obtain a sudden windfall, they usually purchased fortified wine or extra heroin rather than more crack. As a result, many of the whites had larger heroin habits and tended to fall asleep at sunset, unless they were dopesick or belligerently drunk.

On special occasions, the African-Americans injected speedballs to propel themselves onto a roller-coaster high and mesh the sedative effects of heroin with the wide-awake exhilaration of cocaine. They would sometimes celebrate their speedball sessions by "booting-and-jacking" their injections—that is, repeatedly flushing blood in and out of their syringes to provide multiple rushes of pleasure. When we were filming a speedball session on one occasion, Sonny chuckled, "Lady in red give daddy some head," as a plume of red blood flooded into the barrel of his syringe, indicating that his needle tip was safely inside a vein. He then pushed the plunger halfway into the barrel, only to follow it with, "Come back, Little Sheba," as he pulled the plunger back to reflood the barrel with blood. On the final flush, he sang, "Hit the road, Jack, and don't come back." All of the whites dismissed booting-and-jacking as "a nigger thing." In all our years on Edgewater Boulevard, Al was the only white we saw inject a speedball on purpose.

The whole crack package—the rapid spending, the celebratory binges, and the stimulating physiological effect—meshed with the racialized late-twentieth-century persona of the enterprising black "outlaw," which, on Edgewater Boulevard, was mobilized in opposition to the persona of the broken-down white "bum." Most of the homeless in the scene, of course, fell somewhere in between these two stereotyped ways of being in the world, but the African-Americans in our social network strove more consistently to maintain the public appearance of being in control of their lives and having fun. In sustaining a sense of self-worth, they embraced an ecstatic commitment to getting high. Most of the whites, in contrast, considered themselves to be depressed and, indeed, most of the time looked and acted dejected. Furthermore, even though we often observed Frank, Hank, Hogan, Max, Petey, and Scotty nodding after they injected, they usually claimed with stoic boredom that they no longer enjoyed shooting and that they were merely staving off withdrawal symptoms: "I get well. I don't nod no more."

Everyone in our scene had severely scarred the veins in their arms as a consequence of long careers of injection. It was difficult for them to "direct deposit" heroin into a vein. By the midpoint of our fieldwork, most of the whites had given up searching for operable veins and skin-popped. They sank their needles perfunctorily, often through their clothing, into their fatty tissue.

In contrast, the African-Americans, even in the final years of our fieldwork, rarely skin-popped their injections. Instead, they often spent up to forty-five minutes searching for a functional vein. This could become a bloody process as they made a half dozen or more punctures, pulling back on the plunger each time in order to register a vein. An intravenous injection, though difficult, provides an instantaneous rush of pleasure. Rejecting the aura of failure and depression associated with the whites, even the oldest African-Americans continued to pursue this kind of exhilarating high. They also expressed their pleasure openly in public sessions of deep nodding immediately after injecting. Some individuals, such as Carter, Sonny, and Vernon, performed their highs dramatically, collapsing into full-bodied relaxation and moaning with pleasure or jumping hyperenergetically to their feet. The white addicts, however, usually tried to nod discreetly, their chins slowly dipping onto their chests as if they were merely cat-napping. When energized, they might, at most, talk enthusiastically, scratch their noses compulsively, or clean up their camp.

These distinct injection methods and manners of experiencing and expressing the heroin high become physically inscribed on the body. The whites, for example, suffered from more abscesses, because skin-popping traps impurities in the soft tissue under the skin (picked up from dirty fingers, cookers, water, lint, or whatever adheres to a needle point when it is pushed through filthy clothing and unwashed skin) (Bourgois et al. 2006; Ciccarone et al. 2001). In an intravenous injection, these same impurities are usually safely filtered out by the body's vascular system. The disadvantage of an intravenous injection, however, is that it increases the risks of fatal overdose and also of hepatitis C and HIV infection because of the greater potential for blood-to-blood contact when syringes are shared (Rich et al. 1998). Significantly, the Centers for Disease Control and Prevention documented that the rate of AIDS in the United States in 2005 was ten times higher among African-Americans than among whites (Centers for Disease Control and Prevention 2007b).

The HIV prevention mandate that was part of our National Institutes of Health (NIH) funding motivated us to document hundreds of injection episodes in our fieldnotes. The ethnic differences became evident when we began coding these detailed (and often repetitive) descriptions of the ostensibly trivial acts of preparing, injecting, and savoring heroin. The following excerpt from Jeff's notes is merely one of hundreds of descriptions that reveal ethnically patterned contrasts.

Felix opens the door of Frank's van when I knock. They are in the midst of fixing. Felix pulls down his pants and, with a polite "Excuse my ass," pushes the needle of his syringe three-quarters of the way into his right butt cheek.

The radio is tuned as usual to an AM talk show. The right-wing host is attacking President Bill Clinton over the war in Kosovo. While debating the pros and cons of deploying U.S. troops in the Balkans, Felix pushes forcefully on the plunger. It barely moves, however, because it has struck scar tissue. He leaves the syringe hanging unattended from his rear for a few minutes to let the liquid heroin seep around the brittle tissue. When he pushes on the plunger again, it slides forward a few millimeters but starts to bend under the pressure, so he leaves it dangling again for a few more minutes to allow more liquid to seep out. He repeats this push-and-dangle sequence five or six more times until the syringe is finally empty, arguing the whole time with Frank about the war in the Balkans.

Frank meanwhile has jabbed his needle directly through his filthy t-shirt into the flesh of his upper arm, just over his right shoulder. He flushes his heroin solution in one rapid motion. I offer him an alcohol wipe, but he politely declines. Within a few minutes he starts to nod. He periodically tries to lift his chin and open his eyes to pretend that he is listening intently to Felix's commentary, but his chin keeps dropping back down, his eyes fluttering in evident relaxation.

I walk to where Sonny is currently "staying" inside the Discount Grocery's garbage storage shed. He is with Carter and they too are about to fix. Carter taps with his fingertips along the left side of Sonny's neck to increase blood flow while Sonny sucks on his thumb to swell his jugular. Grimacing anxiously, Sonny looks uncharacteristically passive and vulnerable, like an overgrown toddler sucking his thumb. Carter completes the injection into Sonny's jugular smoothly and pats him on the back. "You'll be feelin' better real soon."

Sonny smiles, "That's my doctor." Carter begins to explain to me that it takes longer for heroin to affect you when you are dopesick and "have nothing for it to piggyback onto." Sonny's dope, however, takes immediate effect. His eyes clear up; his voice drops an octave and becomes gravelly. He drapes his arm affectionately over Carter's shoulder to keep from slumping over.

Carter turns his back on Sonny and probes his needle into his own biceps, holding his breath as he concentrates on finding a vein. Unable to register blood after half a dozen attempts, he jerks the syringe out of his arm, cursing.

He plunges the needle deeper into his biceps several more times, reaching almost under his armpit and changing the angle each time while wiggling the point. He tugs the skin in all directions as he repeatedly pulls back on his plunger to check for blood. Suddenly he starts jabbing violently, as if trying to spear a miniature fish in his bloodstream. Unsuccessful, he yanks the syringe out again.

He sits back and holds the syringe chamber in the window light with the needle pointing up. Air bubbles marble into the mixture of red blood and black heroin in the chamber. He mutters

another curse and, with several abrupt chops of his wrist, forces the air bubbles to the top of
the chamber. He then slowly pushes the plunger upward until the bubbles surface one by one
through the point of the needle. He licks it so as not to waste a drop.

He pokes again into the same awkwardly located biceps muscle in his armpit. After fifteen
more minutes of jabbing, poking, and pulling, he finally manages to register a vein and quickly
flushes the heroin directly into his bloodstream. He drops the used needle on the ground, and
I can see visible traces of blood inside the empty syringe. I suggest that he rinse it, but he is al-
ready nodding and moaning with pleasure.

Carter tries to give Sonny a cigarette but nods abruptly in the middle of handing it to him and
mumbles, "Love you brother . . . hmmm . . . done my good deed for the day . . . hmmm." Sonny, who
is also nodding, lets the precious cigarette fall to the ground in mid-grab. The conversation comes
to an abrupt halt; they have both suddenly fallen into heavy nods.

I open the door of the garbage shed to leave, and the noise snaps both of them out of their
postinjection heroin bliss. They immediately stand up to follow me—energetic and ready to go,
as if their deep nodding moments earlier had occurred hours ago. Carter pops the cotton lying
in the bottom of the cooker into his mouth and we walk out.

Techniques of the Body

Bourdieu, following Mauss, would have called these distinct ways of injecting and experiencing heroin "techniques of the body" (Bourdieu 2002:110–126; Mauss 1936). They are
complex, historically grounded sets of innumerable cultural practices that contribute to
the perception of radical ethnic difference. Countless other routine interactions and markers naturalize such ethnic distinctions into an everyday "common sense" that casts them as
genetico-cultural differences infused with moral judgment. In the very same encampment
or on the same streetcorner, the African-Americans were usually dressed stylishly in the latest hip-hop fashions, while the whites often wore ripped t-shirts, dirty jeans, and disinte-
grating sneakers: Frank would never tilt his baseball hat cockily to the side.

Patterns of cultural diversity are a banal fact of social organization and are not necessarily significant in and of themselves. What is significant about the ethnic distinctions in behaviors that we describe among the homeless is that they are "misrecognized" by most people
as the "natural order of things" (Bourdieu 1990, 2004). Most dramatically, as seen in the
injection process, ethnic distinctions become inscribed onto bodies as scars and infections
and are acted out in postures that become associated with racial characteristics. For example, after we made a presentation on ethnic patterns in injection techniques and abscess
prevalence at the medical school where we worked, a laboratory-based scientist expressed
his interest in obtaining a grant for research to discover the "black gene" for resilient veins.

The down-and-out way of being in the world common to most of the whites was reinforced by the absence of a culturally celebrated model for performing outlaw masculinity

on the street among middle-aged white men. The white street culture—the leather-clad biker riding a Harley Davidson and sporting a graying ponytail, or the prison-based Aryan Brotherhood gang member—did not carry mass appeal. In contrast, fashionable hip-hop youth culture in the 1990s and 2000s had created a positively inflected linguistic term for over-forty-year-olds, *O.G. (Original Gangsta),* with which African-American and Latino homeless injectors could self-identify. Whites, however, could not pass as streetwise hustlers or former gang members even when they tried. (See Jackson's [2001:12, 201–205] discussion of reactions to the aging white movie director Quentin Tarantino staking a claim to "blackness" through childhood association with "underclass" African-American men.)

The middle-aged whites sought to mitigate their pariah status as public masculine failures by presenting themselves as traumatized Vietnam veterans. This identity was predicated on their victimization and the pity they elicited for suffering from a psychiatric disability labeled posttraumatic stress disorder (PTSD). When Hogan's multiple abscesses made

him limp, he blamed it on "that round in my hip from 'Nam." He reminisced about "Hamburger Hill 84 in the Aishon Valley, south of Bon Son, Pol Point, not too far from Dan Lok," where he received "three Silvers, two Bronzes, an MOH [Medal of Honor] . . . and two Purples." When drunk and angry, he would call out for "my baby," the name he gave to the M-16 that he claimed to have buried in the brush by the freeway. Similarly, Hank spoke in detail of how he had been demoted from captain to sergeant for "conduct unbecoming an officer." He claimed that "two black soldiers" in his squad reported him when he commandeered a helicopter to rescue wounded comrades trapped in a firefight. During our first year, when Felix was still an honorary white, he told us about "stuffing body bags with body parts" in Vietnam as a "phlebotomist-medic."

Some of the blacks also claimed to be Vietnam veterans. Almost immediately after we met him, Carter spoke with visible trauma of being sent on a covert mission deep inside the Mekong Delta:

> There was no honoring of the Geneva Conventions or nothin'. That shit about cutting off penises and sewing the mouths and de-legging and de-heading people was true. My partner, Hughes, his brains was splattered all over my neck and on the side of my face. . . . [shaking at the memory] "Oh, my mother! Please don't let me die over here!"

We obtained everyone's military records and found that only Vernon, Carter, and Petey had actually been in the military. None of the three was sent to Southeast Asia; in fact, both Carter and Petey had served after the end of the Vietnam War. According to Hank's sister, "Hank was classified 4F, unfit for military duty. He didn't want to go in the army. He fixed into both his hands right before going in for the interview. . . . They looked like balloons." Nevertheless, thirty years later, Hank regularly evoked full-blown Vietnam War PTSD symptoms: "I lived and died in 'Nam. I wanna live and die here, on the street, too." Like Hogan and Carter, Hank interrupted his gory stories with bouts of sobbing and shaking—sometimes even ducking for cover when cars backfired. Arguably, these men did in fact suffer from what could be diagnosed as PTSD, but it had been induced by the continuum of violence in the gray zones of their childhood homes and of their ongoing lives on the street.

Violating Intimate Apartheid

Carter's appropriation of the traumatized Vietnam vet persona may have been indicative of his ability to cross ethnic lines despite the hostility of whites toward blacks. He had grown up on the same multiethnic, working-class block as Felix; and significantly, during several crisis interludes over the years we knew him, he entered into brief running partnerships with whites. Predictably, Carter's longest alliance was with Al, the only white who regularly violated the bounds of intimate apartheid. When Tina temporarily left Edgewater Boulevard to stay in Antioch, a town in California's Central Valley, with her eldest son, newly released from prison, Carter moved with Al into a well-camouflaged lean-to shack nailed into a wall of creosote beams that held up the freeway along an eroded stretch of the embankment. The path to their shack was so steep that they had to attach a thirty-foot rope from an overhanging eucalyptus branch to use as a hoist. The flat perch on which they built their shack was so tiny that they had to sleep head-to-foot with no room to roll over or to take care of bodily functions. They left shards of used toilet paper tangled in the brush surrounding them, fluttering in the breeze.

Like Al's earlier cross-ethnic running partnership with Sonny (described in chapter 1), this black-white friendship elicited disparaging comments. Carter's unusual proximity to one of the whites in the scene worried Tina, and she called Jeff from Antioch for updates:

> I bet Carter be stinking now and still wearin' those nasty-ass overalls. Al's odor is out of this world. My nose can't take it. He's sour. When I used to be next to Al, I could barely breathe. I be like, "I'm suffocating. I need air." He probably has lice and all, and now Carter, he's gonna be carrying that odor too.
>
> All of them are like that. They be too funky for me. But Hogan's worser. He always have them dookie stains in the back of his pants . . . walkin' like there a turd in his butt. I'm like . . . *God!*

Al's decrepit way of being in the world did, in fact, rub off on Carter, who began to stink just as Tina had predicted (see Orwell [1937] 1972:128 on the "smell" of the "lower classes" in England; see also Stallybrass and White 1986:139–140). This surprised us because formerly Carter had made a point of differentiating himself from the slovenliness of the whites, often shouting at Hogan whenever he came too close, "Get your stinky ass away from me before I hit you in the motherfuckin' head!" If Hogan shuffled away too slowly, Carter would raise his fist for emphasis: "I'm tellin' you nice—get the fuck away from me! *Move!*" Carter was embarrassed when we visited him at his shack and overcompensated with a performative account of personal responsibility and hygiene:

> We in close quarters, right, . . . and two men . . . so you want to try and keep things as clean as possible . . . mainly your socks and stuff. So we don't disturb each other, right, and be respectful. I mean, I've wrecked my brains. And I can't see no reason in the world why you should be dirty. There is no reason in the world to be nasty just 'cause we outside. We got these five-gallon buckets where you could soap everything if necessary in the morning when the sun comes up, and you can position to where you can dry all your clothes.
>
> I'll steal deodorant, garbage bags from the restaurant, and spray them first both inside and out with insecticide. And we got a dumpster right there [pointing down the embankment and through the razor-wire fence into the parking lot of the Dockside Bar & Grill]. Sure, you might have to make a trip or two. But so what? We gotta keep it clean here. But Al? He ain't gonna bust a grape in a wine factory!
>
> My mother and father never raised me like that. And I never will be nasty like that. This [pointing to the litter and feces surrounding the shack] is simply pathetic. I can't stand it, honest. When you hungry, how you gonna sit and eat with this smell here? I don't get it. I don't fuckin' get it.

We got this pee bucket here, right, and literally every fuckin' single day I have to grab his jar of piss and dump it. Like I'm his fucking maid. He just lets it sit there two, three, four days, until I empty it [pointing to a plastic one-gallon juice container half-full of urine].

Al shits right where he lays his head. But I don't wait like Al till I gotta go where I gotta go. I walk down the hill and use the bathrooms at McDonald's, the gas station, or the Taco Bell. And I don't make no mess, no sense being triflin' and nasty, 'cause I don't wanna burn no bridges. So I keep it clean, and they give me respect on using the bathroom, right.

They got toilet paper in the bathrooms. So I can wipe. And they got soap and water. So I can wash real good. And then dry off with a paper towel and put it in the garbage. Because I don't leave shit lying on the floor. I treat it as if it was my home. 'Cause I may have to come back.

And if the bathrooms are closed, I walk to the end down there [pointing down the path] and dig a hole.

Masculine Sexual Performance

Sexuality was another visibly embodied ethnic marker among the Edgewater homeless that followed the same overall pattern as drug preference, clothing style, masculine dignity, mood, and hygiene. All the African-American men except Stretch adhered to the macho heterosexual persona celebrated in gangsta rap hip-hop. No matter how old or physically debilitated, all the men publicly sought sexual partners, and a few, such as Carter with Tina, became romantically engaged. Even those who never had "girlfriends" during the years we knew them claimed to be sexually active.

Carter was the most graphic in broadcasting his sexual exploits and fantasies for everyone to hear on the bus, in hospital elevators, and in other public venues. He often cat-called at women walking by on the sidewalk, announcing his explicit sexual desires. He was genuinely surprised by our failure to bond lecherously with him on these occasions and chided, "Well, I still got a dick!"

A sense of patriarchal entitlement pervaded sexual bravado on the street and was often expressed in a romantic discourse of devotion and control that legitimized violence. Vernon, for example, claimed to have been a pimp in his youth and made frequent references to his ongoing sexual prowess with multiple girlfriends (whom we never saw). At the same time, he repeatedly asserted his love for his wife. "I'd kill a dead tree stump behind my woman. I married her at sixteen. I'm the only man she ever had sex with." The feminist and masculinity literatures have documented the ways "subordinated masculinities" fractured by class and ethnic divides mobilize violence to control and dominate women within their social grouping (Anderson 1990; Bourgois 1996b; Connell 1995; Fordham 1996:164–165; Messerschmidt 1993, 1997; Patterson 1998; Wallace 1979). Violence against women is often normalized on the street. It is exemplified in popular culture by the celebration of the misogynist African-American pimp-hustler persona (see, for example, the Hughes Brothers movie *American Pimp* [2000] and the hit songs "P.I.M.P.," from 50 Cent's *Get Rich or Die Tryin'* [2003], and Jay-Z's "Big Pimpin'," from *Collision Course* [2004]).

The white men, like the African-Americans, took misogynist language for granted and routinely used the word *bitch* to refer to women, but they did not sexualize their aggression toward women. They sometimes referred with pride and nostalgia to having been sexually active in their youth, yet almost all of them spoke without embarrassment about having erectile dysfunction: "I don't even masturbate. I just physically can't do it. My sex drive is null and void." They cut short our questions about sex with standard quips: "My old lady is heroin, and I been faithful to her for over twenty years. I've never cheated on her, and I never will." Max put a positive spin on his sexual disinterest, noting that it freed him from having to worry about AIDS.

Ben was the only white man in the Edgewater scene who publicly claimed to have an active sex life. Significantly, he was also exceptionally effective at generating income and spent a great deal of money on crack. He regularly shoplifted, passed false checks, and intermittently worked as a painter on union jobs. He tried to maintain a cheap hotel room in the white working-class suburb of South San Francisco, where he had grown up, and commuted to Edgewater Boulevard at dawn to buy heroin. Halfway through our fieldwork, Ben moved into Nickie's housing project apartment and bragged about having sex with her. Nickie, however, told one of the women on our ethnographic team that none of the white men, Ben included, ever attempted to initiate sex with her, even when they slept in the same bed. She confided, "Sometimes I miss having a warm body next to me."

Of the three middle-aged Latinos in our scene on Edgewater Boulevard, only the two who were most committed to their Latino identity (Sal and Victor) claimed to have active sex lives. For almost a full year, Sal lived with his girlfriend, Carmen. In contrast, Felix, consistent with his honorary identity as a white dopefiend, subordinated sex to heroin. Nevertheless, he found it necessary to justify his disinterest in sex as a principle of honor and responsibility within the logic of lumpen masculinity, and he also racialized it:

> And as far as the pretty girls, I'm glad they're around. . . . But I don't have no cravings for women like I do for my medicine: heroin.
>
> My priority is just not to be sick. How you gonna be with a woman if you're always sick? What are you gonna do? Just pimp her off? Tell her, "Give me all of your money!"
>
> Nah! I can't do that nigger shit. I ain't gonna use or abuse anybody. I already abuse myself with the drugs.

We documented ethnic patterns of sexual expression with caution because racist stereotypes in the United States obscure the historical processes through which differences are produced. The specter of the "hypersexual Negro" is a particularly vicious example: inverting and displacing the sexual exploitation of black women by white men, lynch mobs in the southern United States claimed they were protecting the "virtue" of white women when they castrated African-Americans and tortured them to death (Litwack 2000:22–24; Patterson 1998).

Accessing the Emergency Room

Ethnically distinct techniques of the body resulted in very different patterns of interaction with medical institutions. Most notably, each one of the whites was hospitalized for septic infections on multiple occasions during our fieldwork because skin-popping heightened their susceptibility to abscesses. The whites had enormous medical files at the county hospital. They appreciated the quality of the high-tech care they received and the methadone that was administered to them in the hospital wards (Bourgois et al. 2006). Their primary problem was gaining access to medical care because hospital services for the indigent were strictly rationed in the 1990s and 2000s through a deliberately hostile bureaucratic triage system in the emergency room that lasted several hours. The Edgewater homeless, consequently, usually postponed seeking medical care until they were quite literally dying, in order to ensure admission to the hospital. Otherwise, they risked finding themselves back out on the street after several hours of waiting, in full-blown heroin withdrawal and with no money for their next fix.

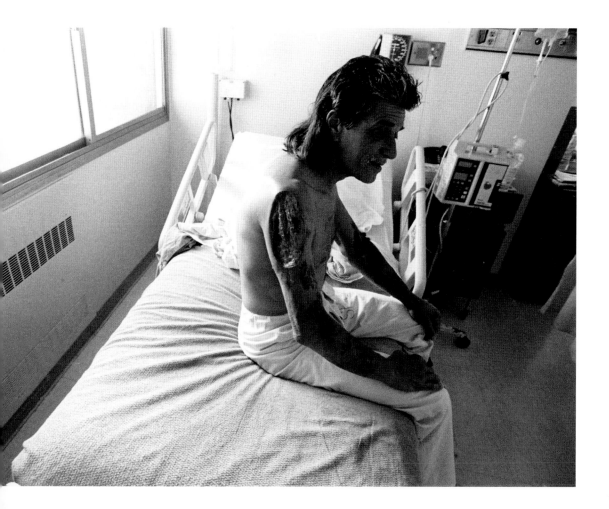

Scotty: When I start swelling up with an abscess, I gotta make sure it's fucking ripe enough— red and infected enough—and that I got a fever that's wicked enough for them to take me in and give me part of the help that I need. We're not allowed to just go in there and try to get help.

Hogan was the one notable exception. His reliance on cotton shots and his extreme filth often resulted in blood infections that qualified him for overnight stays. He increasingly sought refuge in the emergency room after he lost access to panhandling at the corner store during the white flight episode. When an unsympathetic triage nurse would diagnose his shaking and moaning as a simple case of delirium tremens or as heroin withdrawal, rather than as a life-threatening septic condition that warranted admission, he would threaten to "jump off the Golden Gate Bridge." This threat would precipitate a required twenty-four-hour psychiatric evaluation, guaranteeing him a dose of methadone and a night indoors. He claimed that his frequent abscesses were "AIDS-related," but he was not HIV positive. Like so many of the indigent in the 1990s and 2000s who were increasingly falling through the frayed social services safety net in the United States, Hogan had nowhere else to turn.

Overwhelmed by an onslaught of complicated and vulnerable people like Hogan, many of the frontline emergency room personnel became harsh taskmasters. A national-level institutional problem caused by federal cutbacks for indigent care reimbursement, initiated in the 1980s and exacerbated in the late 1990s, expressed itself in interpersonal confrontations and insults at the hospital gates, where desperately sick people with no health insurance clamored, often unsuccessfully, for care. Faced with insolvency in the 1990s, hospitals across the United States had to reorient health care delivery toward high-tech procedures for patients with private insurance while decreasing services for uninsured and publicly insured patients. At ground level, in the growing maelstrom engulfing county hospital emergency rooms, this structural problem caused by federal policy and the market-driven logic of privately financed health care was obscured to patients and service providers alike. Instead, overburdened clinicians disparaged the homeless as malingerers and "manipulative frequent flyers." In response, desperate wannabe patients accused nurses and doctors of being "bitches, bull-dykes, and bastards."

On at least a dozen occasions, we drove members of our network to the emergency room, afraid they might be dying. The first time this occurred, Philippe, unprepared for the institutionalized hostility of emergency room services for the indigent, fell into the trap of interpersonal blame and was evicted by a security guard for angrily berating the triage nurse for being rude to the patients. We learned to take people to the hospital only when absolutely necessary. In another instance, for example, a member of our ethnographic team found Hogan listless and shivering with fever on his mattress in the mud behind the Dockside Bar & Grill. A large abscess on his left leg had swollen to the size of a grapefruit. Earlier that week, he had been denied admission to the emergency room and he was too debilitated to try again: "They'll just tell me I'm fine and send me away. It's not worth it. They won't do nothing for me there." The ethnographer insisted on driving him to the county hospital. As they parked, Hogan began moaning fearfully, "I hope they don't pour ether on my leg. That stuff burns like hell."

When Hogan walked into the emergency room, everyone recoiled from the smell. Recognizing him, the head nurse snapped, "I'm busy. You're gonna have to wait." When the ethnographer tried to intercede, the nurse interrupted, "We all know about him. He's a frequent flyer." Hogan limped back out the door to prevent his smell from disturbing the two dozen patients already waiting for intake. The nurse immediately resumed arguing with an angry man who was leaning drunkenly over the edge of her counter. Moments later she ran into the center of the waiting room and ordered a man dressed in rags to quiet down. He was babbling loudly and waving his arms. She then walked briskly to the far side of the room and ordered two dozing men to take their coats off their heads and open their eyes. This prompted a shower of curses from the exhausted men. She responded by calling everyone to attention, shouting, "Sit up! I need to see everybody's eyes in here!"

The security guard standing behind her was embarrassed by her outburst, and he was intimidated by the large number of patients he might have to restrain if the confrontation escalated. The tension abated, however, because two police officers burst through the entrance dragging an emaciated woman in manacles who was blinking rapid-fire and showing no sign of comprehension. They whisked her past the intake station into the back without a word. Thirty seconds later, the automatic double doors banged open again, and a stretcher careened straight into surgery carrying a moaning man with a bloody head. A well-dressed white couple, running to keep up with the stretcher and clearly panicked, began screaming at the security guard who had stopped them, "Why can't we see our son? We demand to see our son!"

In the midst of this commotion, Hogan stepped back inside the emergency room and the seated patients scrambled away from his stench. Shivering, Hogan apologized to the nurse, "It's getting too cold for me to keep waiting out there, but it's probably a good idea," and he started shuffling back out the door. The nurse stopped him and agreed to process him through triage. An hour later, a Filipino orderly, pinching his nostrils, escorted Hogan to the shower. Hogan's right pant leg was stuck to the abscess on his calf, and the orderly gagged as he cut off the pant leg. Little white maggots were wiggling in the center of the mess. Ten minutes later, while being wheeled away on a gurney, Hogan began pleading, "You don't need the ether. I washed all the maggots away in the shower. You don't need the ether!"

The surgeons performed a skin graft on Hogan's left calf. It was several weeks before he was able to bear his full body weight. A doctor declared Hogan to be "ambulatory," however, within a week after the operation, and he was released, sent back out on the street with a cane. Barely able to hobble, Hogan returned to his muddy camp behind the Dockside Bar & Grill. Bewildered and in pain, he kept repeating, "I wish they'd kept me in longer."

Iatrogenic Pathology

In the weeks following Hogan's release, it was disconcerting to see him injecting directly into the side of his still-festering skin graft. At first glance, it appeared to be a self-destructive, even masochistic, practice, but we soon came to realize that when one's veins are scarred by a lifetime of daily injection and when one's priority is to consume heroin by any means necessary, an abscess is a convenient and effective site for injecting. The body is pumping blood to the area in order to combat the infection. When heroin is injected into this especially vascular site, it provides a rush of exhilaration that is almost as intense as that of a direct deposit into a functional vein. Furthermore, poking a needle into an abscess is not particularly painful because much of the tissue is already dead.

The whites recognized that skin-popping (an act they called "muscling," even though they rarely hit a muscle) caused abscesses, but they managed to construe it as a responsible way to manage their addicted bodies.

> *Hank:* [while injecting into the side of an abscess on his left buttock] My way of looking at it is that you're better off muscling in the first place. It's a slower flow through your body.
>
> *Petey:* Yeah. It makes the dope last a lot longer.
>
> *Hank:* The only thing you don't get is the rush.
>
> I wish I had known about muscling when I was younger. I can get this abscess [pointing to where he was injecting] cut out of me. But what if you shoot that same bacteria directly into your vein and it passes all through your body and lands in your kidneys? You're taking a hell of a chance every time you shoot.
>
> The dealer might drop his dope in dog shit or whatever else is around and he is not going to rinse it off. He is going to wrap that right up and just tell you it's two-tenths of an ounce overweight. And that two-tenths . . . ! That's what can kill you.

Toward the end of our fieldwork several of the African-Americans in our network began to skin-pop, but only occasionally, as a last resort. They spoke of muscling with shame and distaste. The only African-American whom we actually observed with an abscess that required hospitalization during our twelve years on the boulevard was Sonny. He was adamant that the abscess was "not his fault" and that it was his "first ever." He claimed that Vernon had badly administered a speedball injection in his biceps, missing the vein.

After carving out the abscess, the surgeon released Sonny from the emergency room without bandaging the large gash. The surgeon also refused to prescribe any painkiller. The weather was stormy on Sonny's second day out of the hospital, and contact with passing gusts of wind made him wince in pain. He sought advice from Lou, a newly arrived white man who had been nicknamed Spider-Bite because of a gaping, persistent sore on the back of his neck (where three years earlier he had been bitten in his sleep by a brown recluse spider). Spider-Bite Lou dug a small medical kit out of his shopping cart, which was overflowing with aluminum cans fished out of the gutter. His hands were black with grease and dirt, but he did not pause to wash them; there was no soap or running water available. He delicately picked lint out of Sonny's wound and then dabbed antibiotic ointment into it. He then wrapped Sonny's biceps with a shred of gauze. Lou normally avoided interactions with African-Americans, but when Sonny thanked him profusely, he responded warmly: "I know how much it hurts! They done that to me too. I packed it lightly for you to keep the wind out but still let it breathe."

Sonny's mistreatment at the county hospital was an extreme case, but we collected several other surgical horror stories, and a sympathetic nurse in the emergency room confirmed to us that some surgeons deliberately cut without anesthesia: "Most doctors care, and do their best, but a few—especially those on temporary rotations—are frustrated by the self-inflicted pathologies of addicts and punish them." Many doctors in the United States consider it "unadvisable" to give painkiller prescriptions to addicts when releasing them from the hospital, even when their pathologies are objectively painful (see critique in Lander 1990). Epidemiological clinical studies also reveal that U.S. doctors disproportionately undertreat the pain symptoms of African-American patients (Bonham 2001; Todd et al. 2000).

Hank tried to avoid having to deal with the hospital by lancing his own abscesses.

Jeff's Fieldnotes

With his boxer shorts pulled down to his knees, Hank juts out his hip and twists contrapposto to get a clear view of his left buttock cheek. Seeing me take out my camera, he starts describing the gruesome procedure, as he pinches the center of the inflammation:

"First you feel for a pocket, and if it be real kind of mushy like this one, then you know it's ready.

"Yesterday I could hear like a crunch, like a squish when I bent down [squatting to show me]. But nothing was coming out. I was worried that it was an inverted abscess with the pus flowing inside. It has to come to a head like this one. Yesterday I bled it off a little, but then left it overnight [squeezing again]. Now it's ready."

He slowly inserts a pair of manicure scissors into the center of the inflammation, pushing one of the blades all the way up to the handle. He then slowly swirls the blade around to loosen the flesh. Pus flows out of the gash like a weeping eye. He finally pulls the scissors out and, with slow deliberation, squeezes the gash between his two thumbs to "drain it."

After ten or twenty more seconds of grimacing and squeezing, he pokes a toenail clipper into the center of the abscess, using it as tweezers. He pulls out some sort of black gunk and, satisfied, holds it up for me to photograph: "This is the poison causing my pain."

Noting my look of concern and discomfort, he reassures me, "There's not much pain and getting that shit out basically ends the abscess."

He covers the area with ointment and a Sterile Pack bandage left by a visiting nurse as part of a new outreach program for the homeless that is being piloted by the Public Health Department. He then plunges a full syringe of heroin up to its hilt into the edge of the fresh bandage.

No one in the camp thinks there is anything unusual about this procedure. Petey is reading a Danielle Steel romance novel, Al is stripping aluminum from a metal window he is planning to recycle, and Frank is organizing his sign painting supplies to get ready for a new job. I am the only person who has noticed what just occurred.

Initially, we suspected that Hank's self-lancing might represent a form of pathological self-mutilation. We subsequently came to understand it as a logical response to the iatrogenic surgical wounds resulting from the unnecessarily deep and painful procedure for cutting into abscesses that was being taught to medical students and residents during their surgical rotations in the Department of Surgery at the county hospital at that time. Furthermore, despite his filthy surroundings, Hank's lancings were usually successful. Abscesses are a lumpen medical condition par excellence. They are experienced almost exclusively by street-based addicts, and they are self-inflicted.

In the 1990s and 2000s, there was no national standard of care for treating abscesses, even though "soft tissue infections" represented the single largest admissions category at institutions like San Francisco's county hospital (Ciccarone et al. 2001). When we began our fieldwork in 1994, the surgeons at the county hospital were routinely carving and scraping out the abscesses, creating deep gashes. The procedure required general anesthesia and usually involved an expensive overnight stay. It was also painful and disfiguring.

The surgeons believed that the deep carving and scraping procedure was necessary because of the risk of necrotizing fasciitis, caused by a "flesh-eating" bacteria commonly found in feces and dirt. These bacteria reproduce exponentially inside the human body and can spread across the body within a matter of hours, consuming muscle sheaths. Full-blown infections are rare, however, because healthy vascular and immune systems normally clean out the deadly bacteria. In San Francisco, fewer than a dozen of the approximately four thousand abscesses treated each year at the county hospital represented cases of necrotizing fasciitis. Nevertheless, as a preventive measure, all abscesses were subjected to the deep carving procedure until 2001.

In late 2001, seven years into our fieldwork, budget shortfalls provided the institutional impetus to reform the county hospital's abscess-carving procedure. Two senior surgeons obtained permission to open an outpatient clinic at the hospital as a cost-savings initiative. They piloted the simple incision-and-drain procedure that community-based clinics were already delivering routinely. Not surprisingly, the technique proved to be less painful and patients healed more rapidly (Harris and Young 2002). Furthermore, no cases of necrotizing fasciitis went undetected.

During our years among the Edgewater homeless, two individuals, Hogan and Ben, contracted necrotizing fasciitis, nicknamed the "Pac-Man virus." Hogan's life was saved by Sammy, the owner of the Crow's Nest liquor store, which was adjacent to the Dockside Bar & Grill's parking lot.

> I went back behind the chain-link fence, because my landlord was complaining about all them guys back there on the hill under the freeway.
>
> And on the side, I seen somebody layin' down. And I looked over, and I seen Hogan is layin' there. And so, anyways, I tapped his foot.
>
> I was "Hey! Hey, Hogan, you all right?"
>
> "Uuuuugh!"
>
> I was all, "Man, you look like shit!"
>
> He had a foul smell. That's what really attracted me out there. There was urine smell and shit smell and another smell I couldn't even describe. A smell I never smelled before. I knew he had problems with his legs, probably gangrene.
>
> So I came back here to the store, and I called the ambulance. I says, "I think this guy's dyin' or somethin'. Something's not right with this guy."
>
> But they didn't want to come because they know Hogan. He's always callin' 9-1-1. I told 'em, "But I've never seen him look this bad." I told 'em, "Please, you gotta come." Hogan is lucky I called and persuaded 9-1-1. Otherwise, maybe an hour, two hours more . . . he woulda' been dead.

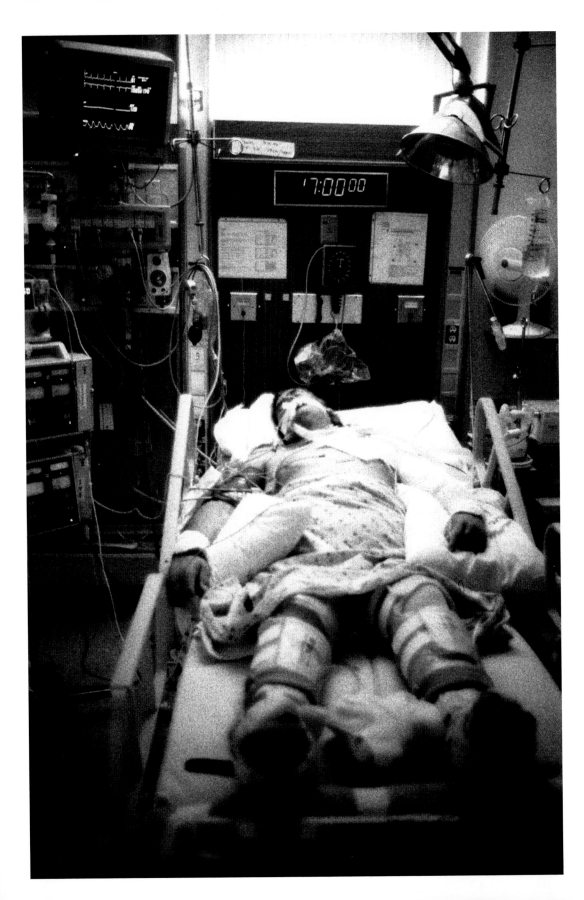

Hogan spent six weeks in the hospital. For the first two weeks, he was sedated in a semi-coma in the intensive care unit, plugged into hundreds of thousands of dollars' worth of high-tech medical equipment. The bacteria had consumed most of his pectoral muscle and also had spread along his muscle sheath into his left shoulder. To everyone's surprise, including that of the nurses, Hogan survived without having his left arm amputated. Five weeks later, he was discharged from the hospital with ten dollars cash in his pocket, sent to him by his mother in Sacramento. The doctors also provided him with a bottle of codeine, a bag of vitamins, and a seven-day voucher for an SRO hotel in the Mission District.

Jeff saw Hogan hobbling down Edgewater Boulevard leaning on Felix's shoulder immediately following his release from the hospital. They were heading to Hogan's old camp in the muddy gulley behind the Dockside Bar, and Jeff offered them a ride. As Felix lowered Hogan gently into the front seat of Jeff's car, Hogan whimpered apologetically his refrain from the previous year when he had been released early from the hospital following the skin graft on his left calf: "I wish they had kept me longer." Felix grabbed Jeff by the shoulder and pleaded, "Jeff, you gotta get him out of here. He's much too sick." To thank Felix for his concern, Hogan handed him a few codeine pills, and Jeff immediately drove Hogan to the address on his hotel voucher.

At the SRO Hogan was barely able to maneuver up the steep staircase. He limped up one step at a time, with Jeff supporting him from behind. The place was a far cry from the county

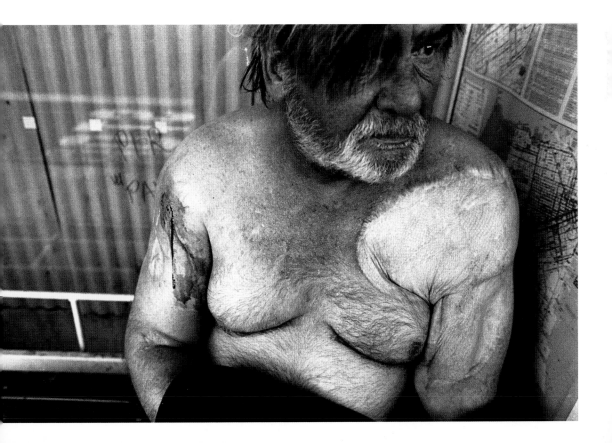

hospital with its three hot meals per day, warm showers, clean sheets, and caring nurses. The stained walls of Hogan's room matched the stains on his thin blanket. He sat on the sagging bed, lit a cigarette, and burst into tears. "I'm scared, Jeff. I'm through with dope."

Hogan managed to stay off heroin for the duration of his seven-day hotel voucher. On the eighth day, however, he was back on Edgewater Boulevard, living in his old camp and injecting heroin directly into the skin graft covering his pectoral muscle. "What else can I do?" he shrugged. "I don't have any veins."

Symbolic Violence of Public Health Outreach

Abscesses are merely the tip of the iceberg of the crisis facing health care for the homeless in the United States. Most patients with abscesses are also infected with hepatitis C, smoke cigarettes, drink large quantities of alcohol, and eat poorly. Consequently, they are at risk for a panoply of chronic conditions as they age, including malnutrition, liver disease, emphysema, tuberculosis, depression, and dementia, not to mention gunshot and knife wounds.

Injection drug users constituted one of the epicenters of the outbreak of HIV in the industrialized world during the 1980s. Epidemiologists identified injectors as a potential vector for spreading HIV into heterosexual populations, and this threat raised the stakes of inadequate health care for the indigent. A worldwide public health movement known as "harm reduction" emerged, modeled on earlier hepatitis A prevention initiatives for heroin injectors in Holland. The movement advocated nonjudgmental engagement with active drug users and hoped to lower the cultural and institutional barriers to medical services. Harm reduction outreach initiatives such as needle exchanges were not predicated on abstinence; they were designed to be pragmatic and inclusive.

Despite the radical, user-friendly intentions of harm reduction activists, their movement could not escape what Foucauldian critics refer to as the "logic of governmentality." Harm reduction operates within the limits of a middle-class public health discourse committed to educating "rational clients . . . free to choose health" (Moore 2004:1549). In pursuit of knowledge and progress, medicalized discourses promote disciplined subjectivities that self-impose responsible behavior (Bourgois 1999, 2002). In short, harm reduction became the gentle strand in the disciplinary web that seeks to rehabilitate the lumpen. The cross-class effects of this form of "positive" biopower, however, are often contradictory.

Knowledge may be empowering to the middle class, but prevention and outreach messages that target the decision-making processes of drug users fail to address the constraints on choice that shape need, desire, and personal priorities among the indigent. Arguably, many of the outreach programs designed to empower vulnerable injectors and to treat them as rational actors shame them as much as, or more than, they help them. Hypersanitary messages clash with the realities of practical survival on the street. Medical social services predicated on "empowering individuals" to make "informed choices" misrecognize the power relations that constrain socially vulnerable populations and that shape subjectivities (Bourgois, Lettiere, and Quesada 1997; Farmer 2003; Farmer, Connors, and Simmons 1996).

For example, healthcare providers and outreach workers routinely advised the Edgewater homeless never to share injection paraphernalia (syringes, cookers, cottons, and rinse water). For the first dozen years of the HIV epidemic, injectors throughout the United States were given little bottles of bleach to clean their paraphernalia. But it is impossible to rinse a used cotton or cooker with bleach if one is trying to inject leftover residues of heroin. Furthermore, in the moral economy on the street, sharing the same cooker is both ethical and pragmatic. From the perspective of the street-based injector, sharing injection paraphernalia, especially the ancillary components such as cookers, cottons, and water, promotes health rather than damages it. The injection practices defined as sanitary by biomedicine were a luxury most street-based injectors could not afford. Even though all of the Edgewater homeless had technical knowledge of the way blood-borne infections are spread, they would often flamboyantly squirt several units of heroin from their used syringe into one another's cookers as a "favor." Their top priority was to avoid dopesickness, and that required them to share publicly and frequently in order to build a generous reputation.

Early in our project, Philippe naively asked Frank whether he shared needles. It immediately became apparent that the standard public health messages we considered ethically important to promote were inadvertently offensive (Bourgois 1998b:2334–2335).

> *Frank:* Oh, c'mon, man! Don't ask me that question. You know damn well I share needles. It happens to everybody a million times.
>
> We always try not to share needles but we still do it. Hey, if you're sick, you're not gonna worry about it. When you gotta fix, you gotta fix.
>
> People gonna share a needle; they're gonna share a cooker; they're gonna share whatever the fuck they got to if they're sick.
>
> I mean, we worry about AIDS, but when you're sick on dope and you got to fuckin' get well, you not gonna worry about that shit right at the moment.
>
> That's the way it is. I'm sorry, man. [handing Hogan the needle he had just used]
>
> *Hogan:* [holding up the needle] Give any motherfucker out here a motherfuckin' taste of forty units of dope and even if the man has any kind of knowledge about AIDS, he ain't gonna give a fuck. If he's sick, he's gonna fix.
>
> I'm sorry, but that's the gospel motherfuckin' truth.
>
> *Philippe:* But . . . but shouldn't you at least rinse that needle with bleach before giving it to Hogan?
>
> *Frank: Shut up Philippe!* I know you're in the AIDS business and all, but water works. I know water works; I've been rinsing with water for years. We all have. None of us have HIV. Water works. I know it. Trust me. We only share with people we know. People in our group.

When we recorded this particular conversation, we thought that the Edgewater homeless were in denial about their objective level of HIV risk. A close reexamination of large-scale epidemiological HIV infection patterns, however, suggests that Frank was probably right about his simple HIV prevention strategy of "rinsing with water." None of the Edgewater homeless contracted HIV during the twelve years we spent with them, and they are not anomalies. Laboratory and epidemiological studies have consistently documented that water effectively flushes the HIV virus out of contaminated needles (Ciccarone and Bourgois 2003).

Furthermore, epidemiological infection patterns from the 1990s and 2000s also suggest that ancillary paraphernalia sharing is probably not responsible for transmitting HIV in the United States. Most likely, in order for enough blood-to-blood contact to occur and to transmit HIV, one would have to reuse a syringe that has not been rinsed with anything (Bourgois 2002). In the United States, HIV rates were two to three times higher in East Coast cities than in West Coast cities throughout the 1990s (Ciccarone and Bourgois 2003). This is because Mexican black tar heroin was the only form available on streets west of the Mississippi River during the 1980s through the 2000s, and its gooey consistency forced injectors to rinse their syringes with water in order to prevent the plungers from jamming. In contrast, the heroin used east of the Mississippi during these same years came primarily from Southeast Asia and later from Colombia. It was in a highly soluble white powder form that did not clog needles. Injectors in eastern states, consequently, did not need to rinse their needles with water on a routine basis in order to reuse them.

Most of the Edgewater homeless regularly volunteered to be research subjects for large public health epidemiological surveys in order to obtain the ten- to twenty-dollar incentive fees paid by these projects. They were required to attend a counseling session on HIV risk before receiving the money. These sessions provided them with enough detailed information to learn that their daily injection practices were self-destructive, but there was relatively little they could do to change their behavior because they lived on the street and were physically addicted to heroin. Most of them were already taking the basic precaution of avoiding direct needle sharing whenever possible. Direct needle sharing between running partners, however, was so routine that they usually did not remember to report it as "using someone else's syringe" when they completed the questionnaires of our epidemiological collaborators.

Hepatitis C prevention campaigns highlight the counterproductive effect of imparting impractical scientific knowledge without also offering resources and structural alternatives. More subtly, the data on hepatitis C prevention suggests that the public health field of drug research and harm reduction outreach suffers from a hypersanitary bias. Halfway through our fieldwork, public health researchers began using a new technology to test the blood of street injectors for the hepatitis virus (HCV), dubbed the "silent killer" by the media and some researchers (see, for example, Hirsch and Wright 2000). All of the Edgewater homeless discovered, to their dismay, that they were infected with hepatitis C. Unfortunately, counselors and doctors had little practical advice to give infected injectors, because the pathophysiology of the virus was poorly understood by scientists. The prevailing statistics at the time indicated that some people fell sick and died of liver disease rapidly; most, however, suffered from no HCV-related liver problems, even when they continued to drink alcohol, and almost 10 percent spontaneously cleared the virus from their blood with no treatment. Interferon, the medication used in the 2000s to treat hepatitis C infection, has uncomfortable side effects and works for only 50 percent of those who manage to complete a full year of the difficult daily regimen. Moreover, the official U.S. federal guidelines for treating liver disease recommended six months of abstinence from alcohol or drug use prior to initiating therapy (National Institute of Diabetes and Digestive and Kidney Diseases 2003; for a critique, see Edlin 2004).

Public health researchers conscientiously educated the Edgewater homeless about the blood-sharing acts that had infected them, but injectors could do little with that knowledge. At the end of their counseling sessions, they were given a card with a toll-free number and ushered out the door back onto the street, where they usually felt compelled to pool the "incentive fees" they had just received for being research subjects to buy heroin and engage in risky injection practices. Combining Bourdieu's critique of symbolic violence with Foucault's insight on the knowledge/power nexus suggests that the harm reduction movement's well-intentioned hepatitis C blood-testing and counseling initiative inadvertently created a dynamic of unproductive self-blame among the Edgewater homeless, which contributed to the conventional misrecognition of the relationship between power and individual self-control. No resources were provided to injectors with HCV. Instead they received a slew of detailed technical information about the micro injection practices through which they had infected themselves. This kind of knowledge-based intervention reflects the historical turn public health has taken under neoliberalism. Rather than investing in structural interventions to protect the health of its citizens, the state frames health as the individual's moral responsibility to choose a lifestyle that avoids risk (Fischer et al. 2004; Lupton 1995; Petersen 1997; Rose 1999).

The Edgewater homeless did not analyze their personal problems in terms of Foucault's biopower and governmentality, or Bourdieu's symbolic violence and misrecognition. On the contrary, they appreciated the respectful treatment they received when they participated as research subjects in public health projects (including ours). Even though they could not change their risky injection practices following the testing, they often felt that they had done something responsible merely by getting tested. Blood testing for HCV and HIV, consequently, engendered a false sense of confidence. Soon, most of the Edgewater homeless came to accept HCV infection as a normal condition (Bourgois, Prince, and Moss 2004; Roy et al. 2007). The hepatitis C prevention campaigns of the early 2000s illustrate how the uneven effects of biopower on lumpen populations often backfire. Polite counselors taught long-term street-based addicts to take personal responsibility for damaging their bodies. This interaction reaffirmed the "hope-to-die-with-my-boots-on" righteous dopefiend subjectivity among the Edgewater homeless. Being willfully and oppositionally self-destructive feels like an empowering alternative to conceiving of oneself as a sick failure who lacks self-control.

For example, we asked Tina upon her return from an HIV blood-testing counseling session, "What do you do to keep from getting HIV?" She immediately asserted her public health worthiness by repeating the standard condoms and bleach message that she had just heard from the counselor. At the same time, she took advantage of our awkward question to tease Carter with a parody of the middle-class, sex-positive discourse of feminine empowerment that permeates HIV prevention messages in San Francisco. Perhaps she was also defusing the biopower insult of having been confronted—in the counseling session and by our question—with the inescapable fact of her daily risk-taking practices.

Tina: I rinse our syringes in bleach. [turning to Carter and scolding] When I came back, all Carter's rigs was so bloody! I had to soak 'em in bleach. . . . [long pause] And I don't have sex with no one else—

Carter: [interrupting] You better not!

Tina: . . . [deadpan] without a condom.

On another occasion at a needle exchange, we saw an elderly heroin injector hold up a handful of condoms that a volunteer had just given him and quip: "What do you people want me to do with these? Throw a balloon party?"

Pathogenic Law Enforcement

Our critique of the limitations of public health, including the best-practices harm reduction component, should not distract from the fact that law enforcement, and not health services, has long been the dominant institutional regulator of poverty and drug use in the United States, in contrast with many European countries. On Edgewater Boulevard, fear of arrest and eviction was a chronic condition. The destabilization of the daily lives of the homeless by the police caused immediate negative health outcomes. Most important, law enforcement accentuated the lumpen subjectivity of the homeless—especially their dopefiend outlaw/outcast habituses—by further dispossessing, humiliating, and angering them. Police sweeps and evictions generally intensified in the fall, around the civic holiday of Thanksgiving, at the onset of California's six-month rainy season.

> *Felix:* This ain't right, them kicking us out like this the day before Thanksgiving. They [the California Highway Patrol] woke me out of a dead sleep. I opened my eyes and see these uniforms.
>
> *Frank:* I'm like, "Whaaat?"
>
> *Felix:* [imitating a rough voice] "You got one hour to get the hell outta here!" We had to watch them stomp our shelter into the ground. Took all our shit . . . the tent with all the blankets in it and all my clothes. . . .
>
> *Max:* [shaking his head] The day before Thanksgiving!
>
> *Felix:* Just to be mean. They smashed everything that was left with their boots: radios, boxes, everything.
>
> *Frank:* And what'd they do afterwards? Go home to their families and give thanks?
>
> *Felix:* And they're all having a good Thanksgiving dinner. [rough voice again] "Ha, ha, yeah. Yesterday we just smashed all these homeless guys up. Thank you, Lord!"
>
> *Frank:* These people pride themselves on being well informed. They think they're the most intelligent goddamn people. [falsetto voice] "Oh, in Northern California we're the most sophisticated wine-drinking, quiche-eating motherfuckers in the whole part of this country." And look at the politicians they vote for. Assholes like our mayor who wants to lock up all the homeless.
>
> *Felix:* I think I'm coming down with pneumonia. . . . I can hardly breathe. I'm hungry, and I've had to spend my fuckin' money faster than I been getting it. I'll totally be broke tomorrow. I'd rather be in jail. I ain't gonna stay out here, man, like a troll under the bridge . . . and die.
>
> *Frank:* Homeless means nothing to them. They have their houses, their swimming pools, their little barbecue pits.
>
> *Felix:* These people are really wrong. They don't have any priorities in their life. All they know is how to pick up a paycheck.

Our fieldnotes include dozens of accounts of police sweeps that sent the Edgewater homeless into survival crisis mode and noticeably exacerbated their risky injection practices. Repeatedly, all their blankets, sleeping bags, clothing, and tarps were ground up in garbage trucks as if they were useless trash. Only the moral economy of sharing kept the Edgewater homeless from total mayhem on these occasions when they suddenly lost everything.

Jeff's Fieldnotes

There has been yet another round of evictions and Hank looks like absolute hell. His eyes are so puffy that I ask him if he has been in a fight.

"They wiped me out again. I went for a drink at the corner, and when I returned, there was the CHP [California Highway Patrol] and Caltrans. I'm tempted to get my gun and shoot the next Caltrans truck that I see."

He tells me that the "Mexican worker" ripping down his shack (probably a prisoner from San Quentin) had already put on his suede jacket. When he asked for it back, the officer in charge threatened to arrest him. "You're on state property! We're teachin' you a lesson."

As he talks to me, he starts shivering so hard that he has to hug himself across his chest to steady himself. Uncharacteristically, he asks me for money. When he sees that I have only a dollar in my wallet, however, he refuses to take it. I tuck the dollar in his shirt pocket, just as he did to me last week when I turned down his offer to treat me to a beer.

Max walks by and when he hears about Hank's eviction, he puts his arm around his shoulder and offers to treat him to a taste of heroin. They immediately head to Max's encampment, where they set a candle on a pizza box and prepare to cook a bag of heroin. Max has only one syringe, and it is clogged. When he tries to rinse it, water sputters out the end.

Hank reaches into his sock and pulls out his needle and hands it to Max, muttering apologetically, "Caltrans took all my clean ones." The syringe has been used so many times that the numbering on the chamber is worn off. Max squints at it, frowning, and notes a burr on the tip of the needle. Hank takes it back, licks the point to confirm the defect, and quickly files it down on a rock, alternately licking and filing until he can no longer feel the burr with his tongue.

Max is the one treating, so Hank hands the needle back to Max and eagerly waits for his turn to prepare a cotton shot with the leftovers.

Max and Hank were not running partners at the time of this interaction, and under normal conditions they probably would have avoided directly sharing a needle. We often saw this kind of promiscuous direct needle sharing, however, in the midst of law enforcement offensives.

More subtly, the pariah status of illegality encourages street addicts to pursue drugs with a self-destructive intensity akin to devotion, as if they had nothing left to lose (Bourgois, Lettiere, and Quesada 1997). The criminalization—not just of heroin but also of syringes— as well as the enforcement of local city ordinances against public intoxication, urination, and sleeping outside, pushes drug users into the farthest margins of public space. Filthy nooks and crannies that are optimal for spreading infectious diseases, such as the shooting gallery dubbed "the hole," become their safest refuges, further reinforcing their outcast and/or outlaw sense of self.

Everyday Physical Suffering

Our fieldnotes and tape recordings contain hundreds of descriptions of being cold, wet, filthy, hungry, and exhausted. We have selected a few excerpts to document how the physical pain of the Edgewater homeless is overlain with a self-administered everyday violence. These excerpts also offer glimpses of their generally hostile—but occasionally solidary—interactions with the outside world of the employed and the housed who pass by them each day.

Jeff's Fieldnotes

Spider-Bite Lou's new running partner, Grant, is huddled under the bus shelter to keep out of the rain. He is wearing only a skimpy windbreaker over a hooded sweatshirt. Lou has on an army jacket with a fur-lined hood which he has covered with one of the bright orange headlight-reflecting garbage bags that Caltrans workers use to pick up garbage by the side of the freeway. He has punched holes for his head and arms, and the bag reaches down to his knees. With his thick beard and scabbed face framed by the fur in his green army parka hood, he looks like a foot soldier from the Middle Ages bearing an orange day-glo body shield. He is negotiating with Hogan to rent his yellow rain suit for a cotton per day.

Grant is shivering wet and limping heavily because his rubber boots have holes in their soles and the heavy rain has soaked through the only pair of socks he was able to save from the last Caltrans eviction. He feels lucky to have obtained a job at the Christmas tree lot, but he complains that the pine needles chafe his feet through the holes and make them bleed.

The drawstring of Grant's hood is pulled so tightly around his head that it forms a tiny port-hole for him to peer through. I can barely make out that his left eye is swollen—a shiner, heavily clotted with blood. When I ask what happened, he mumbles, embarrassed, "I got hit."

"Who?" I ask.

He nods toward his new running partner, Spider-Bite Lou, who, stealing the moment from Grant, announces that he too had a black eye once that was "just as bad—back in '87," as though this camaraderie exculpates him.

I am worried that I might jeopardize Grant's safety even more if I criticize Lou for hitting him, so I walk away silently—angry and ashamed for not knowing how to help Grant.

Spider-Bite Lou runs after me to ask for "ninety-nine cents" to buy a Jumbo Jack special. He claims he has "the runs" and is feeling too weak and hungry to hustle. "Please help me, Jeff, I'm hypoglycemic."

Ethnographic Team Fieldnotes

We run into Frank rummaging through the dumpster at Discount Grocery. He is angry because "they throw a lot of good shit away here: pans of lasagna, macaroni salad, stuffed shells, milk, all kinds of food! But the new manager is dousing it all with Clorox" to prevent them from eating it.

Al and Sonny defecated at the entrance to the supermarket yesterday to "teach the manager a lesson."

Frank: "And I'm starving. I've lost thirty pounds. I barely fuckin' eat anymore. My stomach has shrunk up so much that when I do start eating I lose my appetite. I just take one or two bites and then I can't eat anymore. Then I'll get hungry again, one or two hours later, and take another couple of bites.

"But when I'm doing well and start eating regular I get hungry all the time. I can eat breakfast, lunch, dinner, snacks. But bam! If all of a sudden I run out of food for a week or two and I don't eat, I'll go right back to losing my appetite. Could it be the hep C?"

Ethnographic Team Fieldnotes

Felix has not been able to build a fire to dry his clothes because the wood is too wet. He has holes in the sides of both his sneakers and cannot keep his feet dry. They have started to swell.

We offer to buy him a hamburger, but he refuses. "My stomach is so shriveled up I don't even bother tryin' to eat no more."

An African-American man drives up and, recognizing Felix, gives him a plastic bag full of clothes. Felix pulls out a pair of white socks, an almost brand new pair of Adidas, and a new pair of jeans.

He rips off his decaying Reeboks, throws them in the gutter and pulls on the white socks over his muddy feet. With a smile, he whistles. "I'm surprised. There can be some nice, nice, nice people out here."

Jeff's Fieldnotes

It has been raining all week and Carter is soaked. Someone stole his shopping cart with all his clothes. Last night he woke up in a mud puddle and had to stand wrapped in his plastic tarp for the rest of the night to try to stay dry. He has been sleeping with a knife and a metal pipe because, he says, rats have been running around seeking shelter from the heavy rains.

As we stand talking, Carter is shivering uncontrollably. He says the cold has penetrated his bones and he cannot warm up.

In the store by the farmers market, Carter chooses a beef noodle Cup-o-Soup, but at the microwave station he pauses to contemplate the ninety-nine-cent price tag on the soup. "Fuck it!" he shrugs, and purchases a thirty-five-cent cold hard-boiled egg instead.

While I drive him back through the rain to the A&C corner store, he keeps telling me, "I'm at the fucking end!"

When I stop, he says in a flat voice, "It's not just raining, Jeff. It's cold." Before opening the car door, he pauses to relish the hot air blowing from the dashboard vents for a few more seconds. "God, this heat feels good," he smiles and then jumps out, sprinting to the bus shelter, where he huddles next to Spider-Bite Lou. As usual, Lou is scratching at the bandages unraveling on the back of his neck. They are soggy and gray from the rain and mud. I had originally planned to sleep out with them tonight, but I too shiver and drive home instead.

It would kill my mother to see me like this. —*Felix*

With only a few exceptions, all of the Edgewater homeless grew up poor. Most of their childhood homes were violent, and many had alcoholic parents. A few, however, described their
families as having been stable and supportive.

There were notable differences across ethnicities in how families coped with having one
of their adult members living as a homeless drug user. The majority of the whites had no
contact with their natal families; many no longer knew where their parents and siblings
lived. Al and Ben were the only whites in the core network who kept in touch with their parents. Three others (Frank, Hogan, and Petey) recontacted their families temporarily during
the years we knew them, but only in very exceptional circumstances such as when they were
hospitalized for life-threatening conditions or when they agreed to introduce us to a family
member to conduct family history interviews. In contrast, all the African-Americans maintained ongoing relationships with their families and with extended networks of kin. Several (Reggie, Stretch, and Vernon) lived with aunts or spouses. Two of the three Latinos in
our core group, Felix and Victor, lived intermittently with their mothers. Periodically, they
would be thrown out for stealing or for selling drugs at home, but eventually, sometimes
within a few months, other times a few years, their mothers invited them home again.

White Christmas

It was difficult for us to elicit stories of childhood and family from the whites. Their outcast
status within their families was a source of shame that reverberated with their generalized
sense of failure and depression. On major family-centered holidays, however, they often
came together as a group and reminisced about their childhoods. During our second Christmas on Edgewater Boulevard, Nickie baked a ham that had been given to her by a volunteer outreach worker at San Francisco's Women's Needle Exchange and brought it to the main
white encampment. Her eleven-year-old son was spending the day with his father, now a
recovered addict married to a prison guard and living in the suburbs, and Nickie did not
want to spend Christmas Day alone in her apartment in the projects. While we were eating
Nickie's ham in the camp, an elderly couple we had never seen before drove up and un-
loaded a case of beer from the trunk of their car, calling out a cheerful "Merry Christmas."
This serendipitous holiday gift from housed strangers unleashed a slew of childhood Christmas stories:

Felix: I used to like Christmas morning. All night we'd try to sneak into the living room and take a peek at the presents. Just rip a little corner of the wrapping paper.

Frank: When I was a kid living in the projects I used to dream about getting a bike. It seemed like all my friends had bicycles, nice bikes. And I didn't have a bike. I had these vivid dreams that I got a bike on Christmas, and I'd wake up in the morning and it'd be so real that I'd be looking around for my bike. Then I'd realize that it was just a dream. And I'd be disappointed. [laughs]

Hogan: I always wanted a bike.

Nickie: [waking up from a deep heroin nod] I got a Barbie doll once for Christmas.

Max: I had the flu one Christmas. And I got a bicycle that year. My first one. [smiling] They gave it to me Christmas Eve, 'cause I wasn't feelin' real good. It was a beautiful bike, beautiful bike. I sat on it, and it made me feel better. I remember, man, an expensive bike. . . .

Frank: Never got a bike when I was a kid.

Hogan: Nope. Me neither. Not for Christmas.

Max: I was really lucky. That bike was the best thing I could ever have got. . . .

Hogan: I wanted a bike.

Felix: Oh, fuck! What kid didn't want one, man? I never got a bike for Christmas. . . .

Max: I stripped my bike all down. Took the fenders off. [softly] My father blew it when I did that. . . . [all speaking simultaneously]

Hogan: At that time my parents didn't have no money. . . .

Frank: My parents never had any money. . . .

Max: It was one of those old Schwinns [smiling], with the horn in the middle—*beep!* And it had a spring in the front, had one hand brake and foot brakes. It was a special-made bike, I guess. My father was in business—he had a bar in North Beach—and he was doing well, so I had a nice bike. . . .

Hogan: [taking his sneakers off] Shit! I got a hole in this sock.

Max: Once you get a little hole in 'em, that's it!

Hogan: I always wanted a new bike for Christmas.

Forgiving and Affectionate Families

Unlike the whites, the African-Americans often spent major religious and civic holidays (Christmas, Thanksgiving, Memorial Day, Fourth of July, Easter) with their families. Sonny had an especially warm relationship with his family, and he was fully integrated into all their reunions, including funerals, birthdays, and marriages. He spoke about his mother with affection:

She is one of them old French Creole girls with Indian in her. But I never tripped on that, because she's just an old black woman that I love. But my daddy, he was an old dark-skinned guy, and I used to tease her [giggling], "Momma, what you see in this old black man?"

Sonny's mother had migrated to San Francisco from New Orleans when she was pregnant with him. For the next thirty years, she worked as a registered nurse in private homes. According to Sonny, "All her patients were millionaire folks, you know, like the Swanson family, who make the Swanson pies. They stay in some mansion right there in Pacific Heights."

Sonny's father was also of French Creole descent, from rural Lafayette Parish in the bayou, where he ran juke joints. Sonny described him as "a player who drank." He was proud, however, that his father "maintained his home." Sonny described with emotion his father's death in old age:

> We had the whole family there spending nights. It was a gang of us. I'll never forget it. I was in the ICU with him alone, rubbing his head, sayin', "Daddy, I love you." And I'm crying. Then for about ten seconds, he opened his eyes and looked at me. I started cryin' real hard and callin' my mom. She came in and sat down next to him. It was like my dad was waiting for her, because he passed right after she came in.

The affection and concern of Sonny's mother for her wayward son were poignantly reflected in a tape-recording made by one of the members of the ethnographic team when Sonny called her from a pay phone. The sun had just set and Sonny was supposed to be spending the evening at her house. He had managed to sell a scavenged electronic keyboard for twenty dollars, however, and he now wanted to buy crack.

> *Sonny:* [dialing] I wanna make sure to call so she don't think I don't care. . . .
> Hello, Ma? I'm not gonna be comin' home tonight. . . .
> Yeah. . . . Uh-huh. . . . I got a couple of blankets and stuff. . . .
> Oh, I had lunch. . . .
> Well, mmm-hmm, you know . . . I'm not eating no hot meals or nothing like that. . . . Whenever I can, but . . . mmm-hmm. Well, yeah, I eat enough to keep going. A lot of junk food and stuff, but . . .
> Yeah, do I! [laughing] That seem like the main course, hamburgers, cheeseburgers. . . . No . . . I haven't had no Chinese food in a while. . . . Uh-huh. . . . Yeah. Yeah—
> [long pause] Well . . . mmm-hmm, I will see what I'm gonna do tomorrow Ma, you know, about getting on this methadone and stuff like that.
> Mmm-hmmm, yeah. I'm trying my best. . . . Yeah, to uh, bring myself down to the program. . . .
> Yeah . . . mmm-hmm, like the doctor told me. . . . Mmm-hmm . . .
> [softly] Yeah. Uh-huh. Yeah. 'Cause you keep askin' me. . . . Yeah . . .
> I love you too, Ma.

Even though Sonny failed to fulfill his mother's request that he enter a methadone program, she continued to welcome him home. He was her first-born, cherished son. When her second husband died of smoke asphyxiation in an electrical fire in her home halfway through our fieldwork, Sonny sat next to his mother at the funeral service and comforted her throughout the ceremony, his arm around her shoulders.

Sonny was the only one of his siblings involved in drugs and crime, and he referred to himself as the "black sheep" of his family. His extended family had been part of the large-scale African-American migration from the rural Deep South to the urban Bay Area during World War II. The family members had, for the most part, been successful. Sonny had three sisters and two brothers. One brother was a bus driver, and the other was a roofer, who also helped his wife run a beauty shop. Sonny's oldest sister, born in New Orleans, worked at the San Francisco Public Library. He described her as "the head . . . head supervisor or something like that. She's been there since she was like outta high school—thirty years." His middle sister worked in a bank, and his youngest sister was employed in the San Francisco sheriff's office.

Sonny relished his mother's care and the comforts of her home. He was also proud of the achievements of his extended family. Nonetheless, hustling for drugs remained his number one priority:

I spent the weekend at my Mom's 'cause it was my niece's wedding—my baby brother Gregory's onliest daughter, with his grandkids participating. And I'm glad I got to see my nephew, Richard Jourdan Jr., before he leaves for Germany. He gonna play professional basketball over there. He's taking his whole family with him. He graduated from Balboa High School and got a scholarship to Cal Fullerton. They used to write him up in the papers. He played with the Warriors and the Hornets.

My niece looked beautiful, man. She had a very, very nice wedding. Bride, groom, and all this stuff. She and her man workin' together in the airport. They be having a little janitorial service now for the last eight, nine months. At first, when my Momma invited me, I told her I didn't have no clothes. She said, "Don't even worry about that. We gonna help you get some all new stuff." She didn't want me bringing no shit in her house, no telling what's in my clothes—you know, ticks, lices or something, or little bug eggs in the pockets. I took off all my clothes down in the basement and put it all in a big bag.

And I got into that bathtub . . . ooooh! Lord have mercy, that water turned dirty! But it was so relaxing. Then I let the water out, turned on the shower, and scrubbed down the rings of dirt to where there weren't too much of no more dark black water. Then I ran the tub water again and sat down in there. And man! Talk about dope giving you that good feeling. . . . That water was so relaxing. I went off in some nods in there. Yeah, man.

After all that, Momma got the bed ready. Fresh blankets. Sheets. Turned on the TV with the remote control.

And then I went in the kitchen to get something to eat. She didn't have too much to eat, you know, since she be there by herself mostly. She don't be needing a whole bunch of food, but she had cooked some greens the day before. No, I take that back, it was cabbage.

She said, "Hey, baby, I got some cabbage in there if you want, and some rice."

I said, "Yeah, Momma." For some reason, I was cravin' some cabbage, too. So I got me a big old plate, got that cabbage hot, and I put the rice on top of it. . . . And I had three pieces of ham hocks and two neck bones.

She said, "Eat it all if you can."

But I said, "Well, I'm gonna leave you one ham hock and a little bit of this cabbage just in case."

I got in there in front of the TV. And my plate was like this here, you know [holding his hands ten inches apart]. And then, oh yeah! She gave me some hot water cornbread. It was about half of a skillet of it left, you know. And I was fixin' to cut me a piece, but Momma said, "Go and eat the whole thing."

I put a little juice on top of the cornbread, make it a little softer, put a little hot pepper on there. And got to eatin'!

Next thing I know, man, I'm scraping the last little bit. Damn, that food's gone. I said, "Momma, you sure you don't want none of this?"

She said, "No, eat it all. You must have been hungry, boy, huh?"

I say, "Momma, I was. You know, being out there on the streets, you don't get no righteous kind of a dinner like this here. Plus the price would be too high, and that takes away from money you need to get high."

This mention of money "to get high" triggered Sonny back to hustling:

Sonny: Hey, Philippe, buy these coasters for fifty-one cent [pulling them out of this shopping cart] so I got enough for two beers?

Philippe: Sorry, man, I don't need them—

Sonny: [interrupting] You set them coasters on the mantelpiece. For the price, man, you cannot beat. Buy these from me.

Philippe: No thanks, man.

Sonny: [aggressively] Come on Philippe! Don't do me that way.

Shortly after his niece's wedding, Sonny's brothers and sisters began visiting him under the I-beam where he slept, trying to persuade him to "come back home." They offered to pay for a methadone maintenance program, but Sonny turned them down. He was proud of who he was, a righteous dopefiend and an outlaw. He rationalized his homelessness as evidence of masculine autonomy and self-control:

I can always go home and ask for help. But I don't be trying to put that off on them. I just be struggling with what I have to do on my own instead of just running on into the house as soon as things get rough.

I have to try to make it out here on my own, man, and learn to deal with this shit, man! It's a responsibility knowin' that if I ain't made no money, the next day I'm gonna be hungry.

And I never want to be dopesick in front of my mother. She's never seen me that way. I'll never let her see me that way.

Sonny was an all-American rugged individualist. He took full responsibility for his homelessness. When we asked him if childhood traumas might explain the situation of his peers on the boulevard, he responded aggressively: "I've heard that same old song all my life. People blame other folks for their problems. But once a person get a certain age, then he know right from wrong. Whatever you do is on you. It's not on your parents and stuff. I believe everybody here had pretty good parents."

Inclusive but Abusive Family

Tina was also welcome at her mother's house and in the homes of her extended family members, but they did not offer a supportive environment. Unlike Sonny, Tina had an unstable childhood. Most of her family members had not been upwardly mobile and were perennially engulfed in violent crises. Tina met her biological father for the first time when she was twelve, when he tried to reassert his patriarchal prerogative following an incident in which Tina's "big sister" had been sexually molested.

> We were living with my auntie on Fillmore, and one of my auntie's mens tried to molest my sister, Sylvia. She was thirteen and he tried to feel on her titties.
>
> My mother almost cut his throat and that's when I found out about my daddy 'cause my mother called him. He came right over, hollerin', "I don't want *no mans* around neither one of my daughters!"
>
> But my daddy was a rollin' stone. He was already married to someone else. My mother was his mistress, evidently.

Tina's last contact with her father was also precipitated by the violence surrounding sex work:

> Last time I seen my daddy was at my sister Sylvia's funeral. He never treated me like a daddy treat his daughter, but at the funeral he treat me so sweet because I wouldn't move from the coffin. [long pause] Then he hug me [voice cracking], but I never had a chance to tell him how I felt.
>
> Sylvia was stabbed in the back seven times. It was drug related. It was two black ladies and it was two tricks—a judge's son and a lawyer. And the black lady stabbed Sylvia in the back and tried to throw her in the swimming pool at the Colonial Motel in Antioch, California.
>
> The bitch that killed my sister got seven years. But she's dead now. She killed herself; she ran into a damn telephone pole by the railroad in Antioch.
>
> We went and identified Sylvia on Mother's Day . . . and she lived seventeen more days and died on her birthday. It was thirteen years ago; she'd be forty-two today.
>
> My daddy gave me five hundred dollars at the funeral. But I didn't want no fucking money. Shit! I wanted my sister. And that's the last time I seen my dad, at Sylvia's funeral . . . and I haven't seen him since. . . . And I won't even try to find him, or call. No lookin' up no numbers, no nothin'! Because I know he don't want me. I already failed.
>
> And his wife, she hate me. She was like in her thirties, and my dad, he in his sixties, and she say I look just like my mother. . . . And I do! My daddy used to say, "Tina, looking at you is lookin' at your mother."

Tina sought to reconstruct memories of childhood love and nurturance to redeem the chaos of her family:

> We was living in the Sunnydale Projects and then my mother had another little boy. So it was two stepbrothers and then me and my sister, we had the same daddy.
>
> I had got a tricycle that Christmas and I was so happy. It was red. My baby brother's daddy bought the tricycle for me. His name is Arthur Scott. He was not my dad, but he was my real dad. I still call him "Daddy" today.

Arthur was a bus driver. He provided for us. And took good care of his son. He tried. But then he became an outlaw and his life ventured on.

But still I'll go and I'll see him and his mother, Mrs. Montgomery. I call her "Granny." They used to have this shop across from Candlestick Park called The Candy Shop. They used to make hamburgers, french fries every day . . . real cheap.

Now they just at home, together. Mother and son. Yeah, but they're real sweet to me. They still love me and they want me to do good with my life.

Tina sometimes sought respite from the street in her fictive Daddy and Granny's home. But the stability and emotional support of her adoptive, ostensibly loving kin-figures was imbued with instrumentality and straightforward violence. Tina's commitment to kin reveals that there is nothing inherently positive in "strong extended families" when they are embroiled in drugs and violence. (See Jarrett and Burton 1999 on poor extended African-American families in flux and Stack 1974 for a counterclaim; see Fordham 1996:98 on the "culture of forgiveness.")

Jeff's Fieldnotes

After buying crack on Third Street, Tina decides to introduce me to her "Granny" and "Daddy," who live around the corner. Granny shakes my hand gently and breaks into a welcoming, eighty-four-year-old's toothless smile. She is wearing a blue muumuu with a matching silk scarf wrapped around her head and a gold beaded necklace around her neck. She immediately resumes her place in a rocking chair by the window.

Arthur greets me heartily, "The first man I ever met in San Francisco was named Jeff." He is much shorter than I expected and is very thin. He is wearing a beat-up baseball cap and is carrying a bowl of quartered oranges in his left hand.

The room is covered with old family photographs, including a painted photo of Granny's parents. She says that the image does not do them justice and that they barely look like how she remembers them.

While Granny and I chat, Tina and her Daddy hurry into the side room. I overhear, "So did you bring me anything today?" And a few seconds later, "That's my good daughter," followed by the scratching of matches, the bubbling of melting crack, and deep inhalations.

I ask Granny about the past, and she recounts the classic life story of an elderly African-American in San Francisco. Born in Mississippi, she migrated to New Orleans as a teenager. She left for San Francisco in 1943 and found work as a hospital aide. "At eighty-four," she tells me, "I plan on relaxing and on enjoyin' not working." She has lived in this house, which she rents, for fifty years.

Tina and her Daddy return to the living room. The rush of their crack smoking dominates the rest of our stay: first they want to visit an uncle in the hospital; then they don't; then we are all going to go to church; then we aren't.

When we finally get up to leave, Tina pauses at the door and asks for an orange. Arthur hesitates but then slowly holds out his bowl. She frowns at the two slices in the bottom of the bowl and declares, "I want that one," snatching the slice Arthur is holding in his hand. She then runs across the room and grabs her Bible, a large white volume with an image of Jesus embossed on the cover, and we head back out to Edgewater Boulevard.

The difference in tenor between Tina's and Sonny's family visits is accentuated by gender roles. As the favorite, first-born son, Sonny could graciously accept his mother's nurturance and her desire to indulge him with his favorite foods. He was confident in his sense of entitlement to her treats. At the same time, he protectively made sure that she, too, had eaten her share (see Fordham 1996:147–189 on mothers socializing their adolescent boys to receive the entitlements of "black patriarchy"). In contrast, when Tina went home, her stepfather expected her to bring him crack. Ever since childhood she had gone to the street to escape domestic turmoil. Unlike the men living on Edgewater Boulevard, however, Tina sought to fulfill the role of caretaking daughter and grasped at any signs of reciprocal nurturance. She had to settle for shared drug use:

> Arthur made Granny's place a ho' house! Bitches and niggas be coming in and out of there. That's why I don't like going over there no more. Bitches be suckin' dicks and shit for crack. And Arthur, he gettin' the money.
>
> And then my Grandmama sitting there at the kitchen table, or at the window . . . and they just passin' her by. So I'm like, "Bitch! Get outta here." I'm gonna whip all them ho's ass. Every last one of 'em.
>
> [long pause] All of us fight. Me, my daddy, and my little brother, Dee-Dee. The three of us. But before my brother Dee-Dee went to jail, he and my daddy was so sweet to me. Now that I fix, they hold my arm when I need help.

Granny's rapidly deteriorating health revealed once again the gendered division of labor in caring for vulnerable kin. Arthur often disappeared on crack binges, leaving his mother alone in the house with "nothin' to eat." Tina began to worry:

> You know, Jeff, Granny, she is senile. It's like this [imitating a conversation]:
> "Hi, Grandma! I'm gonna take a bath."
> [feeble, slow voice] "You don't have to tell me. You stay here anyway, don't you?"
> [normal voice] "Grandmother, can I have my clothes?"
> [slow voice] "Why you keep tellin' me, baby? You know where you stay."
> "Grandmother, I stay in the van with my friend now."
> "It ain't no shower in there?"
> "No, what is a shower doing in a *van?*"
> You see, Jeff, I have to make her remember what a van is like. As soon as I walk away she don't gonna remember. I was wantin' to take her walking this week, but she don't want to go out.
>
> Last month, Jeff, I had to call the police on my Daddy two times to kick his ass. He was fussing and yellin' and Granny told him, "I'm gonna kill you in your sleep!" She swung her cane at him and he grabbed at it and she fell.

Six months later, Granny was evicted by her landlord. She and Arthur were saved from homelessness by a city-subsidized housing program for the aged. Consistent with gender caretaker roles, Tina's mother, Persia, who had been separated from Arthur for over thirty years, also stepped in to help her former mother-in-law.

Tina's own ongoing relationship with Persia was framed by the same paradoxical continuum of love and abuse that characterized her relationship with her stepfather. Meshing love and violence and taking refuge in a sense of individual autonomy defined through drug use, Tina had consolidated a habitus that was effective for survival on the street as an addict. Although critical of her mother's mistreatment of her as a child, she, like Sonny, took full responsibility for her drug use. She also held on to her sense of filial love.

> Growing up was a bitch. My mother didn't want me. I overheard her tell my daddy over the telephone, "I wish I wouldn't of had her. I tried to kill her by fallin' down the stairs." I heard her say it several times. That's how I know she don't like me.
>
> She been fucking me up ever since I was a kid. She used to beat the fuck outta me . . . with extension cords and telephone cords. I remember one was real thick . . . and I couldn't dress for gym.
>
> She scald her husbands, too. She stabbed the fuck outta the—was gonna kill one of 'em.
>
> [long pause] Last time I seen her, she put me out of her house. She wanted to kick my ass so I got the fuck out of there 'cause I can't hit her. [long pause again] I think about all that shit. [tearing up] It all comes back to me.
>
> [raising her head] But it ain't my mother's fault I'm like this. I don't blame her. I really don't. I don't blame her for my drugs. That's on me. [lighting a crack pipe] I can't keep putting that burden on my mother. The only thing she could do is just pray for me. She loves me. . . . But when she hurts me, I rebel from that. . . . But I don't want to hurt her. I'm too much like her ass.
>
> I only keep thinking about when she scratched my face up when I was eighteen [frowning]. My face was like a zebra. She thought I was gonna live with her forever, and I thought I was too. But then I tried to move out and she snapped.
>
> I've never ever really told my mother how she made me feel when she beated me when I was little. She made me feel that she hated me. We talk, but I never tell her. . . . But I have to. . . . But if I tell her, maybe she would just really push me outta her life forever.
>
> Yesterday it was Mother's Day and I left a letter by her door on rainbow paper. I told her that I love her, and that I miss her, and that I want to be with her for a while. She was up in Vacaville [at the prison], visiting my baby brother Dee-Dee. He be out in December.

Tina made frequent references to her mother's psychological instability, blaming it on the outlaw behavior of her brothers. "My mother been to Napa [state psychiatric hospital] and all that, Jeff. She snapped over my oldest brother. He worried her to death, that son-of-a-bitch jailbird—a burglar, in and out of jail. But he's a minister now in Modesto."

We took Tina to the beach at her request on several occasions. She wanted to evoke positive childhood memories on these outings. "I used to be at the beach, a little girl jumpin' up and down in the waves. Once my mother was gonna kill her husband, but instead she got herself outta bed and told us, 'Come on, y'all!' And took us here. That's why I love the beach. She used to get us up at three, four in the morning, 'Let's go wade in the water.'"

Tina racialized her explanation for why she suffered so much corporal punishment as a little girl, taking it back one more generation to her maternal grandmother:

My grandmother moved in and helped my mother take care of us 'cause my mother was a single parent. She was a beautiful lady. Oh, I loved my grandma. But she had picked the two oldest as her favorites. And the two babies—my baby brother Dee-Dee and I—we wasn't shit.

[crying silently] My grandma idoled my older brother's ass because he was born with blue eyes.

Jeff: Did your grandmother abuse your mother when she was little?

Tina: My grandmother didn't even beat her, 'cause my grandmother was real black, and my granddaddy he was a white man, so my grandmother thought the world of her. But evidently my grandma was searching for something, and she beat the fuck outta me.

Jeff's fieldnotes from his first meeting with Tina's sixty-one-year-old mother, Persia, reveal a charismatic but emotionally overwhelmed grandmother who was trying to protect herself from the turmoil of her outlaw progeny, whom she could not stop loving. She was also beset by the anonymous violence and drugs that pervade most U.S. inner cities, including the public school system (Bourgois 1996a; Devine 1996).

Jeff's Fieldnotes

In a bustle of high energy, in a half dance, half trot, Persia skips about the kitchen and insists on making me lunch. She speaks in a nonstop stream of consciousness and says that she has not heard from Tina in six months. When I tell her that her way of moving and talking reminds me of Tina, she smiles appreciatively, but then her mood shifts anxiously.

Persia: [softly] "How was she when you seen her last? How is she lookin'? [abruptly changing her tone] But what can I do? She's grown. I can't fuss. I just live in fear. So all I do is hope and pray.

[softly again] "I'm scared to get involved because everyone is on drugs.... [loudly again] My grandson, he's getting drugs at school. [suddenly shouting] What can I do? I'm only one person! I have fourteen grandchildren! And they so bad!

[composing herself] "I don't want no contact with Tina. Because I'm the mother and father, the uncle, the aunt, and all that, you know. Oh, God, I don't know! Where can you escape to?

[softly again] "Is Tina okay? Tell her I love her."

Persia shows me photographs from the time she "ran away" from her children to "take care" of herself. Just last week, she quit her job as a high school tutor because a student was murdered on campus. Seeing the feet under the sheet reminded her too much of her daughter Sylvia's stabbing. "My first daughter, she's dead. I had her when I was seventeen. She was a love baby.... [shaking her head] Tears and devastation ..."

In much the same way that Tina spoke of her childhood, Persia overlaps the traumatic incidents of her daughters' lives and enmeshes maternal love with rejection.

> I got a lot of fightin' over my children comin' up. Drinking beer at an early age. Somebody had kidnapped Tina. Oh God! A nightmare, a heart attack!
>
> [gently] I know she love me, but she'll get rid of me in a minute. [suddenly angry] I've seen somebody early in the morning throw her something; she go get it and hurry up and get rid of me. I finally realized I can't rescue her.
>
> I was runnin' my blood pressure, not sleeping. I just had those crying spells. But I'm over that a little bit now. I cry a little bit, but not every day, all day. I don't make myself sick, 'cause there ain't nothin' I can do.
>
> But I don't want nobody to hurt her. Just don't be out there on the streets with a cup! But if you see her, Jeff, tell her I'm not mad, that I be loving. . . . To take care of herself. And let me know about Carter, too.

Socialization into Drugs

Like Sonny, Carter came from a nuclear family, but like Tina, he was introduced to life on the streets inside his home before he understood what he was seeing.

> My uncles on my mother's side was dopefiends. I be wanting to play in the living room— [opening his eyes wide to imitate a waddling toddler] and they be like [husky voice], "Ah, I'm so tired." That was a cover-up. They was noddin'. My mother knew it, but she never told us nothin' about it.

Carter shared a bedroom with his older brother, A. J.:

> My brother would make me turn over in the bed and make me hide my head under the pillow. But I could hear him making the rig. See, they had to make the rigs in those days. With a needle point, a rubber band, a tube, and baby bottle nipple. It was an art to it. They used a little piece of dollar bill, just the white part, and they roll it up and jam it so it fits snug with the nipple. Then I could hear the *"squish, squish"* sound of him squeezing the baby nipple.
>
> And I used to see him standing in the playground in front of the rec center just nodding and shit. And I used to say, "Damn! Why someone gonna do that?" And I used to always look down on it.
>
> They used to take sides of cows off the meat delivery truck. A whole half a cow with the legs on it and run with it to the All American Meat Market on the hill. These little scrawny, sick dopefiends carryin' a whole half cow.
>
> They used to intimidate Chinese Kim, the butcher: [shouting] *"Cut this up!"* And then go sell it door to door.
>
> This one time they hid one of the cows in the bushes by the playground. It was a leg stickin' out and I was tryin' to drag it to go give it back, right. But I end up fallin' backwards 'cause it was greasy. My brother's other partner, the one who got blown away by a shotgun, caught me. "Little nigga, what the fuck is you doin'?" [motion of punching and kicking]
>
> I'm crying [whining], "I'm gonna tell my brother on you." He answers [deep gravelly voice], "You ain't got to tell him. I'm gonna tell your brother."

Then my brother got on my ass for doing that. "You little wannabe, motherfuckin' innocent bastard." [bending down to slap at an imaginary child with both hands] 'Cause that was their money I was fucking with. That half a side of beef was going to fix them for maybe two or three weeks.

An HIV prevention peer outreach worker who had been a running partner of Carter's older brother, A. J., during the early 1970s remembered Carter as an earnest little boy: "We used to use [heroin] in Carter's mother's house. And Carter used to tell his brother to stop using. [chuckling] 'Stamp out drugs!' But then when we'd be goin' out on a lick, Carter used to always want to follow us. A. J. would have to chase him home."

Carter grew up in a large household beset by poverty and instability. He made passing references to "my father beatin' on my mother," but he also held on to vivid memories of a working-class propriety upheld by the virtuous women in his household:

It was the day before school started. And we was supposed to go to school looking nice and clean. We ironed all those school clothes we was going to wear and show off the next day. Laid them out on our beds. Had our books and our binders ready.

There was eight of us, counting my two nieces, who was living with us. And my mother was the only one working, so everyone had their little summer jobs to get their school clothes and everything.

That's when the whole house burnt to the ground with everything in it and my sister got burnt badly. She was in the hospital for eight months in one of those incubators. She's a nurse now. She dedicated her life to taking care of people.

Carter was proudest of his elder sister, with whom he had been living before becoming homeless, because she ran "a center for wayward girls."

Coming of Age in the Sixties in San Francisco

Most of the Edgewater homeless retained fond childhood memories of growing up in the neighborhood up the hill. Although gentrifying rapidly at the time of our fieldwork, this community of single-family homes was still largely working-class and ethnically diverse. Its main street was lined with all the amenities of an old-fashioned neighborhood: a public library, a community center, a baseball card shop, a bank, a barber shop, a butcher shop, a produce market, a supermarket, and several bars, corner liquor stores, and churches. In the "old days," the neighborhood had been even more self-contained, boasting a movie theater (converted in the early 1980s into a Latino evangelical church) and a gas station (transformed in the early 1990s into the parking lot of a health food grocery).

During her third winter on the street, Tina once again left Edgewater Boulevard for California's Central Valley to take refuge with her eldest son. He had just been released from a six-month prison term for a violation of parole on a four-year bank robbery sentence. Suddenly alone, Carter established a temporary camp behind the ice machine at the Crow's Nest liquor store. He camouflaged his shelter as a mound of discarded cardboard boxes awaiting recycling. Caltrans had confiscated his blankets in a raid the week before. To try to keep warm, he created a cavelike vortex by stuffing small boxes into consecutively larger ones and insulating them with Styrofoam. We had to crawl on our bellies to enter his shelter, but he was proud that he had "hooked it up with music" by running an electrical wire from the ice machine to a boom box.

On an especially cold evening, Jeff and Hank happened to walk by and found Carter sprawled in front of his boxes, drooling in the midst of a heavy nod. With a flick of his cane Hank woke him up, teasing, "Wipe your mouth." Startled, it took Carter a few minutes to shake off his grogginess and recognize us. When he finally stood up, he was stiff and shivering.

"Thanks for waking me up, Hank, I might have froze to death. 'Cause, damn! Caltrans took my jacket too, last week." Jeff bought a round of food and drink, and they went back to Hank's new camp. It was carefully hidden on the embankment behind an Apple Computer billboard featuring John Lennon and Yoko Ono. This reference to the 1960s set Hank and Carter to reminiscing about "life on the hill in the old days."

Carter: Hank was the usher at the Liberty Theater, where the church is now. Everyone knew Hank.

We used to see two major features and two twenty-minute shorts for twenty-five cents—or was it fifty cents? I would work after school babysitting and save all my little earning money to go to the show on the weekend. The line for the theater used to be 'round the corner.

Hank: We had a whole variety of horror movies.

Carter: [excitedly] Yeah, horror movies! *Taste the Blood of Dracula.* I remember that one. Boy, that was good! Christopher Lee was awesome in *Dracula,* and Bela Lugosi too.

The only way I was allowed to go to the movies was if I had gone to church first. My mother and father was like, "If you ain't go to church, you can't go to the show." We had to have the program from Sunday school to show we'd been there.

Hank: We used to play all these religious films like *The Ten Commandments.*

Carter: Hank, remember the five-and-dime store that used to be by the theater? And Bob's barber shop?

Jeff: Did your parents go to the movies with you?

Carter: No, because they was always working. But on the weekends they was like [firm voice], "Take your brother!" Because I was younger. And after the movies, right, you had to hurry to get home, especially on a Sunday 'cause you had to get ready to go to school. It was gettin' dark.

And after the last movie ended, everybody would be in a hurry to get to the door and we used to run down the hill trying to stay together. And you'd be lookin' 'round 'cause you'd be scared, "Aaah! where's Dracula?" [laughing] You might get snatched!

My sisters could run fast, boy! And I'd be like . . . [shrill voice] "Wait for me!"

[taunting voice] "You the last one. Dracula gonna get you!"

Oh man that was great! Jeff, if I could recapture those days. . . . Those are breathtaking memories.

Carter's preadolescent innocence coincided with the height of the 1960s, when San Francisco was the epicenter of the hippie counterculture: sex, drugs, and rock 'n' roll. Some of the legendary rock stars from that era lived or rehearsed in the neighborhood.

Hank: Before Santana was discovered, he used to practice in a basement up here on the hill.

Carter: When Hendrix used to be at the Fillmore, he used to come play in a basement up here, too. They used to make us get away from the garage door 'cause we'd be blocking the street.

Hank: And every Sunday they had the "dope bowl" right at the top of the hill.

Carter: There would be ice chests with beer and wine and plenty of weed and they'd play football.

Hank: A few people would have some cocaine.

Carter: We had go-carts here, and the pole where they put a rope on it and you'd swing an easy fifty foot over the side of the hill. Like a Tarzan. You run and pull back, and you let go and scream, Whooooooo! [laughing]

Hank: And go way the hell out over the drop.

Carter: We'd run up to the pole hoping there ain't nobody there and you was the first.

Hank: Yeah, "firsties!" [slapping a high-five and laughing hard]

Carter: [choking with laughter] Yeah, "firsties!!" We used to have fun as kids. Not like youngsters today. They don't know how to have fun nowadays.

Hank: We oughta' go fly a kite up there. Haven't done that in years.

Carter: And we used to walk down the hill to the swimming pool in the Mission. It only cost ten cents to get in.

Hank: Oh that swimming pool was fun. But now you got motherfuckers hanging outside that pool selling crack.

Carter: This was a fantastic neighborhood back then.

Hank: If I could do it all over again I'd just want it to last a lot more years. Wouldn't trade it for nothing in the world. I have a million memories.

Carter: A lot of the guys who drive by the corner here [pointing toward the corner store] don't have a clue that we knew their parents.

Hank: They walk down here and right past us, but we see their parents in them. . . .

Carter: And they see us, but it's [dismissive gesture], "Oh, the ol' dope heads." But this was a fantastic neighborhood.

Hank: I'm glued to the hill. I don't want to leave the hill.

Carter: Y'know what? I don't think I ever will. I'm gonna die here.

Gangs and Ethnic Socialization into Crime

A more violent world of adolescent street gangs operated parallel to San Francisco's hippie drug scene during the years when most of the Edgewater homeless were teenagers. Following the ghetto race riots, the federal government began funding innovative social programs for at-risk youth, through the Department of Health, Education, and Welfare (HEW). Carter, for example, joined an African-American youth gang that was subsequently recruited into a federally funded program known as Youth Organizations United (Y.O.U.), founded by former members of the Conservative Vice Lords, a Chicago-based gang (Gang Research.net 2006a, 2006b).

> *Carter:* After school they had workshops, and we'd learn different trades so that after growing up we'd be getting into the business field after graduation . . . and being productive citizens and everything. The organization ended up lasting maybe five years or so. There was twelve states represented in the West, and organizations throughout the East Coast and the South. It advanced a lot of kids and students.
>
> We wrote up a program with curriculums and formats and everything and we did fundraising and interchanged ideas. And I swear on my life, my right hand to God, Sammy Davis Jr. wrote us a check for five thousand dollars. [chuckling] Didn't nobody have a pencil, and he wrote the motherfuckin' check out in green crayon.
>
> Then the HEW funding ended and I went back to being a bum.

The experimental social services of the late 1960s and early 1970s that briefly channeled Carter's energies away from gang fighting were short lived. By the age of sixteen, he was incarcerated as a juvenile delinquent on a fast track to a career in crime. Thirty years later, however, Carter still reminisced with pride about his participation in Y.O.U. As we have noted, Carter crossed ethnic and class barriers more readily than the other African-Americans on the boulevard, and he was especially effective at dealing with us. Y.O.U.'s programs may have contributed to his slightly more diversified repertoire of ethnic and class-based symbolic capital (Bourdieu 2000; 2001:1–2, 33–42; Bourdieu and Wacquant 1992:162–173, 200–205).

Adolescent street gangs also propelled Sonny onto the same fast track toward a career of criminality. Sonny's family, however, unlike Carter's, was not overwhelmed by economic crisis, domestic violence, or drugs. His working-class parents had achieved the American dream of owning their own home. But it was located next to a violence-plagued housing project, and Sonny was drawn into the local teenage peer group.

With the notable exception of Al, none of the whites had joined gangs or spent time in juvenile custody. In contrast, all the core African-Americans in our network had been locked up for gang activity as adolescents. Joining a gang had become self-evidently "cool" and brave to black teenagers growing up in poor neighborhoods. This option was not as readily available to white boys because by the 1970s white gangs had largely disappeared from most San Francisco neighborhoods, and the new black and Latino gangs were increasingly segregated. Even those whites on Edgewater Boulevard who came from abusive and alcoholic families had not been incarcerated as juveniles. Significantly, when we asked Carter about drug use among boys in juvenile jail in the early 1970s, he responded bemusedly:

> Drugs was taboo. . . . [squinting distastefully] Pathetic! Heroin, cocaine—I was so down on that shit! [giggling] That was the worst thing a person could do. I don't think too many people up there [in juvenile jail] at that time even knew too much about those drugs.

In short, poor African-American boys were being formed into professional outlaws before they began to use drugs, whereas poor whites embarked on criminal careers later in life, after their drug use had spun out of control. This historical, institutionalized ethnic pattern from the 1970s was a crucial generative force shaping the contrasting dopefiend habituses of outlaw versus outcast that became visibly racialized on Edgewater Boulevard in the 2000s.

The proliferation of segregated youth gangs coincided with President Richard Nixon's declaration of the War on Drugs in 1971 and the shift in funding from social services, education, and job training to law enforcement. Police records from the era note with alarm the disproportionate number of African-American youths being jailed in San Francisco. In 1974, for example, African-American boys were 2.5 times more likely to be held in custody than white youths (Juvenile Court Department 1975:19). A San Francisco task force on juvenile justice from the period warned that disparities in adolescent incarceration rates threatened to shut the current generation of African-American youth out of the legal labor market, "since many employers in the private sector think that commitment to CYA [California Youth Authority facilities] is similar to a prison sentence" (Bay Area Social Planning Council 1969:716). In other words, in the 1970s, the administrators of juvenile justice predicted the long-term criminalization of black youth that became so visibly institutionalized twenty-five years later in California's apartheid-like prison system of the 1990s and 2000s (Public Safety Performance Project 2008:6, 34; see Wacquant 2001a:95–96 on the "hyper-incarceration" and "containment of lower class African-Americans").

The ways that institutional and historical forces channel vulnerable cohorts of youth into crime, violence, and drugs are generally misrecognized. Following the logic of symbolic violence, involvement in illegal activities is usually considered to be a personal choice that reveals an individual's moral defects. The structural political-economic forces that are in fact at work operate "invisibly" at a more subtle, long-term, and incremental level of habitus formation. Drug use, crime, and homelessness, therefore, are widely suspected to be evidence of laziness, lack of intelligence, biogenetic disability, or inadequate impulse control. Following historical patterns of racism, ethnic markers of habitus frequently emerge as stereotypes, which, in turn, are oppositionally celebrated by members of stigmatized groups in a display of resistance or as an assertion of dignity (Katz 1988:ch. 7; Levine 1977:407–419; Marcus 2005:24–30). In routine interactions, the political-economic basis for the racialized habitus formations of middle-aged African-American outlaws and white outcasts on Edgewater Boulevard are hidden because their everyday behaviors express themselves as the purposeful actions and conscious choices of individuals.

The African-Americans did not have a critical awareness of the historical institutional forces that had shaped the last twenty-five years of their lives, as the United States quadrupled the size of its incarcerated population and imprisoned six times more black men than white men (Bureau of Justice Statistics 2004, 2005; Public Safety Performance Project 2008:6, 34). Instead, they reminisced about juvenile jail with nostalgia and masculine camaraderie, as though swapping stories about summer camp or varsity sports.

San Francisco's main correctional facility for juvenile recidivists, known as "Log Cabin," was set in a redwood forest outside San Francisco, surrounded by state parks on the hills above Silicon Valley. Enormous public resources and effort were spent on what became a de facto racialized training ground for professional criminals.

Sonny: The South Park neighborhood was fighting the Medallions from the Fillmore. I was in the Conquistadors and we was helping the Fillmore Medallions. There were two different Medallions, one in the Fillmore, one in Potrero. Anyhow, we all got busted and went to juvenile hall. I did a year behind that shit.

Carter: Were you in the B-5 wing? That's where I was.

Sonny: We were the first ones that broke in B-5. The very first! They called it "high risk." [chuckling] The maximum security wing.

Carter: [explaining slowly] See, they had wings. Like B-1, B-2, B-3. B-1 would be like young, young kids. B-2, a little bit older; B-3 was considered the big boys. Sixteen and seventeen.

Sonny: I went through all of them wings, man.

Carter: [turning to Philippe] It's like a boys' home. You had beds going down rows inside a big dormitory. It was old-fashioned, solid wood.

Sonny: And you used to get what they called gigs on conduct.

Carter: Gigs! [laughing and high-fiving with Sonny] That's right, gigs. [turning back to Philippe] You sit down for evaluation periods every six weeks at the dinner table, and they read off who made what. And after so many gigs you get bounced, demoted. You get gigs for cussin' out counselors, serious gigs that rank you. I got bounced three times.

Sonny: Yeah. I got bounced. That gives you an extra month, like for a fight.

Carter: It wasn't that bad. See, everything was wide open. You weren't behind no bars.

Sonny: It's all redwoods up there. It's beautiful.

Carter: Oooh, some kind of beautiful, know what I'm sayin'? On your birthday they would bake you a big ol' cake and ring a little bell and say [deep voice], "I would like to announce today is the day of your birthday." And everybody sang "Happy Birthday."

No one wanted to run away because out there in the woods there were some brown bears that would come down, and mountain lions too.

And they had everything you wanted up there, man. They fed you three meals a day.

Sonny: And you'd get to smoke six cigarettes a day. Six light-ups a day, and if you get caught smokin' when it wasn't light-up time, they give you a gig. That's a minor gig. . . .

Carter: And they had a little pond where they had some horses, and they'd let you run around the pond on holidays and stuff.

For Carter, incarceration may have been a relief from the substance abuse and fighting occurring in his home. Log Cabin facilitated family bonding and reinforced his budding sense of masculine self-esteem:

Your whole family could visit, and you could walk around and show them the pond. I got a picture at Log Cabin with my mom and dad and sister and girlfriend. They used to visit every weekend. That was a big thing, to be sent away from your family. So they would be there every weekend and try to console me. "Don't worry about it, son. It's gonna be all right. Just hang in there. Only six more months."

I likeded it. You do everything you want to do, you know, work all day, eight o'clock to two. I was on the crew building the rock wall.

Later in Carter's life, many of the major liminal rituals that bring families together, such as funerals and births, continued to be mediated by the prison system. This institutionalized removal of able-bodied males from their families for long periods, interspersed with intense bonding through brief kinship rituals, parallels the way many of the African-American families continued to integrate aging homeless sons, fathers, and uncles into holiday celebrations and periodic family reunions.

Carter: When my father passed away I was in jail. When my mother passed away I was also in jail. But I got to come home for both of the funerals. Then I had to go back again.

Sonny: [softly] I lost my first son, Sonny Junior, God bless his soul, when I was in San Quentin doing a [parole] violation. April 14, 1988.

Gendered Suffering

Mothers bore the brunt of the pain and destructiveness of their homeless, addicted children. Of everyone on Edgewater Boulevard, Felix and Victor had the most intense, on-again, off-again relationships with their mothers. They subscribed to a patriarchal discourse often associated with Latin American and circum-Mediterranean cultures and with Catholicism, which celebrates a son's privileged relationship to a saintly, long-suffering mother whose self-sacrificing love enables her to forgive a son's youthful masculine transgressions (see Belmonte 1989:87–94; Melhuus and Stolen 1996; Stevens 1973).

Felix: My mom's a saint. Oh yes she is! A saint. She's the best woman. . . . She's my best friend.
I don't ever tell her I'm homeless. That'll break her heart. She'll have a heart attack. I tell her I live in a hotel and that I'm trying to get into a program. She knows I'm a dopefiend.
Whatever she says to people about me when she's angry, she still knows I'm her best friend, too. Me and mom are close. I take care of her. Whatever she needs, I'll do it.
I love my mother more than anyone in this world. I wouldn't ever want to hurt her. She's the greatest.

When we first met Felix, his younger brother, a California Highway Patrol officer, had filed an order of protection with the court to keep Felix out of their mother's house. Felix accused his brother of being "nothing but a prima donna, no-good, son-of-a-bitch, too-good-for-the-world Republican." We learned subsequently, however, that a dramatic event had been the straw that broke the camel's back: Felix had sold his mother's furniture to pay for a crack binge while she was away on vacation. Furthermore, throughout much of his twenties and thirties, Felix sold heroin out of his mother's garage. "The police kicked down my mother's door six times," he told us, somewhat proudly.

Nevertheless, Felix still sought out his mother in moments of emotional crisis, and she usually accommodated him. For example, when a peripheral member of the scene who had just been released from prison died of a brain aneurism while smoking crack in Felix's tent, Felix called his mother from a pay phone, begging her to let him spend the night in her house: "Ma. I gotta get outta here. Someone died in my room."

Most of the Edgewater homeless admired Felix's mother and referred to her politely as "Mrs. Ramirez." Their respect, however, did not stop them from hustling money from her for heroin.

> *Frank:* Felix's mother is awesome. Jesus Christ, she put up with Felix's shit for so many years.
>
> Felix would call from a pay phone, but he'd make it sound like he was at some hospital somewhere across town, trying to get into some treatment program, right. Then he'd hand me the phone. I knew the scenario.
>
> [clearing his voice officiously] "Oh, yes, Mrs. Ramirez. This is Dr. Lombardi. And, um, yes . . . your son is here. And, yeah . . . he's applied to enter our program and . . . ah . . ." [voice trailing off] And so forth and so on.

I played so many different characters. I've been doctors, lawyers, psychologists, cops, social workers—you name it. All to get a twenty-dollar or twenty-five-dollar initial payment.

Max: [laughing] But she's a smart lady, really nice.

Frank: Yeah! She's always asking Felix how I'm doing.

Halfway through our fieldwork, Felix was hit by a Pizza Hut delivery car in the alley behind the A&C corner store. The county hospital performed two surgeries on his left knee. The doctor's release order specified, "Maintain leg elevated at home." Felix complied by moving under a freeway overpass and using the support beams as a prop for his leg. He eventually settled out of court for four thousand dollars in damages from Pizza Hut. It was paid to his mother, who doled out the money to him in daily increments of five dollars. She had suffered a heart attack shortly after the lawsuit, and she allowed Felix to move back into her garage "to watch over her." He felt redeemed, reporting the details of her health condition to us whenever we saw him on the boulevard: "Ma's doing much better now. The holidays were stressful for her because my father died and his grandfather died at this same time of year, but we got through it."

Estranged Families

Frank grew up in San Francisco's North Beach housing projects. He described his mother, a painter, and his stepfather, a writer, as "bohemians with a lot of creative friends but no money." He referred to one of his babysitters as "a famous black poet" from the "Beat generation." Like Sonny, Frank was the only child in his family to use drugs; unlike Sonny, however, Frank was not welcome to visit his parents or siblings:

I'm the only black sheep of the family. I haven't called my stepfather in ten years—or any of my brothers. It's been so many years, I don't even know if they have any kids or not. I'm embarrassed to even call. What am I going to say? [long pause] I don't want them to see me like this. I keep putting it off, and the more I put it off and all the years go by I keep getting more embarrassed.

[softly] It's like a trap. I've got to call them sooner or later. [standing abruptly] I need a cigarette; you got one?

Frank's stepfather—whom he referred to as "father" or "dad"—worked seasonally for the Forest Service as a fire lookout when Frank was in elementary school:

We lived in a little house in the forest every summer, in the middle of nowhere. We had no electricity.

No TV or nothing. At night we'd all climb on my mother's bed—me, my mom, my father, and even my little brother who was just a baby, and my dad read a few chapters out of some old classic. I loved it! [smiling] I lived all day for that moment. I'd lie there and just close my eyes . . . just listening, drifting. It was one of the most enjoyable moments of my life.

He read every classic there was: *Gulliver's Travels, Huckleberry Finn, Tom Sawyer, Wizard of Oz, King Arthur's Knights of the Round Table, Connecticut Yankee.* Just every classic you could think of . . . *Alice in Wonderland, Wind in the Willows*—Froggie "Beep! Beep!" [laughing] at Toad Manor.

It's too bad that kids today just sit in front of the TV and the video monitors. They lose a lot. Reading is the best thing you can do for your kid. They get more out of that than watching TV any day.

Frank also had fond memories of his biological father, and he worked for him for several years as a sign painter when he was a teenager and young adult. Frank took us to visit him in a gentrified San Francisco neighborhood a short bus ride from Edgewater Boulevard. As we approached the three-story house, admiring the million-dollar panoramic views of the Golden Gate Bridge, Frank suddenly became nervous about a spot on his shirt.

His father answered our knock, surprised but gracious. He had not seen his son in several years, but he agreed to be filmed on video with Frank at his doorstep. We could hear Frank's stepmother shouting angrily from inside the house, forbidding Frank from entering.

Although father and son resembled one another physically, their very different demeanors in front of the camera uncannily highlighted their distinct positions in the world. Frank's father was a retired self-made contractor, and he stood up straight, looking directly into the camera. He spoke in a soft voice with a gentle, resigned tone, intermittently smiling or frowning at his son. Frank squatted on the ground and remained hunched over throughout the entire interview. He spoke with the gravelly rasp of a long-time heroin addict, looking downward most of the time. Struggling not to argue or interrupt, he occasionally squinted anxiously at his father, flinching at his criticisms and perking up at his compliments.

Frank: You've lost a lot of weight, Dad.

Father: Yeah, I lost about fifteen, twenty pounds.

Frank: [worried] Damn! Are you okay?

[awkward silence]

Father: I really don't know what I could say about what happened to Frank and why he's been on the street for the past twenty years. Because he didn't have to be. I mean, he was a talented sign painter and had at least three years of college and studied photography. He had the support of myself and his brothers. If he had cooperated—but he didn't.

Philippe: It must have been hard for you?

Father: Yeah, you know at first it was. But you see, I was raising another family with three children, and Frank's mother and I had been divorced for a lot of years at that point—ten years I guess. Frank was almost like a stranger in a way when he came to live with us in his senior high school year. His stepfather and his mother had moved to Idaho. . . .

Frank was working for me part time then. In fact, we built this house. He rented a little shack in back with a group of rock musicians in 1970. I guess that's when the drugs started. . . . [smiling uncomfortably]

Frank: [wincing in agreement] About then . . .

Father: Well, or a little before. . . . Then he moved out to live [turning to Frank] with that girlfriend, the beautiful blonde [smiling].

I went over to Frank's new place and saw this table with this giant bowl of cocaine and this big cigar box full of Acapulco Gold. And I said, "Frank, do you know what this does to people?" 'Cause in those days you could go to Haight-Ashbury and see what was happening.

And he says, "Oh, I can handle it."

And I said, "Frank, you *can't* handle it."

But we absolutely couldn't talk, so I finally gave up trying.

But then I bought him a truck and some equipment to go paint signs on subcontract. . . .

Frank: [eagerly] I worked for years doing that. . . .

Father: Well, he worked off and on, except he'd get on these drugs, and . . . [voices overlapping]

Frank: Well, except when I was dealing. . . .

Father: And the jobs wouldn't get done. And I'd lose the accounts. . . .

Frank: Well, it wasn't that bad. . . .

Father: And finally they had a few accidents and totaled the trucks. . . .

Frank: That Yellow Cab hit me. That wasn't my fault! I won the lawsuit. They hit me and screwed up my back for three or four months.

Father: Well, whatever. It's the drugs that screwed your life up, not the cab, not the wreck. . . .

Frank: Well . . . [nodding] absolutely.

Father: He was always getting me in debt, which I couldn't afford. I mean, I had three other kids, small children. Finally I said, "Frank, this is it."

He went his way, and I went mine. And it's been that way for the last fifteen years.

Frank: [quietly] Well . . . yeah.

Father: I try not to see him, and he tries not to see me.

Frank: We still . . . I mean, you know . . . [wincing] I love my dad, but . . . I understand that . . . you know . . . it's not a working relationship. It's kind of tense.

Father: You see, I'm seventy-four years old. I had a quadruple bypass. I got Crohn's disease. I look almost as young as he does! [frowning] I don't know, I can't comprehend it. . . . And I finally gave up trying to because . . .

Frank: [loudly] Tell them how I got started, though.

Father: I don't know how it got started. Oh, you mean your mother and I breaking up. . . .

Frank: No, no, no, no! I'm talking about when I had all that money. The only reason I got into the heroin in the first place was because I was dealing it. . . .

Father: I didn't know if you wanted me to bring that up [pointing to the camera]. But yeah, I remember that.

In the early 1970s he invited me over to his place and there was a drawer full of about a hundred thousand dollars in cash. And I said to Frank, I said, "Well—" [stopping suddenly and turning to Frank]. Are you sure you want me to mention who you were selling to?

Frank: I don't even remember who I sold to.

Father: Well, it was the Jefferson Airplane. And his friend was bringing it in from Vietnam.

I said, "Frank, there's nothing I can tell you that's going to make you do anything differently, but I'll tell you what I would do: I would get rid of this stuff."

Frank: [smiling] No, you wanted me to invest it in real estate!

Father: And what'd he do? He reinvested it in more drugs. And of course his partner got caught and did twenty years in a Bangkok jail. It was terrible.

Frank: But you don't know what you're getting into when you do that sort of thing. I certainly didn't know. I didn't plan on getting hooked on drugs. If I had hindsight now I would never do that again, but I was young and stupid and was having a good time. It was 1970.

I had all the money in the world and I didn't think I was ever gonna work again.

That's how you get started. I started smokin' it, then snortin' it. . . . And then one thing led to another. You don't expect to get hooked on it. You don't expect that to happen to your life. . . .

Father: Well, I certainly would have expected it if I started, so I never did.

Frank: [defiantly] No, you don't expect it. Nobody does! What do you think . . .

Father: [exasperated] What do you mean "nobody does"? Sure you do!

Frank: [loudly] Not one single person out there that's hooked on a drug, or alcohol, or anything expected to be. . . . Nobody does!

Father: [throwing up his arms] I don't know how you can say that, Frank. It's just inconceivable to me that you didn't think that you were going to get hooked on something that you were doing every day.

Frank: What! Do you think somebody's gonna do that deliberately, thinking that they're gonna get hooked? Of course not! I had no idea! I thought I could stop any time I wanted to. I had absolutely [shouting] *no idea that I was ever gonna get hooked on drugs!* None whatsoever!

Father: [gently] Well okay, okay, that's fine. But we just go around in circles on this. [shrugging] What difference does it make? You got hooked and you basically committed suicide. Basically that's what you've done, Frank. Huh?

[Frank shaking his head and clearing his throat as if to say something, but swallowing hard instead]

Father: You've been dying for twenty years.

Frank: I'm not dying. In fact I'm perfectly healthy. I just had my blood test come back. They told me my liver's fine. My cholesterol is excellent. My kidneys are fine. My blood pressure's perfect. Everything's normal. They told me I'm perfectly healthy.

Father: You don't look that great. Maybe you're malnourished. Maybe you're not eating. . . .

What about the drugs and the booze? Are you giving those up?

Frank: Yeah, well . . . I've been working on it. I mean . . . I stopped for a long time. And I kind of fell back again. Uh, I'm trying to stop again. And uh, you know, going to these programs. Y'know, I'm trying to do what I can. But you know, I'm not committing suicide. . . . I guess you could say I'm trying to, but so far I'm not succeeding 'cause I'm healthy.

Father: [turning to Philippe] Frank came to live with us for one year in the seventies when he broke up with his old lady . . . or whatever you call her.

And he kept getting high and fighting with his brothers and sisters. They were only ten and thirteen years old. I'd go around the house, and upstairs in the loft would be little piles of matches where he'd been cooking his—what is it? Coke?

Frank: Dope.

Father: Dope. Whatever. There in the basement, in the bathroom—jeez! So finally, it got to the point where I kicked him out.

Frank: No. I left.

Father: . . . Or he left. Whatever.

Philippe: How did Frank do in school when he was a kid?

Father: I think he did all right. Didn't you, Frank?

Frank: Average.

Father: Average?

Frank: Yeah, average. I had a lot of problems in school. I had fights all the time. Yeah, I got kicked out of that one school and had to go stay with my dad for three or four months. Then I went to another school and had fights there.

Father: [nodding] Had fights there . . . and then he went to Idaho to live with his mom. And had fights there. So they finally sent him to Canada to a special boarding school.

I don't know, [sighing] possibly it's the broken home problem. [addressing Frank] You've had—what? Two half-brothers by your mother and stepfather.

Frank: I always felt like I was on my own. You know, always kind of felt in the middle of everything. . . .

Father: A sense of rejection or something?

Frank: Even when I was a kid, for some reason I always wanted to leave home and go do what I wanted to do. Independent, I guess.

Father: But I hired Frank and gave jobs to all his junkie friends 'cause I was trying to help Frank out. But also because they worked fine. They'd say, "As long as I got the heroin I can function normally. It's when I don't have it and have to look for it and find it and connive to get it, that's when—"

Frank: When you got heroin in you, you can work all day long, like a bastard. But when I was sick I wasn't worth shit!

[turning to Philippe] See, he could never understand that. And I never really wanted to tell him what was going on.

Father: We'd be ten stories up in the air and off Frank would go, sliding down the rope to "get a drink of water" or to "go to the bathroom" or something. It would drive me up the wall.

He went down the wrong rope once, too, and fell five stories. Almost killed himself [laughing].

Frank: I damn near did kill myself that time. Fucked my hands up real good.

Father: Anyway, what can you say? It's water under the bridge.

Frank's father died two years after this interview. According to Frank, in the weeks before his death, his father was in terrible pain and begged him for enough heroin to overdose himself. Two days after the funeral Frank was still dressed in the new clothes given to him by his half-brother. When we visited him in his encampment, he was carefully rolling up the sleeves of his pin-striped button-down shirt to avoid getting it bloody. He had surrounded his sleeping area with religious figurines—a twelve-inch statue of the Virgin Mary and a framed picture of Jesus. Max was consoling him.

> *Frank:* [softly] I miss my dad a whole lot. He was a good man.
>
> [angrily] They fucked up at the hospital. They were giving him the wrong goddamn medication for a long time.
>
> *Max:* [putting his arm around Frank's shoulder] Damn! That's what gets me mad.
>
> *Frank:* [yelling] *It was the insurance company's fault!* His treatment was too expensive. They ought to take the heads off of all those company bureaucrats and shoot 'em. Fuckin' medicine-for-profit!
>
> *Max:* [gently] Frank, you can't bring the man back.
>
> *Frank:* [softly] I wish my father had outlived me. I truly wish it. He was a great man.

Frank received seven thousand dollars as his share of his father's estate. He bought a twenty-five-foot-long 1978 vintage motor home, complete with toilet, shower, kitchen, pantry, closets, and refrigerator. He also rekindled a relationship with his favorite half-brother, the one he used to protect in high school "to make sure he didn't get jumped by two or three of them niggers." The motor home, however, failed to pass California's smog test, making it impossible for Frank to register it legally. Soon the engine stopped running, and within a few months the police had impounded it. He blamed his half-brother for not lending him the money to fix it, and their relationship, once again, broke down. Frank became so despondent that he stopped talking except to ask whether anyone could find an "extra-large" syringe. The Edgewater homeless dismissed this suicide threat as hyperbole. As Max commented, "Where would he get the money to buy enough dope to kill himself, anyway?"

Subsequent conversations with Frank's half-brother revealed that he empathized with Frank's plight and worried about his welfare, but he could not figure out how to help him productively. We gave him a copy of our video of the conversation between Frank and his father, and he called us back shortly after watching it. He wanted us to know that Frank's idealization of his father masked significant childhood trauma. As an example, he told us that, shortly after his father's divorce, on one of Frank's visits home, his father's girlfriend "threw a pot of hot coffee over Frank's head while he was sitting on the floor playing a board game with my dad. She wanted all the attention."

Abusive Fathers

Hank, in contrast to Frank, grew up in a large nuclear household with an exceptionally violent alcoholic father. All of Hank's siblings, four brothers and three sisters, became addicted to heroin. The body language accompanying his accounts of his father's violence evoked his Vietnam vet PTSD stories. Initially we suspected that his dramatic stories of childhood violence might be exaggerations, if not outright confabulations, on par with his Vietnam tales.

Hank: My dad was what you would call a common drunk. The guy worked hard. He did what he had to do in life to support his kids, but he was very stern, and there was no other way but his way. And my mother, she was kind of a . . . moot person. . . .

He broke her fingers one time. And when he done that . . . I said, "Hey Pop. You're a man. I'm a man, right?" I grabbed him by the shirt and I banged him up. "You ever touch my mom again and I'll kill you."

He even pulled a gun out on me. I had to knock the handgun out of his hand, you know. I could have shot him. In fact, I put it against his head and tilt it back and I go, "Hey, I got the power now, don't I? You like the violence?"

"What violence?"

"The violence that you instilled in me."

I'm the youngster, and at that time I was like two hundred eighty pounds. I'm standing six feet. I had a martial arts background. And I'm street savvy.

I never took his manhood pride away from him. He's a French-Polynesian. He would have shot himself before he lost his dignity.

I was scared of my older brother Steve, too. He was extremely violent. He beat me with a baseball bat one time. Beat me with a pipe another time.

He always beat up my sister Barbara. I was tired of seeing her hurt all the time. She was [high-pitched voice], "Hank! Help me! Help me! Help me!"

[speaking slowly] And I did the best I could, but out of fear, out of fear, I wouldn't attack my brother. But one year I did.

Hank's sister Barbara was also a heroin addict and spent six months homeless on Edgewater Boulevard after losing her job of seven years. She had worked as a cook at a private university in San Francisco. She had been sleeping on the couch in the housing project apartment of her PCP-addled eldest daughter. Like Hank, Barbara was affable, generous, and effective in the moral economy. She confirmed Hank's violent, oedipal stories. The brutality reflected in her accounts made us realize that Hank's PTSD was very real—but it had been caused by domestic violence rather than combat in the Vietnam War. For Hank, as for Tina, the street was safer than home during early childhood.

Barbara: [whispering] I remember being picked up by my neck and hung on the wall by my dad. Did Hank tell you about that?

Our father was French-Polynesian, from Papeete. He worked in the shipyards. But see, he wasn't pure, and he came out light-skinned. They do things differently in Tahiti and he went back and forth until he stayed in San Francisco. But he would get drinking and start getting crazy, bust up the house, beat on my mother.

His first wife cheated on him a lot. He caught her in bed with his best friend. And he had this thing about how all women were whores. 'Cause I know when I was young he always called me a whore.

When our little sister Mimi was born, she came out with a lot of dark hair. They had just come home from the hospital, and he picked Mimi up by her legs and threw her, saying to my mother, "This ain't my baby!"

And I thought, "Oh, my God. He's going to kill the baby." And like, I'm crying and begging him, "Please put her down!" And he started in on my mother. And he just ripped off her robe, and my mother's just crying. She had just got out of the hospital. [flat voice] My father was cruel.

[speaking faster] And it bothers me now. I was little and I remember seeing him knock my mom out. I was crying. And then his trip was [deep, friendly voice], "Come here my little whitey-bichette"—that's French for "little deer." "Come sit on my lap." Then he'd give me a Lifesaver. "Oh, your mom will be okay." And I'm looking at my mother, knocked-out on the floor for no reason.

One night, I remember all these lights were coming through the windows. I didn't know what was going on. All of a sudden this big ol' rifle—to me it looked really big—was pointing at me. And I'm against the wall. I'm scared as hell. I don't know what's going on. And all of a sudden someone just grabbed me, blanket and all. And we ran out the door.

It was my aunt who came in and got me out of there. It was my dad who was going to have a shootout with the goddamn police, drunk again. I remember a lot of things. It was horrible.

Philippe: Hank told us your father pulled a gun on him once. Is that true?

Barbara: It's true! My father pulled a gun 'cause Hank was stealing everything out of the house. Everything they worked hard for, Hank was taking it. Because Hank didn't have friends. He bought his friends. He was a loner, and he was a big, fat, pudgy kid . . . real quiet. But he'd do anything for anybody. He's got a heart of gold.

But people take advantage of it. And these idiots would get Hank to go into the house and steal everything. I mean, he stole my mother's diamond necklace. He stole everything they had, projectors, screens, cameras, whatever. But Hank wanted to have friends, and that's what he did to have them.

Philippe: And this is before he had a habit?

Barbara: Oh he had a habit by then. See, my father got really sick of all the thieving. And they got in a fight and my father pulled a gun on him. They were wrestling on the floor. The gun went off. Put a hole in the hallway, and the bullet went right down into the garage.

My mother screaming, "Stop! Stop!" But she loved my father, no matter what. My mother had a real tough life. She'd tell me stories. When she was a kid in Salem, New Jersey, they used to be starving. She would go to a watermelon patch and steal the watermelons out of the neighbor's yard.

She was into God and sent us all to Sunday school—Simpson Bible College on Silver Avenue, where the L train stops. I think it's some Chinese school now.

Philippe: Did Hank ever try to defend your mother when your father beat her?

Barbara: Oh hell yeah. I mean, everyone would. Hank would jump on his back, just like a little puppy dog up there on his back. [laughing nervously] "Dad, leave mom alone!"

And my brother Steve used to beat me up all the time. All he seen was my father whip on a woman. So that's what guys are supposed to do.

But Hank tried to protect me. We used to run into the bathroom to hide from Steve. And we're standing against the door blocking it and all of a sudden here comes a knife right through the door just between us.

All of us got hooked up on drugs. You know, it's really a shame. . . . My brothers blame the old son-of-a-bitch, our father, for their life being all fucked up. And my brother Hank, he still don't know how to let it go.

Our father stopped beating us when he got old and couldn't do it no more. He got real old and my mother could have floored his ass. But she still loved him, no matter what.

What a torture it is in his head, to look at us older now and we're all fucked up. [looking up at the sky] Think about it, old man! Think about why it's like this.

Hank's and Barbara's addiction to heroin and their homelessness could be analyzed in exclusively psychodynamic terms as the socio-pathological aberration of two victimized individuals. Barbara's and Hank's references to skin color, immigration, cultural dislocation, sexual jealousy, masculinity, poverty, and religious faith reveal that even the most extreme forms of interpersonal abuse are shaped by ideological and cultural forces within nuclear families.

We can get any job we want as long as we put our minds to it! —*Hank*

The city of San Francisco lost twelve thousand manufacturing jobs between 1962 and 1972, the years when most of the Edgewater homeless were adolescents (Arthur D. Little Inc. 1975). The Edgewater Boulevard corridor, which had provided employment for most of the residents in the neighborhood up the hill, was particularly hard hit. Most of San Francisco's largest factories were located off Edgewater. It was also the hub for the region's transportation, communications, and utility sectors, including the Southern Pacific railroad and, most important, the shipyards. Throughout the mid-1950s, the Hunters Point navy shipyard was the engine of heavy industry in San Francisco, with eighty-five hundred employees (Military Analysis Network 1998); but in 1974 it closed down. Fifteen years later, the abandoned shipyard was declared toxic and designated a federal Superfund site. The land surrounding the housing projects off Edgewater Boulevard was also found to be environmentally contaminated—a result of decades of unregulated dumping by the area's now-vanished heavy manufacturing sector.

In 1975, when most of the homeless in our scene were in their late teens and early twenties (crucial ages for integration into the manual labor force), a study commissioned by the city of San Francisco noted that the "[Edgewater] corridor" was in a "depressed state." The authors projected the loss of another three thousand jobs by the year 2000, warning that "with modern warehousing techniques there is likely to be relatively little employment except in clerical jobs" (Arthur D. Little Inc. 1975:IV–100, IV–103, IV–107).

Economists have shown statistically that high rents, high levels of income inequality, and low rental vacancy rates are the three variables most consistently associated with elevated levels of homelessness in any given city (Quigley et al. 2001; U.S. Bureau of the Census 2001). From the 1990s through the 2000s, San Francisco County ranked number one in the nation with respect to *all* these variables and, predictably, its homeless population burgeoned. In polls, residents consistently declared that homelessness was their city's most serious problem (National Low Income Housing Coalition 2006; *San Francisco Chronicle* 1999, September 21; see also Marcus 2005, which describes the contrast with New York City).

San Francisco's housing problems were part of a national trend in rising income inequality and real estate speculation that was exacerbated by dramatic reductions in the federal budget for subsidized housing. President Richard Nixon initiated these cuts in the 1970s, and President Ronald Reagan accelerated them in the 1980s. During his first year in office, Reagan halved the federal budget for public housing and for section 8 subsidies (Bipartisan Millennial Housing Commission 2002; Sahlins 1987; Sternlieb and Listokin 1987). He did not, however, reduce federal support for freeways, home mortgages, or the generous tax rebates and monetarist policies that promote suburban sprawl and subsidize suburban lifestyles for the middle classes and the wealthy to the detriment of inner cities (Davis 1990; Sahlins 1987; Self 2005). By the middle of Reagan's tenure, in 1985, there was a shortfall of 3.3 million low-cost rental units across the country, compared to a former surplus of 300,000 in 1977. In 1994, the year we began our fieldwork, eight hundred thousand families were officially wait-listed for the nation's 1.3 million existing public housing apartments (Atlas and Dreier 1994).

Consistent with the consolidation of neoliberalism in the United States, most forms of federal assistance to local governments that funded social programs for the poor—such as job training, legal services, public transit, and Community Development Block Grants— were also reduced. By the last year of Reagan's presidency, in 1988, the federal government was funding only 6 percent of big-city budgets, down from 22 percent in 1980 (Dreier 2004a). Free market forces further depleted the low-income rental housing stock in expensive cities like San Francisco, where real estate speculators aggressively gentrified poor neighborhoods. SRO hotel units, where the poorest of the poor have historically lived, were especially devastated. In 1999 only 19,618 units remained of the 33,000 low-income residential hotel units that had been available in San Francisco in 1975 (Groth 1994:2, 9; Hoenigman and SPUR Homelessness Task Force 2002:15, fig. 11).

Obsolete Manual Workers

The U.S. government's retreat from the provision of services coincided with a major structural transformation in the economy as a result of globalization. The industries that had formerly employed the families of the Edgewater homeless disappeared from the Bay Area, effectively transforming San Francisco into a pressure cooker for producing lumpenized social sectors. The parents and grandparents of the Edgewater homeless, who had worked in shipyards, steel mills, and smelters and on the docks, became a generation of obsolete laborers. For example, Sonny's father was laid off from the shipyards in his forties and was forced to work as a low-paid janitor for the rest of his life. Vernon's father, who had immigrated with his entire family from Orange, Texas, "the last town before Louisiana, where everybody worked in the sugar mill and no one ever had no money," worked as a longshoreman in San Francisco until he was displaced by labor-saving containerized shipping technology. At the end of his life, he found work as a cement mason.

Al's grandfather worked at Bethlehem Steel, the Bay Area's largest steel producer, which, in its heyday, supplied the metal to build the Golden Gate Bridge—over one hundred thousand tons. The plant where Al's grandfather worked, just off Edgewater Boulevard, furnished material for the hulls of dozens of U.S. Navy ships. Nicknamed Gunboat, Al's grandfather boxed for the union team against Jack Dempsey in the 1930s and subsequently became the local union's vice president. A decade later, Carter's father migrated to California from rural Louisiana and also sought work in the steel industry. He remained one step removed from its unionized labor force, finding employment only as a grinder with a company that subcontracted with Bethlehem Steel. In 1970, facing stiff competition from smaller, nonunion producers located overseas, Bethlehem lost a crucial bid to produce the steel for New York City's World Trade Center Towers. Six years later, in a class struggle scenario typical of global industrial restructuring, Bethlehem Steel closed its San Francisco factory in order to punish its union for refusing to accept a 10 percent pay cut.

Frank's father was an independent contractor painting billboards and signs. By the late 1980s, sign painting as a skilled trade was being eclipsed by computer-driven technology, including digital printing. Frank's father was able to retire and supplement his income as a construction contractor during California's residential real estate boom. Frank's half-brothers also successfully retooled themselves: one became an art gallery owner; the other brokered leases for billboard advertising space and was eventually bought out by media giant Viacom for $2.1 million, allowing him to retire in his late thirties.

The Edgewater homeless were unable to adapt to the economic metamorphosis of the 1970s and 1980s. The structural adjustments caused by globalization were rendered even more disruptive by the historical shift in the U.S. mode of governance away from rehabilitative social service provision toward punitive containment. As noted in the introduction, rapid transformations in the mode of production produce the residual and problematic class category of the lumpen, a social sector vituperatively dismissed by Marx and Engels as "this scum of depraved elements from all classes" (Engels [1870] 2000:xii). Economically obsolete, members of the lumpen become unable or unwilling to engage in disciplined productive labor. They do not even form part of what Marx called "the reserve army of the unemployed" that factory owners draw upon to undermine unions and lower wages.

Only two of the homeless in our scene were old enough to have worked in the former industrial economy that had employed most of their parents:

Reggie: I worked at the shipyard. It was union. I welded. But I didn't like it. There were too many fires, and you had to have a tracer when you're hanging and a guy who follows you everywhere.

I fell a whole deck. *Boom!* My teeth was everywhere. They gave me four months of workers' comp. But I didn't go back afterwards.

Hank had the longest history of legal employment. In fact, his relationship to the labor market began prematurely when he was still in elementary school. According to Hank's sister Barbara, the coercive child labor arrangement imposed on her brothers was connected to the transitional kinship obligations engendered by the migration patterns of their father's extended family, combined with his worsening alcoholism.

Barbara: See, the problem was my uncle stayed in Tahiti, leaving his kids in San Francisco. So my father felt obligated to help raise my uncle's boys, because my father's brother had married my mother's mother, my grandmother—they do that in Tahiti.

My father took more to them than his own boys. He had a machine shop, ABC Engineering, over a shop in Oakland, and all my brothers had to work there. But my father let my uncle's boys go to school and gave them money. Meanwhile, the sad part was that his real sons had to work in the shop for nothing until real late and missed a lot of school. They were lucky to get five or ten bucks at the end of the week—he just beat them instead.

Friends and distant cousins would get my father drunk and he'd give you anything you wanted. And my brothers would have to try to run the shop and get the work out. Finally my father lost the shop and started drinking, just drinking.

Even if Hank's father had not been a violent drunk, he and his boys would have lost their business because nearly all the foundries and machine shops producing for industrial markets disappeared from the Bay Area during the last quarter of the twentieth century. In his mid-twenties during the late 1970s, Hank found work as a welder in a foundry. We visited his last employer, who had relocated from San Francisco to a modest warehouse on the Oakland waterfront. Despite the company's proud slogan, "Phoenix Iron Works Castings Since 1901," there was no sign of activity. The semi-retired owner was dressed in army fatigues, and his cramped office was decorated with hunting trophies. He explained, "We don't do foundry work here anymore. We just can't compete with Third World imports. No one can. Now we broker to specialty markets for Hong Kong producers." When we asked whether Hank had been a good worker, he chuckled, "He was a friendly guy, but he wasn't a company man."

Most of the Edgewater homeless were too young to have had access to the industrial work force. Instead, they spent their lives cycling in and out of marginal manual labor. At best, they worked in warehouses and in construction-related trades that were highly susceptible to economic fluctuations. Sal, for example, was an on-call loader at a unionized warehousing firm, "until they went belly-up, shutting and locking the doors without warning in 1992." He had been replaced by labor-saving technology. "When I joined the Teamsters Union," he noted, "there were nine thousand of us in San Francisco. Now there's less than eight hundred fifty." Petey also worked as a laborer in a warehouse and he too was "downsized":

> Me and my dad and my brother used to work at the same place. I was a forklift driver. My father was a truck driver and my brother, he was also a forklift driver. Things got tough and I ended up getting laid off. They call it "low man on the totem pole." I ended up being the last one hired, the first one laid off—not fired. So I collected unemployment for about two years. I was getting three hundred fifty dollars every two weeks. Then I started throwing newspapers for three cents apiece. That's good money—thirty dollars for a thousand.

Like Petey, Victor was laid off after working six years as a forklift driver at a corrugated cardboard box factory in South San Francisco. Felix passed through a half dozen delivery and service jobs: he drove a truck for the *San Francisco Chronicle* newspaper, delivered bread for the Parisian Bakery, and worked as a bellhop in a luxury hotel downtown.

Tina's most stable job had been as a home healthcare attendant:

> I was twenty-seven. I liked it. I got my license. I used to have my own car. You take your patients into your heart, but you not supposed to because they die on you. A couple of them died on me and I just had to stop getting attached to them. I really found out what my job description was talkin' about, so I quit.

Spider-Bite Lou was a licensed plumber. Like Ben, he had served in the Merchant Marine during the Vietnam War. Max bartended for his father in the Italian North Beach neighborhood of San Francisco until they lost the lease when tourism and gentrification drove up the rents. Carter had been employed at Fort Ord, a military base that closed in 1994. He worked as a chef, a hospital orderly, and a firefighter and also did asbestos removal. "I lost my army jobs just being young and irresponsible. If I would of knew what I know now, just a little bit, I would have stayed in the military; best job I ever had. It was 'career conditional' to where I coulda bought a house, credit union, everything." When we first met Carter, he was still on the margins of the legal labor force, working as a parking attendant at a luxury car dealership in downtown San Francisco.

Ben and Frank both worked briefly as carpenters for high-tech firms in Silicon Valley before the dot-com boom of the late 1990s. They reminisced about the electric-eye alarms that protected restricted research areas and monitored their movements. They laughed at the memory of the labor-saving robots being tested in those years: "one delivered shit from floor to floor and another vacuumed the rug."

By the time the Bay Area's dot-com and biotech sectors were in full swing in 1998 and 1999, the Edgewater homeless were too marginal to obtain stable employment. Their subjectivities had long since shifted from being rebellious young members of the disappearing industrial working class, the artisanal contractor economy, and the growing, but unstable, low-wage service sector to being middle-aged outlaw or outcast dopefiends. They did benefit marginally, however, from the trickle-down effects of the economic boom. Construction sites mushroomed throughout the city, and Carter's opportunities for "wood licks" multiplied. Vernon began obtaining steadier, off-the-record house painting gigs from overbooked contractors. All of the whites, as well as Felix, found occasional day jobs cleaning yards, repairing fences, and performing other manual tasks, usually for former friends, acquaintances, and neighbors in the homeowning neighborhood up the hill. Felix lasted for six months as a taxi driver until an elderly woman who lived around the corner from him saw him nodding in his cab and reported him to management.

Ben was the only person on Edgewater Boulevard who managed to gain access to unionized employment, but it was only because his mother continued to pay his dues regularly to the International Union of Painters and Allied Trades. As a level 3 journeyman, he earned fifty-five dollars an hour to hang from the bottom of the San Francisco Bay Bridge and strip asbestos. Hoping that this steady employment would stabilize her son, Ben's mother paid for him to receive methadone maintenance from a for-profit clinic. Unfortunately, Ben enjoyed the speedball effect of boosting the sedative effects of methadone with the stimulus of cocaine, and he increased his crack consumption dramatically (for a discussion of the dopamine-stimulating effects of cocaine on heroin and on methadone in the brain, see Martin et al. 2007; Leri et al. 2007). Soon he was smoking crack every day with Carter and Tina on his way to work, right after receiving his daily dose at the methadone clinic. He also stopped by at the end of the day as he headed home. During one of his after-work crack visits, still dressed in splattered painter's pants and a flannel shirt, he proudly untangled a pile of cables from the trunk of his car to demonstrate to us how he chained himself to the underside of the Bay Bridge for his eight-hour "asbestos abatement" shifts.

Ben was eventually thrown out of the methadone program for "giving a dirty urine" containing cocaine during one of the clinic's random surveillance tests. He was given forty-eight hours to appeal his case and had to request permission to leave work early to file for reinstatement. The methadone clinic readmitted him, but when his job supervisor discovered that Ben was in a drug treatment program, he immediately fired him. The union also sanctioned Ben: "There's plenty of work, but they now see me as a fuck-up and call me last."

He scrambled to find low-budget painting jobs along Edgewater Boulevard, at only a fraction of his former union wage. The manager of the local Pizza Hut hired him to clean up an old paint spill on the parking lot pavement. Kneeling on the ground, scrubbing the cement with a wire brush, Ben held up his hands to show us the skin peeling back from his cracked and bleeding cuticles. "Hell of a way to earn twenty dollars!" He was most irritated by the manager's offer of free food as a bonus: "All they're doing is paying me with pizza. I don't wanna see another pizza. I'm pizza'd out." He appreciated, however, a more substantial fringe benefit of this poorly paid side job: the freedom to take breaks any time he wanted to smoke crack and drink malt liquor.

The classically lumpen relationship of the Edgewater homeless to the organized working class was exemplified when a member of the ethnographic team overheard Felix arguing with Frank about who deserved the fifty-dollar cash payment they had just received for throwing cow brains and blood over the door of the Boilermakers Union hall downtown. "Fuck you. It's mine. I threw the shit. You were too afraid." (See Marx's outrage over the betrayal of the Paris Commune in 1851 by members of "the rabble" who sold their violent services to Bonaparte's military, which Marx describes as the "swamp flower of the peasant lumpen proletariat . . . a drunken soldiery . . . bought with whiskey and sausages" [(1852) 1963:130, 123].)

Patron-Client Relations in the Legal Economy

By the time we began our fieldwork in 1994, Edgewater Boulevard was already in an advanced state of decay. The few local, family-run businesses that still survived on this postindustrial corridor were losing out to suburban-based discount chains and fast-food restaurants. Large lots had been left vacant for over ten years by speculators who were lobbying the city to rezone the area for a shopping mall.

The owners of the remaining small businesses interacted closely with the homeless on the boulevard. Some chased the homeless away whenever they caught them loitering on their sidewalks. Most, however, developed patron-client relationships with their favorite individuals and intermittently hired them for odd jobs. Business owners came to know details of the life histories of the homeless—their family problems, interpersonal feuds, run-ins with the law, and patterns of drug binging. Some business owners offered logistical and moral support. For example, Macon, the owner of a construction supply depot, let several of the Edgewater homeless use his address for receiving welfare checks. He also paid out cash advances that could be reimbursed on a piecework basis by shoveling sand into the sandbags he sold at his depot. During the months when Hogan was pretending to be HIV positive, Macon paid for his enrollment in a drug treatment program. (Hogan dropped out after a week.) Chico's Tunes, a car stereo installation shop, provided mail services and relayed messages from relatives for Tina and Carter. Chico also fenced stolen items, which he sent to his family members in Honduras. Some of the friendlier managers of the fast-food restaurants allowed the Edgewater homeless to use their restrooms; but others called the police on them when they saw them panhandling in their parking lots.

The homeless competed aggressively for the limited number of odd jobs offered by local business owners. Andy, a mover who lived up the hill, was the local employer most favored by the men in our network. He was eighty years old and owned a fourteen-foot van. He had no business license, but advertised his moving services in the free neighborhood weekly paper. Andy paid well by Edgewater Boulevard standards, forty dollars for an average day of labor and as much as sixty dollars for heavy ones. He also accommodated drug use and alcohol consumption. His daughter was a recovered heroin addict, and he hired Hank preferentially because she had been one of Hank's running partners "back in the days." Unfortunately, Andy rarely managed to line up more than a few jobs each month, and it was not unusual for several weeks to pass with no opportunities.

Everyone jockeyed jealously to take Hank's place, and so, to Andy's benefit, Hank pushed himself to extremes to maintain his privileged access to the irregular moving jobs. One late afternoon, Jeff found Hank sitting stiffly in a bus stop shelter pressing his lower back against the glass as if it were an electric heating pad. He had been "carrying pianos for Andy" for the past two days and his lower back was aching. "O-o-h, that warm sun feels good on my back. I just wasn't in any kind of shape to work for Andy this morning but I had to go. If I don't go, how am I goin' to get my money?"

Andy recruited his day laborers by honking his car horn from the curb nearest the largest homeless encampment. Sometimes in the middle of the night, loud honking or backfiring on Edgewater Boulevard would startle Hank out of his sleep. Convinced he was about to miss a rendezvous with Andy, he would throw off his blankets, jump to his feet, and sprint down the highway embankment, screaming, "I'm coming, I'm coming." When his campmates taunted him by shouting the wartime mortar round alert "Incoming!," he would snap out of his altered state, embarrassed by their mockery of his claims to Vietnam shellshock.

Hank's "flashbacks" in pursuit of legal employment, forty years after the bankruptcy of his father's machine shop and twenty-five years after he had been laid off from the foundry (his last well-paid job), reveal the overlapping dimensions of abuse that often contribute to PTSD-like symptoms among the homeless. In Hank's case, this vulnerability is especially "overdetermined" by a mix of political-economic and psycho-affective forces (for classic discussions of overdetermination in marxist theory and in psychoanalysis, see Althusser 1966 and Freud [1900] 1965). These forces include child labor and domestic violence associated with parental dislocation and alcoholism; the disappearance of San Francisco's industrial economy in the post–World War II era; and, of course, the routine and ongoing interpersonal violence of survival on the street—all brought to a head by his extreme dependence on a fly-by-night employer to stave off heroin withdrawal symptoms. Those who employed the homeless invariably believed that they were doing them a favor by offering them work. In fact, these business owners usually paid homeless workers substantially less than they would have had to pay more stable employees, including undocumented Latino day laborers, for the same jobs.

Sammy, at the Crow's Nest liquor store, was particularly adroit at manipulating the moral economy of heroin sharing for his own profit. For an eight-month stretch, he managed to persuade Felix to work for him for ten dollars a day, seven days a week, by "doing Felix the favor" of paying Frank an additional ten dollars a day as "rent" so that Felix could sleep on the floor of Frank's van. Astutely, Sammy insisted on handing that daily rent payment directly to Frank at 7:00 A.M. every morning to ensure that Felix would come to work before the arrival of the beer delivery trucks, free from heroin withdrawal symptoms. Sammy knew that because of this arrangement Frank would be obligated to treat Felix to a morning "wake-up" shot in anticipation of the guaranteed 7:00 A.M. rent payment. Felix was embarrassed at earning the equivalent of two dollars per hour in such a dependent manner and tried to save face by telling us, "It's okay, Sammy also treats me to free cigarettes and beer."

Macon, at the construction supply depot, also engaged in a profitable strategy to maximize the productivity and obedience of physically addicted indigent laborers. Every Monday for almost a full year he "treated" Max and Frank to breakfast at a local diner and gave them enough cash to buy one bag of heroin. Frank and Max enjoyed Macon's Monday breakfasts and considered him to be a generous and thoughtful patron. Heroin withdrawal and hunger are often acute for the homeless on Monday mornings because most businesses have been closed for thirty-six hours, emptying the streets of pedestrian traffic. This creates a long stretch of time with few opportunities to beg, borrow, steal, or work. Macon told us that as a Catholic and a recovered alcoholic who had binged on cocaine during the 1980s he felt a "sense of duty to help the homeless." For several months, Frank and Max faithfully knocked on his door early Monday mornings and eagerly offered to shovel as many (or as few) sandbags as he might need that day. Macon sometimes told them to check back later in the afternoon if sales the previous day had been slow. Market demand for sandbags fluctuates during the rainy season depending on flooding conditions. By supplementing his minimal piece-rate payment system with one free breakfast and a ten-dollar tip, Macon was able to maintain adequate inventory without having to pay extra workers to stand by idly. Convinced that he was in spiritual "solidarity with the poor" and empathizing with the vulnerability of addiction, Macon followed just-in-time production principles, and his business obtained cheap, flexible, and grateful laborers.

Offering employment to the lowest bidder has its costs, however. Macon had to tolerate erratic conduct at his worksite. One busy December, when he hired Hank to shovel extra sandbags, Macon caught him in the main office using the coffeemaker to steam the smog inspection sticker off a customer's license plate. He fired Hank on the spot, and two weeks later Hank's van was towed for not having a California smog certificate. Spider-Bite Lou immediately replaced Hank as a steady shoveler, but halfway through the rainy season the police arrested him on an outstanding warrant.

Over the years, Frank, Max, and Felix proved to be Macon's most stable laborers, despite their often problematic behaviors. Macon paid them eighteen dollars to shovel forty seventy-five-pound sandbags. It was not uncommon for them to take most of the day to complete the task.

Jeff's Fieldnotes

As he shovels, Felix complains about "doin' all the work." Max, dressed in the bright yellow slicker overalls and rubber boots Macon provides to his homeless workers, is supposed to be helping him, but instead he is sitting hunched in the back of the lot on a pile of antique bricks, having thrown out his lower back this morning filling the first sandbag. He is also having trouble standing because of sores on his feet. The heavy rains of the past week have swollen his size 13 feet, making his toes chafe in his one-size-too-small sneakers. The sores on his toes are bright red and they look, as he says, "like cancers."

Frank walks into the depot, flicking his wrist at Felix to flash the glass stem of a new crack pipe. Felix immediately drops his shovel and motions for Frank to follow him to the back of the supply shed. They crouch behind a stack of concrete and mortar sacks and Frank dumps the full ten dollars' worth of crack on top of a bag of Play Sand (used for children's sandboxes). As Frank loads the pipe, Felix reminds him that he had treated Frank to a big bag of dope earlier that morning, "so give me more than half."

There is no front wall to the shed, so anyone walking by—a customer, another worker, or the boss—could easily catch us. Felix crouches lower to light the crack pipe. He cannot see over the bags, however, and when he hears footsteps outside, he jumps up, lowering the pipe to his side. Without skipping a beat, he points to the west, announcing in a clear, friendly voice as if I were a lost customer asking for directions, "…and the Golden Gate Bridge is over there!" I lower my camera to my hip and struggle to keep a straight face so as not to attract more attention to us.

Seconds later, Felix crouches back down, takes another hit of crack, swivels on his feet to peer at an imaginary noise, inhales again, and swivels to peer out again. He repeats this frantic sequence three times in rapid succession, becoming increasingly agitated with each inhalation. Twice he interrupts his smoking to launch into another directions-giving alibi, even though I hear no footsteps anywhere outside. He is now in full-blown crack-induced paranoia and is hearing all kinds of imaginary noises. He launches into a brand-new alibi in an especially loud voice: "Jeff, can you give me a ride downtown to the GA [General Assistance] office?" While talking, he motions dramatically for Frank and me to stay still. He falls silent for ten long seconds to listen before squatting back down to smoke more crack.

Frank angrily demands the pipe, but just as he is loading it, Felix runs out of the shed into the main part of the lot shouting, "Be quick, quick! Macon wants us out of here." Cursing, Frank starts to follow him out, but Felix runs back inside the shed. He is sweating profusely, droplets falling from his forehead. I ask if he is okay. He holds up his finger for me to be quiet, staring fixedly at the ground, trying to settle himself down.

Binging on crack often gives Felix bilious burps. He has to concentrate on holding them down so that he does not vomit. I start to worry that Felix might be having a heart attack or a seizure and I rehearse the procedure for CPR in my head. Felix reassures me that "it's just a bit of indigestion." When his bout of indigestion finally passes, he gnashes his teeth, already crashing from his crack rush. Meanwhile Frank has smoked up his portion and also starts tweaking in his distinct manner—pacing and muttering curses.

Following one of the many Caltrans offensives to rid highway embankments of homeless encampments, Frank and Max began to take refuge at night from the rain in Macon's supply shed. They would wait for the sun to set before climbing the barbed-wire fence to lay their blankets out on the bags of cement. Each morning before the first delivery truck arrived at 5:30 A.M., they stashed their blankets under piles of construction materials and climbed back over the fence to report early to work via the front gate. They were eventually caught. Jeff came upon them that evening, huddled on a discarded sofa under a makeshift tarp in the alley behind the corner store.

Max: We overslept today! Macon walked in to meet the delivery truck and we're asleep right there on the cement bags. "Whoa!"

Frank: Man, it was embarrassing! We started to pack up quickly to leave but Macon said, "Since you guys are already here you might as well get right to work."

Through a "don't-ask-don't-tell" compromise with their boss, Max and Frank managed to continue sleeping discreetly in the shed for three more months. The arrangement worked well until Frank began selling ten-dollar bags of heroin from the premises. Frank's heroin was of such good quality that Sal's customers began shifting over to him. Dopesick addicts would call out for heroin from the other side of the barbed-wire fence at all hours. With this sudden influx of heroin income, Frank stopped shoveling and Max's back fell apart under the strain of the solo workload. Spider-Bite Lou, newly released from jail, jumped at the opportunity to replace Max and Frank. Macon agreed to hire him and evicted Max and Frank for being "fire hazards," pointing to the candle wax on the bags of cement in the storage shed where they slept. Unshaven, scraggly-haired, and shuffling on his still swollen and infected feet, Max went back to "flying a lame sign" on the traffic island, an income-generating strategy that shamed him. He groaned: "I hate it out here. I just gotta find a job." He was not angry at Macon for evicting and firing him. Instead, he blamed Spider-Bite Lou for stealing his job by "badmouthing me to the boss."

During this period, Frank painted a storefront sign for the owner of a printing press up the hill, whose son had died of a heroin overdose in the 1970s. The man became Frank's new patron, lending him seven hundred dollars to buy a pickup truck with a camper shell from a friend of Jeff's, who was a substance abuse counselor and a former heroin injector himself. Frank agreed to pay off the loan by cleaning the printing presses once a week.

Frank's heroin supplier proved steadier than expected, and Frank was able to hire Max to sell for him. He forced Max to stand on the sidewalk some ten yards away from his pickup at all times, and, to further minimize his own risk of arrest, he forbade Max from sleeping in his "new camper." This prompted so much criticism from everyone on the boulevard that Frank relented, although he did not allow Max to enter the vehicle during daylight hours in case the police were monitoring him.

Max received one free bag of heroin for every ten he sold. He did not complain because the bags he sold were cheap at ten dollars and the quality was good. Sales were brisk and Max worked all day long, "jacking up" the size of his habit. Hunger became his main problem, because he no longer took time out to panhandle in the McDonald's parking lot, soliciting gifts of burgers and fries with his old sign, WILL WORK FOR FOOD GOD BLESS. Frank smoked up in crack the profits from Max's brisk heroin sales. On binges Frank would often lose track of how much had been sold and accuse Max of stealing. Frank's relationship with the printing shop owner also deteriorated, and he gave up trying to work off his remaining five-hundred-dollar debt for the camper shell and the pickup.

Despite repeated police crackdowns, Frank stayed in business for over two years. Max, his eyesight poor, his feet always aching, and his shoulders increasingly stooped, was a surprisingly effective salesman. Each dawn before leaving the camper, he would fill his mouth with ten bags of heroin packed in uninflated balloons. When a customer walked by him, Max would discreetly spit one of the balloons into his palm and shake hands with the passerby, exchanging heroin for money in one fluid motion. On a Friday afternoon, three police officers pounced on Max from behind and probed his mouth and under his tongue. Max had only one bag of heroin left at the time and managed to spit it out before being seized and searched. The officers combed the gutter and found the tiny packet in its bright red balloon. They then ripped apart Frank's camper, but found only a few old syringes. At the time, the local police precinct was no longer instructing officers to arrest the homeless for possession of needles, so they left Frank alone when he pleaded, "Ah, come on! Can't you see I'm just an old-time dopefiend? I don't do nobody no harm. I work paintin' signs."

The judge released Max from jail three days after his arrest, because possession of one ten-dollar bag of heroin, an eighth of a gram, is not sufficient evidence to prove intent to sell. Three days in the county jail's holding pen, however, condemned Max to full-blown opiate withdrawal symptoms. Immediately upon his release, he returned to selling on Edgewater Boulevard at the same spot. He was scared of being rearrested, but he was too dopesick not to take the risk.

De Facto Apartheid in the Day Labor Market

The African-Americans tended to be more openly oppositional than the whites to the business owners along Edgewater Boulevard, who in turn often referred to them as "goddamn niggers." Relations with the Yemeni and Palestinian storekeepers were especially antagonistic. The African-Americans routinely called them "motherfuckin' A-rabs" and were frequently 86'ed for shoplifting, badgering customers for change, demanding free matches, or cursing over high prices. The whites adopted more subservient, dependent attitudes toward the storekeepers and were sometimes rewarded with odd jobs such as sweeping the sidewalk or stocking new deliveries. Some of the whites were also periodically 86'ed, but usually it was for being malodorous rather than for being oppositional. Nevertheless, out of earshot, they too engaged in xenophobic rants:

> *Frank:* These fuckin' A-rabs don't know how to spend American money. They'll give you twenty dollars for a whole day's work if you're lucky.
>
> *Spider-Bite Lou:* All A-rabs are the same. They're worse than the Chinese. They think you're just a junkie—just shit! "Just give the man a Cisco; he'll do anything for it."

During our twelve years on Edgewater Boulevard, only two local businesses hired African-Americans from our social network, and they did so only at the height of California's dot-com boom, when no whites were available. Sammy, at the Crow's Nest liquor store, gave Carter "a chance" when Felix, his former steady worker, left to drive a taxi for six months. It was during the period when Frank and Max were selling heroin and when Andy, the mover, had enough jobs each week to keep Hank, Petey, and even Al busy most days. Ben was working at his unionized asbestos removal job under the Bay Bridge, and Spider-Bite Lou was shoveling sand at Macon's.

After three weeks, Sammy confronted Carter and accused him of stealing bottles of vodka. In response, Carter quit the job in self-righteous outrage. Despite vehemently condemning "thieving niggers" when he told us this story, Sammy continued to commission large orders of stolen wood from Carter. He was remodeling his home and also placing special orders for discount wood for neighbors and cousins. With Sammy's "help," consequently, Carter reentered the illegal economy full time and rekindled his outlaw romance with Tina.

Carter: They got a gang of two-by-fours, two-by-sixes, four-by-fours, two-by-twelves out by where they're [earthquake] retrofitting under the freeway. And after about four o'clock or four-thirty ain't nobody back there. The workers kick off early. And with all the busy traffic and people coming and going, we just put on one of their construction hats, an orange one and a white one, and their reflector jackets, and we have a field day.

Tina: Yup, we put five of them six-by-twelves all up onto two carts. Bust our butts!

Carter: Discount Grocery's shopping carts are the best ones for that because they're all steel. . . .

Tina: We had one cart in the front and one in the back. I was pushin' it. But then Mr. Big-shot-pocketful-of-money didn't want to just issue me money when he got paid.

Carter: [angrily] Because Sammy backed out of his full order! Son-of-a-bitch only paid five cents a foot because he said the wood was damaged. It ain't no money, and I didn't take them penitentiary chances on motherfuckin' state property just for that! Can't be expecting to get top-notch, top-grade motherfuckin' shit all the goddamn time. It don't be that way.

But it's okay because he set me up with another contractor who puts in bigger orders, and Sammy lets me store the wood behind his shop now.

Tina: Shit! Crow's Nest Sammy even make Carter pay him to store his wood there.

The only other local business to hire the homeless African-Americans on Edgewater Boulevard was a Christmas tree seller who arrived each year to set up shop on the first Friday after Thanksgiving in the empty lot across from the A&C corner store. He paid just above minimum wage but offered steady work for ten hours a day, plus tips—all tax-free cash. More than half his workers were heroin injectors, and he accommodated their multiple lapses and petty rip-offs. This enabled him to tap into an inexpensive, just-in-time, seasonal labor force in order to sell several thousand trees during the four-week Christmas rush. The Edgewater homeless eagerly anticipated this opportunity for full-time work, even though few lasted for the entire month. Those who did gained weight and improved their relationships with the surrounding businesses on the boulevard.

Of all the homeless in our scene, Felix worked hardest and most consistently at the lot: "It's fucking good money, slingin' those trees, and it pumps you up." This "worthy worker" persona allowed Felix to fleetingly reassert his Latino second-generation immigrant identity during the Christmas season. He would once again start referring to the "lame whites" and the "scandalous niggers." He also asserted his wannabe-legal, Latino working-class identity by frequently referring to losing his taxi job "last year, when that old lady squealed on me," many years after the fact. While Felix worked at the tree lot, the Mexican owner of the taqueria next to the A&C corner store, who just a few weeks earlier would have called the police on him for panhandling in front of her door, began treating him to an extra large bowl of her "soup of the day" before the start of his shift. Felix's temporarily rehabilitated worker status during the Christmas season energized him and enabled him to gain weight, but it also exacerbated his unsanitary injection practices. His heroin supplier began fronting him a half dozen extra ten-dollar bags every morning to resell to co-workers from other neighborhoods. This allowed Felix to parlay free tastes from his new, outsider customers.

Jeff's Fieldnotes

In a hurry on his mid-afternoon fifteen-minute break, Felix motions for me to accompany him into the abandoned shack in the alley behind the corner store. "Watch my back, Jeff."

The floor of the shack is wet and slimy. Feces, soiled clothes, bottles of urine, and used cookers are scattered about. Two syringes are stuck in the wall, mimicking coat hooks. Felix is furious about the filth. Yesterday he walked in on Lou defecating in the corner. "There's no excuse for that kind of behavior. Anyone can go right over to the McDonald's and use the bathroom."

I can tell he is feeling the preliminary symptoms of dopesickness. He is yawning heavily, and his nose is dripping. He clears each of his nostrils onto the ground, apologizing for being so messy. Steady wages have jacked up Felix's habit, and he is already worried because this steady work ends in two weeks.

Sitting on an overturned computer monitor, Felix searches for a cooker among the debris. "Shit! There's no water!" he mumbles, and kicks an overturned plastic bottle across the floor. He proceeds to poke his fingers, black from Christmas tree sap and mud, into each cooker to locate leftover water. Finally something inside one of the bottle-cap cookers jiggles with what looks for a second like jelly. It is water. He quickly dumps a full bag of heroin into the cooker and smiles as it splashes with a resounding clink.

When Carter was hired on the Christmas tree lot at the height of the dot-com boom in 1999, Jeff went to photograph him. He was in a rear annex to the lot, nailing tree stands. He called over to his fellow workers, who were serving customers in the front, to come pose for a group portrait. They ignored him. He called out several more times, practically pleading. Embarrassed, Jeff snapped a solo portrait.

As Jeff was walking away, Felix ran up to him, whispering that the boss had "fired Carter yesterday for going AWOL on his lunch break." Apparently, the boss had caught Carter attempting to sneak back onto the lot an hour before closing time, pretending that he was returning from a fifteen-minute break. The next morning, Carter had returned to work, begging for a second chance. According to Felix, the boss made Carter confess in front of all the workers.

> *Felix:* [imitating a nervous, stammering Carter] "I . . . I . . . guess . . . I guess . . . I really did take a five-hour break yesterday."
> [imitating the boss] "That's more like it; now say it louder."

Carter was rehired, but the boss placed him on "work punishment," stacking deliveries and hammering stands in the back annex. He was explicitly denied contact with customers in the front lot, thereby losing the opportunity to earn tips. As Felix was explaining this, the boss suddenly noticed Jeff and walked over, politely warning, "If you're not here to buy a tree, you gotta move on, buddy. Sorry, but I got to keep Felix working before I lose him." The boss thought of himself as disciplining his workers fairly on the basis of performance— and Carter was, objectively, a lousy worker. Nevertheless, the only black employee on the lot was confined to the back annex, working for the lowest pay, performing the most menial task, and was not allowed to talk to the mostly white clientele. (For a discussion of "de facto apartheid" in the workplace, see Bourgois 1989:129–136; Holmes 2006). In later years, pressured by community action groups to diversify his labor force, the Christmas tree seller hired an African-American foreman, who successfully recruited a network of unemployed African-Americans from the nearby Hunters Point–Bayview neighborhood. This successful implementation of affirmative action infuriated the homeless whites on Edgewater Boulevard, convincing them that the world discriminates against white men.

Only three hours after Jeff was thrown off the Christmas tree lot, Philippe ran into Carter in front of the A&C corner store, where he was taking yet another extended impromptu break from work. Their conversation reveals their very different class-based dispositions toward risk and anxiety. Philippe was eager to document Carter's experience with legal employment. He hoped Carter would prove to be a "worthy worker," and he was nervous that Carter might get in trouble for taking an unscheduled break. He did not realize at the time that Carter had already been placed on work punishment, and he steered the conversation to the subject of earning tips, because he figured that eliciting tips was the aspect of the job most analogous to the excitement and sense of achievement found in street hustling (Bourgois 1997, 1998a:43, 64–65; Wacquant 1998). Philippe thought Carter would enjoy discussing how effective he was at "hustling tips." Instead, Carter responded with an outburst of masculine bravado and a reasoned critique of economic exploitation:

Philippe: What's up, Carter? Are you on break now?

Carter: No. I just took one 'cause I seen y'all from across the street.

Philippe: [laughing nervously] We're gonna get you in trouble? You'll have to go back to work soon.

Carter: Man, you know what? Just fuck 'em! What they gonna do, send me home? Fuck it. Pay me off, and I'm going.

Philippe: Well, if you're not going back, let's at least walk around the corner so the boss doesn't see you. I don't want you to get fired.

[walking to the back alley] The tips must be good? Are you earning good money slinging trees?

Carter: Oh, they been okay. . . . Uh . . . uh . . . uh, I mean, they been okay. . . . Uh, they ain't all that great either.

I mean, the law of averages and chances on shit I do out here [pointing down the alley], on takin' penitentiary chances . . . stealing, I do better than what I get over there [pointing toward the lot].

It's just that this work is steady and keeping me out of trouble. It's, uh . . . an hourly wage, and I know that's guaranteed money.

Philippe: Isn't it kind of nice to have a steady income?

Carter: Yeah. . . . [imitating a "whiter" voice] Yeah, yeah. [both laugh]

Philippe: But Carter, seriously, isn't it a relief not to have to be hitting licks all the time? I mean, doesn't stealing give you anxiety?

Carter: It gives me—[long pause, and then thoughtfully] a rush, Philippe. A fuckin' rush! I mean, actually working over there [frowning in the direction of the tree lot], I be, in a way . . . bored. Unless I run across a little fine ol' chick buyin' a tree, or this 'n that. Otherwise I be bored.

Philippe: Explain to me the difference between working legally and hitting licks.

Carter: Taxes! [laughing] Fuckin' taxes.

I don't know. Shit! What the fuck you asking me for, Philippe? I'm the lowest man on the totem pole! You're the professor workin' legal.

Philippe: Well, is working boring for you?

Carter: No. It's not boring to work, right, but if I had a motherfuckin' dental plan, a benefit package, a credit union, and all of that . . . no motherfucker could pull me from my job. I'd be workin' twenty-four/seven, with all the overtime I could get.

A job like this here is only gonna last a month, but I'm tryin' to get all I could get. Save up enough money for a methadone program.

Philippe: Why can't you save just as much money when you hit a good lick?

Carter: It depends on the lick. You gotta backtrack from what you had to do to survive up until the time that you was able to hit the lick, right.

If people took care of you up until that time, you gotta take care of them, naturally, right. And then you go from there on whatever you got left . . . to carry yourself along until you gotta do somethin' else, right.

But I have a debt right now. I got a debt every morning. Shit! I wake up and start getting to sniffle—dopesick! I got a debt!

Philippe: Come on, let's go back to the lot.

Despite Carter's jesting about the boredom and exploitation of off-the-books legal day labor, he made a concerted attempt over the next three weeks to "go legal" while employed on the lot. He began saving up for the down payment required at that time by most private, for-profit methadone maintenance programs in San Francisco, about one hundred twenty dollars.

Here's sixty dollars, Jeff, that's a gram [of heroin]. Hold it for me till next week and I'll have the other sixty. You see, I'm serious. I'm gonna try to get back on the stick. I swear it. I'm going to try this time, while I got a chance to do it, right now! The methadone will keep me from buyin' dope and takin' breaks to fix every day!

I can focus on bein' clean, on goin' and getting a valid driver's license, on getting a driving job, and bein' able to take a drug test and come up clean.

Carter stayed at the lot through the end of the Christmas season, even though he was never taken off work punishment and was never able to hustle tips. By the time his name finally came up on the methadone program's month-long waiting list, his job had ended. He no longer had the stable income to pay for the program or the pragmatic motivation to "go clean." In short, despite a plethora of good intentions, institutional and structural forces—the inadequacy of treatment programs and the instability of unregulated day labor jobs—had once again rerouted Carter into being an outlaw.

Abusive Bosses

Like most patron-client relationships across steep divides of power and vulnerability (Scheper-Hughes 1992:98–127), the interface between homeless drug users and their employers ambiguously spans conviviality, compassion, exploitation, and humiliation. The worst employer on the boulevard was Bruce, the owner of a warehouse that sold repossessed furniture. For the last six years of our fieldwork, Al worked for Bruce for twenty dollars a day, moving furniture onto the sidewalk for display each morning and stowing the unsold items in the evening. It was an easy job, but he had to be on call all day to run errands and unload new shipments.

Every morning, Al jolted awake at 5:00 A.M., his chronic lower back pain exacerbated by oncoming heroin withdrawal symptoms. He had to wait until Bruce opened the warehouse at 7:30 A.M. to receive his previous day's wages. Al did not drink alcohol, and Bruce knew that twenty dollars was sufficient to cover his daily dose of heroin as well as a nightcap of crack and a quart of milk at bedtime. Bruce not only paid badly but also was verbally abusive. Early in the employment arrangement, in order to avoid triggering an employer's tax liability, he had refused to confirm to the welfare department that Al worked for him. Al consequently lost his monthly food stamps for failing to participate in welfare's required workfare program. He began to express serious interest in entering drug treatment. "It's like I'm a dog on a leash, a slave. All for twenty dollars each morning. Bruce gives me just enough so I can go cop, fix, and return to work."

We visited Al at the warehouse at closing time to offer him a ride to a detox center. Caltrans was in the midst of an eviction offensive, and he had lost all his blankets:

Al: Carter hid the blankets last month when Caltrans came. And last week, I got lucky—a new Mexican guy on the boulevard grabbed my blankets for me just in time when he saw Caltrans drivin' up. That was nice. So this week I been carting all my stuff here in the morning down from the camp. But I was late for work yesterday so I left a sign: "Caltrans: I'm at work. Please call [the warehouse telephone number] so I can get my stuff." But they just cleared me out. They ripped down all the shelters.

Bruce, a burly fifty-year-old man with a thick Brooklyn accent, interrupted this conversation without saying hello: "You's the guys writin' stories about heroin addicts? Huh? What is there to write about junkies that people don't already know?" We tried to explain diplomatically the public health and HIV prevention goals of our research, and Bruce exploded:

Why should society help? It's their fuckin' problem. No one holds a fuckin' gun to their head and makes them shoot up! Who got them into the drugs? All they gotta do is look into the fuckin' mirror. [shouting at us] *I don't want nothin' to do with you! Get the fuck outta here!*

[turning to Al and pointing to us] He and his buddy are just tryin' to make money off a' scumbags like you.

[turning back to us and pointing to Al] These guys are habitual criminals. They don't need no fuckin' breaks. Leeches, bloodsuckers, and snakes. . . . They'll never change. Anything you give 'em for help they just put right back into their arms. Welfare, SSI, shoot up, drink up— what else they want for free?

Get the fuck outta here! You're part of the fuckin' problem. You don't see the reality of their destruction.

Throughout the harangue, Al had continued moving the last set of overstuffed couches inside Bruce's warehouse. He then sat on the curb to the side, waiting for us to finish, as if the argument had nothing to do with him. Later that evening, Al felt compelled to apologize for his boss's tirade:

I don't understand why he's acting like that. I must have hit a nerve somewhere. He was just joking. You know in January his rent was raised from twenty-five hundred dollars to six thousand a month. Now he's gotta earn twenty-four thousand just to break even with all his other stores.

Bruce eventually rewarded Al for his subservience by allowing him to sleep in the delivery truck parked in front of the warehouse, and Al stopped talking about wanting to quit heroin.

Carter was Al's running partner at the time, but Bruce specifically forbade Carter from sleeping in the truck with Al. Carter was mystified by Al's willingness to tolerate exploitation and subordination:

Al works his ass off. He's a honest hard worker, right. But his boss literally fucks with him.

Al can barely motherfuckin' get by to stay fixed and well in the morning where he can lift them heavy-ass credenzas and armoires.

And that motherfucker Bruce likes to make Al wait for his money. Al be sick, shittin' on himself, waiting to get his heroin.

I don't like that. That boss is chickenshit. He's got Al living in his truck now. Al thinks that's great, but it ain't like his boss is doing him no great goddamn favor. He doin' it for his own advantage on keeping Al close by. He didn't want to have to start looking for Al when he needed him. But now if the boss decides at any given time that he needs to use the truck to make a delivery or load furniture, then he'll throw Al's shit out of the truck. That's treatin' Al fucked-up, right.

The boss got this Filipino broad and her mother or cousin or whoever it is also working for him. And those two gook bitches in there is gettin' by flashin' titties and fucking the boss. They got something to work with. They got a pussy. They don't do shit!

Al ain't got no pussy, so naturally he's the motherfuckin' likely subject to have to do all the work. Because he damn sure ain't going to suck Bruce's dick, right.

Carter's insistence on sexualizing Bruce's exploitation of Al in racist and misogynist terms was a common oppositional refrain we heard from the African-Americans in response to demeaning relationships in the legal labor market (see Bourgois 2003b:146–147). Their acute sense of insult can be understood as the painful sediment of the history of slavery in the United States. Unlike the whites, they frequently used the word *slavery* in everyday speech. In the 2000s, contemporary outrage over the unresolved brutality of U.S. slavery and racism often expresses itself in an idiom of sexual subjection. (See, for example, the work of African-American artist Kara Walker [2007–2008].) The African-Americans on Edgewater Boulevard also had an active social memory of the Jim Crow racial regime that their parents and grandparents fled when they migrated from the rural Deep South to San Francisco in the World War II era (Beck and Tolnay 1990; Broussard 1993). They occasionally returned to their parents' hometowns for family reunions, many of them in eastern Texas, which, according to historical sociologists, had been "the center of Ku Klux Klan killings during the heyday of lynching" (Patterson 1998:173).

Many of the same African-American families had been subjected to indentured debt peonage as sharecroppers or rural plantation laborers. It was especially noxious to find themselves forced, two generations later, to reenter oppressive and unequal labor relationships, whether it be with openly demeaning patrons like Bruce, moralizing ones like Macon, or manipulative and openly racist ones like Sammy at the Crow's Nest liquor store. Furthermore, after they arrived in the Bay Area, many of the parents of the African-American homeless worked in unionized industrial jobs. Decades later, they retained a memory and consciousness of workers' rights and benefits.

Most of the whites were also second-generation descendants of poor rural immigrants; but, unlike the African-Americans, they did not retain a salient living memory of that migration experience, nor did they maintain contact with their parents' and grandparents' communities of origin. More important, most of the parents of the white addicts had been able to establish themselves as small-scale entrepreneurs by the 1960s and 1970s. When we asked them to tell us about their first job, most of the whites replied with a shrug of their shoulders, "Workin' for my dad." Global economic and technological transformations, however, broke up these small family-owned businesses.

From the perspective of class, both the African-Americans and the whites on Edgewater Boulevard were downwardly mobile, second-generation rural/urban migrants who had been lumpenized by their inability to maintain a foothold in a labor force restructured by multiple shifts in the mode of production. Despite sharing the subjectivity and habitus of the righteous dopefiend, they had very different conceptions of exploitation and subordination at work. Displacement from the unionized industrial labor force is a very different ideological experience from failure as a small-scale entrepreneur in a rapidly growing economy dominated by high-tech, finance, and services.

Poorly paid workers often become demoralized and blame themselves, at least partially, for their economic subordination. Under these conditions, a worker's "bad attitude" in the workplace is understood and experienced by both employers and employees, irrespective of ethnicity, as either an individual moral characteristic or a cultural/racial essence (or both). Active racism in the day labor market remained a public secret on Edgewater Boulevard, because not hiring African-Americans was considered a "logical" business strategy.

On only one occasion were we able to elicit self-reflexive criticism from an employer of the homeless on discrimination in the day labor market:

> I'm not like the other storekeepers. Whenever I have a chance, I always hire a black man because I feel that they are discriminated against. Racism is the great scourge of America. Homelessness, too! And if they are black, forget it! Here, people do not tolerate them.

This particular store owner represents the exception who proves the rule. He himself had suffered directly from nationalist discrimination in his youth. Born and raised in Cairo, he had been expelled to Lebanon when Egypt evicted its ethnic Lebanese citizens in a wave of nationalist jingoism during the 1960s.

Panhandling

Passive begging was an income-generating option that the African-Americans actively shunned. Most of the white drug users on Edgewater Boulevard generated a large proportion of their resources (money, food, clothing) by flying signs at passing cars: WILL WORK FOR FOOD. VIETNAM VET. GOD BLESS. They often spent hours at a stretch, their eyes on the ground, with an empty fast-food soda cup held aloft. They usually raised enough money to "stay well." Although passersby were sometimes willing to contribute spare change to visibly needy whites on the street, they rarely spontaneously gave alms to even the oldest, feeblest African-Americans on the boulevard, because blacks were deemed intimidating or unworthy. The police also enforced public nuisance and panhandling laws more rigorously against blacks.

The African-Americans in our scene did not discuss their rejection of passive begging in terms of limited options resulting from racism. Instead, they referred to it as a function of their way of being in the world and of their natural sense of dignity. Furthermore, they reduced their opportunities for receiving charitable gifts and for avoiding police detection by engaging in flamboyant or oppositional behaviors such as conspicuously drinking alcohol in public and talking loudly on streetcorners. Once again, the outlaw habitus that offered them a sense of self-respect through asserting control of public space convinced those who interacted with them that they deserved their fate.

Philippe: How come you never fly a sign?

Carter: I just never, ever could do it. To me that's just too odd. It's just too . . . un-me. And I hate being told fuckin' "No." It really makes me mad.

I don't give a fuck how desperate I am. I rather go take something instead of waitin' on somebody who's looking at me like I'm a piece of shit tellin' me, "I ain't got it!" or "Go get a job!" when they just stuffin' some money in their pocket.

"Motherfucker, you got it and I'm takin' it!"

That's why I could never beg. It's the rejection. I'm not going to be standing out there for two dollars here, or three dollars, when I know I'm gonna get fifty or hundred in one *whomp!* [smiling and slamming his fist]

Go for it! You just going to have to parlay and take penitentiary chances, right? I'm not bragging or actin' like I'm better than nobody, but I just didn't grow up on doing things like that—begging.

When the African-Americans did panhandle, they distinguished it from passive begging by engaging passersby actively, offering a service, a friendly quip, or a threat. Routine fieldnotes capture these distinct ethnic styles.

Jeff's Fieldnotes

Max, Nickie, and Frank are all flying signs, positioned at opposite sides of the freeway's entrance and exit ramps. Expressionless, they all lower their eyes or squint, unfocused, into the distance, with an expression of boredom or anxiety. Max complains in a low voice that he has been out for three hours and has raised only three dollars.

I walk farther down the boulevard to the gas station where I see Sonny carrying a blue ny-lon bag full of clothing, presumably scavenged and/or stolen items for sale. The worn red han-dle of a windshield squeegee is sticking out of the zipper of his bag. He offers to share a can of malt liquor with me, and we step behind a dumpster to keep out of the gas station atten-dant's view and sip together.

A pickup truck with the name A-1 Glass stenciled on the door drives up to the pump, and Sonny calls out: "Hey, Mr. A-1 Glass, can I pump your gas?" The driver, a middle-aged Latino, chuckles but shakes his head. A half dozen more cars fill up. The drivers all turn down Sonny's personalized offer to help.

Sonny complains that he has been hustling for four hours and has made only seven dollars. In the same breath, he proceeds to try to sell me an assortment of objects that he pulls out of his nylon bag as well as from the bulging recesses of his brand-new Gore-Tex winter jacket as if he were a magician: a 1921 Buffalo nickel, a 1901 Indian Head penny, a pack of dominoes, a large metal compass (which he describes as "an architect's tool"), several tie clips and class rings from St. Ignatius High School. When I try to interrupt his sales pitch, he scolds, "Don't go bein' like them people, Jeff-er-y! Let me finish!"

Passersby from all ethnic groups, including other African-Americans, gave more easily and more generously to whites than to blacks. Flying a sign was especially lucrative on national holidays.

> *Spider-Bite Lou:* Christmas is a great time for flyin' signs, but Thanksgiving is even better. People are more—how do you say, giving. Last Christmas Eve, I made forty-four dollars in an hour and a half.
>
> People surprise you. You might see someone in a junked-out car, you know. And it looks like the only difference between them and you is they got a vehicle. And all of a sudden, they'll whip out a five-dollar bill.
>
> Yesterday, one of my regulars, a Korean storekeeper, promised to give me a trailer if his busi-ness goes well. He gives me five dollars every Saturday evening; says it brings his business good luck.
>
> The Chinese give real good, too, and the Filipinos are okay. I get a lot of hits from black women. Yesterday I got a ten-dollar hit from some white guys on their way to the 49ers foot-ball game.
>
> There's a Chinese guy on Sundays who's usually good for a ten or a twenty if I catch him. I introduced myself last time when he handed me two twenties. He's just a real humble kind of man.

Most of the homeless whites subsisted primarily on the food given to them when they panhandled in fast-food parking lots. They rarely visited soup kitchens because they found these institutional environments unwelcoming and excessively time-consuming. Sometimes private individuals came down to Edgewater Boulevard spontaneously to give the homeless clothes, blankets, or sleeping bags or to pay for haircuts and rounds of laundry at the laundromat. One of Petey's "regulars" took him to a San Francisco 49ers' football game. It was Petey's first time at a professional sports event, and the seats were on the forty-yard line. The African-Americans, however, rarely received free food, clothes, or random acts of kindness from people whom Carter called "good Samaritans." They resolutely refused to present themselves as pitiable, down-on-their-luck panhandlers. As a result, they often remained hungry and dopesick.

On rare occasions, motorists took seriously the entreaties for work displayed on the cardboard signs held up by the whites. An elderly white woman hired Nickie to clean her house once a week. One of Philippe's neighbors, an African-American man who lived up the hill from Edgewater Boulevard, picked up Petey from his regular panhandling spot at the Taco Bell exit ramp and hired him to paint his backyard fence. During the second half of our fieldwork, a middle-aged white man named Paul brought Hogan into his home and allowed him to live in his garage for several years.

> *Hogan:* Paul's spent most of his life taking care of his mother. She died last year and he didn't have no one else to talk to after work. He'd come by the Dockside's parking lot at the end of the day, and I'd borrow a dollar or two dollars. And after a few years it got to where I was borrowing tens and twenties. That's when he offered to let me stay in his garage.
>
> He gives me twenty dollars every morning for my hit. He buys me clothes, shoes, cigarettes. So I help him around the house. He's left his mom's room just the way she had it. He cooks meals every night, frozen pasta. He's Italian. So at least I eat once a day.

Paul was gay, but he made no sexual advances toward Hogan. His only requirement was that Hogan remain quietly in the garage when sexual partners visited.

In contrast to the generosity of private citizens, public welfare entitlements were difficult to access. Rarely were more than two or three individuals in our network receiving public assistance checks or food stamps at any given time. The whites negotiated the complicated, and sometimes humiliating, bureaucratic hoops more frequently than did African-Americans. Few, however, managed to remain on welfare for longer than a few months. Case managers have significant leeway in interpreting eligibility rules. When Frank was thrown off welfare one Christmas, he attributed his "bad luck" to the "bad mood" of his welfare worker: "Maybe it's the holidays. I was an hour late, and usually he doesn't care about that as long as my paperwork's in order. But this time he said, 'Maybe . . . I should send you through triage again.' I was too dopesick, so I got up and left." Heroin withdrawal symptoms made it difficult to fulfill the workfare requirements legislated by the Personal Responsibility and

Work Opportunity Reconciliation Act passed by the U.S. Congress in 1996. It took Frank over a year to successfully requalify for public assistance, but his payments lasted only three months because he failed to comply with workfare recertification.

Nickie was the only member of the Edgewater scene who stayed on welfare throughout the entire duration of our research. Women can qualify for support from welfare bureaucracies when they obey scripts of "worthy [single] motherhood" (Passaro 1996). Somehow Nickie successfully hid her heroin addiction from her social workers and maintained custody of her child. She never lost her housing project apartment despite repeated incarcerations for shoplifting. She also complied with her workfare obligation, washing city buses at the municipal depot for twenty hours per week.

Honor among Thieves

The Edgewater homeless did not recognize the complex array of structural forces around ethnicity, gender, economy, public policy, law enforcement, and social stigma that shaped their subjectivities and habituses and constrained their survival options. Instead, as we have shown, they acted out socially structured roles through their everyday practices, confirming to themselves and to those around them that they deserved their fate. They also talked about race and culture in moral, essentialized terms. The whites condemned African-Americans for being thieves, and the African-Americans criticized the whites for "lacking initiative" and for "being too stupid and lazy to hit licks." Both groups, however, engaged in petty, opportunistic theft. The whites pretended that they did not do so, whereas the African-Americans exaggerated their professional skills as criminals. They often reminisced about the dramatic criminal escapades of their youth, whereas the whites generally spoke in hyperbolic terms of past successes in the legal labor market.

Occasionally, the whites also celebrated memories of youthful illegal exploits, but their outlaw nostalgia differed from that of the African-Americans, reflecting distinct reservoirs of ethnic cultural capital. Frank, for example, spoke of smuggling kilos of heroin in a yacht from the Golden Triangle and claimed that *Rolling Stone* magazine had run a feature on his partner in crime, who had been arrested in Thailand. We were unable to locate the *Rolling Stone* article, but as chapter 4 describes, Frank's father confirmed that his son had sold drugs to the Jefferson Airplane rock group and at one point had a "drawer full of about a hundred thousand dollars in cash." Hank recounted a fantastic story of drilling a hole in the roof of San Francisco's de Young Museum to heist antique dolls. Barbara, his sister, told us that Hank never burglarized the museum, but she confirmed that he was arrested for insurance fraud when he faked the theft of valuable porcelain dolls from his brother-in-law's antique store.

Sonny referred to his glory days of being a big-time drug dealer. According to a 1987 police report, he was merely selling ten-dollar packets of heroin from his girlfriend's housing project apartment. His supplier owned the garage where Sonny's father had his car repaired.

Carter sought respect as an O.G. through braggadocio accounts of having been a "stick-up artist" (see also Katz 1988:263–273):

I did three banks. One was two days before New Year's Eve. We watched it on the news on the seventeenth floor of the Hyatt Regency, drinking champagne. The rush! You actually living out a movie, right—you open the bag and throw a stack of money, like playing a food fight.

It was great, but after doin' a couple of banks, we robbed a House of Pancakes on Lombard Street and got caught. The police put a hundred seven holes in my van. Looked like a piece of Swiss cheese. Had us face down on the ground in the middle of the freeway. They had a SWAT team on our side and a helicopter landing on the other side of the guardrail. It was a do-or-die situation, you know, living on the edge. That's the rush.

My partners was in the back of the van on the floor with two Samsonite thick briefcases full of ammunition. Boxes of bullets, brand-new bullets. Anything from twenty-two shorts to twenty-two longs to three fifty-sevens to nine millimeters, thirty-eight specials. We even had a motherfuckin' German Lugar in there. And a sawed-off shotgun with a custom holster.

The D.A. messed the case up. Plus the witnesses had their stories all fucked up. I went to court every day for three months. I had three lawyers 'cause it was two codependents [sic]. The judge was mad. He said, "It's motherfuckers like you that I'd like to put away forever."

But we beat the robbery. They gave me a year for possession of firearms. They even gave the money back. "Robbery dismissed!" [pounding an imaginary gavel] It was seven thousand dollars cash because we did really detailed casing. That's why we chose Thanksgiving morning. We knew they wouldn't turn the money in till after the holidays.

According to the police report, only 596 dollars was taken from the International House of Pancakes that Thanksgiving morning, and a portion of the money was in "traveler's checks and charge drafts." Carter's yellow van was, indeed, shot many times, but only in the tires, and only after it accidentally lurched forward when Carter forgot to shift out of gear after being ordered to get out of the car and crawl onto the ground. There is no mention in the police report of a getaway attempt, but there is a description of "two briefcases . . . containing seven handguns and a large amount of ammunition. Two of the handguns were identified as previously stolen weapons."

The court records also confirm that the robbery charge was dismissed. Carter and his co-conspirators benefited from the inability of the white witnesses to distinguish the three black male defendants from others in the police line-up. Ironically, according to the court records, Carter and his accomplices had originally been arrested precisely because of their skin color: black men running down the street often prompt suspicion in the United States.

[Witness X] testified . . . he was one block from the IHOP [International House of Pancakes] in his pickup truck. . . . As he started to turn left . . . a black man ran alongside the driver's side of his truck. He saw another black man running on the sidewalk on the passenger side . . . the running men looked strange to Mr. [X] and he copied down the license plate of their van . . . and circled the block. When he saw a police car arriving at the IHOP [Witness X] . . . gave the officer the license number.

Sonny's personal style was more gentlemanly than Carter's, but he was no less committed to being an outlaw rather than a beggar: "It's not beg, borrow, or steal. It's beg, borrow, *and* steal. But I still like to think of myself as having morals. I never steal from people I know." Court records confirm Sonny's accounts of participating in an armed robbery and home invasion in the mansion of a wealthy, politically connected San Francisco socialite: "Entry was . . . made through a window. . . . Owner was tied up and threatened on numerous occasions and . . . bound in her own home. . . . [T]hey took . . . personal property . . . [and] also took an automobile." Sonny considered himself to be a professional, and he favored intimidation tactics over violence. In addition to being an effective hustler, he was a friendly, good-humored person. He even expressed empathy for his victims:

We ransacked in and then, fuck! Somebody was in the kitchen. There she was. But she still hadn't seen us, and we didn't want her to see us. We told her, "Be cool about it. . . . Make no noise. . . . No one's gonna get hurt. . . . Turn your head away."

I could imagine the lady was pretty scared. We surprised her in her own home and we had a gun. I could imagine if somebody came in my mom's home like that. She'd probably shit bricks!

But she tried to run away, so I grabbed her hair and told her to lay down while we tied her up. We didn't want to tie her up too tight, just enough so she could get loose, but not while we were still there.

So then we got to ransackin' and got to loadin' up shit in her car, in the garage—jewelry, stereos, and even some stock exchange things.

We got her ring, worth about five or six thousand dollars, and my partner drove off to pawn it. Get us some quick cash. I made it back to my apartment, but the lady got loose too soon, and the police was swarming around. They stopped my partner. He drivin' all crazy, right, through a red light. And he on parole and he got a warrant on him and got his billy club in his car. And so they got him for a weapon violation and he was locked up.

So then his mother and his brother had came to where I be stayin' at my mom's house, askin' [whining], "Can I have this? Can I have that?"

I said, "Sure, that's your son's part."

I gave both of them a lot of shit, whatever they wanted—stereos and TVs, because I had the good shit, like the nice jewelry, stashed to the side, so I just went on about my business.

About a week and a half later, I drove to my mom's house and I'm coming down the hill and I see this white undercover police car parked. I opened my door to make a mad dash right by them, but then from behind me, "Click, click." A police in plain clothes drew down on me with his gun.

We enter through the garage of my mom's house. "You on probation," they say. "Search and seizure." I say, "Yeah. I know that, but you can only search me and my person and *my* place of residence, and I don't stay upstairs. I stay right down here in this room in the garage." And I say, "Mama, all you got to do is tell them you don't want them searchin' your house."

But she doesn't know nothin' about this law stuff, but she finally got on that and said, "No. I don't want y'all searchin' my house." And one of the police—they was actually acting kinda nice—says, "Well, he's right and we can't."

So they didn't search upstairs. In my room they started taking pictures of shoes, 'cause when we made the lady lay down, she was looking at our shoes. She never saw our faces, but she gave them a description of my shoes.

Well, the police are looking up and down, checking their list with jewelry and stuff like that. They lookin' all up on the shelves. And suddenly I say to myself, "Goddamn. I got her husband's watch on!" And they did *everything* except check the fuckin' watch.

They did a whole interrogation. I'm tellin' them I don't have nothing to say, but they keep interrogatin'. Nothin' about no memorandum [Miranda] rights. And in court, my lawyer, he played their interrogation tape to the judge. That's how I beat the burglary case. I was never read my memoranda rights, man. But I also had probation, so the judge gave me the maximum on that previous drug sales charge—three and a half years.

See the lady, she was scared. She told the judge we was threatening to cut her finger off because we wanted to take her ring, and it wouldn't come off.

But I had told my partner, "Fuck that ring!" It wouldn't be worth it to cut the lady's finger off to get the ring. I'm not into that violent kind of shit. It would make things worser than what they are.

She said in court, "I was really thankful to him that he said that. If not, I might have been missing a finger."

Also, the lady, she a personal friend of the mayor, that Feinstein lady. And the judge, too. They all friends. They came out together in the parking lot. I saw them. They all belong to the same country club. They play tennis and golf. . . .

So the mayor had the police movin' on it. It a top priority case. They wanted to wash my ass. And that's why the judge sent me back to the pen again for three and a half years on a probation violation. I went to Soledad.

Superannuated Outlaws and Wannabe Workers

Shortly after this conversation, Sonny was incarcerated for breaking into a parked vehicle. This time, however, he ended up as the victim of violence and he spent a week under police guard in the county hospital's surgery ward to have a metal plate inserted into his forehead. When he was released from county jail eight months later, he was partially blind in his left eye. The police report contains a handwritten statement by the owner of the vehicle, a contractor with a Spanish last name and limited English literacy skills. Sonny emerges from between the lines as a broken-down old man no longer capable of defending himself effectively, a far cry from the gun-wielding burglar of his youth:

> Saw black male with toolboxes. . . . Relized they were mine . . . saw back window in Van broken. . . . Person tryed to run, grabed & pushed. . . . Made set down on butt. Jumped up and Tryed to run again. Shoved down & held him W/knee on chest by Throat . . . person when to corner, Tryed to run again (comb in right hand raised up in air) & Thought it was a knife, threw him against concrete. Grabed hand & removed comb. Made set down again.

The police report continues with a list of what Sonny was carrying in his jacket pocket:

ITEM: CRACK PIPE. DESCRIPTION: THREE-INCH PIECE OF ANTENNA TUBE WITH A RUBBER
MESH AROUND ONE END AND COPPER AROUND OPPOSITE END.
ITEM: TWO OFF-WHITE ROCKS WRAPPED IN MUNI TRANSFER.
ITEM: ONE HYPODERMIC NEEDLE FILLED WITH 30 CCS OF A BROWN LIQUID.

The African-Americans rarely discussed employment spontaneously or sought jobs during the years we knew them. Nevertheless, when we collected their work histories, they spoke positively about past involvement in the legal labor market. Their nostalgic reminiscences provide additional evidence that their celebration of an outlaw persona, which proudly rejected subordination and exploitation in the labor market, was not a personal choice. Rather, it was imposed on them by a legacy of exclusion from legal employment. Sonny spoke with fondness of his emergency employment in 1983 following a toxic chemical explosion in the Del Monte building downtown (*New York Times* 1983, June 2; *San Francisco Chronicle* 1983, May 16):

The best, most paying job I ever had, as far as making money, was when they had that chemical spill down there at One Market Plaza. Ten dollars twenty-four cents an hour. We worked ten hours a day, six days a week. Got paid every Friday.

And the job was easy as shit, you know what I'm sayin'. Wiping down a lot of chemicals. They called it PC . . . something. . . . Oh, yeah! PCB.

The first six months, everybody was working, but during that time you had to take . . . what was it? Biopsy! You know, they cut a little piece of meat off your ass. And if you were well, then you worked the last six months. You were the last one to be fired. Not fired, but let go.

I was okay, so I worked the second six months too. I worked security, and that wasn't nothin' but directing cars. Telling people walking by, "Go back this way. . . . You can't go through this way. . . ." And we had straight overtime. Time-and-a-half, to fifteen an hour.

When pressed for more details, Sonny admitted, with some embarrassment, that this one year-long stint in toxic cleanup was the only legal job he had ever held. According to newspaper reports from the 1980s, the toxic risk of Sonny's "best, most paying job" was not limited to "wiping down . . . PCBs." He and his fellow workers were also exposed to "the more toxic tetrachlorodibenzofuran . . . a chemical relative of dioxin . . . known to cause cancer, liver damage and birth defects in laboratory animals" (*San Francisco Chronicle* 1983, May 16). Reggie and Carter, two other African-Americans, also spoke with pride about working temporary, but "well-paid," toxic jobs: they both worked on U.S. military bases removing asbestos.

An additional indication of the lumpen status of the Edgewater homeless is apparent from the way so many of them referred to the prison system as one of their primary, long-term, "legal" employers. Much of their work while incarcerated had been routine. Nonetheless, they spoke of it with relish: Carter parlayed "mail delivery" into trafficking contraband; Frank worked in "agriculture" and fermented moonshine in the seedling sheds; Ben manufactured freeway signs and referred to those skills when applying for unionized tinsmith jobs; Hank worked in the cafeteria and laughed about the power that this position gave him over other inmates. The prison jobs they were proudest of were the most dangerous ones: Carter and Al had fought forest fires while in juvenile detention, and Sonny and Frank had done so as adults. They were paid only a fraction of the minimum wage to perform these dangerous jobs, yet their eagerness to talk about them suggests that they yearned for the sense of worth they achieved through engaging in this socially respected and quintessentially masculine hard work.

Frank was serving two years for first-degree burglary when the Loma Prieta earthquake hit San Francisco in 1989. He was sent to salvage materials from the wreckage:

They sent us to the Marina District, where all those buildings were crumpled down and shit. It was like a ghost town. All the buildings cracked, with big jacks holding them up. They had the streets barricaded, and our job was to go in there to haul stuff out.

The institutionalized racialization of the California correctional system and the normalization of extreme violence by prison guards also emerge between the lines of Frank's prison work reminiscences:

The Busters, the Northern California Chicanos, controlled the pen. They knew how the system worked and had the best jobs. One of their fathers was a heroin dealer that I used to buy from, out on the street, and his son saved me when they tried to put a snitch jacket on me.

First, I worked in agriculture. But we got raided for fermenting pruno from fruit, sugar, and yeast that we'd get from the kitchen workers. I didn't even get a chance to drink it.

Most of the guards were white, though, and they liked me. So they went easy on me, and I was assigned to firefighting as special work duty instead of being chained down for the pruno.

You see, the blacks used to fight the blacks, the Mexicans used to fight the Mexicans, and sometimes the Mexicans fought the blacks. The guards just stood by, laughin'. "Let the toads fight," they'd say. And the Mexicans were swingin' fence posts studded with barbed wire. But I was white, and they didn't usually get involved with white guys.

In the mountains, we worked side by side with regular firemen, who got paid good. We only got a dollar an hour, but when you're in prison that's pretty good money, because we'd be out there twenty hours straight, cutting a firebreak. Sometimes for a week or more.

You gotta go through a training program. They give you these old fire tents. Some of them were so old they'd get rotten, and we called them Shake-n-Bake because the flame goes right through the holes. When the winds change, and there's convection currents when you're on the side of a hill, all of a sudden, the fire shoots right up that hill, and *whap!* Runs right over you. Two or three times I've heard of crews getting wiped out like that. You can't get out of the damn way. And you're gone.

Globalization: Undocumented Latino Day Laborers

Undocumented immigrants were the most visible, face-to-face competitors for the day labor jobs that the Edgewater homeless strove to obtain from local businesses and homeowners. On any given day, at rush hour along the boulevard, there were dozens of Asian and Latina women waiting at bus stops on their way to and from the few remaining factory sweatshops in the adjoining warehouse district. A half mile away in the Mission District, hundreds of young, healthy men, newly arrived from Mexico and Central America, lined the main street, waiting hopefully for employers. They were prepared to work hard for low wages.

This competition for day labor generated a palpable ethnic animosity. Petey, for example, in response to a passing motorist's offer of three dollars to clean his car, "inside and out," answered, "I ain't no bean-and-rice-eating illegal!" A week before this incident, Andy, the mover, drove by Petey and picked up an undocumented laborer instead: "I know he saw me, because I was where I always am, standing here by the Taco Bell exit sign. He always passes up and down the boulevard at least twice lookin' for me. But this time I saw that he had some Mexican sitting next to him in the van." As a U.S.-born Latino, Felix aggressively differentiated himself from the undocumented: "I ain't working for no wetback wages." Max, consistent with his gentler personality, was more charitable. When he came back from a day of moving furniture for Andy, he marveled: "I never moved such heavy stuff in my life, but we got some Mexican kids from the Mission to help. They were good workers, and that made it much easier."

The Edgewater homeless often preyed on Latino immigrants—even if not always successfully, as in Sonny's beatdown over the toolbox. On another occasion, Jeff was an unwilling witness to a spur-of-the-moment theft of tools belonging to new-immigrant laborers.

Jeff's Fieldnotes

I accompany Carter as he cases out a junkyard he plans to burglarize for recyclable metal later tonight. From behind a camper, we hear three men talking in Spanish. They are celebrating the end of the work week on this warm Friday summer evening, drinking beers.

At the foot of the warehouse loading ramp, there is a small green and tan canvas duffel bag. Its straps are crisscrossed and twisted to form a more secure single reinforced strap. Carter looks at the bag intently and slows down, but keeps walking. With feigned disinterest, he casually turns his head to the right and then to the left. Detecting that the bag is not within the view of the three men, he slowly walks back to inspect it more closely, patting it softly with the palm of his hand. I hear him mutter something about a drill, and then a more audible, "Please help me, God."

Scanning once more in both directions, but this time more openly and more tensely, Carter whispers to me, "Why would they leave the bag back here out of sight and be sitting just ten feet away?" I pretend to ignore him, but remember that some of the guys say the toolbox that led to Sonny's beatdown had been bait, left out by the construction worker to catch him red-handed.

Carter takes a deep breath, grabs the bag, spins around, and cradles it in both arms to his chest so that it is not visible from behind. Hissing, "Jeff, watch my back," he walks briskly down the street.

A nervous smile fixed on his face, Carter deliberately slows his pace as he reaches the middle of the block. His back has now come into full view of the three Latino workers sitting on the warehouse loading dock. I hear him murmuring, "Oh, please, Lord, just let me get around that corner; please, please!" I can tell that his insides are coiled and he is ready to burst into a sprint at the slightest noise behind him.

Rounding the corner and out of sight, he lunges into a sprint. An empty rusted shopping cart happens to be lying on its side in the gutter, and he drops the canvas bag into it. He pushes it rapidly at a trot for another two blocks. After rounding two more corners, he finally stops to examine the bag's contents. A well-worn leather work belt is neatly folded on top as a protective cover. Underneath is a power drill with an orange extension cord coiled into a tight ringlet. Further below lie a masonry hammer, a screwdriver, and some heavy-duty wire cutters.

I follow Carter three more blocks to an auto body repair yard that fences stolen goods. The owner, an Asian man, is busy with a customer, and we have to wait for an hour. Carter, still nervous, tells me he is planning to ask for forty dollars for all the stuff but will settle for thirty-five.

Feeling terrible for the workers who have just been ripped off, after what must have been a week of hard work, I ask Carter how damaging he thinks it will be to those workers to lose these tools. He pretends not to hear my question and giggles, "My ass was scared, walking with my back to the Mexicans."

Carter leaves the fence's shop cursing, with the duffel bag still underarm. Apparently, my camera "spooked the owner," and he told Carter to leave and never return. "Motherfuckin' chink," Carter grumbles, "I'll get your shop, later."

We walk ten blocks to Chico's Tunes, where Carter settles for ten dollars without much negotiating. He is visibly suffering from heroin withdrawal symptoms, and Chico knows that ten dollars is the current price for a bag of heroin. Cursing, Carter heads straight to Sal the dealer.

The Edgewater homeless and undocumented Latinos were confined to the same marginalized public spaces, sought the same poorly paid and unstable jobs, and scavenged for recyclables in the same gutters. This kind of structurally overdetermined setting acts as a pressure cooker for racialized ideologies. It is a microcosm of the larger, long-term patterns of immigration and inequality that have shaped U.S. history and helps explain the ongoing valence of racism in the United States. Ironically, Chico, a new-immigrant business owner, profited the most from the victimization of the undocumented Latino workers. Nonetheless, in manipulatively out-bargaining Carter (who had already vengefully vowed to burglarize yet another immigrant entrepreneur), Chico unwittingly fueled another round of racialized antagonisms.

Sonny was aware of the structural forces that limited his access to stable, well-paid employment. He specifically identified the multinational corporate logic for the deindustrialization of the Bay Area, where tens of thousands of factory jobs were lost in the 1970s and 1980s (Self 2003; Walker 1990; Wright 2004). Sonny could not stop himself, however, from echoing the conspiracy theories and anti-immigrant vitriol that prevailed on right-wing talk radio in California during our dozen years of fieldwork:

> A lot of these companies move they business overseas where they ain't got to pay all that money that they would pay here. And that takes jobs away from a lot of people.
>
> It creates a lot of problems, too. It seems like these company people should want to think about home first.
>
> They want to know why we got so much turmoil, so much problems, so many homeless people in this country. And that's the reason why. Company people being greedy. Each day that go by, they sendin' more and more people out in the streets to be homeless, where a lot of them turn to crime. A lot of them would do shit like we doin', push a buggy to get cardboard, bottles, and shit like that, to try to more or less stay within the legal guidelines.

But don't nobody want to starve, man. Hunger ain't nothin' nice. I used to take shit like that for granted a long time ago, you know, when I was coming up, until I became part of it, being out here [pointing to the cans in his buggy] and bein' hungry; and it ain't nothin' nice, man.

Plus them companies got a lot of those illegals working for them. That's where they save money. It keeps a lot of other folks from getting jobs. They don't pay them right. But the illegals don't care. Compared to what they would make at home, you know, they doin' pretty good here.

And then they work for a good little ol' while and then go back home with that money. That's a nice little ol' bundle they have within a year. They can live pretty good on that back home. They take care of they family.

I don't blame them, you know. I'm just sayin', them companies that do that, they keepin' a lot of other folks from getting jobs. They hire twenty or thirty of them illegals, and that's twenty or thirty other people that could be workin' that's been here all they lives and stuff but can't find nothing; because they hiring all these aliens, because they ain't got to pay them that much. Everywhere you go just about now you see a lot of them. . . . What do they call them? Foreigners. From other countries and stuff like that.

Even down at the welfare office. Shit! The majority of the people that work in there . . . you can't understand what they be sayin' when you talk to them.

And then they be actin' like the money is theirs and shit, like this here [high-pitched voice], "You can't get no money."

[resuming normal voice] "Oh, you motherfucker. Shit! I been here all my life. And I got to go do all this here, just to get a few dollars from you all. And then you all come here. The government give you all money when you get here."

They set 'em up with a little old business, give them a little old house where nine or ten of 'em might be staying, poolin' they money together and shit, to open up a business.

And here we are. Out here in these streets struggling. Trying to do this, trying to do that, and can't do nothin' 'cause they giving all the jobs away to other people.

As an individual, Sonny was a polite, gentle man, who stole and scavenged aggressively to maintain his addiction to heroin and crack. Understanding him or any of the homeless on Edgewater Boulevard in absolute moral categories, such as worthy worker, or thief, or xenophobic dopefiend, overstates the parameters for individual agency and obscures structural forces. Sonny's predicament is framed by a restructured global economy, institutionalized racism, a shredded welfare safety net, gentrification accompanied by a speculative real-estate market, and draconian drug laws. Depending on which fieldwork moment and theoretical lens one might select, consequently, the Edgewater homeless can be construed as exploited victims desperately seeking the dignity of legal day labor or as conniving, lazy, good-for-nothing addicts. In fact, like people everywhere buffeted by their moment in history and bounded by their personal fallabilities, they struggle to sustain some sense of agency and moral logic within the chronic crises enveloping their immediate social network.

I can't take care of my children. Look at me! —*Tina*

In the 1990s, income inequality grew more extreme throughout the United States, and the number of children living in poverty in California rose by almost half a million (Kids Count 2002). All of the Edgewater homeless except Hank had children, and most had been married and divorced. None maintained regular contact with their progeny. They were the "deadbeat dads" and "crack monster mothers" vilified in the press for failing to support and nurture their children (in an era when social services for impoverished and abandoned youth were severely cut back) (Bourgois 2003b:276–286). Everyone in our scene prioritized heroin over family. Most had simply been neglectful, but several of the men had been brutal to their children, wives, and girlfriends. Nevertheless, on the rare occasions when they discussed their children, they expressed tenderness and love for the sons and daughters they had abandoned.

Absent Fathers

Consistent with the ethnic family patterns discussed in chapter 4, the whites, with the exception of Ben and Nickie, were rejected by their offspring, whereas the African-American children sought intermittent contact with their wayward parents. The whites rarely broached the subject of their absent children, and several years passed before we managed to record stories about their families. Holidays elicited painful family memories. One Christmas Day, Philippe brought his twelve-year-old son, Emiliano, to Frank's camper, prompting Frank to comment that he had not seen any of his own children (two sons and one daughter with three different women) "in I don't know how many years." Max, who in deference to Emiliano's presence quickly put away the cotton shot he was about to inject, joined the conversation enthusiastically:

Max: I've got three kids too. One's in England. I've never seen him—

Frank: [interrupting] My middle son is the only one I really raised. I had him every weekend. I loved that kid more than anything in the world, man. He used to have my last name. I don't know what last name he's using now.

I bought him a red cart one Christmas.

Max: [talking simultaneously] Yeah! I bought my daughter a red cart, too, for Christmas. When she was three . . . or four . . . something like that. The old-fashioned Radio Flyer red wagon. That's what she wanted. She pointed it out one day in the store.

Frank: Yeah! The red wagon I bought Dougie had the stake sides. It was used, only about three or four years old. Cost me thirty dollars.

Max: I made sure my daughter had a brand-new one.

Frank: While I was assembling Dougie's wagon, I thought of my parents and parents all over the world putting their children's presents together on Christmas Eve. I thought, "Yeah, my parents used to do it for me, and now here I am doing it for my son." I did it in the basement, where all the tools were. I had a big place.

Max: I had a hard time assembling my cart. . . . .

Frank: Nah! It was easy for me. . . .

Max: I also bought my daughter a bike; a red bike, a brand-new one. She was too young for it [laughing], but ol' Max had to get it anyway.

Al: [overhearing us as he climbed into the camper] I bought all my kids their first bikes. Even when the ol' ladies took 'em away from me.

Frank: I used to play with Dougie until I stopped having contact . . . when I started living out here.

Philippe: How does that make you feel?

Frank: So much shit happened. It's kind of a weird trip. I don't really want to think about it.

But anyway, when he was a kid I used to take him with me everywhere. I'd even take him to bars with me. You could ask people about this up the hill.

I would like to be in touch with Dougie again. If I really straighten myself out, I would take care of him. I gotta get myself together. I gotta get out of this rut and start making it back to my family.

Later in our relationship with him, Frank resurrected his lost masculine sexuality by talking about his children:

My youngest son doesn't even know what I look like. His mother was gorgeous. Everybody was trying to get into her pants, but I was the only one who did. I had just got out of the joint and was doin' good. I used to dress in slacks and sports coats. I took her home one night from the bar. I'm Italian. She liked that Italian thing.

When I was a youngster I was a pretty good-looking guy. I'm not trying to brag, but I had some fine bitches in my time.

Frank's relationship with his oldest daughter was just as anonymous:

I can't remember exactly how old my daughter is. I was eighteen when she was born. Her [mother's] parents had money, and one of the arrangements was that I didn't come around. So I never really got to see her. So I guess I don't really have a daughter.

When asked about child support, Frank dismissively denied any sense of responsibility: "They don't need me for child support." A follow-up question, however, triggered a longing for redemption:

Philippe: Do you miss your kids?

Frank: Yeah. . . . But . . . I mean, you get used to it. . . . I mean, it's easy to kind of separate yourself.

But I loved Dougie, my son. The first two girls, it doesn't really bother me, because I never really knew them. But Dougie, I'd like to have him with me right now. He's about fifteen. That really bothers me. I can't just stay away forever, just disappear.

I've got to start . . . reuniting. Reestablishing family ties that I've put off for years.

Man! I've got to stop doing this [holding up his syringe]. It's so hard to do. . . .

These other guys out here, they don't give a shit. They don't really have any family ties. But I've got things I gotta take care of.

On another Christmas visit, Philippe found Max clean-shaven, with his hair neatly combed and his clothes freshly laundered. Philippe complimented him on his appearance, and Max smiled widely, revealing splintered teeth along his entire upper gum line.

Max: [probing for a vein] My girl was voted "most beautiful" in her class and I was voted "best hair." We got married in Reno. I was eighteen and she was fifteen, half Mexican, half Irish. My father drove us, and her mother came too. When we got back, I went home with my dad, and she with her mom.

Frank: Watch out, Max! Don't drip on the furniture.

Max: What are you talking about?

Frank: [pointing to Max's arm] Where you fixed. There's blood dripping.

Max: Oh, really! [wiping the blood]

Philippe: Did you have kids with your wife?

Max: Two daughters. I haven't seen them in years. I was a teenager. They live down the peninsula somewhere. They've got a beauty shop, I think. I hear my girls are beautiful.

Although the African-American men had some limited contact with their children, they did not support them financially or emotionally any more than did the whites. None of them had lived with their children for significant periods. Nevertheless, when their children occasionally sought them out, they responded with excitement. Their sense of patriarchal masculinity was not a distant, wistful memory of a macho past enveloped in depression and failure, as it was for Frank and Max. Instead, they basked in a shared sense of entitlement as fathers and as jealous heads of households, despite the fact that they had all subordinated the economic and logistical responsibilities of patriarchy to heroin and crack.

Jeff's Fieldnotes

Trying to protect himself from the rain, Carter is standing under the overhang of the cashier's booth at the gas station. He is ebullient. He tells me that he is "doin' great" and "has a story for [me], but first," he says, "buy me one too [pointing to the beer in my hand], so we can drink together." When I hand him my beer, he calls Sonny over to share it and begins in a loud voice:

Carter: "I'm walking with Sonny and Tina and this car parks next to us. I'm wondering who the dude is getting out of the car. He start walkin' towards me. I look and I start walking towards him and I say [in a soft whisper], 'My son . . . my son!'"

Sonny: [smiling] "Yeah. Yeah."

Carter: "And he calls out, 'Carter James?' See, he's got my name, a junior. 'How are you, Daddy? I'd always recognize you, Daddy.'"

Sonny: "Yeah. He said that."

Carter: "And he is fuckin' huge… six foot three and two-seventy-five."

Sonny: "Yeah, but he look like Carter. He do."

Tina: [reaching for the beer in Carter's hand] "Let me have some of that."

Carter: [raising the beer out of Tina's reach] "Yeah, yeah, Jeff. My son's gonna come back around at five o'clock. We gonna get together at the corner store. I want everyone to meet him. It's his birthday today. He said, 'Daddy! Dad!'… Oh, Jeff, you gotta meet him."

Sonny: "Jeff, it was somethin' beautiful if you woulda' saw it with your camera, the father and son."

Carter: "He was turning into the parking lot at Taco Bell and we was going down the street. And he spotted me, Jeff."

Tina: "Come on! Gimme some of that beer!"

Carter: [turning to Tina] "You know what? You'se fuckin' rude!"

Tina: [shouting] " You fuckin' rude! Shit, motherfucker!"

The commotion prompts the gas station attendant to threaten to call the police. We apologize, and Carter offers more details on his son's visit this morning. He is excited because his son's fiancée, who was sitting in the passenger seat, was "already sticking out," and he anticipates "soon being a grandfather." He is also proud that his son runs a barber shop in Oakland, where he lives "either with, or by, his mother."

    Tina continues grabbing for the beer. She is irritated by Carter's paternal gloating and in retaliation raises the specter of Carter's insolvency as a male provider.

Tina: "And I didn't grow up washing no windows, or gettin' no cans and bottles."

Carter: "I didn't either."

Tina: "Oh, yeah! You have me doing it."

Carter: [laughing] "And you right. And I do."

Tina: "That's right! And I didn't grow up shooting dope neither. I'm so angry with myself." [stomping off]

Carter: [ruefully watching Tina walk down the boulevard] "I did grow up with heroin."

Tina returns ten minutes later, smiling and flashing a ten-dollar bill. "Time to get me some crack." She has "hit a quick lick," fencing a plumber's monkey wrench and a pair of pliers that she grabbed from the back of a pickup truck parked at the discount lumberyard. We board the bus to Third

Street, where they have "a new connect, who gives a good count. Ten dollars worth for seven dollars."

Half an hour later, they are clinking their pipes in a three-way "cheers." I remind Carter on several occasions that we have to hurry to make it back to the corner by 5:00 P.M. to see his son. Instead, over the next forty minutes they spend their bus fare on crack, and we have to hike back to Edgewater Boulevard, arriving more than an hour late. The corner is empty.

Carter's eldest daughter, Charlotte, maintained a warm relationship with her half-brother, Junior. She also regularly visited Carter's aunt, who still had a home on the block where Carter and the mothers of his first two children had grown up. Charlotte's mother, Serena, had lived two doors down from Carter. Fourteen years old when she became pregnant, she broke up with Carter and hid her pregnancy from him. He found out about Charlotte several weeks after she was born, when one of Serena's cousins beat him up over it. Serena raised her daughter alone, with no help from Carter, and never had any more children. She describes Carter as having been "handsome, but very arrogant." To impress her, Carter had pretended he was sixteen years old, but in fact he too was only fourteen.

At that age, Carter was already fully invested in street life. He belonged to a gang, but Serena kept in touch with him because she did not want her daughter "to grow up not knowing her father." According to Serena, Carter would sometimes appear on her doorstep, promising help: "I'll be back in a few hours." The "few hours" turned into days, the days became months, and the months grew into years. When Charlotte was sixteen, Carter mistook her for one of his cousin's "cute girlfriends" at a family holiday reunion party. Serena had to reprimand him: "No, Carter, this is your daughter, Charlotte."

Carter was oblivious to the pain and disappointment he had caused his daughter and her mother. During our fieldwork, Charlotte was in her mid-twenties and was herself the mother of two young children whom she was raising alone, as her mother had done, trying to protect them from exposure to drugs and crime. She maintained warm relations, however, with Carter's extended family. On the way to visit her aunt up the hill from Edgewater Boulevard, she sometimes saw her father "pushing a shopping cart" or "nodding on the corner." Whenever this happened, she would call her mother for moral support. Nevertheless, halfway through our fieldwork, Charlotte introduced her children to their grandfather on the street.

Carter: I'm a grandfather! My grandsons, they're beautiful; four and one years old, very, very well-mannered and smart.

Sonny: It was like this, Jeffrey. Carter's daughter walked down the hill this afternoon to invite him to a family reunion. It was a beautiful moment. When she invited Carter to meet her children, he started to cry.

Carter: My daughter is beautiful. She works downtown at Bank of America. And she's going to school now, Laney College, in theatrical arts or something. She got in, paid her tuition. She wrote a screenplay and she sent it to Spike Lee.

She's been struggling. Life is hard. But she's been real supportive of me. But I was really kind of avoiding her, 'cause I been out here like this.

She told me, "I know it's been hard for you, but regardless of that, you're still my father and I wanted to see you. I love you for being my dad." She know what time it is, bein' a mother herself.

Sonny's daughters and grandchildren also sought him out, despite his failure to reciprocate. One Thanksgiving, he disappeared from Edgewater Boulevard for three months. It was rumored that he was "on the run" for stealing money and drugs from the crack sellers on the corner, that he was in jail, and that he had died of an overdose. When he finally returned to the scene, he had gained weight and looked revitalized. He spoke eagerly of having reunited with his grandchildren and expressed his affection in a discourse of paternal pride that Carter shared vicariously:

Sonny: I was at my mom's house for Thanksgiving. My brothers and sisters and all they kids are there, and my mom's house is kind of crowded.

Carter: [interrupting] They rocked the house!

Sonny: And I'm thinking, "Here I am at Thanksgiving and none of my kids or grandkids is here."

So I try to enjoy everything, but I'm wishing, "Damn! Wish it were my kids that's here." So it got to be something like five o'clock in the evening, and the doorbell rang and I look through the peephole thing.

I'm thinkin', "I guess it some parts of the family I don't know, because it's guys and girls with kids." And I'm walking away, after opening the door, and they come in and they say, "Happy Thanksgiving, Grandma!"

And I'm hearing this, and thinkin', "My brothers and sisters, they all here. And they kids is here. . . . So who is this here tryin' to say, 'Happy Thanksgiving, Grandma'?"

Carter: It was a surprise!

Sonny: And here come my son, coming through the door. "Hi, Daddy."

Carter: Yeah! Must a' felt great!

Sonny: "Ma, look, it's Raymond." And whoo! Whoo! Whoo! We hug, and we shake hands. And Raymond says, "Daddy, this is little Clarence. This is little Raymond Junior. And this is my wife, Louise, and this is your granddaughter"—I can't even think of her name right now.

Anyway, in comes two little girls behind Raymond. They looking almost like twins 'cause my two daughters—no way in the world that you couldn't tell that these two girls were sisters. And their daughters, they look like twins too.

And I'm, "Oh, my girls!"

And they see me, "Hi, Daddy. Happy Thanksgiving."

Everyone is hugging me and everything. And my spirits come from down here [patting the sidewalk] to way up here, way beyond the sky, if there was such a thing beyond it, you know. I mean, really, man! I am floating now you know.

And the little ones are calling me, "Sonny, Sonny." I say, "Girl, you call me 'Sonny' one more time, I'm going to turn that little old bottom up and spank that tail. Call me Granddaddy 'cause that's who I am."

Before I know it, they was sittin' on my lap. Hugging me, kissing me. "Granddaddy, I love you. Where you been? Granddaddy can you buy me this?"

And we getting connected. And then they runnin' all around the house saying, "Granddaddy, tell him to leave me alone." You know, a house full of people, and instead of running to great-grandma or grandma or momma or uncle or something, they runnin' straight to they grand-daddy. Like they picked me out from everybody in the house.

Carter: I feel you! I feel you!

Sonny: It was like as if I had never been away from my grandchildren. Like I had been know-ing them all the time. And, man, that something that made me feel so . . . so . . . indescrib-able! That was something I'll never forget. I'll always treasure that moment. No kind of drug or nothing could give me that kind of feeling.

The next day my daughter took me back home with her to San Diego.

Carter: Great!

Sonny: We catch the Greyhound 'cause my daughter, she's like me. She don't like to fly.

And I had brought my habit down and I didn't get as sick as I thought. I just had to go get me a spot in the back of the house and go lay down. Being around them kids, I don't want them to know, so I'm trying to be strong. They always knew what I did. "The old man mess-ing around." But I tell them, "Do as I say, not do as I do."

Carter: [nodding wisely] " . . . Not do as I do!"

The last time Sonny had seen his grandchildren, they had been infants. He used to babysit them, and he cherished his memories of their toddler milestones, including the first steps of his firstborn grandson:

I told my girl, "You're going to have to sneak out, baby. 'Cause your little boy goin' to cry."

And after she left, my grandson got to walking around the house, lookin' for his momma. And he not supposed to be able to do that, but he is actually walking around. And all of a sud-den here comes a brand-new world opens up. Like, "What am I . . . doing? Oh!" [opening his eyes wide and spreading his arms]

Oh, that was great! I noticed so many new things he was doin'. And his little sister, too. [making peek-a-boo gestures to an imaginary baby] "Right here is the same thing I used to do with your mom." We had fun!

According to a police incident report from these years, the housing project apartment where Sonny babysat his grandchildren was also a retail heroin sales spot. Three officers forced entry into the apartment and caught him flushing heroin down the toilet. They also seized "packaging materials such as balloons, sifters . . . Semi Automatic pistol cal. 25 auto Raven . . . clip with six live rounds ammonn [sic]" and a crack pipe. Following this arrest Sonny served a five-and-a-half-year sentence in Folsom State Prison. He was never able to reestablish him-self either as a successful dealer or as an occasional babysitter for his grandchildren.

Despite his daughter's entreaty that he live with her in San Diego, Sonny returned to San Francisco's Edgewater Boulevard. At first, he was full of positive resolutions:

They is so beautiful. I guess everybody would say that about their children, but my kids all came out beautiful. I really enjoyed that close bond. But instead of having that great moment and then not having it no more, not seeing them again for the next nine or ten years . . . I'm going to try my best to be with them as much as I can.

Like I said, they knew everybody else but their granddaddy. I was the only one not around.

Sonny's commitment to heroin and crack prevailed over his love for his kin, and he did not increase his visits to his grandchildren. Instead, he remained full time on Edgewater Boulevard, pushing his shopping cart full of cans and hitting licks whenever possible.

When pressed to reflect on his children, Sonny expressed his emotional vulnerability:

Philippe: Tell me about your son who died.

Sonny: I was sitting in my cell, and the guard came and told me the Jewish chaplain wanted to see me.

And I says, "Want to see me! For what? I'm not Jewish."

And he made an ol' remark 'bout how "I've seen some black Jews before."

I say, "Well, you ain't see none right here."

So he asked me, did I want to go over there or not?

And I told him "No" at first. Then I thought about it and I say, "Well, it a chance to get me out of my cell for a little bit."

So I went over to the chaplain's office and he wasn't in at the moment, and I seen a little strip of paper on his desk with my mom's number on it. And I started tripping, and I say, "*Da-a-amn!* I hope there ain't nothin' wrong with my mom."

The chaplain came in about five minutes later. He say, "Are you Sanford Jourdan?" That's my real name. "Well, I think you oughta have a seat."

I say, "Nah. I'll stand."

He say, "Uh . . . ah . . . I hate to inform you of some bad news, that your son Sonny Junior was killed."

And when he say, "Your son Sonny was killed," that's all I heard.

I didn't hear. . . . It's like somebody hit me with a ten-pound sledge hammer and just knocked me down in my seat. I started crying; couldn't stop. [wiping tears from his eyes] It hurt. It hurt. It hurt.

I never been hurt like that before in my life and it still hurts today. God bless his soul.

He was my Junior. My dad, me, and him, we all Sanford Jourdan. He didn't have no kids. Dad passed in '77. Sonny Junior was killed in '89, and now it's just me. As far as any more Sonny Juniors—the third, the fourth, stuff like that—there ain't no more.

Philippe: And do you miss your ex-wife?

Sonny: I do sometimes . . . whenever I think about her. She's a good girl. She raised all those kids good, too. And I didn't have to worry about her fuckin' around.

But a lot of times, I be so busy now, hustling, you know, collecting bottles and cans, I don't have time to think about anything. I've got to think about me, you know. And try to make some kind of preparation for me. . . . I'm getting tired of this shit.

[slowly] I don't think anyone that have any kids would ever want to go through that feeling. 'Cause to lose a kid is just a hurtin' thing. I hurt today as much as I was hurtin' when I first

got the news. It's not something I want to even think about. Because I miss him too much. Even when I was a kid, I used to say I hope I would die before my mom and dad.

The guards took me into lockdown for three days. It's what they do so you don't go off.

At this moment in the conversation, Sonny motioned for us to turn off the tape recorder. He stooped over his shopping cart, shoulders shaking. To calm himself down and hide his tears, he began rummaging through the recyclables in his cart. By the time he had filled a bottle on the bottom of the stack with sand, he had fully recomposed himself, and we hurried with him to the recycling depot to have his materials weighed. After an hour-long wait in line, he received eleven dollars in exchange for the bottles and cans in his cart (which represented a night of full-time scavenging), and he ran off to split a bag of heroin with Carter.

On the tenth anniversary of his son's murder, Sonny asked Jeff to take him to the cemetery. Carter accompanied them.

Jeff's Fieldnotes

We cannot find the grave in the miles of tombstones, but the rolling hills of the cemetery's perfectly clipped lawn are soothing. We walk past the Arab section, where carved script flows on pink and gray marble. The Chinese section features portraits of the dead, framed by horizontal lettering.

Sonny stops suddenly before a headstone. It is his father's, not his son's. He kneels down on one knee, tears welling, "I miss you so much, Daddy. After this, I'm going to see your grandson." Placing his hands on Sonny's shoulder, Carter says gently, "Sonny, he's a lot better where he is down there than where we are up here."

Perpetuating Patriarchal Abuse

Several of the men on Edgewater Boulevard talked about having beaten up their children, girlfriends, and wives in the past. Rather than interpreting their violent behavior as harmful, they saw themselves as rectifying inappropriate gender roles. They invoked the morality of violence through a recurrent set of patriarchal values with classically oedipal resonances. Experiencing and perpetrating domestic violence were central to their construction of masculinity. They felt an urgent need to use violence to teach their sons how to be strong, virile men respectful of both their mothers and their absent fathers. They were convinced that the mothers had "sissified" their sons and deserved punishment. Only they, as the male heads of household, however, were authorized to administer that punishment. Significantly, none of the men admitted to hitting a daughter.

In the childhood stories presented in chapter 4, many of the Edgewater homeless emerge unambiguously as victims of scarred childhoods. When these same individuals speak of being parents, the roles are reversed. The perseverance of domestic violence across multiple generations turns victims into perpetrators.

Arguably, the levels of bodily pain (cold, hunger, abscesses, exhaustion) that the Edgewater homeless endure daily as drug users can be interpreted as self-punishment from unresolved childhood trauma. In many cases, abandoning children for homeless heroin injection and crack smoking was less toxic than attempting to maintain the patriarchal nuclear family ties that perpetuate domestic gray zones. Hank, for example, broke his father's spiral of violence by becoming an outcast heroin addict on the street and never having girlfriends or children. Tina, like Hank, suffered exceptional physical and emotional violence as a young child, and she was explicit about the importance of protecting her sons and daughters from her drug use: "I can't be with my kids. The baby's only three years old. But I don't want them back. Because I tried it. And I got 'em back, and I let 'em down again—and I refuse to do them like that again."

Similarly, perhaps we can understand why Carter and Tina kept telling us, "We always have a place to stay, anytime we need it," in reference to their extended families, but very rarely took advantage of that opportunity, even during moments of crisis. As children, both of them appear to have taken refuge in the street, fleeing families beset by domestic violence. Years later when they were on the path to becoming dedicated outlaws and addicts, they began to inflict the same kind of harm on their own households. Even Sonny's difficult-to-comprehend "choice" to remain on the street, despite the entreaties of his loving family, may also have been a self-imposed exile to mitigate his destructive influence on his kin. In short, there may have been a protective logic among the Edgewater homeless for abandoning their children and failing to reciprocate attempts to reunite.

Sal, who maintained no contact with his family, spoke eloquently about his violent relationship to his sons. Despite his exceptionally small physical stature, he had a domineering personality on the boulevard. Within his circumscribed social network, bounded by homelessness and drugs, he differentiated himself from those around him by exercising the arbitrary personal power available to a small-time heroin seller. As many male batterers do, he considered himself a victimized man and asserted the patriarchal values he understood as self-evident: filial respect (for *both* father and mother) and a father's monopoly on violence against a mother. By beating his son and tongue-lashing his son's mother, he may also have been seeking to redeem himself as a failed head of household in a home that had long ago expelled him.

Jeff's Fieldnotes

Sal limps out of the A&C corner store with his ever-present twenty-two-ounce bottle of St. Ide's malt liquor. His pit bull, My Girl, follows two steps behind, attached by a leash made from a three-foot fragment of chain. To avoid a ticket from the police, he unhooks from his belt loop a plastic travel mug with a Deloitte and Touche Consulting Group logo and fills it with malt liquor, tossing the bottle to the ground. He pops in a straw and sips while surveying passing traffic.

I ask permission to tape-record the story he told Philippe and me yesterday. "I don't want to talk with these bozos around here," he replies, motioning with a tilt of his head toward Felix and Vernon, who are nodding on the corner.

We walk into the alley to the shipping container in which he lives. It sits on a vacant lot, surrounded by a ten-foot-high wrought-iron fence. While unhitching the padlock, he pauses to yell at Vernon, "Get the fuck out of here! Stop making such a commotion in front of my place." Vernon is doing what Hank calls "the chicken." It is his bizarre way of nodding when the heroin is strong. Eyes closed, he bobs his entire body in rhythmic slow motion at the knees, while alternately flailing his arms and daintily scratching the tip of his nose.

Vernon snaps back, suddenly wide awake: "I look like a judge compared to him!" He points to Felix, collapsed in an even deeper nod in the gutter, surrounded by trash. "If anyone looks like a dopefiend, it's him. I look like a preacher compared to Felix!"

Sal holds open the gate and invites me to pass first into the "patio" in front of his container. He pulls out his only chair, a white plastic garden model, shakes off the puddle of water pooled on its seat, wipes it with a rag, and covers it with a dry piece of newspaper. He then stretches out his palm waving me to be seated and stacks two cinder blocks for himself.

Throughout the tape recording, Sal maintains his gaze just beyond me, never catching my eyes, as though the action he is describing is taking place over my shoulder. He animates his story intermittently by jumping to his feet and acting out the dramatic moments. Periodically, he interrupts his account to peer through the fence at the customers who are pacing in front of his gate, waiting for him to "open up." They see him peeking at them but remain quiet and stare at the ground. They know not to bother him, lest he explode in anger and arbitrarily refuse to sell to everyone, leaving them all dopesick until tomorrow morning. Among the anxious clients outside, I recognize a disheveled public works maintenance laborer, who became addicted to Vicodin (an opiate painkiller) during a hospital stay after a work-related back injury.

Sal registers no facial expression during these interruptions and resumes his story without losing his train of thought:

"My ex, she couldn't handle my son. She was talkin' about throwing him out, and she been in court. He was talkin' back to her, and violent, too. So she called me. And I went over there to talk to him on the front steps of her trailer home.

"My son said, 'That bitch takin' out on me, Dad, what she wants to take out on you.'

"I said, 'I figured as much, but check it, amigo; you can't be callin' your mom a bitch. That I don't tolerate! You should know that.'

"And my son goes, 'Well, you gotta go teach her a lesson—'

[interrupting his son in the conversation] "'No, no, no no, that's my business with her. You're my kid. You don't get involved. Even if I was sixty-five years old and you're thirty-five, you don't get involved between me and your mother's business. That's the way it goes, buddy. That's your mother, right or wrong. You don't say nothin' against your mom. You probably gonna have kids one day. Then you'll understand. I'm just trying to give you an example. I don't understand how the hell you could ever come out like this, 'cause I wasn't raised like this. I never talked back to my mom. And I never ever dreamed about touching my mother. No fucking way!'

"I told my son, 'Till you turn eighteen, you can't be talkin' like that to your mom. First of all, she's your mom. You do what she says. And second, she's feeding you and everything else.'

"So then, right then, his mom comes out of the house, and he goes, 'Get outta here, you bitch!'

"I go, 'You don't call her a bitch.'

"Then she goes, 'Hit him, Sal. Hit him! He's a little monster.'

"And he goes, 'Old man, you're a weak-ass dude. You let her walk all over you.'

"I go [gritting his teeth], 'What did you say?'

"And he said [mumbling], 'You heard what I said.'

"I said, 'No, I didn't. Say it louder.'

"He said [shouting], 'I said, fuck you, Dad! All right? Did you hear me now?'

"And I said, 'Yeah!' And I go bam! And I slapped him. [swinging his fist in slow motion toward the bevy of customers outside the gate]

"He's like, shocked. [widening his eyes and stumbling backward with both hands on his cheeks]

"I go, 'Don't you ever, ever talk to me like that again.'

"He goes, 'You ever hit me again, Dad, I'm gonna fire on you.'

"I go, 'I'll hit you all I want. I'm your father. If I think you're wrong, I'm gonna beat you all I want. And I don't want to hear that language no more, either. You talk to me with respect.'

"He goes, 'I don't give a fuck.'

"I go, 'What?' And I slapped him again.

"And he grabs my hand and he goes [clenching teeth and spitting the words], 'Don't hit me again!'

"And I go, 'I'll hit you.' And I went to hit him again, and he socked me on the left side of my face.

"Then my ex-wife, she goes, 'Sal, Sal! I told you, beat his ass. Beat his ass!'

"I go—to him—'Who the hell do you think you are to hit me? I'm your father!'

"And he goes, 'Fuck, I don't care. You don't care about me.'

"And then he goes to put his hands up again, and bam! I hit him again. I dunno if I hit him with the open hand or with the fist. The next I know, he socks me again.

"I said to myself, 'Damn! My kid's fast.'

"So I says, 'You think you wanna mix the men with the boys, huh? You little motherfucker, I'm gonna hit you with my fist closed, son. You say you're sorry right now.' But he puts his hands up in order to defend himself. As far as I was concerned, that was his answer. I go bam! And I hit him in his face. And he flew back.

"And he goes, 'Ow! You hit me!'

"So then it was on, and we started fighting. We rolled down the steps. He was punching me and everything. And I hated to hit him. But every time I hit him, ya know, I didn't want to break his nose or blacken his face, so I kept hittin' him in his chest. I hit him hard.

"And every time I hit him, he go [grunting], 'Oh! Unh!'

"And his mother the whole time is sayin', 'Beat him, Sal. Beat his ass. That's what he needs!'

"I go—to her—'Get the hell outta here!'

"Me and my son were boxing toe to toe. And I said to myself, 'I can't believe this. That I'm hitting my son. And this kid's hittin' hard, ya' know. Hittin' me a lot.' Because I'm a man, I outweighed him and stuff at that time. Then boom! I caught him right here [pointing to the side of his stomach], and that made him double up. That's when I held him down. It seemed like it was forever.

"And he was crying, 'Let me go, Dad. Let me go. Just let me go. Just let me go. You hit me, Daddy. You don't love me. You don't love me. You don't love me.'

"I go, 'Now I'm Daddy, huh? You're always gonna be my son, whether I hit you or not. No matter what happens.' He was bleeding a little bit from his nose. I was bleeding more from my nose and from my mouth.

"His mom finally comes out of the house again, and when she sees that he bleedin'… [high-pitched voice], 'Oh, my baby! My baby! Look what you did to my baby. Oh-h-h…. You son-of-a-bitch!' She turns on me. [flailing his arms]

"'Fuckin' snake-ass-motherfuckin'-punk-bitch.' That's what I said to her, and I just left."

Sal had two other sons, ages twenty-nine and fifteen, at the time of this conversation, and both were incarcerated. He referred to the oldest as "an asshole, a real fuck-up" and to the youngest as "a fuck-up, too. He's in Log Cabin [juvenile detention]." He took no responsibility for their outcomes; he considered himself a good father, following the logic of patriarchally scripted violence that he believed would bring moral order and inculcate the proper succession of masculine values into younger generations: a father's role is to dominate the mother; the son's role is to sanctify the mother and to respect the father until the father is no longer strong enough to beat up the son. Sal himself was imbued as a young child with the common sense of these violent masculine roles. Now in middle age, he struggles with the memory of being unable to defend his own mother from an abusive father figure, and he seeks redemption through violence:

I was raised by my stepfather. He used to beat me every day of my life, though. *Every day of my life*. I wasn't his kid. That's why he used to beat me.

Jeff: Did you ever think about hitting back?

Sal: Yeah, I did. But I never got in a fight with him, because my mom got divorced while I was thirteen and a half. So I never had a chance. I was already thinking about killing him when he was in his sleep.

He used to beat my mother. One time he was choking her. He was killing my mom. I told my little brother, "C'mon, c'mon. He's gonna kill mom. He's gonna kill mom."

[swinging an imaginary object] *Bonk!* She hit him with the copper pot. Knocked him flat on his ass, walked to the telephone, called the police. They came, and when he talked shit to them, they whooped him up, because they seen how he hit my mom, right? You gotta realize this was back in the sixties.

After that, my mom got a restraining order against him and he wasn't allowed back in the house.

The literature on domestic violence emphasizes the importance of transgenerational cycles of violence (Earls and Barnes 1997). Our theory of lumpen abuse goes beyond the individualizing psychological frame to link psycho-affective experiences—including those that express themselves in oedipal frustrations—to political-economic and cultural forces as well as to gender power relations. Violence in Sal's account is not simply sociopathy or a universalized masculine drive for domination. It is mindful, targeted, effective, and ethical within its own logic. Abuse within families is not reproduced as blind, imitative behavior, but rather as a resource for making order in the world. It is rewarded by prevailing cultural values that pass for common sense and for universal ethics. The valence of violence around gender and generational authority becomes especially charged when avenues for asserting hierarchy and achievement are limited by poverty, chronic drug and alcohol use, and social marginalization—all of which shape lumpen reality at the everyday level in the United States in the early twenty-first century.

In chapter 1, for example, Carter presented his decision to leave his sister's house and become homeless as an assertion of his masculinity in response to his niece's lack of respect for him. More dramatically, in chapter 4, Hank's account of fighting with his father also reconstructed individual moral worth through a patriarchal understanding of masculine roles rendered more violent than the norm in the crucible of childhood abuse. Hank's story, like Sal's, resonates oedipally when he describes the epiphany of putting a gun to his father's head to defend his mother. Violent, sexualized masculinity organized around patriarchal themes pervades much of the routine interaction on the street, such as the bantering among Felix, Reggie, and the Yemeni storekeeper described in chapter 1 or, more subtly, the threateningly playful, parent-like edge in Carter's voice when he was first falling in love with Tina and would call out to her jealously, "Don't make me come get you!" when he saw her talking for too long to other men on the block.

The failure to live up to the patriarchal ideal of autocratically controlling women may explain the routinized misogyny prevalent among lumpenized men on the street. This was the case for Al, who was otherwise exceptionally generous and was always hospitable, helpful, and thoughtful when we visited. He cheerfully related many particularly offensive accounts of his violent treatment of women. He assumed that we shared his common sense and would bond with him as fellow victims of unworthy "ol' ladies." His stories contained the familiar domestic themes of instilling masculinity in a son and accessing female sexuality hierarchically within the family. Significantly, Al's lumpen subjectivity, molded in a lifetime of ongoing abuse, expressed itself in a version of masculinity that explicitly contradicted the conventional obligation of providing financial support for spouse and progeny, and he triumphantly flouted the incest taboo:

My son's twenty-one now. His name is Eli Sunshine. I named him Sunshine because he's the light of my life. I always wanted a boy.

He's been pretty wild, dealing weed and crank. But he was a sissy when he was little. Used to cry like his mother whenever I did anything to him.

He works in a warehouse now. His old lady has him by the ears. I told him to never get married. "Don't be a fool. All women do is take you in, take your fuckin' kids, and leave you."

Last time he visited, he asked for money. I told him, "Get the fuck outta my life. Get outta here."

Last year I took him and his girl to Reno. We got a hotel room for three days. I gave him a hundred dollars. "Why don't you and your old lady go downstairs and have a party?"

He says, "Why don't you stay here and poke my old lady and I'll go downstairs and party?"

His mother left me because she was strung out. I was fixing Harleys [motorcycles] up in Clearlake at the time, building them from the bottom up. My first was a 1947 Knucklehead. I told her, "Drugs or me? Take your pick." So she left . . . and I took her daughter—my stepdaughter—with me. She was fourteen, but the mother didn't even care about her own daughter or nothing. So I took care of her till she was about seventeen. And then me and her got together.

We had two babies. They were about eight months apart. The second baby was born premature. He weighed like two pounds when he was born. They kept the old lady in the hospital for a month. And we already had my son, Eli Sunshine, not yet a year old. I had to take care of both of them.

The second baby died of crib syndrome. I was in jail at the time for an old warrant. But my partner who fixed Harleys with me told me about it. The baby choked to death because she propped the bottle up in his mouth and then went in the other room to shoot up speedballs with my partner.

That's when I just said, fuck everything, and went to pot. The old lady come to visit me in jail. A special visit. She acted like nothing happened. She goes [high-pitched voice], "Hi, how ya doin? Guess what?"

And I go, "What?"

And she goes, "Noah died." Just like it was nothing.

I said, "Get the fuck out of here!"

The county jail didn't even let me out for the fucking funeral, and when I finally got out, the old lady was fucking around with someone else. Every time I go to visit her, I got about nine dudes after me, plus her old man, who won't let me see her.

We were able to confirm through California county birth records that Al's stepdaughter turned "wife" was actually sixteen, not seventeen, when she gave birth to their first child, Eli Sunshine.

Al spoke only briefly about his own childhood, but his account contained the familiar themes that promote (and reflect) lumpen outcomes: absent/criminal/violent/ incarcerated fathers, alcohol and drug use in the family, poverty, and job loss. He also specified the recurring imperative to monopolize violence against women and children within the family:

I grew up with my grandma because they sent my dad to Folsom Prison. He beat the fuck outta some lady. Robbed her blind, her house and everything.

My grandma married nine times and never had any money.

My sister is ten years younger than me. She's been a dopefiend for twenty-five years. And she's had AIDS for over ten years. She still does half a gram when she gets up and half a gram in the afternoon, plus her AIDS medicine.

Her old man cut her eye out. Took a beer bottle, stuck it in her eye and turned it. His mom lives up the hill, so I'm watching out for him to kick his ass.

When I used to tease my sister, my grandmother would get my grandfather, Gunboat Al, the boxer, to come to the house . . . and he had these big old fingers, man . . . and would go *boom!* [swinging his arm] up against the head. Felt like somebody socking me; knocking me out.

Mother Love and Addiction

Society condemns mothers more than fathers for using drugs and for abandoning children. All the women on Edgewater Boulevard internalized this condemnation and had more pro-longed and emotionally engaged relationships with their children, even though they, too, like the men, ultimately subordinated responsibility for children to drug consumption. Nickie's son, Alexander, for example, lived with her for the first four years of our fieldwork until he was fourteen years old. She thought of herself as protecting her son from her lifestyle and successfully obtained public housing for the two of them, after she and her infant had experienced homelessness together:

> It makes all the difference not to be sleeping on the ground. Keeps you from shivering all night. When I was on the street with my son, when he was a baby, I laid down cardboard—anything to keep our sleeping bags off the ground so we wouldn't freeze to death.

She stopped "turning tricks in the Tenderloin" when her son turned six, "old enough to understand." She could not, however, protect Alexander from the fallout from heroin in her life:

> *Nickie:* I met his father in a drug rehab program. But we started using together when we got out.
> I found out I was pregnant after I swallowed a bag of dope when my husband and I got pulled over by the cops. Later, I took an Ivory dish soap bottle and gave myself an enema to get the dope out. Afterwards I was having this pain, and *it did not feel right.* I thought it was from shoving that bottle up there, so I went to the emergency room. That's when they told me I was four months pregnant. Alex was born dopesick.
>
> *Philippe:* What happened to Alex when you were locked up earlier this year?
>
> *Nickie:* My ex took care of him, but there is a lot of conflict with his wife. She's a guard at the county jail [chuckling]. I saw her last time I was arrested. She's a stone-cold bitch, and Alexander can be a handful—so he spent most of the time in my apartment alone when I was in jail.
> My ex brought Alexander to visit me once when I was in the new county jail, you know, the one they call the "glamour slammer." Alex was really impressed with all the security. He really enjoyed coming there. But when I was sent away to Chowchilla [women's prison], I told him not to come, and I like it like that.

Nor could Nickie protect her son from the ubiquity of drugs and violence in their hous-ing project:

> Alex is twelve and has always been in gifted classes at school. I try to keep him away from the other twelve-year-olds in the project who have already quit school and sell crack. They're all black.

He hangs out at a card shop in the Avenues on the other side of town till dark time. I asked him if it's safe, you know. And he says, "Yeah, because over in that area it's the white gangs." So they don't mess with him. Whereas over here he gets messed with by the black gangs.

[walking into her son's room] See, this is his coin sorting bank. I'm just gonna take a dollar eighty-five out to go buy a Cisco. I gotta remember which coins I take 'cause I gotta put the exact same ones back before he gets home. He counts the coins every night and gets upset if any are missing or even if they're in a different combination.

On one occasion, a member of the ethnographic team was in Nickie's apartment when Alexander came home from school. The boy walked in just as Felix and Nickie were about to inject, and they ran out of the room. Alexander was polite to the ethnographer but complained matter-of-factly, "I hate Felix and all the other junkies my mom brings home." His stepmother, the county prison guard, eventually allowed him to move into her house in the suburbs halfway through our fieldwork. Nickie continued to speak with pride of Alex's teenage milestones, but her commitment to heroin trumped her mother-love discourse and she rarely saw him:

Alex is having a great summer out in Vallejo. They even have a swimming pool in the backyard of their complex. I might get to go visit there. I see him on the weekends sometimes, 'cause his father drives him in so he can volunteer at the zoo. He's been doing that for four or five years. I'm sure when he gets out of high school, they're gonna hire him. Ben's brother is a big shot at the zoo, and he did the same thing when he was a kid.

Alexander takes care of the sick animals, bringing them their food. He likes doing that. Last week he was walking one of them things that got real powerful hind legs, like a kangaroo, and it took off running. And Alexander can't let him go. He's runnin' with him, and then the animal went one way and he went the other way into a tree. And they knocked each other out [chuckling].

I guess everything must be hunky-dory over there now at his father's. I wish I could go visit. . . . Maybe one of these years. I'm really happy.

Tina also expressed tenderness and longing for her children in a strong mother-love discourse. She had seven children by five different fathers, and she was not in contact with any of them when we first met her. Despite multiple attempts, we were never able to elicit a complete accounting of where they lived or their precise birth order and paternities. Tina was often overcome by tears when she tried to enumerate them on her fingers, pausing, repeating, stuttering, and backtracking. She would locate each child in her memory, arranging and rearranging them by birth order, gender, or father as well as by particular trauma.

My first two boys, Ricky and Antoine, they's Richard's kids.

Then I got Persia, Jewel. Oh! [counting on her fingers] . . . Wait a minute . . . okay. Ricky, Antoine, Persia, Jewel. But I got another girl. Oh! . . . Sylvia. Yeah, yeah, I forgot about Sylvia. Sylvia came after Persia. Persia is thirteen and named after my mother. And then came Sylvia. She's eleven and named after my sister. Then Jewel; then there's . . .

I have five fathers. No, I don't, I have four fathers because . . . my two oldest boys is by one. . . . Two girls is by one, so that's two. . . . And Antoine is a Williams, too; but I put him as Gordon because I was upset at his father and all that shit. But the father knows . . . the whole family know that he a Williams.

She would jump from an account of one child's crisis to that of another, in a manner hauntingly similar to how she talked about her own exposure to violence and sexual trauma in early childhood. As if to reassure herself, she would often interrupt her accounts with the non sequitur "But they safe. They have everything; they not without nothin'."

All Tina's children lived with relatives in formal foster care arrangements, except for the eldest, Ricky, who was twenty years old. "He do what all the youngsters do, he a baller [crack dealer]." None of her children still lived in San Francisco or Oakland. The cost of working-class housing had forced all her extended family members to move to the exurbs of the Bay Area in the Central Valley of California, well beyond commuting distance.

Reminiscent of Tina's childhood story of being socialized into the common sense of sex work, her account of her marriage to Richard conveys the way a particularly violent "pimp" version of outlaw masculinity endures across multiple generations:

> I never had a pimp or nothin', but I married a pimp, Richard, at the age of twenty. And didn't know it until he told me.
>
> Richard was so slick. I never caught him at nothin'. I just couldn't believe it. It was like he spent so much time with us, he didn't have time to sneak around. But he did. He got about fifteen kids. It wasn't the kids I didn't like. But I wasn't fit to be no wife to no pimp and take care of all his bitches' kids while they out givin' fucks. They the ones wanted to pay him. I didn't!
>
> When I had my second son, Antoine, one of Richard's ho's was pregnant at the same time [shaking her head in disgust]. It ain't nothin' new. I didn't know that ho' was pregnant, but my son, Ricky, he like, "Mother, Mom, my Daddy's girl told me next time she see me I might have a little sister."
>
> I'm like, "Boy, shut up! I'm gonna have a boy, what you talkin' about?" And that's when I found out.
>
> But ain't was nothin' I could do about it. It's just like, oh, well, I'll remember this name, this birthday. It was my stepchild. [loudly] *Shit!* My kid's half-sister.
>
> Richard took little Ricky with him wherever he went. Every week, we had to get whitewalls for our tires. We had a El Dorado, and we'd be at Big O Tires because he'd done flapped them tires off ridin' up and down the highway, checkin' out his ho's. Ricky'd be sittin' right up alongside his Daddy on this little seat thing. That's how he learned from his Daddy. All the ho's that be hangin' out, they just loved that little boy.
>
> Richard was a bank robber, too, but I didn't know, till I seen him on the news when he got caught.

During Ricky's infancy, Tina struggled unsuccessfully to control her consumption of alcohol and pills. Her extended family intervened against her in favor of the outlaw father because she was seen as the unworthy mother. They set the foundation for Ricky to follow his father and his uncles into pimping, bank robbing, and eventually into crack dealing:

I'll never forget. My oldest brother came to see me and told me he knew I was usin'. And he went and told Richard, and Richard came and took Ricky from me. That was real awful, ugh! Ricky was only one years old. That time, it wasn't the county that took him away from me, just Richard.

But then I went back home to live with my momma in the John Muir apartments with Rick and Antoine, and my mother convinced me to put Ricky in a daycare, 'cause I had went back to school. He had all the activities and everything. My mother always tried to make us happy. We the ones fucked our lives up.

My baby brother, Dee-Dee, took Ricky under his wing. Dee-Dee's not really blood—his daddy is Arthur—but you know how it is when someone grow up with you. Anyhow, Dee-Dee potty-trained Ricky and got him out of the daycare to bring him home and everything.

This brief period of stability for Tina's two youngest children ended in a conflict that precipitated contact with Child Protective Services (CPS). The outcome of state intervention proved disastrous for little Ricky:

See, I had broke my boys' daddy's damn window 'cause he had went to Texas. And then someone called the damn housing authority and I was drunk and they took me to jail.

So the next day the CPS was at the house and took Ricky. They had him stayin' at my cousin's in Oakland, and I could see him when I wanted. But my cousin's husband tried to molest Ricky. That's when all the mess hit the fan.

My son tried to kill him with a butcher knife. Ricky always slept with a knife under his pillow. He remember me sleeping with a knife under my pillow.

My baby brother, Dee-Dee, say that man better stay in jail because I think Dee-Dee got molested, too, when he was little, because he hate punks . . . faggots. And that's not supposed to go on under foster care.

But then Ricky started acting up easy, you know trippin', like a bad, obnoxious child. He wanted to be like his mother, and he was like his dad, too. He has his own mind.

He went to Arizona to be with his fuckin'-ass daddy, but Antoine, his little brother, stayed here with my brother. Ricky's daddy's a baller. He set Ricky up dealin' crack . . . pounds and pounds and pounds. Got him shot with a nine millimeter in the leg.

See, in Arizona they wear scarves—Bloods an' Crips. It was a Blood that shot Ricky, 'cause they dropped a red scarf when they left.

Richard almost got his own son killed over some dope. That's how my life is: for some dope!

Tina particularly cherished her memories of a period of domesticity and independence when she was legally employed as a nursing home attendant following the birth of her first daughter, Persia. She was living with her sister, Sylvia, a sex worker, in a San Francisco high-rise housing project nicknamed "the highrise from hell" (dynamited by the city of San Francisco in 1998 [*San Francisco Chronicle* 2000, April 28]):

My sister always took care of me. We lived on the seventeenth floor in the Geneva Towers. Sylvia made sure that I continued to take care of my children. Nobody else did. I had no man in my life. I messed around, but I didn't have no man, especially not living with us when I'm a single parent. I didn't want no man because I was able to take care of us, my own self.

I got me a job. And I was a woman, independent; got my own car. I had a bank account, A-1 credit, brand-new furniture. Ricky and Antoine had they bunk beds, you know, them little twin sets with them pillows, and a radio and record player with them big ol' disks. And here's a couch [walking over to the fire hydrant], and you take the pillows off and it's a bed [leaning over the hydrant to an imaginary bed]. And I had my room. We had a car.

I done all of this. I worked graveyard. And I got two hundred dollars of food stamps. And I lived in low rent. My rent was eighty-nine dollars, three bedrooms that I shared with my sister, Sylvia, and her three kids.

Tina's domestic stability ended abruptly when Sylvia was stabbed to death by a fellow sex worker. Tina tried to adopt Sylvia's children, but the biological father kidnapped them:

That was so wrong! I dressed us all alike. Sylvia's three kids and my three kids. They sneaked her kids away from me. My niece was running from 'em, "No! I stay with my auntie!" They grabbed her and put her in the car. Why did they done it like that?

That's when I blew it. That's when I started usin' again. And I had stopped usin' anything.

Tina named her next daughter Sylvia, in memory of her murdered sister. By this time, however, she was homeless and smoking crack, the new drug of choice in the late 1980s. The proliferation of crack coincided with the consolidation of neoliberalism in the United States during the Reagan years (Bourgois 2003a). Housing policy had followed the recommendations of the president's blue ribbon housing task force of developers, landlords, and bankers (Atlas and Dreier 1994). The federal government was slashing investment in public housing in favor of "free and deregulated" markets, and the result was predictable. Across the country homelessness and street-based drug use soared.

I was stayin' at the Richmond Rescue Mission because Ricky and Antoine was in Vallejo with my brother, and Persia was in Antioch with her Daddy. I just had Sylvia to myself. She was a infant.

And this one time, I came back too late to get in. So instead we stayed over to this guy's house. He was selling crack. And I just had him smokin' with me, and he gave me money and crack. I lingered along the way. He was so nice. He gave me and my daughter his room. He didn't come in.

Me and Sylvia didn't have nowhere to go at nighttime to get out the cold. And he was like, 'Get your baby out the cold.' And like, eventually we ended up together. We hooked up. He was the daddy for Jewel, my third girl.

It took two years. He would beat me with a cane stick, beat me with a hanger. I guess he was real angry because I didn't stop using drugs when I was pregnant.

I fought back all the time. I wasn't lettin' nobody hit me without me hittin' them back. But you know, Jeff, my bones . . . my bones are so small they break and he broke my jaw. It was wired up for six weeks, an awful feeling.

Then he felt bad so he cried every time he seen me. But I didn't let him. I hated him ever since. He didn't just break my jaw. He broke my heart. Because my kids had took to him. Ricky and Antoine would come visit on the weekend. My brother, the minister in Modesto, would bring them. Persia's daddy would bring her by, too.

And he treated them like they was his kids. And Sylvia, he loves her to death, because that's the one that he took in, right? She was an infant and he raised her up.

Jewel was my first crack baby. They took Persia from me, too, because she had crack in her, too; but she wasn't no crack baby, 'cause she didn't have withdraws. Jewel had withdraws for a whole year.

I called my cousin from the hospital. She wanted all my kids, 'cause every baby she had, she lost, right. And I was able to have babies, and she was able to get my kids outta the hospital.

"Come get this baby, Genevieve, I can't take care of it." She come right down there and pick 'em up. My mother, she always say, "You shoulda let me get 'em." But she going to college and shit. She don't want my kids. And I wasn't going to take it. On my drugs! *Shi-i-it!* I was still smokin' crack and shit.

Ricky and Antoine, my boys, took care of Jewel at my cousin's when she had her shakes. She had to go in the, um . . . whirlpool, for nine months. And when she had her shakes, they'd wrap her real tight in the blanket.

And one time I was over there visiting, and Jewel was shakin' and Antoine be like [softly], "Mother, it's okay, she just havin' the shakes." And they wrapped her up real tight in a blanket to make her stop shakin'. O-oh-ee! I ran outta there.

Now she so darn hyper; she be runnin', bouncin' off of walls. But she smart as a lark.

My cousin get money from foster care and take care of them real good. They adopted. They got their names. They never seen me like this. I don't go around there.

But you know, my cousin, she would never keep my kids from me. And the only thing they know is that they mother is sick.

In this whirlwind of foster care arrangements, Ricky, who was a precocious teenager, fell through the state's institutional cracks and became his mother's primary financial provider.

Ricky was robbin' banks at seventeen; served nineteen months as a juvenile. He became a grown man making babies. That's just how his daddy was.

He had got several banks when we was staying out in Antioch. I would wake up and that boy have a table full of money. And I'm like, "Why you doing this?"

"Oh, mother, I'm making money. You know that."

He told me I wasn't going to never be broke, and he was going to take care of me for the rest of his life. Because I was taking care of him as a single parent back when I worked graveyard in a nursing home so that he could have what he wanted, you know, what the other kids wanted.

And I'm like, "Oh, baby, you don't have to take care of me now." But even when we got evicted because of his dope dealing, he kept me in a motel. He was probably still robbin' banks, because him and his partner used to case them out. And he was an artist. He would draw everything.

There was nothing I could do about it. I just didn't want nothing bad to happen to him, that's all. That's the type of son I had and I still love him. He's like his mother and daddy. I robbed and stealed, too.

Ricky'll be out of jail next month. When he was arrested the first time, I had to go to court and everything. He was in YA [Youth Authority]. He was just seventeen. I was the last one that testified. And the judge told me I was good. I was a good parent, because everything my son told me, I said. Everything! We practiced. But his little girlfriends who was testifying, they got mad at each other 'cause his little grown ass go and kiss one of his bitches on the elevator, and the other bitch right there. So she go an' get mad and then say somethin' else, different, to the judge.

Carter was afraid of Tina's son and anticipated being punished by him. His public expression of fear represented, on a deeper level, an admission of his failure to live up to his responsibilities for the woman he loved. Carter, like most of the men on Edgewater Boulevard, subscribed to the doctrine that compels a son to fight any surrogate father whose relationship with his mother makes her "unworthy." To alleviate his sense of guilt, Carter invoked Tina's transgressive autonomy as a woman on the street:

Tina's son is getting out of prison next week. He's been out by Susanville, fighting fires. I don't know what he's gonna think about me, right, on the strength of her being on drugs, right. I'm the dude she with. He's gonna think that I'm the one that got his mom on drugs. That's going to be the conflict between me and him.

I told her it's gonna be up to her to tell him. You know Tina, with the strong head and macho-ness. She tries to take it three miles at a time instead of that inch and a mile. But I thank God that we still together and everything. Under that exterior, she's a beautiful person, I mean, a treasure. She really is.

What makes me feel so fucked-up is her saying that she started fixin' to get to me. Come on, Tina, you more smarter than that! I opened up and told her, "Look, I ain't never puttin' you second, but this [pulling a syringe from his sock and holding it up] is something I came accustomed to do. It's been a period of years, and I done did it. I've been trying to slow down and stop on the strength of us being together. But don't expect me to do this and that, right." And she agreed, but all the time in her mind, she figuring, "I'm gonna be the one to curb this." [holding up the syringe again]

He's twenty-two and that's his momma, right. What she say she loves, he likes. But I don't know how I would take to the man who my momma was being on drugs with. I would assume it's his fault.

When Ricky came out of prison, he immediately began looking for Tina, just as Carter had predicted. Carter escaped unnoticed because Ricky's search for his mother fueled another round of intrafamily strife. Ricky paid his uncle Dee-Dee to help him find Tina, and while they were roving the streets together, Dee-Dee warned his nephew about her heroin use. Rather than condemning his sister for her behavior, Dee-Dee admonished her son, "Don't you never let your mother be sick." The next day, Tina, furious at Dee-Dee for revealing her addiction to heroin, attempted to burn him with a hot iron. Dee-Dee burst into tears, apologizing profusely, and mollified Tina by giving her all the money and crack he was carrying—an act Tina interpreted as a true sign of remorse. In recounting the incident to Jeff, she sighed, "I have a messed-up family, but we love each other."

Tina thought of her current separation from her children as a strategy for breaking her family's transgenerational cycle of abuse and for managing her oscillations between maternal love and anger:

I didn't whip my children. It was because you could talk to them. That's what I wanted to be done with me by my mother. But she didn't talk to me. She'd only hit me, beat me. I'm angry at her, but I love her, too. And I swore I wouldn't do my children like that. I wouldn't let them feel that pain and let them go to school with welts.

I only whooped Ricky and Antoine probably five times. But I never whooped my girls. I wasn't abusive. I wasn't that type of parent. And I never left my kids alone—not long, not for over thirty minutes. I thank God for that.

My kids, they're so mannerable. They still say, "Yes, mother" to me, 'cause that's how I taught them. That's how my mother taught us.

Halfway through our fieldwork, while she was living in the Chinook with Carter, Tina expressed her frustration with motherhood by creating an imaginary household with her lost daughters.

Jeff's Fieldnotes

I've been away for three months and, as usual, nothing whatsoever has changed in the Edgewater scene. Carter and Tina are about to smoke crack when I walk up to the Chinook.

Tina excitedly grabs a large, plastic garbage bag and begins pulling out dolls retrieved from the toy factory's dumpster. They are, with one exception, all black, and Tina has christened them with the names of her daughters. She affectionately smoothes the wrinkles on their clothes and props them against Carter's knee so that they are sitting up as straight as possible. For the first time, she doesn't stumble over the names or confuse their ages:

Tina: "This is Persia. This is Jewel. Ashley. Sylvia. [switching to a horror film voice] And this!… This is the little white bitch."

Carter: [laughing] "Crazy, isn't she?"

Tina: [handing Jeff a doll] "Sonny, Frank, Max, they all held my babies. Come on, Jeff, now it's your turn.

[speaking softly to the dolls] "Say, 'Hi, Uncle Jeff.'

[holding up the white doll and resuming the horror film voice] "'About time you got your fuckin' ass here! I'm the angel.'"

When we manage to stop laughing, Tina pulls me gently aside to whisper: "Ricky's back in jail. It makes me feel real fucked-up, Jeff. 'Cause that's like his daddy is. And then his mother is no better. So he followed it through our genes.

"I wrote him a letter yesterday, and I put my lips with my lipstick on it. I learned that from my mother. She used to always seal my oldest brother's letters with a kiss when he was in Folsom [state prison]. But my other children, they doing fantastic. Like Antoine, he's got his scholarship playing college football."

Jeff: "Where?"

Tina: "He… somewhere, I don't know. Ricky liked football at first, and Antoine wanted to be a fireman. And Persia—she's what? eighteen years old—and I haven't seen my beautiful girl in… shit… five or six… no, eleven years.

"The last time I saw Jewel was three years ago in Antioch in the welfare office, 'cause my oldest brother, the preacher in Modesto, [is] going through CPS and all that shit, fixin' to start getting my kids once a month so that he could probably end up with all my girls. So I had to give their birthdays and, you know, their names and stuff.

"No! I ain't goin' to CPS for no shit! Nobody tell me a damn thing. I'm hard-headed. [softly] But it's no excuse, because I put myself in this position. And I pray to God that he help me along the way. Okay? I don't wanna talk anymore, Jeff. Let me smoke this crack. It frees my brain. I don't think about nothin'. I don't think about all this, what I shared with you… my children, my kids."

At first sight, the mother-love ideal weighing on women on the street appears to differ from the discourses available to lumpen men, who primarily seek to reassert lost patriarchal stature through violence, sexual bravado, and misogyny. In fact, however, both men and women on Edgewater Boulevard, despite their uprooted domestic lives, subscribed to conventional nuclear family values. To them, it was self-evident that children ought to be dutiful, subordinate, and respectful to both their parents; mothers were meant to be sexually virtuous, self-sacrificing, nurturing, and drug-free; fathers were supposed to discipline the transgressive behavior of unworthy mothers and to harden sissified and disobedient sons. Men also strove to provide lavish gifts (bicycles and red wagons) on birthdays and holidays for their young children. The normative assumption that the dominant male will provide stable, long-term economic support for his family was once again left out of the equation.

The psycho-affective component of family violence and neglect is not solely psychologically bounded or interpersonally driven. It is structurally overdetermined by poverty, unemployment, household evictions, incarcerations, dysfunctional social services, and chronic drug and alcohol consumption. The pain in the intimate lives of the Edgewater homeless is exacerbated by the dissonance between their valuation of traditional kinship roles and the reality of their lives. The nuclear family ideal has never been an option for Tina or for most of the Edgewater homeless. The family as an institution is a crucial network for resources and for the reproduction of cultural and ideological values, but it is also often a crucible for violence.

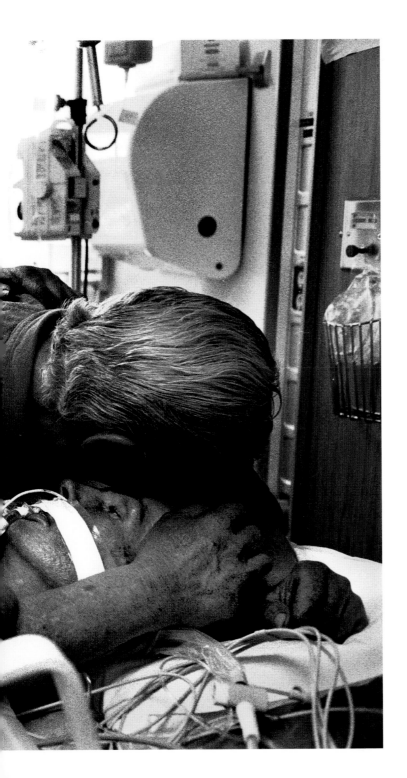

I never let anybody get close to me. But when Petey walked into my life . . . I couldn't stop it. It is hard to put it into words. It's a close-ness thing. It's not about sex, never was. I really love that guy. —*Hank*

During our first year of fieldwork, the city of San Francisco undertook its first major evictions of the Edgewater Boulevard homeless encampments. Following the "zero-tolerance" policies pioneered by Mayor Rudy Giuliani of New York City, the mayor of San Francisco, Frank Jordan (a former police chief), instituted the "Matrix Program" (*San Francisco Independent* 1997, October 21). The city's police force began issuing tens of thousands of tickets for "quality of life crimes" such as jaywalking, loitering, panhandling, and drinking and urinating in public. The rusted shopping carts many of the homeless used to keep their possessions safe were defined as stolen property. When homeless individuals failed to appear in court to pay misdemeanor fines for possession of stolen property, their shopping cart citations became bench warrants that triggered felony charges and arrests.

With bulldozers and backhoes, Caltrans clear-cut the brush along the freeway embankment bordering Edgewater Boulevard, exposing dozens of formerly camouflaged camps. Garbage trucks ground up several tons of mattresses, tents, blankets, and clothing along with the scrap lumber of ramshackle lean-to shelters. We thought this law enforcement offensive would break apart our homeless community and anticipated having to refocus the study. To our surprise, the social network survived. Its members temporarily split up into mobile groups of twos and threes, following the micrologics of alliances in the moral economy.

"Who's the Killer?"

On the morning after the first large-scale eviction, we arrived on the corner in front of the A&C corner store to find Petey crying. During the night, Scotty had died of an overdose in Petey's arms. They had been sharing a blanket to keep warm on the floor of the rented room of one of their regular customers, where they had taken refuge.

> *Petey:* Scotty told me there was no more dope, but I guess in the middle of the night, while I was asleep, he just gave himself a shot and went out. It had to have happened early in the morning 'cause he was rock hard when I woke up. You couldn't move a bone in his body. I hate to even think about it, man.
>
> Lost my best friend. We depended on each other [choking with tears]. Sorry.

The initial explanation for Scotty's death explicitly blamed law enforcement and the structural forces impinging on homelessness:

Frank: It wasn't no O.D. Absolutely not. The guy's too damn smart to overdose himself. It was a murder. The state killed him. They wiped out our camp and the next day he dies. He freaked out—he killed himself.

Hank: He was a little puny son-of-a-bitch, and people stepped on him. The police around here stepped on him.

Frank: The camp was destroyed by the state. [grabbing the tape recorder] Pete Wilson the governor, Frank Jordan the mayor, all the politicians are takin' away the poor man's money.

Hank: In one night we lost one person. The littlest man that's been picked on before. They say good riddance, we belong in prison. We're all homeless. They're kicking us on the street. What are we supposed to do?

Almost immediately, however, a second version of Scotty's death emerged. The day before his overdose, Scotty had told everyone that he had been assaulted and robbed "by the niggers" in the housing projects down the boulevard.

Felix: It was the niggers that knocked him down. Whatever happened was brought on by the beating the crack dealers gave him the day before.

The niggers knew we were gonna get kicked out and when Scotty went to buy crack that morning they beat him down. They thought they could get the whole cha cha cha right then and there. There's no doubt in my mind it was the niggers. They took his life for a little bit of money.

Within a few more days, the Pandora's box of interpersonal abuse burst open with the assumption—logical in the moral economy—that Scotty would have lied about the money stolen by the crack dealers in order to hide his crack binging from his running partner, Petey. Why else would Scotty have gone to the projects alone, without Petey?

After a few weeks, the polemics of interpersonal blame had fully obscured the force of the "state" invoked the day of Scotty's death by Frank and Hank. A consensus grew that "Petey killed Scotty" by failing to revive him. Perhaps by assigning individual blame for Scotty's death, the Edgewater homeless were able to hide their anxiety over their own everyday vulnerability to accidental overdose. In societies throughout the world, anthropologists have noted that sudden deaths caused by "bad luck" often generate accusations of witchcraft that give order to an uncertain world and also reflect preexisting patterns of interpersonal strife (Ashforth 2000; Evans-Pritchard [1937] 1976). As further proof of Petey's malevolence, some in our network claimed that Petey had known that Scotty was dead but had left him under the blanket they shared in order to eat a free breakfast and receive a free shot of heroin from the host. Supposedly, to add insult to injury, Petey then sent their host to wake up Scotty.

The coroner's report registered Scotty's death as an "apparent accident" and described a physically devastated body. He was thirty-six years old, five foot seven, and weighed 115 pounds. His blood contained "morphine, codeine, ethanol, cocaine and Benzoylecgonine," a metabolite of cocaine. He had "acute pancreatitis, an inflamed liver, edema of the lungs, and marked congestion of liver, spleen and kidneys"—painful physical conditions. In the months before his death, Scotty had been prone to "doing the tuna," that is, convulsing spasmodically, as if he were having a seizure. His left arm had also gone limp, and he suffered from night sweats and bloody stools. He had been complaining of not being able to "get the help I need" at the county hospital. As a "hope-to-die-with-my-boots-on-dopefiend," however, he had continued to flood his body with heroin, crack, and alcohol up to the very last moment (Pearson and Bourgois 1995).

Homosocial Romance

Before meeting Scotty, Petey had been snorting methamphetamine and collecting unemployment in his hometown of Simi Valley, a conservative, white working-class suburb made famous as the venue of the trial that sparked the 1992 Los Angeles race riots, when a predominantly white jury acquitted four Los Angeles police officers of beating a black motorist, Rodney King. Petey's wife had thrown him out for failing to support their son. Scotty, a homeless drifter from Ohio, introduced Petey to heroin, and when Scotty left for San Francisco (via Albuquerque and Santa Cruz), Petey followed.

Despite having "good veins" that were easy to locate, Petey had never learned how to inject himself. Instead, he relied on Scotty, who enjoyed lording his power over Petey, especially when Petey was dopesick. Scotty would insist on injecting himself first and would often fall into too deep a nod to proceed with Petey's injection. Ritual subordination in the act of injection is well documented among male-female running partners and is often intertwined with romantic relations. It illustrates the kind of intimate petty brutality that is common among friends and lovers on the street and also reflects gender hierarchies (Bourgois, Prince, and Moss 2004; Epele 2002).

The physical and emotional intensity of Scotty and Petey's relationship confused us at first. They appeared to be a gay couple, but they were living in an explicitly homophobic environment. None of the Edgewater homeless saw anything unusual about their homosocial romantic intimacy. Over the years, several other male running partnerships displayed similar levels of homosocial affection. Many of the men hugged and spooned for warmth and comfort at night. They would sometimes publicly engage in intimate mutual grooming, such as pimple popping, nursing wounds in the groin area, or cleaning soiled underwear. At the same time, almost all were explicitly homophobic. They levied the epithet "homosexual bitch" only at their worst enemies.

Petey fell apart emotionally after Scotty's death and was unable to continue selling heroin. Felix began referring to him as "Scotty's bitch" and calling him "baby Petey" to his face. Hank came to Petey's rescue, treating him to heroin and offering to inject him. Soon the two men established a running partnership with even more homosocial intensity and intimacy than Petey had had with Scotty. In retrospect, we noticed in our fieldnotes that Hank had always been exceptionally kind to Petey and that Scotty appeared to have been jealous of Hank's advances. Hank inherited eight thousand dollars from the sale of his parents' house shortly before Scotty's overdose and purchased a motor home, a motorcycle, and ten grams of heroin with the money. He was an especially desirable running partner at that moment, and everyone was jealous of Petey, accusing him of "sucking up" to Hank.

Hank spoke about Petey in openly romantic, almost chivalrous terms, and Petey responded appreciatively:

Hank: Early one morning after Scotty died, I came down to the corner on my motorcycle and there was Petey. He was standing on the corner against the wall, his head down, deserted by everyone. Feeling bad for him, I said, "C'mon!" And took Petey into my motor home.

Now, people out here, they don't know Petey like I do. They pick fights with him, treat him like dirt. But I'll slap any motherfucker upside his head with a two-by-four if they mess with Petey.

[handing Petey a five-dollar bill] Go get me a Cisco. And pick up a beer for Jeff, too.

[pausing until Petey has left the camp] So after a week in my motor home, we're just sitting around, and Petey says, "Hank, I love you, man." And I tell him, "Petey, I love you, too. I wouldn't ever leave you behind."

Initially, their relationship was framed by the other men in a discourse of masculine domination:

Carter: I saw them at it up there [pointing up the embankment]. Hank has a dick this fucking big [spreading his hands a foot apart]. Petey was on his stomach and Hank had the entire thing up inside him, just pushing, pushing, pushing. And Petey was just lying there—still.

Ben: [clarifying for Jeff] Hank's not a homosexual. He does that just to discipline Petey, to show him who's boss. Hank has Petey well-trained. He stands for sixteen hours at the Taco Bell drive-thru flyin' a sign. Once he's got enough money for a bag of dope, he won't do anything with it. He'll just go look for Hank so that they can go fix together. Once in a while, maybe, Petey'll go get himself a Cisco. But Hank has him running scared.

Carter: Yeah, I leave in the morning to go hit a lick, and when I return after dark, Petey's still out there flying his sign at the same spot.

Eventually, however, disrespect for Petey dissipated, and the two men were reintegrated into the scene as long-term running partners similar to any other stable duo who contribute effectively to the moral economy of sharing.

In *The History of Sexuality,* a book that redefined the field of sexuality studies, Foucault argued that sexually defined subjectivities (heterosexuality, homosexuality, queer identity, and so on), whether considered "normal" or taboo, are not the product of a set of "natural" inclinations. Sodomy, for example, was "an utterly confused category" in the Middle Ages (Foucault 1978:101). Not until the late nineteenth century, with the emergence of biopower, were sex and romantic love between men defined as a perversion. The specific subjectivity of male homosexuality developed out of "the reciprocal effects of power and knowledge" to become "a quality of sexual sensibility . . . a hermaphrodism of the soul . . . a species" (Foucault 1978:43, 101; see also D'Emilio 1983; Rubin 1984).

Historians have argued that gay identity in the United States emerged after World War II. Formerly, men who had sex with one another might maintain a fully masculine social identity (Chauncey 1994). In fact, sex between men was relatively common in the largely all-male communities of the marginal lumpenized working class. Among hobos and tramps in the 1910s and 1920s, there was a linguistic term, *jocker,* for older, aggressive men who dominated younger males sexually (DePastino 2003:85–91), but the word had no implication of a "gay" identification.

In the 2000s, these same "pre-gay" patterns persisted. Lumpen and poor working-class men might, under certain conditions, have sex and fall in love with one another without altering their masculine self-conception. They could even remain aggressively homophobic. Sex between men who do not self-identify as gay or bisexual has been well documented in a range of contemporary lumpen settings, such as prisons (Donaldson 2004; Schifter 1999; Wooden and Parker 1982), sex worker strolls (see review by Kaye 2003), and transient labor camps (Bletzer 1995). Although it is frequently described, this form of masculine sexuality remains undertheorized, and it is not generally analyzed as a class-based phenomenon. It is often presented as an ambiguous cultural phenomenon or is framed as the domination of one participant by the other. For example, the literature on Latin American and circum-Mediterranean masculinities distinguishes "passives" from "actives" in the sex act (Brandes 1980; Cáceres and Rosasco 2000; Faubion 1993; Lancaster 1992; Padilla, Vasquez del Aguila, and Parker 2006; for an example of portrayals in the U.S. press of African-American "down low" scenes, see *New York Times Magazine* 2003, August 3).

The men on Edgewater Boulevard engaged in romantic and affectionate displays with one another without interpreting these practices to be identity markers signaling a transgressive sexuality. Their sexual flexibility offers another window on the uneven effects of biopower among the lumpen, who have not internalized the exclusive distinctions between homosexual and heterosexual subjectivities that have prevailed since World War II in the middle and upper classes and, to a lesser extent, in the stable working class.

If lumpen is a subjectivity as much as a class category, it can be understood as emerging out of a negative relationship both to the mode of production and to biopower. We might expect, consequently, that lumpenized populations would have more transgressive ways of being in the world than normatively disciplined citizens for whom biopower is generally productive and rewarding. The same effects of governmentality that give rise to the phenomenon of the righteous dopefiend might be what allow the Edgewater homeless to find no contradiction between homophobia and homosexual-like relationships. Similarly, this understanding of lumpenized subjectivities helps contextualize our discussion in the previous chapter of how men can remain resolutely patriarchal despite having no sense of normative responsibility for maintaining their children economically, and why middle-class rules concerning the scope of the incest taboo did not prevent Al from talking triumphantly about having a son with his sixteen-year-old stepdaughter or being offered the sexual services of his daughter-in-law by his son.

Within the field of sexuality studies, an approach known as queer theory dedicates itself to theorizing and documenting transgressive sexualities (Seidman 1996; Spargo 1999). Class dynamics have been, for the most part, absent from this body of literature. Queer theory is heavily influenced by Foucault, who, except in publications written during the radical political ferment of the post-1968 decade (Paras 2006; Foucault 1975), generally avoided using social class as an explicit category in his analysis of power. Foucault came of age at the height of the Cold War and was reacting against the stultifying shadow of the French Communist Party's Stalinism on marxism in France (Turner 2000:45–46). Nevertheless, despite his rejection of "grand narratives" and economic functionalism, Foucault was deeply influenced by marxist critique, and this explains the passion with which he theorized the effects of power across history (see Foucault 1975:33; Foucault [1981b] 1991). Unfortunately, as noted in the introduction, many readers in the United States, unlike many European readers (see, for example, De Giorgi 2006; Garland 1997:204–205, 209 n29), interpret Foucault's theory as being antithetical to marxism and class analysis. Recognizing that class is a crucial manifestation of power-effects as well as a relay of power in the constitution of subjectivities, however, helps explain the phenomenon of lumpen male love.

Domestic Running Partners

During the first few weeks of their new relationship, Hank and Petey drove up and down the California coast and spent the last of Hank's inheritance. Their honeymoon was cut short when Hank's license was revoked for a "driving under the influence" violation and his motor home was impounded. They took refuge in a new "white camp" that had been reestablished behind the Dockside Bar & Grill.

Hank built a weatherproof compound with multiple layers of privacy. He pitched his old red pup tent inside an oversized family tent, which he surrounded with a plywood wall nailed to the sides of upright pallets. He then covered the entire construction with blue plastic tarps. Levolor blinds marked the entrance, opening and closing on a still-functional drawstring. The interior of this shelter simulated a one-bedroom apartment, complete with separate living room and bedroom. Later, Hank added a kind of foyer, an outdoor sitting space raised from the mud by wooden pallets covered by carpet remnants. Three yards behind this structure, just beyond a clothesline stretched across a clearing in the brush, Hank built a "bathroom," using a two-by-four wooden frame with white polyester sheets tacked on for privacy. The toilet consisted of a metal platform seat for the disabled perched over a five-gallon paint bucket. By the smell and sight of feces scattered around the perimeter of the camp, it was evident that few people used the outhouse.

Hank decorated their new home with the symbols of bourgeois domesticity. Soon they had two easy chairs, an upright vacuum cleaner, a golf bag, and Christmas decorations dangling from the branch of an overhanging scrub oak. Hank also framed and hung a group photo Jeff had taken of their Thanksgiving barbecue, positioning it as if it were on the mantle of a fireplace. As a final touch, in the place of honor Hank posted a regulation-size American flag.

Hank's reputation for generosity attracted a wide network of former acquaintances, and his shelter soon became a center of social life. Many of the "friends" passing through were newly released from prison. They represented the human fallout from the dysfunctional bureaucracy of the California Department of Corrections' parole violations system. Between 1980 and 2003, the proportion of reincarcerated prisoners in California increased almost threefold as a result of stringent new statutes regulating technical parole violations (*New York Times* 2003, November 14; State of California, Little Hoover Commission 2003). California began reincarcerating 67 percent of all parolees—twice the national average. Most of the parole violators we met in Hank's camp were sent back to jail without trial for "giving dirty urines" to their parole officers on random drug tests. On one occasion, Jeff slept in Hank's "foyer" next to a man called Crazy Carl, who had just been released from prison.

Jeff's Fieldnotes

We wake up drenched by the fog and I nestle under the covers Hank gave me for another half hour, feeling cozy despite the morning chill. Crazy Carl, however, lying on a broken-down La-Z-Boy, is having a very different experience: "I'm scared. I'm scared," he keeps whispering to himself, his eyes bugging with genuine fear. "I hate waking up! Another day that I'm broke. I don't know how I'm gonna stay well. I don't want to go back to jail, but I got to get well."

Mistaking my look of concern for anger, he begins apologizing profusely and then apologizes for apologizing. I reassure him, to no avail.

It is now 5:30 A.M. Petey emerges from the tent, his head hung low, a squeegee and a bottle of Windex tucked under his right arm and his cardboard sign, WILL WORK FOR FOOD, dangling from his left hand. Hank has already gone to meet the dealer at the pay phone on the corner, having sold a television set he scavenged from a dumpster during the night.

Upon his return, Hank offers Crazy Carl a taste of his wake-up shot of heroin to decrease his rising panic level. Crazy Carl asks Hank to inject him in his jugular. He is scared that if he muscles, he might get an abscess and be "violated" by his parole officer. He also has to borrow Hank's needle because his "warrantless search condition," which allows the police to search him on sight and without probable cause, makes it too risky for him to carry a syringe.

A few minutes later, Crazy Carl's anti-psychotic medication is mixing badly with the heroin, and he is staggering around the camp, his eyes rolling back into his head. "I'm fine. I'm fine. It's just my meds." When he falls and begins "fish-flopping," we drag him onto a mattress. I run to call an ambulance, but they stop me, worried about the police.

Luckily, Bonnie, one of Crazy Carl's former running partners, walks into the camp at this moment and announces that she is going to call 9-1-1. This prompts Crazy Carl to stumble back to his feet and sprint out onto Edgewater Boulevard. We run after him, but he has disappeared. Seeing our alarm, the attendant in the gas station across the boulevard points to a two-foot-high shrub next to the air hose. Crazy Carl, in a crouch and still trembling with his head in his hands, is trying to hide, but with the effectiveness of an ostrich putting its head under the sand.

We surround the shrub to guard Crazy Carl until the ambulance finally arrives. He refuses to stand up until the paramedic promises not to call the police, because that would automatically trigger a parole violation.

Within a month, Crazy Carl was reimprisoned for failing a routine urine test. We saw him a half dozen more times over the years, but we never got to know him well because he never stayed out of custody for longer than a few weeks. Carl is an example of a "dual-diagnosis" addict whose medical problems were being handled punitively in the criminal justice system rather than by public health services. Not all of the peripheral people cycling through the revolving door of California's parole violation system into Hank's camp were as harmless, or as clearly mentally ill, as Crazy Carl. Some, like Little Vic, described in chapter 1, were scary. This was also true of Leo, another newly released prisoner who moved into Hank and Petey's tent and began bullying all of us incessantly. To everyone's relief, he was "violated" within a few days.

> *Felix:* The cops got Leo last night. They came in blazing after dark. The whole bit, police, parole agents, the Special Security Unit . . . all their motherfuckin' lights flashing like they're filmin' a movie. You couldn't even fuckin' twitch, blink, fart, move—nothing!—without them seeing every fuckin' thing.
>
> Leo was out taking a pee. When he seen the lights coming up the hill, he went into the bushes. But he couldn't make it far because he was barefooted.
>
> Leo's gone. They caught two of his partners and they snitched on him. He's a two-striker, and they got a case on him of armed robbery and home invasion.
>
> Now we're fucked because he's brought the cops on us. They warned us, "We'll be back every time there's a parolee at large."

Ironically, as we saw in chapter 1 with Little Vic's violent assault, one of the many unintended consequences of the bureaucratic logic of California's parole system during these years was to process arrests for violent crimes as routine parole violations rather than as new crimes. Consequently, only four months later, Leo was back in the camp intimidating all of us. On this second parole release, however, fifty-two-year-old Leo lasted only three hours free on the street before dying of an aneurysm while smoking crack in Hank and Petey's tent. As with Scotty's overdose, Leo's death precipitated a gray zone polemic of interpersonal blame.

Felix: Leo was a no-good snitch. How else could he have gotten out of jail in four months? He was a third-striker.

Carter: Leo was flashing a roll of cash, over two grand.

Tina: I think Hank took Leo's money. Petey didn't work for two fuckin' whole days after Leo died.

Carter: They rolled his body. I would have rolled him, too, before the cops took it. Leo ain't gonna be spendin' that shit.

An explicitly sexualized rumor was added to the mix, alleging that Leo had been receiving a massage from both his uncle and Petey in the pup tent at the moment of his death.

Political Offensive against the Homeless

The sudden death of an acquaintance or friend is merely one of the many crises that engulf the Edgewater homeless virtually every day and produce a chronic state of emergency normalizing conflictive relations. Leo was quickly forgotten, overshadowed by the actions of law enforcement, the most pervasive destabilizing force in the lives of people on the street.

In 1996, Willie Brown, a machine Democrat, was inaugurated as mayor of San Francisco. The conservative Republican governor of the state, Pete Wilson, was determined to upstage Brown, and the homeless became pawns of yet one more of the many get-tough-on-crime political media campaigns that rocked the 1990s. The governor ordered Caltrans, an agency he controlled through the state's Department of Transportation, to evict all the homeless living on state-owned "public land" within the San Francisco city limits. Newspapers published front-page stories with battlefield-style maps peppered with red dots to indicate the locations of targeted homeless encampments throughout the city (*San Francisco Examiner* 1997, March 26). The *San Francisco Examiner* (1997, March 31) conducted a telephone survey asking, "Should the homeless be allowed to live under the freeways?" and 67 percent of the respondents (more than one thousand residents) responded "No."

Hank and Petey's encampment was identified by Caltrans officials as one of "the largest concentration[s] of homeless of any of the Caltrans sites" (*San Francisco Examiner* 1997, March 26). The nightly news on local television featured human interest stories of disheveled men, huddled around garbage bags and shopping carts, poised to flee. One of the segments included a twenty-second sound bite of Hank with Caltrans bulldozers behind him, confabulating that the state was evicting "defenseless women and children" from his camp.

The public debate on San Francisco's homeless policy during these years offers an example of the micropolitics of governmentality in action. The soft left hand of the state, in the form of public health and social services, was jockeying with the hard right fist of law enforcement, and the interplay between these positive and negative manifestations of biopower became especially perverse. The first salvo was fired by the city's new district attorney when he dropped 39,020 citations and bench warrants for the seven "quality of life" violations targeted under the previous mayor's Matrix Program (*San Francisco Chronicle* 1996, April

17). The new mayor, Willie Brown, also unveiled a "comprehensive homeless services program" to address "root causes" of the problem. In response, the governor tried to justify evicting the homeless from Caltrans property by declaring their encampments "public health hazards." The mayor parried that the governor was disrupting his new service programs. At the last minute, the Department of Transportation compromised by agreeing to desist from evicting those encampments that complied with minimal sanitary standards. The Coalition for the Homeless, a left-wing grassroots organization, mobilized a cleanup campaign in the camps, and the city offered to supply portable toilets (*San Francisco Examiner* 1997, March 26).

Eager to support the public health side, we naively mobilized with the white members of the Edgewater homeless to join the coalition's cleanup initiative. The encampments at this time were still fully segregated, and the African-Americans expressed no interest in getting involved.

The city sanitation department has provided the guys with dumpsters, garbage bags (embla-zoned with the state cleanup logo "Care for California"), shovels, rakes, gloves, hard hats, dust masks, and white hazmat [hazardous materials] suits. One of the coalition staff members comes by for a site visit while I am helping Felix and Hank lift a charred box spring mattress into the dumpster. The guys are excited by the cleanup campaign and have put in a full day of work. Even the toilet area is nearly spotless.

Two weeks later, the California Highway Patrol tacked an official twenty-four-hour Notice to Vacate sign onto the "mantelpiece" tree by Hank's flagpole. The following day, a Caltrans work team arrived, flanked by two Highway Patrol officers and trailed by television cam-eras. Hank and Felix donned hard hats for the occasion, and Hank also wore a San Fran-cisco Fire Department sweatshirt, but their attire won them no sympathy. One of the Cal-trans workers found a syringe full of heroin in the dirt by Max's tent. At the request of the television reporters, he held it up with his metal "debris nabber" for the cameras. Oblivious to the media circus, Max sighed that he wished he had found the syringe.

By early afternoon, all the shelters had been razed, and all the possessions had been churned up in the garbage trucks. To add insult to injury, one of the Caltrans workers joked, "The homeless did a good job cleaning. There wasn't much left for us to do." Several other Caltrans workers, however, expressed empathy for the homeless: "We're in bridgework. We've been torn from our trained positions. I know what these guys are going through. Hell, I'm just two paychecks away from being here myself."

Over the next several months, Caltrans returned several more times with teams of prison laborers from San Quentin to clear-cut the trees along the embankment. They arrived with chain saws, pitchforks, and prefabricated Cyclone fences topped with barbed wire. When Jeff attempted to photograph, the supervisor admonished, "If you don't stop taking pictures of my men, *they* will be punished." The crews left vegetation only on the steepest parts of the embankment, assuming that no one could possibly live there. Those became the spots where the Edgewater homeless carved out, once again, a precarious niche. Noting the per-sistence of the homeless colony, several of the local business owners paid Hank, Felix, and Carter twenty dollars each to cut down the remaining pockets of brush. They were eager to earn the money: "If we don't do it, someone else will." In short, they definitively reevicted themselves from the embankment for enough money to buy their next bag of heroin. What originally had been a thickly overgrown two-mile-long hillside was now an eroding hillside, fully exposed to surveillance from the freeway above and the boulevard below.

Law Enforcement and Health

At the time of this eviction, the dot-com boom was gathering momentum, and Mayor Brown, attuned to the neoliberal tide of the era, reversed the priorities of his policies to reduce homelessness. He reinstituted a law enforcement campaign following the zero-tolerance model of his predecessor. The San Francisco police even requested that the neighboring Oakland Police Department lend them its Argus helicopter, "equipped with special heat-detecting technology, known as forward-looking infrared" for nighttime detection of homeless encampments in Golden Gate Park (*San Francisco Chronicle* 1997, November 8). Moving anxiously from temporary site to temporary site, the Edgewater homeless lost most of their blankets and sleeping bags, all of their tents and tarps, most of their needles, as well as all of their contact with the Department of Public Health's mobile health van.

At the time, syringe possession was a misdemeanor, but the local precinct captain directed his officers to issue felony charges of "possession of controlled paraphernalia with intent to sell" to anyone carrying more than two needles. Fearing police reprisals, the city's needle exchange activists began enforcing their program's official one-for-one syringe exchange policy. As a result, the Edgewater homeless did not dare carry more than a few needles, and they stopped regularly visiting the needle exchanges that formerly had been their primary source of clean needles—as well as their gateway to treatment and primary care services. As Frank explained when we asked why he no longer went to the needle exchange: "Maybe you ain't got a dollar to catch a bus across town to get to the exchange. It just ain't worth it for a couple of needles, especially if you're feeling sick."

For the remaining half dozen years that we followed the Edgewater homeless, they were not able to maintain large, stable camps for more than a few weeks before being evicted. This instability reduced their access to outreach services, but the numbers of people living along the boulevard did not diminish. They shifted their shelter strategy and began seeking semi-functional and abandoned parked vehicles in which to sleep. The transition was difficult for everyone, but it was particularly hard on Hank and Petey. During the six months following the Caltrans offensive, all the whites were hospitalized for abscesses. Interpersonal relationships in the network deteriorated as daily life became even more precarious and isolated. Hank and Petey oscillated between nurturing one another tenderly and squabbling bitterly.

Jeff's Fieldnotes

Using sash rope scavenged from the dumpster of the window company, Hank has strung a web of blue plastic tarp hammocks under one of the few remaining thickets of scrawny pines that Caltrans left to prevent erosion. The Highway Patrol has forced Hank and Petey to move six times in the past three weeks, and the hammocks can be disassembled and packed at a moment's notice. To camouflage their access path (and to slow the police down), Hank has replaced the Caltrans padlock on the gate of the new Cyclone fence with a lock of his own.

They feel stable enough to invite me to spend the night, and Hank strings up a newly woven hammock for me. An infected abscess on his rear makes him unable to support his full weight. He has a cane, but his leg quivers nonstop.

During the last eviction, Caltrans had confiscated Hank's medical kit, including the scissors he used to lance his abscesses. Frustrated and in pain, he tears a piece of aluminum from a crushed soda can and presses the jagged edge into the side of the abscess.

"Hank, stop! Let me take you to the hospital."

"Jeff, in battle, if there is a bullet lodged in your body, you just take care of it."

I remind Hank that this is not battle. He nods his head and admits, "I haven't showered in over thirty days, Jeff. I'm too ashamed to go see a doctor."

Petey rolls out of his hammock and walks up behind Hank. Kneeling, he helps squeeze the sides of the abscess on Hank's left buttock, leaving his comic book open on the ground so that he can continue reading in between squeezes.

Half an hour later, Hank is grumbling that he was not able to get "the core" out of his abscess and that it still "hurts like hell." I can see he is very upset because this pain will prevent him from working tomorrow. For the past several months, Andy the mover's jobs have been his primary source of income. A few weeks ago, he cracked a disk in his lower back "lifting a grand piano" on a job. The doctors in the county hospital emergency room gave him a cane and ordered him to stop lifting heavy weights. Hank, however, hung onto Andy's moving jobs for a few more weeks, until he could no longer stand the pain: "I'm just not up to it anymore." The duo, consequently, has become completely dependent on Petey's panhandling to support their habits. Although still publicly subordinate in the relationship, Petey is now insisting on injecting more than Hank since he generates most of the money, causing tension.

Hank rummages through a pile of dirty clothing for a syringe. He finally finds one and, frowning, puts his ear to the chamber to listen for a hole as he runs the plunger up and down the barrel. "Shit! It's cracked." When Petey tells him he does not have a needle, Hank flies into a rage.

Hank: "Goddamned liar! [turns to me] I've had enough of Petey; he drags us both down."

Petey: "I'm sorry, Hank. I'm sorry."

Hank: [shouting] "If you could slap the shit out of me, you'd do it."

Petey: "No, I couldn't. I don't have it in me, Hank. Like you said, I'm too passive."

Hank: "Oh, boy! I never should use those words around you."

Hank attempts to stomp out of the camp but can only limp because of his abscess and back pain. When he reaches the chain-link fence, he hands me his cane and struggles to climb over. Seeing that this is going to take a while, I hop the fence to stand lookout for the police, who drive past here on their way to the neighborhood up the hill.

Hank buys a Cisco at the corner store. For a couple of hours we watch the crack dealing on the corner increase in tempo as night falls.

When we return to the camp, Petey is already asleep in his hammock. Hank immediately complains that Petey goes to bed too early. "He should be out right now flying his sign. We don't have anything for tomorrow's fix. He didn't go to sleep sick, but I will. I know he's doing things behind my back. He probably fixed while we were out."

Hank smokes a cigarette, and I lie down in my hammock. Light from the Lotto billboard above the highway is reflecting softly through the foliage, and when I close my eyes, the smell of the eucalyptus trees almost masks the diesel fumes.

Hank comments, "The freeway is not too bad here. This is all you hear: whoosh, whoosh, whoosh. Down where Felix stays, the traffic makes a terrible noise. There's a bump down there and the cars hit it, and it's loud."

Indeed, the creosote railroad ties that support the embankment at this spot muffle the sound of the cars speeding by on the freeway next to us. It is an almost soothing murmur, like the ocean lapping on a nearby shore.

I drift to sleep watching rats scuttle about the branches above my head and barely hear Hank mutter: "Gotta get a cat in here."

As the night progresses, Hank's dopesickness worsens. I am awakened several times, at first by his tossing and turning and later by his sighing and cursing. Occasionally, he gets out of his hammock to pace. At one point, I awaken to the sound of rustling and see Hank crouching on the ground by Petey's hammock, his head in his hands. But he becomes silent as though hiding, and a minute later he returns to his hammock.

Around 2:00 A.M., a Caltrans road crew begins jack-hammering on the freeway above. They sound like they are only a foot away. The voice of a foreman is audible above the hubbub. One of the workers is complaining: "Where the fuck is Jeff? He said he'd meet us here." I feel a twinge of paranoia. Luckily, we are too well camouflaged for them to notice us from over the edge of the freeway.

Petey is the first to rise in the morning. He has slept with his boots on—big jackboots that Hank picked up on a moving job last week. Before heading down Edgewater straight to the Taco Bell drive-thru to fly his sign all day, I see him carefully, out of Hank's sight, hiding two syringes in a hole in the quilt lining of his shirt.

Hank and I enter the Taco Bell, where Hank has to pay only twenty-seven cents for a cup of coffee, the senior citizen discount. He asks me if I saw Petey wake up in the middle of the night to fix. I shake my head no, but this does not assuage him. His nose is dripping from dopesickness and he is hunched over and shaking: "It's the second time that I've caught him. I'm gonna leave him behind. He doesn't carry his own weight. I'm ready to cut him loose. I'm beyond hurt. I'm angry now."

I can see Petey shivering outside as Hank and I sip our warm coffee inside, and I wonder if Hank is becoming delusional. An hour and a half later, Petey signals to Hank that he has enough money for a bag. As we are walking to the copping corner, Hank launches into yet another furious tirade at Petey for "doin' things behind my back… never helping me out or even pulling your share."

Petey breaks through Hank's diatribe by asking in a soft voice, "Hank… Hank… Tell me, Hank; who else is my friend? Tell me… who else is my friend?"

This soothes Hank, who responds in an almost reassuring tone, "Well… Jeff is your friend."

Petey: "No, Hank. Who's my friend every day?"

Hank: [softly] "But what are we going to do when I wake up sick again tomorrow morning?"

Petey: [gently and slowly] "I'll do my best, Hank. I'll go back out there with my sign. [turning to me] Things have been bad, Jeff. It's been raining so hard that no one wants to take the time to dip into their pocket to give me a nickel or a dime. They don't even wanna crack their window open."

Petey notices me looking at his teeth in alarm. The gums have rotted black. He points to the three or four twisted teeth on the bottom half of his mouth. "I need to get these pulled." His gums have been bleeding, and he thinks this might be why, for the past week, he has been throwing up when he wakes up. I offer to drive him to the homeless clinic, but he shakes his head, gesturing toward the corner where Sal is selling heroin.

Over the next few weeks Petey's health continued to deteriorate with bleeding gums, chronic vomiting, and incessant shivering. Hank's Vietnam references also became increasingly vivid. On one occasion, Jeff found Hank behind the A&C corner store in the throes of a PTSD panic attack.

Hank is sobbing so hard he has to grip the chain-link fence to keep from falling. Moaning, he explains that he is looking for Petey, who is "AWOL" from his usual panhandling spot by the exit sign at the Taco Bell drive-thru. "I just know it. I can feel it. I know my Petey. He's gone to the hole. I told him . . . I warned him never to fix alone. He's dead!" Heaving from the sobs, Hank doubles over as if he were about to vomit. He then straightens himself up, shouting, "I won't leave a man behind! I'll carry him home, on my shoulder back to the corner. It's just not right to die in a place like that." And he begins marching down the boulevard.

Luckily, Petey arrived in the midst of this outburst. "Calm down, Hank. I didn't go anywhere. I was panhandling behind the McDonald's all day." Flashing a quarter-gram bag of heroin in his open palm, Petey added softly, "I got you a fix. Everything's okay. You're not in Vietnam." Hank spread his arms. Oblivious to the pedestrians passing by, they embraced in a deep bear hug for several minutes, nestling their faces in the crook of one another's neck, Petey stroking the crown of Hank's head and whispering, "It's okay. It's okay." Hank continued sobbing, but now with relief.

High-Tech Emergency Health Care without Social Services

Over the next year, Hank became a frequent flyer in the county hospital's emergency room, with over a half dozen long-term admissions. First his back condition became compounded by double pneumonia; then came a diagnosis of colon cancer, followed by radiation therapy. Soon he was also complaining of mysterious seizures that he called mini-strokes. We assumed that these were either delirium tremens from alcohol or a confabulation. The seizures, however, were accompanied by spiking fevers that the doctors could not diagnose. Hank claimed that they had found a rare virus in his spine and that there were only two other known cases in the world, "both men my age who were also in Quang Tri province [Vietnam] in 1970." The county hospital deployed its expensive, state-of-the-art technology (electrocardiograms, computerized axial tomographies, magnetic resonance imaging, biopsies, and innumerable blood tests) but was not equipped to address the social context for Hank's physical distress, and he became a disruptive, "nonadherent" patient. Most of Hank's hospital stays lasted two to six weeks, long enough to control his fever and get him standing once again.

Hank was often undermedicated for heroin withdrawal symptoms during his hospitalizations. When we visited him, we would usually find him semi-conscious, moaning in pain, or alert and wincing, gripping the side of his mattress:

> The nurse screwed up my medication again. She only gave me twenty ccs of morphine. That won't do anything for me. It's like a ten-dollar bag. If I was out on the street with this pain, I'd shoot myself. I wouldn't put my worst enemy through this. Finally, she agreed to speak to the doctor and she apologized. I get eighty ccs now.

It was an ordeal to draw blood for tests and administer intravenous medications. The IV needle would bend as it hit the scarred tissue in his forearm. Most nurses would give up and call a doctor to insert the IV in Hank's jugular with local anesthetic. Only doctors were allowed to perform this procedure at the county hospital, prompting Hank to chuckle, "Jeff, you should show these people those pictures of me hitting Sonny and Crazy Carl in the neck."

The doctors suspected that a fungus resistant to antibiotics had cracked the disk in Hank's lower back. They feared it might be spreading to the neighboring disks, and they proposed a surgical intervention. They did not, as usual, discuss with Hank the surgery's potential effects on his chances of surviving on the street:

> [whispering] I can't understand what the doctors tell me. I'm confused all the time. Do you think the medication might be messing with my head? I think the doctor said there's a fifty-fifty chance I might end up crippled. Jeff . . . ? Do you think I'll survive for even one day under that freeway as a cripple?

Meanwhile, Caltrans's evictions continued unabated, and Petey lost all their blankets during one of Hank's hospitalizations: "They didn't even put up no warning signs or nothing. I hope it's not cold tonight." For several nights, Petey managed to sleep undetected in Hank's room. Hank hooked his IV antibiotic-morphine drip into Petey's arm and ratcheted up the dial, "so that Petey can work for Andy tomorrow." On one occasion, a nurse forgot a bag of medication. "Look what she left! The morphine! Quick, Petey, hide it in the bathroom." This stroke of luck allowed Petey to stay by Hank's side for a full forty-eight hours without having to panhandle in the rain at the Taco Bell drive-thru or move furniture for Andy. In a last-ditch attempt to prevent surgery, the doctors intensified Hank's antibiotic regimen. The nurses had to change his IV drip every hour and a half throughout the night, and they caught Petey sleeping in the easy chair. He was immediately evicted and sent out into the rain with no blankets at 2:00 A.M.

Two weeks later, Hank was back out on the street, nodding and swaying on his feet. With Hank's permission, we asked the physician on our ethnographic team to consult Hank's medical record from the past sixteen months. According to Hank's file, the neurologists originally thought the seizures were caused by "localized lesions in his brain" but could not locate them on a CAT scan. His repeated "spikes of fever" suggested an infection and were diagnosed as an "empyema"—a brain abscess. They conducted a lumbar puncture to test his cerebral spinal fluid and also found meningitis. They prepared to conduct brain surgery to drain the pus from his brain, but he had, meanwhile, responded well to an aggressive new regimen of triple-therapy antibiotics. This was what prompted the hospital to release him back to the street with instructions to take his antibiotic cocktail orally (ampicillin, vancomycin, and ceftriaxone). Hank's official discharge papers stated: "psoasmyositis and lumbar osteomyelitis and clostridium bacteria, copd L2–3 and L4–5 disc protrusion."

Three days later, the police confiscated Hank's medications.

Hank: There was nothin' I could do. They see my pill bottles and see my name all over it. They even spread my pills over the hood of their car, taking their pictures like they're somethin' illegal.

I asked him, "Can I have my medication?"

They told me, "No. This is evidence. We think you are dispensing drugs here."

"What do you mean dispensing drugs? It's got my name on the bottle!"

"Then why do you have it hidden here on state property?"

"So no one will steal it. This is my safe spot in the woods. Do you expect me to carry all these pills?"

Jesus Christ! I went to Vietnam. I deserve better. I got shot up, Philippe, four fuckin' times. I was in a bomb blast. I fell out of a helicopter, and I fell out of an LST [Landing Ship Tank]. The LST wasn't an accident. I got thrown outta that troop transport. . . .

Jeff: Let's go to the hospital right now. Better yet, I'll call an ambulance for you so you don't have to wait five hours in triage.

Hank: Why? So they can send me right back out again?

Petey was still vomiting blood when he woke up each morning and was now severely underweight. With infected sores on his feet and aches in his legs, it was getting harder for him to stand panhandling with his sign for so many hours on end. Formerly the object of scorn among the Edgewater homeless, he now elicited pity. The women and the African-American men, who had formerly refused to have anything to do with Petey, started helping him.

Jeff's Fieldnotes

I walk in on Felix, Ben, Sonny, and Hank fixing in the shack in the back alley. While they each muscle into their rears, Ben says, to no one in particular, "I saw Petey shitting in here last week."

Hank: "My Petey?"

Ben: [pointing his chin at a soiled pair of long johns in the corner] "That's Petey's job."

Felix: "He was in here yesterday looking to pound the dirty cottons."

Sonny: "He looks terrible, Hank. Ready to drop." [sucking his face in to make his cheeks concave]

Hank: "It's the alcohol. He's drinking too much. I'm gonna have to start force-feeding him—gotta get milk and nutrients in him, wheat germ. I'll use our wake-up fix money for food if I have to."

We hear persistent honking outside, and Hank runs out. It is Andy, the mover. Hank is supposed to go to the hospital for his weekly radiation therapy for his colon cancer this morning, but instead he is going to work for Andy, who assures him there will be no pianos to carry in today's job.

I walk with Ben down the boulevard to where Tina is sitting in the sun with Spider-Bite Lou on a sliver of grass in front of the Taco Bell. The two have been binging on crack together and are drunk, sipping malt liquor out of a plastic water bottle with a squirt tip. Tina is applying eyeliner and lipstick, and Spider-Bite Lou is scratching at the scab on the back of his neck. The tops of his hands and his upper lip are covered by crusty yellow sores from a newly infected case of impetigo. Ben and I join them, to warm ourselves in the sun. We watch to see if Petey is having any luck flying his sign at his usual spot. Hank has scribbled PETEY'S SPOT in black magic marker on the back of the exit sign at the Taco Bell drive-thru.

Tina tells me that the police arrested Petey for panhandling yesterday and found three used syringes in his pocket. They charged him with selling syringes, and he has a September 10 court date. With sympathy, she adds, "And his GA [General Assistance welfare check] was cut off this month for missing his appointment."

Ben: [muttering] "Petey'd give someone a blow job with bad breath!"

Lou: "Fuckin' pussy!"

Tina: "Be nice! He's sick."

Ben: "He's probably got that hep C."

Tina: "Shit! We all got it."

Noticing us looking at him, Petey walks over to say hello. He looks older than he did just a few days ago, new lines etched into his gaunt cheeks. Ben shoos Petey away before he can sit down: "No one invited you over." Petey leaves in a huff. Ben resents Petey because Nickie, worried for Petey's health, has invited both him and Hank to stay over for a few nights in her apartment, where Ben has been living for the past few months.

Petey, ten feet away from us, grimacing with his emaciated face covered with open sores, suddenly throws his hat and sign onto the sidewalk. He is crying, uncontrollably.

Tina runs over and takes him into her arms. "Ben hurt your feelings. Don't worry, Ben was only joking."

I follow suit, hugging and reassuring Petey. Through his tears, he moans that he is dopesick, "and I'm tired of all this shit [pointing to Ben and Lou]. And I don't know where Hank is. He is supposed to have been back from working with Andy by now."

Leading me gently by the elbow a few steps down the block, Tina whispers: "This boy needs to eat. I been givin' him burgers. He'll eat it while you watch, but the second you turn your head... he throws it to the pigeons. Can you help him out, Jeff? Lou been takin' his money. Hank saying he going to hit Lou with his cane. I told him, 'You go back to the hospital, Hank. I'll take care of Lou. Don't you worry.'"

Shaking her head sadly, she adds, "Petey can't take care of hisself. That's a shame."

I hand Petey four dollars, and Tina grabs one of them, kissing me on the cheek, "Thank you, Jeff. Love you!" She runs off to catch the bus to Third Street to buy crack and blows us kisses through the window.

Shifting his weight from foot to foot to ease the ache, Petey gags and heaves a mouthful of blood into the gutter.

Jeff: "Petey, let me take you to the hospital right now."

Petey: "I'll go next week after I pick up my hep C results. I promise, Jeff."

There is no arguing with him. A public health research project is paying drug injectors fifteen dollars to pick up their hepatitis C test results and be counseled. Petey will not forego that guaranteed income, regardless of his health.

I ask Petey about his arrest yesterday for panhandling. He blames himself for provoking the officers. They had asked him if he had "points [syringes]" on him before searching him.

Petey: "When cops reach into your pocket and find a rig [syringe], after you've said no, they fuck with you. He cuffed me. I was scared, but he didn't take me in because of the sores on my face. I told him I also had abscesses. [smiling] He told me, 'I don't want to have to wait all day for you at the hospital.'"

As a result of a lawsuit, a new directive has been imposed on the police that mandates treatment for all arrestees suffering from abscesses—another example of the conflictive interface between law enforcement and public health.

Petey suddenly falls silent. When I ask him if he is okay, he starts talking about how much Hank's colon cancer scares him. Then, in the middle of the Taco Bell parking lot, with the afternoon sun beating down, Petey unsuccessfully tries to hold back a new round of tears, his fingers pinching at his eye sockets, his chest heaving.

Carter and Vernon have walked over and the three of us stand frozen, surprised by the sudden emotion. Carter breaks the ice by embracing Petey: "Everything'll be all right."

After a pause, Vernon also takes Petey into his arms. This is the same Vernon who routinely refers to Petey as a "bitch."

That night as I drive home, I see Petey, still at his spot, flying his sign. He is standing on one leg, flamingo style, to relieve the ache, wobbling weakly with his eyes closed.

Ricocheting between the Street and Intensive Care

Two weeks later, Petey was unconscious in his hammock:

Hank: He's laying there, not moving around. I figure he's dopesick, so first thing is I give him a shot. I tell him, "Pick up your blankets and put them behind the wall in case Caltrans comes."

But he is stumbling, mentally gone. "That's it, Petey. You're going to the hospital." He collapsed on the damn bus. When I picked him up, I realized how light he was. I undressed him in the emergency room on the gurney to put on his hospital gown. He was comatose. It fucked my mind over how skinny he was!

A guy can only take so much. What am I, a black widow? I can't even keep myself fixed anymore. I'm mentally fucked up. I'm physically fucked up. I'm just fucked! I don't even got a blanket. Caltrans came again when I was visiting Petey in the hospital. I'd only had the blanket for two days. Got it at the hospital when I brought Petey in. Caltrans has found the spot where I hide my stuff [pointing to a crevice in the retaining wall]. They come every day now.

Petey won't survive another battle like this out here and I won't survive either. I mean, I can't. And now [grimacing] I'm gonna lose Petey.

Hank visited Petey in the intensive care unit (ICU) every day. Most people on the boulevard expressed their solidarity, but the only ones who actually visited Petey, besides Hank, were the African-American members of the network—Carter, Sonny, and Stretch. In fact, they often moved around the city actively. They visited family members and sometimes explored different neighborhoods or tourist sites for fun and for opportunities to steal. Their proactiveness contrasted with the passivity of the whites, who rarely left the six-square-block perimeter around Edgewater Boulevard that bounded their universe. Once again, these ethnic distinctions, operating at the level of habitus, were expressed as racialized moral attributes. Carter, for example, grumbled that the whites "can't even take just five fucking minutes to visit Petey."

Jeff's Fieldnotes

I hop on the bus with Hank and Sonny to go visit Petey in the hospital. Hank gives me a transfer ticket that is still valid from his trip earlier this morning and pays the thirty-five-cent senior citizen discount fare for himself. Sonny pretends to look for change from an overflowing gym bag that he has been carrying for the past few days. He pulls out a squeegee, which he hands to me, followed by a North Face down vest. It is 3:30, and the bus is packed with school kids. Sonny fumbles with a Styrofoam take-home container from a restaurant and pops it open, letting a half-eaten piece of garlic bread drop out. Irritated, the bus driver waves him through.

Inside the ICU, Hank rushes to Petey's side. Petey's legs dangle like twigs from his protruding hipbones. He weighs only ninety-four pounds. Tubes run through his nose and in and out of his neck and chest. One eye is shut, while the other is a quarter open and rolled back, eerily revealing the white part of the eyeball. His paper-thin lips form an uneven opening, barely wide enough for breathing. A gray-black scab, the color of pencil lead, has formed over his gums, spreading across his lips and tongue. His beard is growing unevenly, just a strip of whiskers on his sunken cheeks: the bones look thick and protruding. A blue and white tube stretches from a machine to the side of his bed down into his throat, suctioning his breath. The room resonates with the whoosh of the pumping air.

Hank kneels down and places his cheek next to Petey's, pleading for "Bubba, Bubba, my Bubba" to regain consciousness. Sobbing, he gently strokes Petey's hair to make it flow neatly back over the crown of his skull. His caresses change to a playful tussle, the tips of his fingers intermittently massaging and tangling the hair. "Promise me, Bubba, that you'll hang in there. Keep your promise to me. I love you."

Throughout this, Sonny is holding Hank's shoulders from behind saying, "Look Petey, Hank loves you and he's holding you; and I love you and Hank; and I'm holding Hank; and Jeff is here too; and he loves you. Everyone's rooting for you. Lord, please protect our Petey."

A pulmonary specialist enters with a resident and an intern, and they use Petey, with his pneumonia and spiking fevers, as a teaching case. The specialist removes the tube from Petey's throat and asks the intern to "reintubate" Petey. They are polite. Before rushing off to the next patient, they conscientiously provide us with a slew of technical medical information on Petey's condition that we do not understand.

Petey lets out a rasping groan. With a Q-Tip, the nurse gently swabs his lips, tongue, and the inside of his cheeks with Vaseline. She cannot give him water because it will cause the blood clots on his lips, in his mouth, and down his throat to burst.

In comprehensible language, she explains the consequences of Petey's cirrhotic liver: His bloodstream lacks the crucial proteins that stop bleeding, because the liver produces the body's clotting factors. Furthermore, the blood and other bodily fluids that can no longer be filtered through Petey's liver are being pushed through the cells into his stomach and through the lining of his throat. Luckily, Petey has self-cauterized his throat by burping up acids. Otherwise, the nurse explains, his throat would be bursting with blood too. This explains why his lips are oozing blood.

Hank (who presents himself as Petey's stepfather) asks the nurse why Petey's stomach is no longer bloated. She explains that yesterday they stuck a needle attached to a catheter in the space between the abdominal wall and the bowel to drain the trapped fluid. She tells us that Petey will need this procedure, called "tapping," for the rest of his life because of his damaged liver.

Later, the nurse tells us that the guest visiting with Hank yesterday "stole a tray of food from a patient." It was probably Stretch; every morning he comes to the hospital to check the roster for someone to visit, hoping to steal meds—or anything else of value. Last week he walked off with two telephones.

Hank pulls the covers off Petey's legs to rub the calluses on his feet and exclaims, his voice rising in a songlike sob, "They're cold!" The nurse gives Hank a bottle of baby oil, which Hank massages into Petey's legs up to his thighs.

Hank leans over to pop a pimple on Petey's ear. Noticing me watching, he says, embarrassed, "But that's what we do out there, Jeff."

Politely, the nurse asks us to leave. They want to keep Petey unconscious so that he does not burst the clots in his throat and mouth. She shows us how his heart rate becomes erratic when he is agitated. Petey is safer sedated and undisturbed.

On the drive back to Edgewater Boulevard, Hank becomes anxious about Caltrans. He decides to "dig a hole like a squirrel and line it with cardboard" to hide his belongings.

During the second month of Petey's hospitalization, Hank's cerebrospinal infection flared up again. He found himself on the fourth floor of the hospital, in the skilled nursing ward, with Petey downstairs, finally out of the ICU. To everyone's surprise, Petey had regained some strength and mobility. The two running partners took turns visiting each other, towing their IV drips behind them. Jeff watched awkwardly on one of his visits when a nurse caught Hank adjusting the dials on Petey's analgesic IV drip. They struggled for control of the mechanism until Hank finally wrenched it out of her hands, knocking over his own IV stand: "I can do whatever I goddamn please to my son!" The nurse ran screaming for a doctor, with Hank chasing after her, shouting, "Go get him! I ain't scared! I've been attacked by the FBI and the CIA! Our government trained me in Vietnam, and let me tell

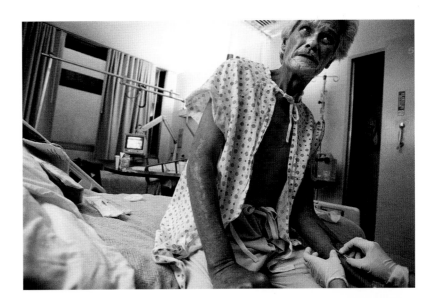

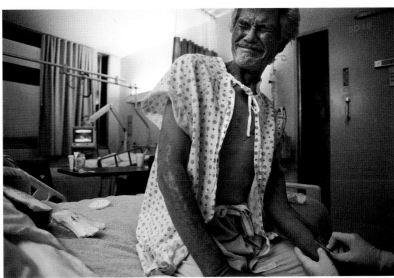

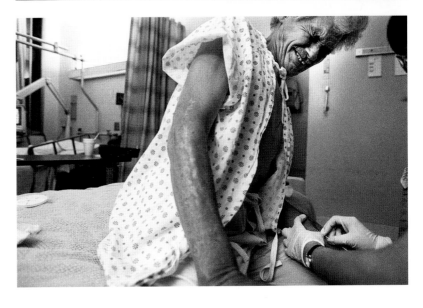

you something, they trained me very well. I can take pain and dish out pain." Hank stomped back to his room upstairs, yanked out his IV, and left for Edgewater Boulevard, his hospital gown spilling below his leather jacket.

Two weeks later an ambulance brought Hank back to the hospital after he collapsed while panhandling at Petey's spot. This time, in addition to the IV antibiotics, the doctors included an extra heavy dose of opiate-based painkillers. Once his heroin withdrawal symptoms were fully alleviated, Hank morphed into a friendly, cooperative patient. Clean and neatly shaven, color returned to his face. He hotwired the television set in his suite to bypass the hospital's service fee, and his room became the ward's hangout scene for recovering addicts. On several occasions, Hank shared a bag of heroin with visitors in his bathroom.

Jeff visited the hospital on Hank's fifty-fourth birthday.

Jeff's Fieldnotes

Pointing to three pink carnations in a vase on the counter by his bed, Hank announces proudly, "They're from Petey." Petey, who is visiting from his room downstairs, blushes shyly. Hank points to another bouquet on the window sill: "They're from Carter and Tina."

Petey's clotting factor is still weak, and he goes to the bathroom to stanch the flow of blood from a shaving cut. He stays for at least a half hour, prompting Hank to quip, "You jackin' off in there?" Without missing a beat, Petey responds, "I'm tryin'," his voice a rasping whisper as a result of his seven weeks of intubation in the ICU. Laughing, Hank retorts, "I'll help you. I used to choke chickens for a living; let me try choking yours."

Before ending this birthday visit, Jeff stopped at the nurses' station to inquire into the status of Hank's SSI disability application. His query was dismissed by the overworked, harried head nurse: "The social workers do that. Not us."

Public Health Budget Cuts

The brief period of medicalized respite in the lives of Hank and Petey was cut short by the trickle-down effects of neoliberal "reform." The federal government's Balanced Budget Act of 1997 had initiated a long-term reduction of $112 billion in the Medicare budget. Federal Medicare and Medicaid reimbursements no longer covered costs (Guterman 2000). In response, private for-profit and nonprofit hospitals began diverting more of their uninsured and Medicaid patients to county hospitals, which were still required by law to treat the indigent. In 1999, the year Petey and Hank were cycling through the emergency room, San Francisco's public health budget shortfall was projected to be between $26 million and $29 million (*San Francisco Chronicle* 1999, May 5).

Hospital administrators pressured doctors and nurses to institute "early release plans." Petey was discharged from the hospital as soon as he was taken off his IV. Hank, who was still on the skilled nursing ward, was furious: "Some doctor told the nurse they needed Petey's bed. 'If he can walk, he can leave.'" Hank was still attached to his triple-antibiotic drip but knew that his own early release was imminent. The hospital was unable to provide Petey with its usual seven-day hotel voucher. There were no low-budget rooms available in the city because for the past several months a series of fires of suspicious origin had been sweeping through San Francisco's SRO hotels, allowing their owners to bypass rent control laws and renovate their properties into luxury tourist establishments. Petey, consequently, was sent to a shelter in a neighborhood overrun by drug dealing. A public health van from a pilot outreach program known as the Homeless Death Prevention Project was supposed to shuttle him to the hospital's outpatient wound clinic every morning. But Petey immediately fell through the cracks.

Ironically, these medical and social service cutbacks occurred at the height of the Bay Area's economic boom. The mayor of San Francisco was celebrating a $102 million surplus for the city even as the county hospital was implementing draconian cuts (*San Francisco Chronicle* 1999, May 5). Sixteen county hospital maintenance workers were laid off, and one of the pharmacies was closed (prompting the hospital to hire four security guards to control the crowds of indigent patients who now had to wait in line for up to four hours to receive free prescriptions). A co-payment plan was instituted to force uninsured outpatients to share the cost of their prescriptions. Doctors' salaries, however, were increased. Coincidentally, Philippe at the time had recently become chair of a department in the medical school that staffed the county hospital.

Philippe's Fieldnotes

At this month's Chairs' Meeting, the chief administrator presents an Armageddon scenario of the county hospital's finances. The hospital is having trouble retaining doctors and nurses because of burnout; the shortage of medical staff has caused them to divert 41 percent of emergency medical vehicles to other sites. There is no longer any trash pickup in nonpatient areas. They had an epidemic of antibiotic-resistant streptococcus in the ICU and were forced to shut down cleaning services in the rest of the hospital in order to assign all the limited cleaning personnel to the ICU. One of the ICU rooms has been closed, and they are now treating ICU patients in postoperative care rooms. (I remember the ICU nurse explaining to Jeff that the secondary pneumonia and throat infections that complicated Petey's liver condition had probably been contracted inside the hospital.) An internal survey revealed that 22 percent of patients sick enough to be admitted to the hospital waited eight hours in the emergency room.

Just before this presentation of what the dean calls the "inhumane conditions at San Francisco General due to federal Medicaid cutbacks," he announced that the university was raising its mortgage subsidy limit for newly hired clinical and research faculty to $900,000 on the grounds that "it is a hardship to relocate to San Francisco and be forced to buy a $1.5 million three-bedroom home."

This institutional budget crisis for social services for the poor occurred in the context of one of the most rapid accumulations of regional and personal wealth in U.S. history. It had a predictable impact on Hank and Petey.

Petey has missed all of his clinic and SSI appointments. My stomach turns when I find him panhandling at his old spot by the Taco Bell exit sign in the pouring rain. His brown leather jacket is waterlogged and is taut against his shrunken, bony frame. His hospital crewcut highlights his pale, gaunt features. The scabs on his face have reopened, and he still cannot talk clearly because of the scarring in his throat. This reminds me that medical students have told Philippe that their supervisors instruct them to practice their intubating skills on unconscious indigent patients. Petey's teeth are chattering, but he does not complain of being wet or cold.

Petey: "I don't know what the fuck to do, Jeff. They threw me out of the hospital after two months in a coma. They gave me a prescription and told me to move on. They never told me to return for an appointment. And I can feel my liver going. My liver is going, Jeff!"

I offer to give Petey a ride to the county hospital, where I have arranged to meet Hank at the pharmacy, but he refuses to leave his panhandling spot. He is scared of being left dopesick, because he is not sick enough to be admitted into the hospital for an overnight stay.

Frustrated, I drive to the hospital alone, hoping Hank will show up. At the hospital pharmacy, more than one hundred people are waiting in snake coils of lines to get their prescriptions. Hank walks by without noticing me. He is carrying an old briefcase with a broken handle overflowing with his SSI papers. He was released only a week ago but already looks like a wreck. Loaded on both heroin and Cisco, he slurs his words and smells awful. While in the hospital, clean, warm, and well-fed, he had looked rested. He had eaten, bathed regularly, and been adequately medicated for opiate addiction (a combination of methadone, morphine, and Fentanyl). He had also stayed completely free from alcohol, even if he did "chip" an occasional hit of heroin in the bathroom.

After three hours in line, we finally make it to the bullet-proof Plexiglas pharmacy window. Hank is handed a piece of paper outlining his "rights to medication," but he does not have the fifty-dollar co-payment for his morphine sulfate prescription, and neither do I.

We head to the hospital social worker's office and wait in front of the desk until she finally has time to talk to us. She tells us that Hank still has an "incomplete dossier" and that his "reconsideration hearing" for missing his last set of SSI appointments is in only two days. He needs to complete yet another set of forms before that meeting, but they must be picked up in person at the downtown SSI office.

I have trouble starting my car as we head back to the boulevard. Hank tells me to pop the hood and walks down the block, looking in the gutter. Moments later, he picks up a hollow pipe and places it on my revving engine like a doctor with a stethoscope to diagnose my ailing car's problem. He reassures me that it is "only the distributor points or the spark plugs that need to be cleaned—nothing serious."

When we drive up to the corner, Tina immediately intercepts us to announce that she caught Petey with a Cisco in his jacket pocket. She tried to confiscate it, but he guzzled it in front of her. "And I offered to buy him a beer instead, because that Cisco will kill him, and this here [holding up a sixteen-ounce can of Olde English malt liquor] is more like water." Hank bursts into tears. Petey has started throwing up again in the mornings. Hank shoplifted Maalox for him at the Walgreens a couple of days ago, but it is not helping. Petey claims that his nausea is caused by eating too much Taco Bell hot sauce, but it is obvious to all of us that his liver is starting to fail again.

Hank confides, his forehead straining at the memory, that Petey defecated in his pants yesterday because the manager of the Taco Bell no longer allows his workers to "buzz Petey in." Petey rushed to the McDonald's across the street, but the bathroom was occupied. "This is the second time this week that Petey has had an accident. He just crawls into bed and weeps. I told him last night. 'I'll clean you. I'll wipe your ass for you, but you need to tell me what's wrong.'"

Tina has been giving Petey the two cans of Boost, a fortified high-protein drink, that she picks up each week at the needle exchange, but Petey is not gaining weight.

Petey returns from panhandling accompanied by Philippe, and Hank invites us to spend the night. We walk across the street and pick up carpet padding from the dumpster at the rug store and then climb over the chain-link fence to reach the encampment. Petey is skinny enough to squeeze through a gap between two corner fence posts. Their new camp, nicknamed "the nest," is ingeniously camouflaged as a heap of rubble. Hank has gathered branches, twigs, and dried pine needles onto a heap of dirt and sand, excavating a circular concave structure. It is just deep enough for us to duck our heads when the police drive by.

In the candlelight and with the reflection of passing car headlights, we try to sort through Hank's mess of SSI papers, but it is too complicated. I show them some photos of Petey in the hospital, and Hank bursts into tears.

Petey squints closely at each picture, asking for extra copies to send to his father, who was contacted by the hospital social worker when the doctors thought he was going to die.

Hank tells us that when he and Petey are cold at night, they rub their bodies up against each other. On some nights, he reaches out to touch Petey's body to make sure that it is still warm and that he is alive.

Petey: "Without Hank, I'd be dead."

Hank: "If Petey died, I'd be dead."

Unfortunately, by the late 2000s, there had been no improvement in the crisis in funding for social services and medical care for the indigent. Across the country, private hospitals continued to scramble for profits, and public hospitals struggled to stay solvent. Access to basic medical care became even more difficult for the uninsured (*New York Times* 2007, February 23). Furthermore, there was still no systematic coordination between high-tech medical care and social services. At the local level, law enforcement continued to dominate public spending and political discourse to the detriment of public health. At the national level, for the first time in half a century, military spending reached levels comparable to those of World War II (*New York Times* 2008, February 4).

I wanted to reach Carter, to get closer to my man, to feel what he was feeling. So I started to shoot dope. I even wanted to have a baby. I still haven't reached him yet. And now, Carter and I . . . we's just hustlers and dopefiends. —*Tina*

To convey in raw detail the daily challenges of obtaining heroin, crack, and alcohol as well as the basic resources for survival, we present a selection of extended fieldnotes and tape recordings in this chapter with minimal analytical discussion. We return to the period of our fieldwork described at the end of chapter 2, when Tina confessed to Jeff at the Thanksgiving picnic that she had started injecting heroin. Our selection of notes and tape recordings proceeds chronologically with the story of Tina and Carter's love affair over the next five years. We hope to portray the creative agency of the lumpen that both takes a destructive toll on them and on society and is also imbued with a fleeting joy of living and a sense of dignified oppositionality. Many new names appear in this chapter because we wanted to offer a glimpse of the wider range of street people who pass through interstitial public spaces like Edgewater Boulevard. Consequently, for this chapter, we decided not to edit out interactions that involve individuals peripheral to our core social network. The wider transient population contributes to the serendipity of hustling opportunities and consolidates the logic of danger and mutual betrayal in the gray zone of the street.

Jeff's Fieldnotes

Tina is in her "comfy-clothes," the kind she reserves for times of sickness and "staying home" when she is menstruating. She has on a cotton terrycloth nightgown with a large, round, ruffled collar; a robe; and a blue ski cap pulled below her eyebrows.

The Chinook's radio is tuned to an AM talk show skewering President Clinton for being a "womanizing pervert."

Carter: "And Jeff, he also got an illegitimate son by a hooker in Alabama. Tina heard it last night on her favorite new talk show—right, Tina? It's wild. Clinton's in deep shit. . . ."

Taking out two syringes from Tina's imitation Chinese silk—embroidered trousseau, Carter explains that while he goes out "to work," Tina listens to late-night radio talk shows, "'cause it's informative and you get up-to-date information as to what's going on." To provide an example, he asks if I have heard of the little boy whose father "injected him with AIDS-tainted blood."

They are both in a great mood, and Carter slides eagerly into a story about the kindness of strangers.

Carter: "I only needed five more dollars to be able to get a bag. And I walk by the McDonald's parking lot where I seen my friend Manny standing by this lady's car. Her battery's dead. It was like a 4×4, a big truck. We pushed it for her to jump-start it. And she reached into her pocket and handed me some money. It was five dollars, exactly the amount I needed in order to get a bag. But I had to give Manny some of it because we had both pushed. But he said, 'You go ahead and keep it,' because he was just fixed and I hadn't fixed yet, and he knew that Tina was waiting for me at home, sick. So now I had just enough to cop and come back to my girl."

Tina: "I was asleep, and he just watchin' me sleep…. And I woke up with a smile on my face 'cause he was there and I was happy he was there. I didn't know that he had already gone out and got some dope or nothin'."

Carter: "But she knows I ain't gonna come home unless I got somethin' to wake her up with."

Tina: "And I looked at him and he was like, 'Look right there,' and there was my outfit ready with my dope."

Initially, Tina made no effort to learn how to use a needle and became totally dependent on Carter. Having Carter inject her was a way of expressing their romantic intimacy and further reinforced Carter's assumed responsibility to generate enough income for her new heroin habit (as opposed to her previous crack habit). (On the romance of injection prac-

tices, see Bourgois, Prince, and Moss 2004; Epele 2002.) Tina eventually managed to mobilize help from other men in the Edgewater scene, including some of the whites who appreciated the way she anchored a traditional, romantic partnership: "If Carter isn't around, Al or Felix will come by and check up on me. Al hits me real good."

Within a few months, however, Jeff's fieldnotes began documenting how the romance of Tina's new heroin habit was fraying under the everyday pressure of physical addiction. The injection act became a source of tension rather than a ritual of hierarchical bonding.

Jeff's Fieldnotes

Carter insists on fixing himself first, just as Scotty used to do with Petey. Today he nodded off in the middle of injecting Tina. With the needle dangling out of her arm, she grabbed an empty forty-ounce bottle of malt liquor and threatened to "crack" him "upside the head." He snapped out of his nod into a rage. I was scared that he was going to pummel Tina, and I pleaded lamely, "Calm down, guys! Please calm down!" He finally stopped when I raised my camera to my eye.

Jeff's Fieldnotes

Tina and Carter, like Hank and Petey, often accuse each other of "half-stepping"—that is, shooting heroin behind each other's back. Sometimes they will scream back and forth for hours, making it unpleasant to be around them. "How could you do this to me, you motherfucker!"... "I'd never do you like that!"

Today Tina tells me in a fit of anger, "I saw Carter on the corner with—guess who! That white motherfucker Lou! He was fixin' to fix Lou and leave me sick.

"I been supportin' that ol' sad ass for too long. It's like he just been not knowin' what to do with his hand when wipin' his ass...just waitin' for me 'cause I been hustlin', I been washin' windows every day, and been coming with the fix. He even pretend he sick when I know he ain't sick. I could tell; I'm a dopefiend. And when I'm sick, everybody be, 'Why you sick, Tina? Carter not sick.'"

Tina and Carter's relationship is deteriorating. Today, as soon as I arrive, she complains about being dopesick, right in front of Carter, in order to embarrass him for not "taking care of his woman." Carter scolds back, "She just wants me to fix her again." He then whispers to me, "Which I'm going to do. But she doesn't know that."

Exasperated by our whispering, Tina exclaims, "You men don't know what it's like. I'm the lady! I deserve to be taken care of! You be a bitch for a day!"

Eventually, they abandoned their attempt to mimic a domestic division of labor and instead reestablished their initial pattern of romance, as outlaw partners. The change was first noticeable as a transformation in Tina's techniques of the body.

Jeff's Fieldnotes

Tina tells me, with some ambivalence, in front of Carter as they are both about to fix, "Jeff, I learned to hit myself so I don't have to wait for Carter no more. He doesn't like it. I learned by watching over his shoulder how to cook it and fix it. When I first showed him, we both laughed. I looked pretty silly. I thought he'd be mad because he feels bad about me fixing."

They are each holding full rigs and the conversation ends abruptly. Tina rolls up the sleeve on her left arm. I am taken aback by the sight of her track. Contrasted against her brown skin, the scar along the vein where she has been injecting for the past few months looks like a thin cord of dried black tar stretched halfway up her forearm all the way to her biceps.

Squeezing her left fist to make her veins bulge, she slowly slides the needle into the endpoint of the track in her biceps. Her fingers hold the syringe chamber conspicuously, almost fumblingly, and she is squinting in intense concentration. Tina's awkwardness reveals that she is still a novice.

In contrast, Carter's fixing is as natural and unself-conscious as a long-time smoker lighting a cigarette. The hitch comes at the end. He has to make quick, sparring jabs to pierce more than twenty years of accumulated scar tissue, and his dopesickness escalates with each frustrated attempt to find a vein.

Tina's final moments of injection are very different from Carter's—the advantage of being relatively new to shooting heroin. The needle slides fluidly into Tina's vein because its walls are not yet scarred. Her eyelids flutter with relief as the heroin rushes through her bloodstream. She leans backward and sighs.

For the past few weeks, Carter and Tina have been supporting their habit by "pulling spreads"— buying clothing with high resale value on stolen credit cards. They receive the cards from Tyrone, a man whom Tina describes as "the scary-ass guy who hangs out at the Dockside Bar & Grill and dresses all fancy and stuff." They drive the Chinook to a gas station to run the cards through the "pay at the pump" mechanism to verify that they have not yet been reported stolen. They then rush to a mall to buy the clothes. In return for giving Tyrone a half dozen high-end items (some of which he keeps for his personal use), they are allowed to keep whatever else they manage to charge on the cards.

Last week Tina was arrested buying a cashmere bathrobe and slippers that, she claims, she was planning "to use one day when I go into treatment." The cashier recognized her from a previous credit card scam and called security. The transaction was recorded on the store's surveillance camera, and both Carter and Tina were detained on the spot.

Tina: "They let Carter go right away. At first I was going to run, but I decided, 'I put myself in this and now I gotta go through with it.'"

Carter: [still injecting] "Yup! My girl took the rap alone."

Tina: "One of the security guards was going off. He was holding me by my arm and he hurt me. I told him I found the card in a phone booth on Twenty-fourth Street, and the other guard told him to cool down.

"My man sure missed me. We haven't fought since. I guess you don't notice the water till the well runs dry. [smiling reproachfully at Carter, who is still probing for a vein] Good thing I learned to fix myself or I'd still be waiting."

Without interrupting his jabbing or looking up, Carter adds, "I was goin' crazy. I called everyone to try and O.R. [release on own recognizance] Tina—her brother, her mother, her grandmother, her daddy. Even Hank, Felix, Al, Frank, Max. We all crowded around the phone booth when I called the jail."

Tina interrupts, "I started to get real sick. They had me strapped to the gurney and I'm gettin' the pain in my stomach. They gave me Librium and it didn't help. [nodding from the heroin] But they was real nice to me because they've had a lot of people die from getting sick. Jeff, did you know Tall Jim? The dealer with the van and the dog? He died last month after being busted. That's why they took me to General Hospital after a day and a half in jail, because they didn't want another dead person.

"The police dropped me off at the hospital and I waved goodbye. Then I just started to walk back to Edgewater to get me well." She leans over to kiss the back of Carter's neck, which is still bent over his needle.

Carter: "That's right, I can't tell you how crazy I was. Bein' up in here all alone, knowin' Tina is locked up sick."

Carter and Tina's romance rebounded as they became an even more effective outlaw team, escalating their drug consumption.

Jeff's Fieldnotes

The camper is still a mess from last night's binge, and entering it is a challenge. I have to wrench open the passenger door because a blue airline blanket has been stuffed into the newly broken top third of the passenger-side window to keep out the chill of San Francisco's summer fog. All kinds of junk tumbles onto the pavement as I maneuver myself into the front seat.

They are sitting cross-legged side by side on the mattress in the back, wearing red bandanas around their necks, bandit style. They would look like young socialist revolutionaries if the bandanas did not read "1-800-Call Collect."

The dot-com boom has filled San Francisco's port with containers slated for next-day delivery to luxury boutiques downtown. Yesterday Tina and Carter "hit" a NikeTown shipment container on the loading docks, and both of them are wearing shiny new Nike high-tops and socks. They saved a white collared golf shirt with a Nike swoosh over the heart for me. I try to turn it down, but this offends them, so I quickly accept it politely.

Carter is writing a note with directions to the San Francisco Unified School District's waterfront warehouse. He holds up the note for me to see. "If someone asks why we're driving around there, I'll show them this and tell them I am making a pickup for some schoolbooks but got lost. Come with us, Jeff?"

Larry, an old white heroin dealer newly released from prison, drives up in a pickup truck. He has elaborate Nazi tattoos on his forearm. Tina whispers, "Watch me get something from him," and jumps out of the Chinook and walks over to the passenger-side window of Larry's truck to say hi. I slump down in the cab of the Chinook, nervous about my camera in front of this dealer I have never met before. Carter whispers, "Don't worry. I'll tell him you're okay."

They chitchat for a couple of minutes. Before driving off, Larry tilts his head toward Tina and asks Carter half-jokingly: "Why don't you just give me a couple of hours with her alone?" Tina immediately climbs back into the Chinook announcing triumphantly, "I got me a sack." We all laugh; neither Carter nor I had managed to see Larry slip Tina the bag of heroin in the middle of the conversation.

When I ask Carter if Larry is racist, given his tattoos, he explains: "In the joint, maybe so. He's Aryan Brotherhood... white power. That's how they do. You gotta stick together. But out here, man, he's all right with me. He don't have no thing against... no blacks or nothin', right.... Well, to me he don't show it. I deal with him every day."

After fixing, Carter and Tina proceed with their burglary plans. We have to drive in the Chinook because the pickup truck they usually use for licks has a flat tire. We weave slowly through the warehouse district along the waterfront. We approach a shipping container that looks promising, but a security guard in a golf cart drives up behind us and Carter takes a quick left turn, causing the lumbering Chinook camper to careen. "Another time, maybe tomorrow," he mutters with a cuss.

When they feel themselves being surveilled, they often shift to dumpster diving, so Carter pulls up to a garbage dumpster and they both hop out. Collecting cardboard, cans, and discarded wooden pallets makes them look less threatening and generates extra change.

Tina, determined to make the best of it, finds a white plaster face mask and announces with a smile: "For my niece; tomorrow's her birthday."

We drive back to the parking lot behind the McDonald's on Edgewater Boulevard. Noticing my yawns, Tina invites me to take a nap while she and Carter purchase crack, heroin, and beer. I am exhausted, having spent the previous night in the main white camp, where I was kept awake by bickering over who "is shitting too close" to the camp.

An hour later, I am awakened by the sound and smell of crack smoking. They are planning another lick because they have had no luck today, and they have only three dollars remaining from the five sheets of plywood they sold yesterday to the used lumber depot. Tina suggests a "visit" to MacFrugal's, a discount store on Mission Street. She has not shoplifted there in quite some time. We drop her off and wait nervously, parking half a block away.

Moments later, Tina walks past us briskly but makes no eye contact. A few more long minutes pass until she finally feels safe enough to double back. She jumps into the front seat and we drive off. She triumphantly pulls out a dozen pairs of children's socks, a set of handkerchiefs, and a large package of underwear.

We stop at a gas station where she gets five dollars and a St. Ide's wine cooler for the socks. She unloads the underwear and the handkerchiefs for ten dollars in a bar. On our way to the waterfront warehouses, searching for a bigger lick, Tina and Carter stop first to buy crack—Tina's priority with her handful of cash. They then move on to buy heroin for Carter, who is already sniffling and stifling yawns.

Tina enters the sales office of a baked goods distributor to use the bathroom. Moments later she bursts out the front door, chased by a man, presumably the office manager, who is yelling and wagging his finger at her. She waves her fist back at him and jumps into the front seat of the Chinook. Carter lurches us forward, gunning the gas pedal, and we leave the office manager shaking both his fists at us. Laughing, Tina opens her purse to reveal a half-empty bag of coffee that she grabbed from behind the office coffeemaker.

We park a half mile away in a wasteland of abandoned warehouses and garbage-strewn empty lots. Carter announces that we now have to wait until dark. They take out the crack and clink their pipes in a toast.

I suggest we take advantage of the once-a-week needle exchange that is held every Wednesday afternoon on nearby Third Street before sunset. On the way, Carter pulls over next to a man working on his car to ask if he needs a battery. They make a twenty-dollar exchange with no bargaining. Tina rolls down her window as we drive off and says cheerily, "If you need another, we can get one for you any time you want."

At the needle exchange, Tina hands me two used syringes so that I will qualify for one of the rationed cans of Ensure, the high-protein drink the program distributes to the homeless, one can per person per week. She admonishes Carter, "Don't forget to ask for a can, too, this time."

Boxes of alcohol wipes, vitamins, tampons, condoms, and dental dams are laid out on the table, guarded by the volunteers. Tina grabs a handful of tampons, emptying the box. When she asks if there are any more, a volunteer shoos her away: "You've already taken five!"

Tina runs behind a dumpster. When she returns, she explains that she is bleeding too much and "needs privacy." Her menstrual cramps are hurting more than usual, making her urinate frequently. "My body goin' through the changes. I get hot. That's what a fuckin' woman do when she go through a change of life. Shit!" She giggles, "I wanna kill someone now."

She uses a loading pallet as a ladder to climb into the dumpster. Dressed in her clean green and yellow striped angora sweater and a pair of nicely tailored dark slacks, she dons rubber gloves and immediately gets to work while Carter, eager to start hitting licks with the approach of nightfall, waits impatiently in the Chinook.

While shifting through the garbage, she tells me, "I've gotten so much shit out of here, Jeff. Last week, I found meat—ten little-bitty cans of the pretty, pretty golden hams. I gave them to Hank to sell."

Tonight's garbage is bountiful. She pulls out a large plastic bucket of Charms lollipops, several flats of Otis Spunkmeyer wild blueberry muffins, one flat of poppyseed muffins, a flat of Hawaiian Punch Tropical Fruit flavored soda, a half-empty extra-large bottle of Excedrin, several cans of Lysol, a box of lightbulbs, an enormous bag of chocolate chips, and a bag of pistachio nuts.

We enter the Discount Grocery Outlet to buy candles. There are boxes of maxi-pads on sale at the checkout, prompting Tina to exclaim, *"That's what I need!"* She refuses to let me buy them for her, however: *"They are too expensive. But I'll take a dollar from you for a beer."*

When full darkness finally sets in, Carter drives us to the waterfront where the most active warehouses are located. Spying an open shipping container, he jerks the Chinook to a stop and runs to check it but returns shaking his head, *"Empty."* He repeats this two more times before he decides that the port must be closed this week because of some change in international shipping patterns.

We head over to the wealthy neighborhood of Diamond Heights, with its sweeping views of downtown San Francisco. Carter is looking for a construction site that he cased a few days earlier. When we reach it, he grumbles, *"Nothing here for my client."* He does, however, tie a large window and some two-by-fours onto the roof of the Chinook.

We drive back to the block where he grew up, on the hill overlooking Edgewater Boulevard. He motions me to stay out of sight and knocks loudly on the front door of a house. I close the curtains and slump into the seat. It is close to midnight, but a man and a woman do not hesitate to come out and inspect *"the merchandise."* Soon I hear the scraping of wood on the roof

above my head. The couple is buying the window and the two-by-fours for twenty dollars. Carter immediately drives to buy more crack.

That evening Carter and Tina shoot heroin three times and smoke crack on at least four different occasions before dropping me off at the white camp at 2 A.M.

The next afternoon I stop by the Chinook to say goodbye before heading home. The van is a mess—clothing and melted candle wax everywhere. They are still asleep, having stayed up the rest of the night hitting licks and continuing their crack binge.

Groggily, Carter calls out, "Thanks for spending the evening with us, Jeff." Tina adds, "We always enjoy your company."

Two days later I find Tina in the Chinook, scraping the resin from her crack pipe. It is a ceramic tube from an obsolete knob-and-tube electrical system of the 1910s. I can tell she has been smoking a lot today because, after taking a hit, she immediately starts "doin' the chicken"—picking at pebbles on the ground, thinking they might be chunks of heroin or crack.

As the afternoon wears on, Tina becomes increasingly anxious that Carter might have gone off to fix by himself. He returns before sunset, huffing and puffing, practically sprinting. He barks as if he were a surgeon in an operating theater: "Tina! The cooker. The water.... [extending his hand without looking up] The rigs!" His dripping nose confirms the onset of dopesickness, reassuring Tina that he has not "half-stepped" her this afternoon.

When Carter hands Tina her syringe, she complains loudly, "That's all I get? I bet once I get through all of that foam at the point [pointing to bubbles in the syringe chamber], it won't even be thirty units."

Carter's syringe contains twice as much heroin. He snaps back, "I don't want you to be goin' out [overdosing] on me. I'm just lookin' out for your safety."

Outraged by Carter's patronizing response, Tina retorts: "You lying! You a selfish motherfucker," and she spits on the ground.

Exasperated, Carter adds water to the cotton, pounds it with the back of the plunger, and refills Tina's syringe to the brim. This satisfies her, even though he has kept the more concentrated first draw of heroin for himself. Carter is evidently still taking advantage of the fact that Tina does not yet fully understand the logistics of preparing heroin.

Tina's mood lifts immediately as soon as she injects. She steps out of the Chinook and starts dancing to the radio. Carter interrupts his attempt to locate a vein to admire her. "Look at her, Jeff! How can you stay mad at her?"

While dancing, Tina sings sarcastically, sweeping her arm over the garbage in the gutter, "Carter promised to get me off the streets after we got our food stamps. He sure took me away from all of this."

Carter ignores the jibe by affectionately telling her she is "nuts" and "a kook." But Tina remains aggressive: "That needle is your pussy. You won't give me none. I need to get me some. At first we sexed it up. We kicked it, but now it's slowed down."

To save face, Carter ignores her and leaves the Chinook to strip the plastic off a bale of stolen copper wire so that he can sell it as scrap at the recycling depot.

Tina mutters, loud enough for Carter to hear, "Shi-i-t. I'm'a go on a mission tonight, hang on Third Street and find this young brother I been knowing and get rid of this headache. I gotta do what I gotta do."

Predictably, Carter and Tina's most prolific period as burglars ended abruptly with Carter's arrest. According to the police report, Carter's guilt was confirmed by the boots he was wearing when the police seized him; they belonged to the victim of a car burglary from the night before. The police also impounded the following stolen items from the back of the Chevy Luv pickup truck: "a handbag, a prescription medicine bottle, a checkbook, several wallets, and a Saturn car radio." The arrest report also notes that Carter stashed "an illegal knife behind the seat of the patrol vehicle" that transported him to jail. Detectives subsequently linked the "red/orange public works pick-up" to unsolved burglaries at a half dozen additional construction sites over the past several months.

According to the court record, Carter listed his occupation as "House Painter; Cook; and Truck Driver" but admitted that he had been a heroin user since 1981 and was "employed for less than 25% of the time." He reported "Zero income . . . Total Assets: zero." Although he accepted a plea bargain, he remained unrepentant in his final declaration to the judge:

> The stuff that was stolen was in my truck, but I do not know how it got there. I pled guilty because my attorney told me to and said I could get out of jail quicker. Although I feel I am innocent, I am willing to comply with the condition of probation and even though I know I did nothing wrong, I'm willing to pay restitution to the victim.

During Carter's stint in jail, the city impounded the Chevy Luv, and the Chinook was towed a week later for multiple parking violations. Tina did not know how to drive a stick shift, and it was no longer possible to push the Chinook out of the way on street-cleaning days because its axle had been damaged while turning a corner on a lick getaway several weeks earlier.

Suddenly without shelter, Tina was in a jam. There were no other African-Americans available in her immediate social network: Sonny was in jail; Stretch visited from the Tenderloin only irregularly; Reggie was in prison; and Vernon was back full time with his wife, the nurse. On any given day, three or four additional African-Americans might pass through the Edgewater scene to smoke crack or inject heroin, but they were too transient for Tina to trust them.

Desperate, she moved into Hank and Petey's camp. Although she treated them generously to crack, they soon regretted their hospitality. The police evicted them because, according to Hank, Tina had been stealing too aggressively from the pickup trucks belonging to the construction workers retrofitting the freeway overpass next to their camp. Shrugging his shoulders, Hank referred to it generically as an instance of "niggers shitting where they eat."

Tina next sought refuge with Hogan, who had just been thrown out of a residential treatment program and was in a deep depression. They formed an unlikely alliance imbued with multiple habitus-level tensions, centered on personal hygiene. Tina tried hard to make their temporary partnership work by invoking a gendered script of motherly nurturance and scolding.

Jeff and Philippe's Fieldnotes

Tina has spruced up Hogan's filthy camp with what she calls a "woman's touch." Within a week, it is overflowing with the bric-a-brac of recycled domesticity that she always manages to scavenge. Tina appears to enjoy taking care of Hogan, who is always polite and thankful for her attention. He eagerly smokes her crack and "stays well" on her cottons. In contrast to Tina's high-energy, twenty-four/seven resourcefulness, Hogan reluctantly leaves his mattress only to panhandle change at the A&C corner store in the late afternoons.

Today, however, Tina is "sick of being Hogan's momma."

She complains: "If I wasn't around he wouldn't do a damned thing. He just a big baby. I got to remind him just to clean his abscesses. I practically got to wipe his ass for him.

"I been making him wash up and change clothes and stuff—you can't be dirty like that around me. I seen him just puttin' the deodorant on his clothes. I'm like, 'Hogan, that's gonna smell real bad. You supposed to put it under your arm, not over your clothes.' And he a grown man! Ain't that a shame!"

Six weeks later Carter rejoined Tina in Hogan's camp. The judge, overwhelmed by the city's heightened enforcement of quality of life statutes, had decided to clear his overcrowded docket of homeless addicts by remanding them to treatment and dropping their misdemeanors and felonies. Carter spent only sixteen days in jail. Ironically, his arrest on serious, multiple burglary charges resulted in clearing his legal slate, which was full of outstanding warrants for drinking in public, urinating, and jaywalking. Furthermore, within a week he had fallen through the cracks of his court-appointed treatment services.

Jeff's Fieldnotes

I run into Tina on the bus as she is returning from Third Street with ten dollars' worth of crack. She invites me to Hogan's camp "for a surprise."

I walk through the bushes to find Carter, who hugs me warmly. He claims that the counselors in his residential treatment program were former "Oakland gangbangers" who discriminate against patients from San Francisco. I ask him if he was offered any other treatment services and he says his sister offered to take him in, "but I missed my girl too much."

Energized both by crack and by the pleasure of being back out on the street with Tina, Carter talks nonstop. He quickly changes the subject away from his failed attempt to "go clean" and shows me two "I ♥ San Francisco" t-shirts that he has just shoplifted in the Fisherman's Wharf tourist district.

"I'm only hitting quick, surefire licks, on and off the bus. Tonight I'm gonna fill an order for a friend of Sammy's of the Crow's Nest liquor store for eight-foot plywood planks and keep my girl well.

"And I'll be out late tonight on the lick, so I'll need to get up by 8:30 in the morning to wash up over there at ol' faithful [pointing to McDonald's], where I got my personal bathroom [chuckling]. I'm supposed to meet my new client at the used lumber yard early tomorrow and I gotta look decent. To get to the lumber yard I gotta cross the freeway maze, which by 9:00 A.M. is like Market Street at lunchtime. It has a million cars turning the corner at that spot.

"You gotta pretty much stay in the middle of the street when you got a eight-foot, thick piece of plywood stickin' out on both sides of your buggy. You got traffic behind you honking and you acting like, 'Hey, I got access to the road, too, right?' But you just a pedestrian.

"And you know they automatically figure you homeless. 'Damn, this motherfucker got balls with his big, long-ass piece of plywood nearly taking up both westbound lanes.'… And you tryin' to stay in your lane … which ain't really your lane 'cause you on foot. And then you get some momentum going on a little bit of hill. So anything coming from around the corner better screech to a halt, or have on brakes, 'cause if they hit me—I'm a pedestrian, right.

"They pretty much stop. Some people blow they horns, say, 'Fuck you!' and get mad, but I just keep on going. They still stop.

"And if they don't stop, and providing I survive the impact, and somebody is a good Samaritan and gets the plates and the color of the car—which, nine times out of ten, that's what they do nowadays—I be in pocket. There are so many goddamn good Samaritans out here it's pathetic."

Carter finishes his riff by inviting me to accompany him to case the construction site he plans to hit tonight. Meanwhile, Tina heads back to Third Street to buy more crack with the seven dollars she had been saving for her next bag of heroin. She earned the money brokering "a forty-dollar rock for a nice white couple from Sacramento who were at the corner with a guitar looking for crack."

On our way back from the construction site, Carter and I are intercepted by Ben, who is waving from his car. He is going to the hardware store to fetch nails to fix the roof over his daughter's room at his mother's house. We climb into his car and, to our surprise, find Tina. They met on Third Street, and Ben is treating.

Several rocks later, Tina and Carter start worrying about impending dopesickness. They figure they can persuade Sal to sell them a bag "two dollars short," so they need only four more dollars "to get well." Tina agrees to hustle up that amount washing windshields, but they start arguing when Carter insists on "holding the four dollars" they already have until she returns.

Tina slams the door behind her and stomps off in a rage. When she reaches the sidewalk, however, she shifts into a steady stride born of routine, her shoulders straight and her head bent forward. A squirt bottle of pink hand soap taken from the McDonald's restroom is dangling by its trigger out of her back pocket along with the squeegee taken from the Citgo station. Halfway down the boulevard, she suddenly shifts course when she sees Little Earl, an African-American *crack smoker new to the Edgewater scene, and jogs over to him. Carter was smart to have in-sisted on "holding" the four dollars.*

Carter and I head toward the A&C corner store. He is sweating, walking lethargically, his head hanging. He suddenly turns to me and pleads with an intensity that catches me off guard, "Please, Jeff, what can I give you to get the last four dollars? I'll give you anything! I got some backpacks, a belt, an exacto knife… I'll give you anything."

Carter never hustles me this way; I am convinced that he must really be hurting physically. It feels wrong to refuse to give him the money.

I leave Carter at Sal's and head to the gas station where Tina is window washing with Little Earl. She hands me eighty cents to buy her a can of malt liquor because she has been 86'ed once again from the A&C, this time for throwing fruit at the cashier when he caught her steal-ing an egg.

On our way back to the camp, we see Carter in the distance receiving a ticket from a heavy-set, African-American female police officer. The officer takes the paper bag out of Carter's hand, twists the top of the bag, and returns it to him. We stand back cautiously until Carter motions with his head to meet him back at the camp.

Carter is furious: "Can you believe that bulldagger bitch? She gave me the beer back with the citation! Shit! The judge just cleared out all my old drinking tickets, and now I got a new one. One of my old ones had gone up to two hundred and something dollars."

After fixing, Tina and Carter fall into a deep nod, arms interlaced, foreheads almost colliding with the slow-motion bob of their heads. Carter emits his guttural moans of sheer pleasure.

The intimacy is broken by Max rushing into the camp announcing, "I don't want to talk to any-one. I been moving furniture all day and I'm sick. I got a twenty piece and I'll give a third if you cook it for me. My hands are shaking too hard."

Carter snaps out of his nod and jumps into action as though the king himself had just arrived. Tina pulls a new syringe out of her purse, forgetting that a few minutes earlier, while fixing with Carter, she had told him that she did not have any extras when he complained that his needle was no longer sharp.

A moldy sugar smell rises from the cooker as they heat it, prompting Carter's appreciation: "When you can smell it like this, it means it's good quality." He adds some water to dilute the heroin that Max has left for him in the bottom of the cooker and draws most of it into his sy-ringe. Tina screams, "Save some for me!" prompting a cursing match. Carter angrily pours more water into what is left in the cooker, diluting Tina's portion even more. To my surprise, this satisfies her. She has still not learned to recognize Carter's sleights-of-hand with respect to heroin dilution.

Carter probes for a vein in his arm while Tina stores her half-filled syringe in her purse. Tina asks Max where he is going to sleep tonight now that Frank's camper has been towed. He an-swers matter-of-factly, "I don't know. I don't even have any clothes. They took everything. I had only one blue suitcase left and they took that. Now I don't even have a clean t-shirt. I never used to look like this. I can't stand people seeing me like this."

He cheers up immediately when Tina hands him a cigarette. Incongruously, he announces that he has quit smoking because of "high blood pressure" and starts counting the remaining dollars in his pocket: "At least I'll be able to buy a razor and shave for work tomorrow. It's a big job. They say it'll last two more days."

Carter falls into one of his loud groaning nods right after injecting again. Tina becomes furious when Carter nods so far backward that he falls in the dirt. I am scared that he might really be overdosing. Tina jumps up to pour water down Carter's back from the plastic bottle they use for preparing their fixes. Carter does not respond, so together we hoist him to his feet. He finally groans and drapes himself over Tina, knees buckling. It looks like they are slow dancing. Tina begins punching and slapping at his back and head, screaming, "Carter! Carter! Wake up, you motherfucker!"

While all this is happening, Max suggests in a matter-of-fact tone that it would be better to "lay Carter on the ground and blow air in his mouth, hold his nose, and then pump his chest. I've done that a couple of times with a couple of people. It works."

Tina reaches into Carter's pocket, searching for some matches to light her cigarette. Carter snaps into full consciousness, shouting, "Never, ever, ever…" Unable to complete his sentence, he scratches his nose and falls back into his nod. We are reassured, though, because now he is moaning steadily, like a foghorn. Tina hisses, "That's the devil, Jeff! Take pictures so we can show him."

Yawning, Tina declares that she is going to "hustle up some change." Carter again snaps out of his deep nod, and this time he stays alert. We follow Tina down the boulevard. She stops to inspect some boxes piled against the door of the flower shop: "Those are nice boxes. Jeff, why don't you stay with us tonight? This cardboard will keep us dry." When I tell her I have to head home because I gave Carter my last four dollars, she laughs and hands me a dollar. "Go get some candles with Carter and set up the camp. And don't worry about your morning wake-up; I'll go hustle you some money at McDonald's for your coffee. [laughing] I'll come back when I got enough for all of our wake-ups tomorrow."

It turns out that Carter, like Tina, also had extra money squirreled away in his pockets when he hustled me earlier for four dollars, because he not only had enough money to buy the beer that got him the ticket, but he also had enough money, with the addition of the fifteen cents' change I gave him after buying the candles, to get a Cisco for one dollar and eighty-five cents. He hurriedly guzzles the bottle before Tina returns from panhandling to avoid having to share it. Hogan, who has had a bad day panhandling at the corner store, joins us back at the camp.

During the daytime they divide up their possessions and hide them to minimize loss "in case Caltrans comes." They unpack everything again after nightfall. Carter pulls out a mattress and a large piece of plywood from a clump of bushes behind the chain-link fence. He then fetches blankets and sleeping bags out of some brush higher up the embankment and sends me to look for more cardboard boxes in the dumpster.

Half an hour later, Tina returns with two hamburgers from Burger King. She hands one to Carter and one to Hogan and pulls out a handful of bills. Smiling, she says, "Let's go see Memphis." Mem-

phis is a new African-American in the Edgewater scene who sells heroin. There are three sellers on the boulevard right now, and the price for a quarter-gram has dropped to ten dollars. Quality is up, too. "We got enough for some crack and a bag of dope for our wake-up. So first thing in the morning we can go straight to the welfare office and try to get on food stamps."

Tina places a handful of change in my palms: "And Jeff, this for your wake-up and your bus fare home. Don't say no!"

Jeff: "How'd you hustle so much money so fast?"

Tina: "I'm telling you, Jeff. The wind blows money. I be finding twenties and a hundred dollars and shit. It just blows from outta somebody's pocket. [laughing] Y'know how they have these money clips. I found a hundred-dollar bill right there in front of McDonald's by the Outs sign. Then I found twenty dollars the other day. Then this man gave me twenty dollars."

Jeff: "Just now?"

Tina: "No. About a month ago. And this pregnant lady gave me twenty dollars last month, too. She surprised me, all pregnant like that, giving me so much money. I didn't want to take it. But she started crying; she said, 'Just take it, take it. You was concerned about my pregnancy! Just take it. Just go, go. You keep the money.' And I started crying, too."

As Tina walks out of the camp to go buy heroin from Memphis, Carter calls after her, "Give him only nine dollars!" But Tina wags her finger: "I can't do Memphis like that. His bags is straight up."

With Tina gone, we sit back on the blankets to listen to Carter's favorite nighttime radio dramas, replays from the 1950s on an AM station. First they run Orson Welles's The Third Man, followed by Eve Arden in Our Miss Brooks, and then a Sherlock Holmes story, starring Orson Welles as Moriarty, the Master Criminal.

Carter knows the sequences of all the shows by heart, repeating along with the narrator in a baritone voice, "Now the intermission!" He even mimes the chiming sounds, banging on an invisible xylophone, "bing, bong, bang," and does not miss a beat.

There is an awkward moment when we hear the vintage radio show audience laughing at Eve Arden's interaction with a "hobo": "Here, give that hobo this three cents' change. He's just bumming around for some soup."

The hobo responds with comic dignity, "No, thank you. I just had breakfast." None of us laughs.

The entire Sherlock Holmes show, on the other hand, sets both of us to laughing. Carter comments on the "gentlemanliness" of the characters as they discuss murdering one another. I doze off just as Holmes and Moriarty "plunge into the abyss" in hand-to-hand combat.

Tina returns empty-handed. Memphis was sold out of heroin. They are disappointed because they are quarreling with Frank, the only seller "in pocket" right now. They will have to wait until 6:00 A.M. to buy from Sal because he refuses to serve customers after sunset.

Hogan curls up on the edge of the mattress, and we lay ourselves out head-to-foot—four sardines in a can. As it grows colder, Tina asks Hogan, "I bet you wish you was in that treatment program now?"

Hogan replies, "Nuh-uh. No. You guys are my friends, my family. I don't got no family there in that program."

Tina whispers under her breath, "Hogan lyin'. I know I wouldn't want to be out here on the street if I could be in a program." It is indeed a cold night, and it is lucky that Caltrans did not locate their caches of blankets today.

We execute a Walton-like goodnight: Tina starts it with "Goodnight Jeff…," and we chime in right after with our "Goodnight Carter," "Goodnight Hogan," "Goodnight Jefferey," "Goodnight Tina."

At daybreak, Carter rushes out of the camp to be first in line at Sal's. I am surprised that Carter does not look even mildly dopesick. I suspect that he fixed on the sly while we slept, but his four-dollar hustle of me yesterday may be oversensitizing me to his half-stepping. Tina sits up and tells Hogan that his coughing kept her up all night. But she put her time to good use: "I had a cigarette and prayed for all of us." She points to her Bible, propped up on a rack flanked with candles illuminating the image of Jesus on the cover, "so that he could watch over us as we slept."

When Carter returns, Hogan immediately compliments him for "getting our wake-up." This is his way of laying claim to at least a small taste of the heroin Carter and Tina are about to inject. Tina hands me a stick of Wrigley's Winter Fresh gum, in lieu of tooth brushing, and I hurry off to get my coffee. The cashier at the produce store cautions me to "be careful around here" with

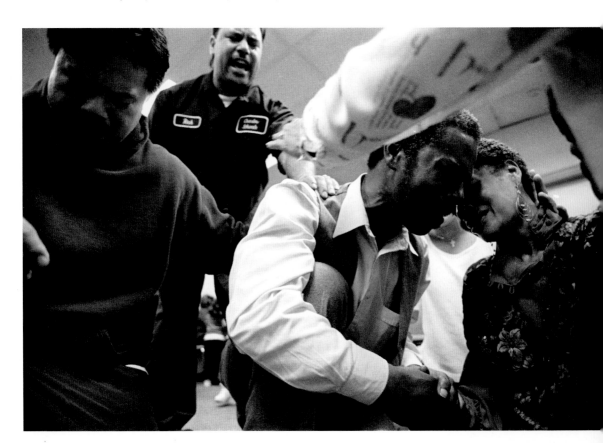

my photo equipment as she hands me my coffee. I tell her about my relationship with the home-less on the boulevard. She responds, saying that things are getting much worse on Edgewater: "Not with the homeless, but with crime. And business is down, the big chains are putting us out of business. Now everyone just buys sodas and chips and do their real shopping at the Discount Grocery Outlet across the street. But you'll like my coffee, it's good and strong."

When I return to the camp, Tina is still moving sluggishly. I give her and Carter a sip of my coffee, but they don't like it—no sugar. I remind them about their resolution last night to apply for welfare today, and we set off for the office downtown. The office is packed and we have to wait thirty minutes to get an appointment for later that afternoon. I head home, unable to bear a three-and-a-half-hour wait just to fill out forms.

During these months, Ben's twenty-one-year-old daughter, Crystal, invited her father "and all his friends" to come to her church, which was preparing to send her to India as a missionary. Tina was thrilled, telling Carter, "Time to exorcise the devil from our lives." Ben was unusual among the whites because he lived most of the time in his mother's home with his daughter.

Jeff's Fieldnotes

I arrive early, thinking I am well dressed for church, clean-shaven, with my freshly ironed button-down suit shirt tucked into clean blue jeans. Carter and Tina, however, are in a different league, and I am embarrassed by my lack of style. For the occasion, Tina has selected a blue floral dress cut just below the knee and a gold and turquoise vinyl jacket with puffy, padded shoulders and a wide Victorian collar. She slips knee-high stockings over her black tights and asks me if "the runs show too much." She puts on blue-gray, low-heeled cowboy boots with pointed toes and horizontal, multicolored stripes.

Carter is carefully checking his neatly combed hair in a small mirror. He is graying quickly, and the salt-and-pepper flows elegantly in stripes from his forehead to his crown. His sideburns, thick with gray, stop below the middle of his ear. He is wearing silvery gray polyester suit pants with a bright white, wide-collared, button-down shirt. He leaves his gray vest open, and on his feet he has clean, white tennis shoes.

Finding a jacket proves to be the fashion dilemma of the afternoon. Carter has three coats, looted a few days earlier from a burned building. He tries on a brown jacket, but the color clashes and it smells musty. A black leather coat fits well, but it too smells smoky, and he fears that the odor will rub off on the rest of his clothing. The third coat—a woman's brown leather with sheepskin lining—is rejected for being too effeminate, and its lining is filthy. We pass the coats around from nose to nose to gauge their smell. Between the three of us, we decide that the smoky odor of the black leather jacket is worth tolerating, since the jacket has the nicest cut.

Carter grabs a paper flyer tacked to a telephone pole in the alley and pours water on it. He lays the jacket on the bare ground and wipes it from top to bottom with the soggy piece of pa-

per. I see that the flyer is advertising a community meeting tomorrow night to discuss plans for constructing sixty-six condominium units in a vacant lot where Spider-Bite Lou has set up camp, across from the farmers market.

They continue their toilette with care, achieving ersatz privacy by facing out toward the ivy-covered chain-link fence that separates the camp from the highway embankment and hunching their backs to the parking lot of the wholesale flower shop.

Tina checks the time and announces, "Good. I have enough time to get me some crack." Carter starts chastising her for wanting to smoke crack before going to church, but she snaps back, "I don't care. I still want my crack." He acquiesces, muttering, "Yeah, and I sure could use a fix," as though proposing a polite cocktail from his wet bar.

I mention that I am hungry, and Tina suggests we eat at "the Colonel" [Kentucky Fried Chicken] on Third Street. Just as we are leaving to fetch heroin, crack, and fast food, Ben walks into the camp wearing blue jeans and a conservatively striped button-down shirt, untucked. He is also carrying a sixteen-ounce can of Olde English malt liquor. I feel a little less underdressed. Tina tells Ben that she is "two dollars short for a seven-dollar rock," and Ben hands her some money, urging her to hurry because he has left his daughter waiting in the car. Tina scolds him, "Ben! How you gonna smoke the crack with Crystal there?"

"I'll find a way," he answers, and Tina rushes off.

An hour later, with Crystal still waiting in the car, I hear Ben from behind the bushes complaining to Tina that her crack pipe is clogged. Tina refuses to give him a pipe cleaner, scared that he will scrape off her precious resin and smoke it. While they bicker, Carter quickly fixes some extra heroin by himself, out of their sight.

When we are finally ready to leave, Hogan walks into the camp. He has just completed his daily routine, attending the outpatient clinic at the county hospital to clean a wound on his pectorals that is still suppurating from last year's necrotizing fasciitis muscle transfer. He also managed to fill out papers at the welfare office downtown. Tina asks him for a Vicodin, which he obligingly gives her.

With maternal concern, Tina asks Hogan if he has eaten today and if he has any money. "No, darlin'. I ain't got nothing. But last night my friend Paul took me to Denny's for dinner. I had chicken livers and onions."

Tina scrounges in her purse and hands Hogan some change. Carter and I both give him a few more nickels and dimes. Carter advises Hogan to get the "Rodeo Burger, on sale for only a dollar and seven cents at Burger King."

Hogan declares that he wants to go to church too, but Carter tells him, "You need to stay behind at the camp. Barry stopped by this morning asking if we had an extra blanket. And bein' he's so desperate, I don't trust we'll come back and have anything left if you don't keep a sharp eye out for him." Tina protests, "That's a shame! That's the work of the devil. Hogan got to go to church, Carter. God'll watch our stuff! Poor Hogan is now all sad 'cause he can't go to church." Hogan shrugs and obediently sits down on his mattress.

The church turns out to be a small, rectangular room borrowed from an evangelical religious school. It has excellent video and sound hook-up because it serves as the school's music room. About thirty-five people, mostly Latino and Filipino, sit rapt with attention while a young Filipino preacher, a short man with slicked-back hair, dressed in a black suit, announces a new fundraising goal that would allow them to rent a larger, permanent space. His eyes sparkle intensely as he invokes God, sinners, and the devil.

Tina and Carter immediately join in the crowd's call and response: "Unh huh!"... "That's right!"... "Amen!" Tina whispers to me in awe, "This preacher is ordained!"

A middle-aged Latina steps up to the piano and starts to play, and the room begins to rock. The preacher calls "all the sinners" to the pulpit, and Carter and Tina lead the throng. His voice rises as the sinners line up. Suddenly he begins speaking in tongues and at least half the congregation joins in with him. The woman on the keyboard is now jumping up and down, swiveling from side to side as she bangs the synthesizer, singing at the top of her lungs.

The preacher works his way down the line, healing people one by one. A young Filipino man, wearing a blue work suit with his name, "Joe," stitched above his right lung and the name of his employer, "Charles Schwab," stitched above his heart, stands behind each "sinner." He catches them when they fall to the floor in rapture under the preacher's blessing.

Carter and Tina await the preacher with their hands in the air. He grips their heads together with both of his palms to "force the devil out of them." Nothing happens.

His voice reaches a crescendo and he grips them tighter, forcing their bodies backward. They both begin to quiver. He pushes even harder, gritting his teeth, with his eyes closed and his brow knit. But still they do not fall. Finally, after five minutes, he gracefully moves on. I feel sad for Carter and Tina, hoping they do not now feel hopelessly "trapped in the hands of the devil."

Ben is in the far corner jumping up and down, his hands raised in victory, dancing in time with the music. We make eye contact and he flashes me a smile, freeing my restrained, nervous laughter, which pours out of me. It is now absolute pandemonium. People are screaming, speaking in tongues, crying, jumping up and down, shaking tambourines, clapping. The preacher continues to move through the crowd, healing as he passes. Joe, from Charles Schwab, has begun mumbling softly in tongues, all the while trailing behind the preacher and skillfully catching everyone who falls.

Determined, the preacher spins around to face Tina again. She is holding her stomach, rocking back and forth, "the spirit of the Holy Ghost in her belly." She is wailing in full swing with her rocking, and the preacher lifts his hand up to her brow, bows his head in deep silent prayer, and strains his eyes shut. Beads of sweat appear on his forehead, and a crowd forms around Tina as she finally tumbles backward into Joe's arms. He lays her down gently on the floor.

Writhing, with tears streaming down her face, Tina sits back up with the assistance of a woman who is also in tears, embracing Tina from behind. Carter joins them on the floor, weeping and shouting, "Praise the Lord!" and holds up Tina's hand in triumph while others join in to form a huddle. They all speak in tongues, tears flowing.

Ben is still jumping up and down, snapping his fingers, his arms flailing, bent at the elbows. Crystal, his spitting image, is flailing right beside him. Tina rises to her feet and starts dancing around the room toward them. As always, Tina steals the show. The congregation follows behind her. At the end, Carter and Tina stand holding hands, rocking back and forth to the music as the momentum gently eases to a stop.

We exchange hugs all around. Joe tells me he has seen Carter and Tina before but cannot quite remember where. He asks me where they live. I avoid the question, telling him I live in Oakland and asking him where he lives.

"In the ghetto, Double Rock, Bayview Hunters Point. Pray for me, brother." Double Rock, off Third Street, is precisely where Carter and Tina often buy crack. As we walk out, Ben hugs his daughter and thanks her for inviting us. He suggests, "Maybe we could get more of the guys from Edgewater to come next time." She blushes and holds on to his shoulder gratefully.

In the car, Tina says that the preacher has taken the devil out of her and that she "feels light." She keeps asking me if I too had "felt the spirit of the Lord." I nod politely. Tina talks about how she "always was a church girl," adding, "the Holy Ghost was in me until I became a backslider— you know, smoking these cigarettes and stuff." Driving past a construction site, Tina turns to Carter: "Let's get us some wood!" Carter hesitates, "We can't do that after church."

But he promptly starts calculating the size and resale value of the two-by-fours lying unguarded and grins: "I guess we ain't in church no more." He adds, as a tease, "But if the devil ain't in you, I guess you don't need that crack no more now, huh?"

"Hell no!" Tina shouts back. "I want my crack."

Eventually Tina and Carter left Hogan's camp, disgusted by his filthiness and laziness. They moved into a nonoperative Honda Civic lent to Carter by one of his cousins, who sold crack by the corner store. To save face, Hogan accused Tina of stealing his last blanket, which in fact had been confiscated by the police during the last eviction. All this happened during the Christmas season of 1999, when the Silicon Valley economy was booming (as described in chapter 5). Employers in the Bay Area were recruiting entry-level workers aggressively, and Carter had obtained his temporary ten-hour-a-day job selling Christmas trees. Tina was also hired on a part-time schedule to clean the restrooms at the Kentucky Fried Chicken on Third Street, across from where she bought crack. A sympathetic night manager had noticed her washing windshields in the parking lot and wanted to "give her a chance."

Jeff and Philippe's Fieldnotes (Early December 1999)
Tina is so thrilled about turning over a new leaf through legal employment that she has started to keep a diary in a two-year-old executive planner that she found in the garbage. To make the calendar current, she has had to renumber all the days of the week. Her entries reveal marginal literacy as well as what she calls "my dylesia [dyslexia]."

The first entry begins with the imprint of a red lipstick kiss in the middle of the page followed by large block lettering: "SUNDAY: KISSES AND HUGS."

Wed 23: AT 2:00, I went to KFC were I surpost to fell out my paper work for my job and go for my or-reatakison [orientation].

Thursday 24: Came back and told my Daddy about the good news and he was Hi Hi Hi way up there, but God, Pleas help us through this Cristit's [Christmas] CJ [Carter] Very Bery happy for me a God we are going to make it with your help. Love you Jesus always.

She is full of resolutions, "to cut out the crack" and "get on welfare" and "always go to work on time." Excited, Tina tells Carter, "I'm gonna eat all the food. I'm never gonna skip a meal. Maybe we won't have to be homeless no more now that I'm working. Huh, Carter?"

She plans to sell her first allotment of food stamps to make a down payment for a methadone maintenance program: "Shoot! I can't stop work in the afternoon, fix in the bathroom, and then go back to work all nodding out." She adds, with some pride, that her welfare benefits will probably be reduced after she receives her first Kentucky Fried Chicken paycheck. She eagerly recites the history of "the Colonel" that she learned at the orientation.

Jeff's Fieldnotes (mid-December 1999)

Returning from work in her brown Kentucky Fried Chicken uniform, Tina poses for us on Edgewater Boulevard, a detached pout on her face, like a fashion model. She then frames her arm around the bright red heart painted on the door of the flower shop, tilting her head back to show off her "natural" hairdo.

She rustles through her purse and pulls out one of the pats of butter that are served with Kentucky Fried Chicken biscuits, vigorously rubbing it into her hands and along her forearms to hide her track marks. Tina often complains of dry skin from living outside in the cold weather. She shines a pair of brand-new high-heeled boots with the last of the butter. She bought them last week at Payless for eighteen dollars to wear at work, "but they don't want me wearin' these; they only allow soft sole shoes." Pointing her toes to admire the gleam of the butter, she asks me if I remember the "stomping" she and Carter gave Bugs in the alley behind the corner store two years ago over the cocaine rip-off. "Boy, Bugs wouldn't want to be under these!"

Tina tells me proudly that she is "doin' everything right: bein' early for my appointments at KFC, getting on GA, getting food stamps." She has been going to the dentist to fix her teeth. She removes her bridge to rub her finger along the ridge of the toothless part of her gum. "The dentist says my roots is coming out. I was eatin' some candy in the parking lot and I almost chewed my tooth."

She will not have enough money to pay for her next dental visit, however, because the day manager has reduced her hours. "He is fucking with me at work. The man just hates me."

Sonny walks up, pushing a shopping cart. He was just released from prison last week, and we greet each other warmly. He immediately feigns dopesickness, hoping we will treat him to a few dollars, but he is too excited at seeing us to maintain his hustling pose. We walk down the block to where Ben and Felix are painting the A&C corner store's brick wall a bright red. Frank, with a full Cisco in his pocket, is eyeing their work critically.

Frank: "They should have painted it chartreuse."

Felix: "Yeah. Fuckin' A-rabs! It's rustic brick that people are buying these days, not this tacky red color."

Frank: "How much they paying you for this, twenty dollars?"

Ben: "They said fifty."

Frank starts putting up "wet paint" signs, suddenly eager to earn a taste of the heroin they will be buying with the fifty dollars.

In the back alley immediately behind the corner store, Memphis, pushing a hand truck, is unsuccessfully attempting to barter several cases of orange and white cakes he scavenged from the Discount Grocery dumpster for a bag of heroin from Sal.

Carter and Tina's precarious attempt at stability through legal employment was shattered by a police sting operation aimed at Carter's grand-nephew, Smokey, the owner of the most active crack sales spot in the alley behind the A&C.

Jeff and Philippe's Fieldnotes

We arrive to find Carter very drunk. His chest is heaving in gasping sobs, a deep wail emanating from his throat. When we try to comfort him, he starts banging his head against the billboard on the outside wall of the corner store. Incongruously, his forehead is striking the silhouette of a bravely smiling African-American man announcing the classic public health HIV-testing slogan KNOWLEDGE IS POWER.

Carter: "I don't know what to fuckin' do, man! Tina's gone and snitched on Smokey. Why did she have to betray me this way? We always came through clutches with each other. I made her part of the family. Everyone accepted her, and now she's brought shame onto me. They see me as a traitor on account of my feelings, my love for her.

"And Smokey is my blood... a nephew, close to my bones. He respects the elders. He provides for the family, takes care of his mother, buys food, pays rent and bills. If someone needs it, he buys clothes for the kids. And his mother just lost her job with that city youth program."

Jeff: [hugging Carter] "Calm down. Tell us what happened."

Carter: "Oh, Jeff! We kickin' it in Smokey's car. The white ghost [unmarked police car] came right up on us. And these two aggressive, motherfuckin' big, burly, no-thinkin'-ass goddamn cops jacked me up against the fence and cuffed me. They got on black jump boots and shit and everything, blue uniforms, right. Lookin' like little twerps with their pants stuck up in they ass. They lit the corner up like Market Street at lunchtime and found five hundred dollars' worth of rocks up under the seat from where Tina was sittin'. Smokey wasn't in the car. He had just gone to get us some more beer. So they snatched Tina up.

"And they make Tina dump everything out of her purse, right. Oh, Philippe! She got every-thing in this motherfuckin' purse with the kitchen sink, right? I mean paraphernalia, with a cap-ital P. Pipes fall out. Outfits fall out... caps from other outfits that ain't even there to 'fess up to the needles that they belong to in there.

"They took Smokey and me to jail, and Tina in another car to another motherfuckin' station. They kept me locked up seven days. Sick! Going through livin' fuckin' hell.

"Smokey's mother come to find me. She had talked to her son's parole officer, and the officer showed her a signed affidavit paper, on a statement given by Tina Gordon!... on she gettin' the drugs from Smokey, right, and everything.

"Smokey only had three days left on his parole. They had set him up. That's why they chose Tina; they picked on the weakest. And Tina sang, blew it wide open! Smokey got seven months in the pen. The judge gave me three years probation."

Tina fled to Antioch, a suburban town forty-five miles northeast of San Francisco with a grow-ing African-American population of rent refugees from the city. Tina's son, Ricky, newly re-leased from two years in prison, sheltered her. She managed to find legal employment for a few weeks at a Taco Bell but quit to sell crack for her son. He gave her a fifty-dollar chunk each day for only forty dollars. This allowed her to get high and generate a little bit of extra money by breaking off crumbs for resale in three-, four-, and five-dollar allotments.

Suddenly alone, Carter urgently sought to form a new running partnership and, once again, crossed ethnic lines. At first he stayed in Spider-Bite Lou's camp, but he soon left, "because Lou shits where he lays his head." Next he moved to a camp newly settled by Buddy, a white peripheral member of the Edgewater scene who supported himself by scavenging for alu-minum cans. Buddy had negotiated permission to sleep on the premises of a defunct fac-tory by promising the owners he would protect the site from burglary. Ironically, he and Carter would have been the first to strip the copper and brass from the abandoned struc-ture's plumbing and electrical systems, had they been denied the right to squat there. Ini-tially, Carter adapted to Buddy's drug consumption pattern. He stopped buying crack and ceased injecting speedballs. He sounded almost like a white righteous dopefiend, criticiz-ing Tina's predilection for crack in front of Buddy.

Jeff's Fieldnotes

Buddy's camp is tucked into the far corner of a loading dock in the guts of the factory. The back wall of their living enclosure consists of twisted steel pipes bunched in a tangle of bent arms and elbows attached to moon-faced gauges and emergency shutoff valves. Several piles of fe-ces lie in a corner at the perimeter of their camp. Buddy has taped a photograph of two middle-aged white men to a slab of plywood. He calls them "my uncles" because they periodically help him with food and clothing. I hear a low, repetitive beep emanating from deep inside the fac-tory; it is a device to repel rats. I ask Carter if he misses smoking crack.

Carter: "Tina had a real thing for crack. We used to argue on the strength of her wanting to go buy a rock after I get her well and on not spending the wake-up money. 'You're just going to run out of what I hustled so hard for to get you well.' That defeats the fuckin' purpose!"

Buddy: "Uh-huh! 'Cause that morning comes around too quick."

Carter: "Uh-huh!"

Jeff's Fieldnotes (two weeks later)

Carter is trying not to blow up at Buddy. Despite their attempts to accommodate each other, their relationship has deteriorated. Carter complains that when they are out on licks, "Buddy's heart beats too fast. Makes me nervous, and that's when accidents can happen."

   Tonight they are planning to hit a nearby junkyard to get a half dozen used carburetors stacked in the rear corner of the yard. They will have to haul the carburetors back to their camp in their buggies, one by one, and then strip them of recyclable metal.

Carter: [gruffly] "You ready to do the motherfuckin' lick tonight?"

Buddy: [mumbling] "Yes."

Carter: [shouting] "You sure!?"

Buddy, who is about five foot five and weighs about a hundred pounds, nods his head. Cowering, he slowly wheels his shopping cart half full of cans and bottles out of the camp. Carter stops him and fills three brown bottles with sand, burying them at the bottom of the cart. Buddy complains, "Don't overdo it. You're gonna get me 86'ed."

   Shaking his head in disgust, Carter invites me to come with him to case the junkyard one last time. He needs to reverify the alarm system and confirm that there are no watchdogs. At the yard, he whispers for me to ask the manager for a Volkswagen alternator. I pretend not to hear, and he does not insist. Instead, we walk around the block to the back of the yard. From the outside he measures the gap between two fence posts, murmuring, "Buddy's small frame will just squeeze through."

   Continuing down the block, Carter inspects a discarded water heater lying in the gutter, but he does not have "the right tool" to remove the copper fittings. Back at the camp, he anxiously turns on the radio to get the six o'clock news because a serial killer has been targeting female sex workers in Antioch.

Carter: "This is the third motherfuckin' murder inside of a month in Antioch. The last one was at eleven o'clock this morning. I was praying. Prayin' to God, 'Oh, please! Please! Don't let Tina be done got in a fuckin' situation. She's smarter than that.'... [softly] I miss my Tina.

   "I was thinkin' all kinds of shit, until they finally said it was a Caucasian girl that got killed. That's all I needed to hear. So I could relax... a teenage girl, five foot six. They found her by the tracks in Antioch. Slain. Her fuckin' neck and head was severed. And it was close to the area from what I had known on where Tina's folks live."

Tina stayed in Antioch for only three months. The town was the site of too many traumatic memories. "Shoot! I don't like that town. There a couple people I wanna kill over there. They fucked me real bad. . . . I don't wanna talk anymore, Jeff." Later Tina explained that ten years ago she had been kidnapped and raped by a "Mexican drug dealer" who left her for dead on the Antioch railroad tracks, not far from where the serial killer in the news at the time was leaving his victims. Antioch was also the place where Tina's only sister, Sylvia, had been stabbed to death. During this last stay, Tina was harassed by a jealous ex-boyfriend who "used to kick my ass every day." She "hired" a bodyguard because she did not want her son to get involved for fear he would kill the man. Her son eventually did find out, however, and "only put his eye out." The next time Tina saw the ex-boyfriend, he "had an eye patch and just ignored me." The final straw that sent Tina back to San Francisco was watching her son beat up his pregnant fiancée: "I screamed at him to never do that again, and I left Antioch."

For the first month after her return, Tina stayed at her Granny's house and held only surreptitious rendezvous with Carter. As Carter put it, "If Tina was to be seen out here, and me be seen with her, oh, man, we both be filled with so many holes, like Swiss cheese." True to form, Tina was unrepentant:

> They say I'm a snitch 'cause I didn't take Smokey's rap. But I wasn't fit to tow all that dope. He ain't my man. What the fuck they expect? It wasn't mine. Shit! And the police knew the crack wasn't mine. . . . It was such a big bag. They know I'm a dopefiend. That's the bottom line.
>
> I came to the conclusion that whatever happens in the world to me, it gonna happen to me. I'm gonna try and make the best outta my life while I'm alive. And I'm not fit to let no one scare me away.

Smokey's mother paid Stretch to locate Tina, and then she confronted her:

> That bitch come by with a broken bottle saying she gonna beat my ass. I been smoking crack all night long. And I was dressed for fighting. [raising her fists up] Either you talk or you fight.
>
> "Bitch, come on! Fuck you, bitch! I ain't scared of you, motherfuckin' old asshole. Eat my ass! Bitch, if you gonna whip my ass, you better shoot me first."
>
> Bitch ain't gonna whip me. I'm a ghetto chile'. She a child who live in the house all her life. I live in the ghettos all my life. We different peoples. I had to fight my way through my life.

The showdown over revenge was finally defused when Smokey called from San Quentin during a birthday party for Carter held at his sister Beverly's house. Over the phone, Smokey forgave Carter for loving Tina. When she heard this, Tina moved in with Carter at Buddy's camp.

Jeff's Fieldnotes

Women's clothing now dangles from the factory's pipes. Tina's beauty supplies are laid out on the shelf of a discarded plastic display case from the Discount Grocery Outlet, which still has

*$1.99 RAID PEST CONTROL price tags on it. There is a crushed lemon on one of the shelves, indi-
cating that Tina and Carter are back to shooting speedballs—something Buddy would never do.*

*Tina complains that her menstrual cramps have been getting progressively worse each month.
Last month her clotting was so bad that she almost went to the emergency room, and she won-
ders if she should go now, but she is scared of being dopesick during triage.*

*Today there is the usual tension. Carter is threatening to beat up Buddy because Spider-Bite
Lou stayed over last night and Buddy borrowed a syringe from him instead of from Carter or
Tina, thereby obligating himself to give a taste to Lou rather than to either of them.*

The next set of fieldnotes laconically documents a repetition of the white flight phenomenon similar to the one we witnessed during our first year on Edgewater Boulevard (described
in chapter 1).

Jeff and Philippe's Fieldnotes

*Two weeks ago, Buddy abandoned the factory camp permanently. It is now home to a dozen
additional squatters, all African-Americans, including Sonny, and it is overflowing with shopping
carts, plywood lean-tos, and strung-up tarps. To make the space feel homey, Tina has posted
Jeff's last batch of photos on the factory wall, surrounding each picture with blue tape as a
frame.*

*The whites no longer visit here anymore. Coincidentally, however, the night we choose to sleep
in the camp, a white ex-con crack smoker named Roy is visiting. Carter had met him at one of
the treatment programs he failed. Despite his balding gray ponytail and Hell's Angels/White
Power allure, Roy is comfortable in this all-black scene and is treating Carter and Tina to crack.*

*As the night wears on, however, Roy begins to suffer paranoia from smoking too much crack.
He jumps at the noises of car doors slamming. Carter calms him down by interpreting the surrounding street noises outside the tarp like a seasoned woodsman listening to nature: "That's
a pickup truck parking; that's kids walking by... a little old lady."*

*We lay out our beds next to Sonny in front of the tarp but still inside the protection of the
loggia. Sonny's bedroll is neatly folded on a box spring mattress. He has set up a tidy nook. A
cardboard box serves as his nightstand next to his pillow, and he has laid out his crack pipe,
lighter, watch, and wallet. Once he is snug in bed, he pulls the covers over his head and takes
a deep hit of crack before resting his head on the pillow. He must have bought a separate supply of crack because throughout the night we hear him lighting up.*

*Carter, Tina, and Roy also stay up smoking. Talking in animated whispers throughout the night,
they reminisce about past licks. Roy announces that he is ready for full-time work because he
has stolen all the tools he needs and he has "a friend who has a friend who is with the carpenters union—and that's twenty-six dollars an hour!"*

*A few days ago, he scored an electric saw that he claims "is worth about sixteen hundred
dollars" from a job site where he was working as a day laborer. His girlfriend had just picked him*

up from work when the boss, who had left early, paged him to tell him to pick up the saw that he had forgotten at the site. Roy said, "I told my girlfriend, 'Turn around, I just got me a new saw!'"

The next day, Roy told his boss that the saw was gone. "I pointed across the street to where a line of Mexicans stood waiting for work. My boss nodded his head and said, 'I think we know who took the saw.'" Carter slaps Roy a high-five, laughing, "The Mexicans took it!"

That same day, Roy had also obtained a power drill from the back of another worker's truck. "I saw it just sitting there… like in an Easter basket. I just had to take it, it was like cupcakes and milk."

Roy and Carter begin planning their next lick, a cops-and-robbers fantasy of charming receptionists for information on payroll deliveries, disarming alarms, and wrenching ATMs out of brick walls with metal cables attached to pickup trucks.

The stability and size of the all-black abandoned factory encampment prompted a police sting operation. Carter was arrested, entrapped by one of the contractors who regularly paged him for lumber supplies. Luckily, the encampment had also attracted visits from the outreach van of the Department of Public Health's Homeless Death Prevention Team, providing Tina with the opportunity to seek treatment.

I believe that with strong determination and willpower, I could get clean one hundred percent. I think I could do it in twenty-one days. I'm going to try my damnedest, Philippe. Let me say that. —*Carter*

In 1996, the San Francisco Department of Public Health declared that it would provide "treatment on demand" to drug users. During our dozen years of fieldwork, however, treatment on demand was never available for the homeless (see critique by Shavelson 2001). Addiction is not simply biologically determined; it is a social experience that is not amenable to magic-bullet biomedical solutions. Although many heroin and crack users (no one knows the proportion) eventually manage to cease using drugs permanently, most of them fail treatment most of the time. Treatment advocates argue that relapse is "normal" and that every single day of sobriety should be considered a success. The challenges of treatment are exacerbated by inadequate public funding and by a lack of coordination between detox programs and long-term social support services.

Accessing Detox Treatment

All of the homeless on Edgewater Boulevard asserted on many different occasions that they wanted "to go clean." Almost all entered treatment programs more than once during the years we spent with them. They were often motivated to seek help by sudden life crises. This was the case, for example, with Tina's decision to seek help when she suddenly found herself alone in the abandoned factory camp after Carter's arrest (described at the end of the previous chapter). She benefited from the exceptional support of a pilot public health outreach team. Even with the team's advocacy it still took her six weeks to get access to an inpatient detox program.

When Tina was finally given a date for an intake interview at a treatment center, Jeff offered to pick her up in his car on the morning of her appointment to make sure she did not miss it.

Jeff's Fieldnotes

Tina is waiting for me outside the Mount Hope Baptist Church, where she just received ten dollars for picking up her HIV test results from blood that was drawn two weeks ago by public health epidemiologists. She hugs me, declaring loudly that she has already drunk an entire bottle of vodka and is "driving everyone crazy." It is only 9:00 A.M., but I am relieved to see that she has brought a duffel bag with her.

*Hopping into the front seat, Tina announces: "First I'll get my crack. Then a hit of hop [heroin]....
We goin' to my program and I'm fit to get loaded on the way! This is my last for two years."*

*I start driving rapidly toward the treatment center and try to talk her out of her plans. Out-
raged, she threatens to jump out of the car if I don't turn around "and let me have my last hit of
crack." Scared to let her out of my sight, I reluctantly agree to drive back to the crack-dealing
stretch of Third Street.*

*At a busy intersection, Tina crumples a handful of one-dollar bills and drops them under her
seat. The next thing I know, she has jumped out of the car and is flashing money and cursing
in the middle of the street surrounded by four young men. The shouting suddenly stops, and
they all turn around to look at me. One of the young men slowly walks over, knocks on my window, saying matter-of-factly, "One more dollar." Furious at Tina for putting me in this position,
I reach under the seat and carefully pull out only one dollar from the clump of crumpled bills
she left behind. I hand it to him through the corner of the window, terrified he will see my camera and tape recorder at my feet.*

*Back in the car, Tina immediately loads her pipe. Ignoring my protests, she asks me to raise
my window to maximize the concentration of crack fumes. I insist again that we must leave for
the program, and this triggers a rant: "And I'm gonna spend my money on me!" Her first hit of
crack escalates her anger, but it dissipates as quickly as it flares. In a quick change of mood,
she is chuckling about how she is faster than any of the men at hustling money when she washes
windshields at traffic intersections: "I can get five dollars in a half hour because women don't
like to stop and give money to a man."*

*Seizing on her mood swing, I interrupt: "Okay. There are tons of cops out; let's get to the pro-
gram right now before it closes." She ignores me. She opens the car window and yells out to a
middle-aged woman who is standing on the corner wearing a gold mesh top with a black brassiere
underneath. "Hey, Pauline! It's me. You got an outfit for sale?" Pauline holds up two fingers and
Tina shakes her head, frowning, "I only got one dollar, baby, but I'll give you a little hit of crack.
Come on, please! It's me."*

*As Pauline climbs into the back seat, Tina opens her hand to show me a few specs of crack
in her palm, giggling in a whisper, "This what I'm gonna give her for the rig, Jeff." Pauline's face
has one scar running along her right cheek and a second scar wrapping around her neck. She
immediately grumbles about the size of the specs of crack, but scrapes resin from the stem
of Tina's pipe and manages to eke out a decent hit.*

*Tina is genuinely happy to see Pauline and proposes enthusiastically, "Come help me look
pretty for going into the program. Help me choose my shoes and do my hair." Without pausing
for an answer, she grabs Pauline's hands affectionately and points to a bevy of dealers on the
far corner and asks, "How much money you got?" I protest again that we have to hurry to get
to the treatment center before it closes.*

*Tina: "See, Pauline, Jeff ain't no trick. The only thing he is worried about is getting me to my
program on time. But I want my hair done. [pouting at Jeff] And I go get my crack, my hop, with*

Pauline. [suddenly happy again] Pauline gonna dress-braid my hair! I wanna be pretty, Jeff. [turning to Pauline] Will they let you do my hair in the program? You wanna go to the program with me?"

Jeff: "Come on, Tina! Enough!"

Pauline: "If you quit talking and go do what you doin', I have all your hair braided by three o'clock."

Jeff: "Three o'clock?! No way! It's eleven o'clock now."

Tina: "See, Pauline, Jeff want me in treatment—"

Jeff: [interrupting] "By eleven-thirty!"

As we drive to Pauline's house for her to pick up clothes and hair-braiding supplies, I explain to her that I am a researcher at the medical school. Pauline responds, "My old man has HIV and they want to do a study on me of why I don't have it." Tina hands her another pipeful of crack.

While Pauline is in her house, Tina takes out a mini Ziploc bag, the kind used to package crack, and fills it with little chunks of white plaster. I realize she is preparing to take advantage of the moment before going into residential treatment to "burn" someone and avoid retaliation. Pauline comes back carrying a roll of toilet paper, a piece of ivy to plant, a large metal comb, and some clothes. We circle around the neighborhood for another half hour until Pauline finally finds her "old man," selling heroin in a liquor store parking lot.

At Tina's camp, Pauline picks her way through the collapsed tarps and piles of soggy clothes and wet furniture and bursts into tears.

Pauline: "No, no. Tina, no-o-o-o! You was staying down here and I got a big ol' house? If you didn't have no income, you know I would… [angrily] Carter had you out here? Look at this! You outside! Living like a motherfucking dog! [shouting] This ain't cool, dude! If Carter were any type of man, he woulda' been trying to get to a motherfucking program for his motherfuckin' own self. [turning to Jeff] Am I right or wrong? [turning back to Tina] I'll slap him with my dick when I grow one! [to Jeff again] Excuse my language, but that's how we talk…. I'm not trying to be funny or nothing, 'cause I know you not no trick or nothin', 'cause you trying to get Tina into a motherfucking program…."

Tina: [softly] "See, Jeff, that's why I asked Pauline to come with me today. Pauline, tell Jeff about my sister, Sylvia."

Pauline: [lowering her voice] "I ain't gonna talk about Sylvia because there be more tears…. I called her Chocolate; she called me Cream."

Tina: "If Pauline had been around, my sister would be alive. Pauline would have killed that bitch before she got my sister. 'Cause her and my sister beat everybody up. They was tough sisters, always together."

Pauline: [gently] "I had went to the penitentiary so I wasn't with Sylvia the day she got stabbed by that ho'. God called her."

Tina: "God put Pauline in her life for my sister."

Pauline: [hugging Tina] "You my nigga."

Tina: [turning to Jeff] "Pauline and my sister whoop Third Street niggers. They got battle scars."

Pauline: [louder] "Mens cuttin' us up. [touching the scar on her neck] But they couldn't whoop us. Now I couldn't whoop no man no more, but back then I weighed two hundred twenty-five when I got out of the pen. And when I was pregnant I weighed two sixty."

Tina: "How much did my sister Sylvia weigh?"

Pauline: "Sylvia weighed a good… hundred eighty, but don't talk about her no more or else I'll go to the Fillmore right now and try to find that ho' who killed her.

"Bitches was jealous of us. I'm tacky now, okay. But I was raised in a middle-class black family, which she… [pointing to Tina and shaking her head in disgust at the camp] was too!"

Pauline opens the balloon of heroin she just bought and, as she hands it to Tina, deftly pinches off a small chunk from it with the tip of her fingernail. She then gives Tina instructions on how to "cook it up good," as if teaching her how to bake a cake.

Pauline: "Stir it up, girl? Good. Now put a little cotton in there. Okay, good; now wipe your arm off…. [turning to Jeff] I used to be an LVN [licensed vocational nurse]."

Tina: "She and my sister took me to nursing school with them."

Pauline: "But Sylvia didn't want to stay after we had to deal with dead people."

Tina falls into a deep nod immediately after fixing, her head dangling between her legs and her forehead practically scraping the ground. Pauline, in contrast, is barely affected. She asks me to fetch "kindle" to build a fire to heat the comb for Tina's hair, and I despair at ever getting Tina to the program.

Pauline pulls a wire mesh out from under a pile of clothes to use as a grill to heat the comb over the flames of her makeshift fire. This prompts Tina momentarily out of her nod: "Don't do that! There some rats might come up through there. Leave that shit alone—it's Carter's."

Tina starts trying on the clothes that Pauline brought for her—a red, strapless, shoulder-baring cocktail dress; black panty hose; and black patent leather high heels. The clothes reveal how emaciated Tina has become. Her jutting collarbone forms a shadowy concave ring at the base of her neck and her skin has become almost translucent, making her veins stand out. Pauline compliments Tina on her new purse. Tina smiles, "It's mine. I just stole it at Walgreens yesterday."

Finally, Tina begins packing her belongings for the program. As she grabs her syringe, I warn her, "You can't take that rig in there, Tina."

Tina: "I'm not, Jeff. I'm just settin' it here so's that I can do my next hit."

Jeff: "What! Your next hit!? No way! We got to go to the program!"

Tina: "Yeah! But I only did forty ccs and I saw Pauline settin' some aside. And I gave her ten dollars and my crack."

This provokes a twenty-minute cursing match between Tina and Pauline. The pain of their lives pours out as they argue about their fair shares of the twenty-dollar quarter gram of heroin Pauline bought from her husband.

Tina: [tears streaming] "Don't do me like that! [in one breath] I'm-a-fuckin'-dopefiend-but-I'm-fit-to-go-to-the-program-and-I-ain't-got-no-more-goddamn-dope-and-I-just-want-me-one-more-hit-of-dope. And I want my hair done now!"

Pauline: "Good Lord, have mercy. Look at those tears. [pointing to Jeff's camera] Could you please take a picture of those tears!? Motherfucker crying about motherfuckin' dope...."

Tina picks up a half-eaten blueberry pie, and Pauline jumps to her feet.

Pauline: "Don't you throw that pie. 'Cause you goin' to a motherfucking program and I don't give a fuck about you getting no attitude. [turning to Jeff] She's been pulling that shit ever since she was a little girl, picking up things, throwing shit."

Pauline finally gives in and starts tearing apart her purse, looking for the missing pinch of heroin.

Pauline: "Jesus, please let me find this hit. God, please! I don't ask you to help me find no drugs, but I need to find this right now. [finding the speck of heroin] Here you go. Take it all. I ain't never seen you clown behind no narcotics like this. Never! If I'd knew it was gonna be like this I woulda' got me a piece of crack instead. I don't have to play no games. [turning to Jeff] My man got dope and my son deal heroin. Tina hogged it. I did not beat [hustle] her! [sobbing] And she makes me feel like a scandalous dog."

Tina: [crying too] "What did I do to deserve this? I just wanted some more dope. Why you trippin'?"

Pauline: "I'm not trippin'. I got fucking feelings."

Tina: "You gave me less. I swear on my dead sister you did."

Pauline: "I swear on my dead baby! I gave you half. I swear on my dead grandson that you got half! [turning to Jeff] Please just take me home."

Tina: [calm again] "Let's say we didn't hear each other...."

Pauline: "I'm through with it. I'm through with it. I still love you...."

Tina: "This dope ain't comin' between us...."

Pauline: "No, the dope ain't comin' between us, but we can't do no narcotics together no more. No more. Because I want you to come out of that program clean and I want you to stay clean."

Tina: "You watch and see. I'm gonna stay clean."

After we drop off Pauline at her house, Tina manages to fix one last time in the front seat of my car and then breaks off the needle tip and throws it out the car window. With relief, I watch in my side-view mirror as the syringe rolls to a halt in the gutter. Tina falls into a deep nod, and I speed to the intake office before it closes at 4:00. We arrive at 3:15, with forty-five minutes to spare. In her red strapless dress, Tina stumbles on her high heels up the stairs to the second floor office. I follow, carrying two ripped black plastic garbage bags full of clothes, with a pillow and a stuffed teddy bear spilling out.

The counselor, surprised, invites us to sit on folding metal chairs. Tina moves hers closer to mine and bursts into tears. I put my arm around her shoulder, lamely reassuring her, "It's okay to be scared.… Everything will be fine." She pouts, explaining to the counselor, "My tears are both happy and sad."

I am relieved to see that the counselor is empathetic and spends a few minutes easing Tina's nerves. He then calls the detox center to confirm whether Tina's bed is still available. They inform him that Tina cannot be admitted without a blood test. He hangs up the phone, shakes his head, and sighs. I plead with him to make it work and describe the ordeal of the last six hours trying to get her here. The counselor appears moved and rushes downstairs to the public health clinic.

We wait nervously for ten minutes and Tina cries silently until the counselor returns with the good news that the nurse has agreed to squeeze Tina in at the front of the line. Before medical intake, however, Tina still has to complete a formal "social work readiness interview" in another office down the hall. There is also a long line at that office, but in yet another stroke of luck the security guard, who has overheard our commotion, pushes Tina ahead of everyone. As we walk into the social worker's office, she is chastising a patient for coughing: "Go over to triage and get yourself a mask. I'm not getting sick because of you."

Tina cannot find her identification card (she forgot it in her purse upstairs), and the social worker, irritated, calls out, "Next person in line." Luckily, the counselor has accompanied us and he runs back to his office, returning just in time with the purse. Tina rifles through it, shivering uncontrollably, and in the process tears off the strap of her new Walgreens purse. Finally she holds up her ID triumphantly.

After completing the readiness interview, Tina runs to medical triage, where the nurse accidentally drops the thermometer that she is about to place in Tina's mouth. Tina protests, "Could you wipe that off first?" and then turns to me and mouths silently, "Lesbian." By the time Tina finally emerges with all her paperwork, the driver of the van from the detox program is waiting outside impatiently. She refuses to climb on board, begging me through her tears to drive her. She finally gives me a long hug and jumps in, sobbing.

Seven days later, Jeff sent the following email to Philippe:

> Just got off the phone with Tina and she's kicked! She sounds great and even had the wherewithal to apologize for what she put me through last Wednesday with Pauline: "I'm sorry you got upset, Jeff. Pauline somethin' else! She sweet 'cause of my sister. At first she thought you were a sucker 'cause you white, till she found out you really wanted to help me get in a program."

At Tina's request, Jeff brought her mother, Persia, to the detox center on the first open visiting day.

Jeff's Fieldnotes

Mother and daughter greet by hugging and nuzzling noses. They sit on the couch, arms interlaced. Tina then serves us coffee and jelly beans, and Persia asks Tina what she does all day. Tina answers laconically, "Go to groups." They are anxious to be nice to each other, but neither quite dares to hope that maybe this time they might avoid yet another hurtful exchange.

In a picture frame designed to look like the back pocket of a pair of blue jeans, Tina has affectionately placed a photograph of two very young girls posing together. She tells us that the girl on the left is the pregnant fiancée of her eldest son, Ricky. Persia comments that "they are going to hell" for not being married—"I won't let anyone unmarried have sex in my house."

When Persia goes to the restroom, Tina tells me she faced her big temptation yesterday while being escorted on the morning stroll to a coffee shop in the program's upscale neighborhood. She found herself face to face with the coffee shop's tip jar. The escort was serving as a "perfect decoy." In the old days, "I would have run off with the jar."

Toward the end of the visit with her mother, Tina suddenly turns sullen. She attributes this to "mood swings." Persia hesitantly asks, "Why should I give my precious love when you are killing me slowly?" She then pulls out a little bottle of holy water from her purse and places crosses on our foreheads. She instructs Tina to read from "Psalms and Revelations 1, 2, and 3." She promises to discuss the passages with her over the telephone next week.

As we step out the door, Tina hands me a pair of nurse's shoes that she found at the intake center and asks me to take them to her Granny. She is scared that her stepfather might try to con me and warns me, "Just leave them outside the door." She also tells me to alert Ben and Max that two beds were vacated this morning at the detox. Both of them are currently wait-listed for treatment by the Homeless Death Prevention program, with instructions to call this detox program each morning before 9:00 A.M. "to check on space." Two weeks have passed with no vacancies, and Tina is excited that they could be admitted tomorrow.

On the drive home, Persia tells me: "Round and round we go, to no avail. I'm tired! I can't get with somebody. I can't let myself go. It's just hope and pray, hope and pray. This is the last time. If my family does not get it together, I will run away and not tell anyone where I go. That's what I did for two whole years after Sylvia died."

As I park, she invites me into the apartment and offers me a brand-new photographic enlarger that she bought after taking a photography class at City College. She has never used it. "I prefer you have it, instead of the Goodwill."

Jeff relayed the good news about the empty beds at the detox to Ben and Max. When they called the next morning from the pay phone outside the A&C corner store, however, they were told there were "still no available beds." Ben snapped back, "Do I need to grow a pussy to get admitted?" and was immediately thrown off the waiting list by the receptionist. Ben was desperate because a judge had mandated him to serve eighteen months in a treatment program in lieu of the same amount of jail time for shoplifting at Nordstrom. He had been unable to locate a program willing to accept him, and he now had only three weeks left before having to serve the jail sentence. Ironically, later that same morning when he went to a community-based clinic to have an abscess lanced, the intake nurse scolded him, "So, now do you want to get clean?"

Ben's problem was not unusual in San Francisco. Treatment programs are subject to a punitive "audit culture" (Strathern 2000) and must justify their limited funding by their success rates. They purposefully exclude risky patients by institutionalizing artificial obstacles. One common strategy is to require patients to call their prospective treatment center at 9:00 A.M. each morning for three weeks to "prove readiness." The logic behind "screening" is not explained to the homeless when they seek treatment. As a result, the byzantine bureaucratic rules imposed by funding imperatives become yet another friction point fueling mutual resentments in the idioms of race, gender, and sexuality. We often heard whites claim that programs were partial to "niggers" and heard heterosexuals denounce treatment counselors as "bull dykes and faggots." No one recognized that the root of the problem was the precarious funding of treatment services in the United States.

Facing imminent incarceration for "failing" to find a treatment slot, Ben went on a shoplifting spree. In the middle of the Discount Grocery Outlet, he pulled out two backpacks that he had stuffed down his pant legs and filled them with butcher knives. His running partner, Nickie, was waiting outside by the automatic entrance doors and triggered them open so that he could sprint out without setting off the electromagnetic merchandise alarms. Three days later, Ben was detoxing "cold turkey" on the floor of a jail cell while awaiting arraignment. He and Nickie had attempted unsuccessfully to repeat their heist at Walgreens later that same day. Nickie escaped just in time. When she told us the story a week later, she referred to Ben affectionately as having had "a fuck-it-all-take-no-prisoners attitude" on the day of his arrest but also expressed relief and pride at his finally being "clean." Her equivocal emotions encapsulate the lumpen subjectivity fostered by neoliberalism's punitive version of biopower, in which law enforcement dominates health services. She admires Ben's outlaw masculinity, and that includes the ability to endure five days of unmedicated withdrawal symptoms in jail—"cold turkey."

The Absence of Post-Detox Services

Tina's counselors at the detox program spent hours on the phone placing her name on waiting lists for long-term residential treatment programs throughout the Bay Area. They could not release her to her mother's care because of the history of trauma in that relationship; they could not send her to her adopted grandmother because her stepfather, Arthur, had turned that house into a sex-for-crack den. Tina's eldest son's apartment in Antioch was obviously not an option since he sold crack. Nevertheless, the program's bylaws required the counselors to "graduate" Tina within thirty-one days. They were unable to locate any subsidized counseling or follow-up services and had no alternative but to discharge her to a women's shelter located in San Francisco's Tenderloin neighborhood, a hotbed of drugs, alcohol, and crime.

Coincidentally, ten days earlier, Carter had been released early from jail, and he returned to the abandoned factory camp. He too had not been offered follow-up treatment services. A work referral program for ex-cons, however, had placed him on a construction job, and he was thrilled. Unfortunately, his first weekly paycheck coincided with a three-day downpour of rain that halted construction. Suddenly idle, Carter's newly earned legal cash burned a hole in his pocket. He went on a three-day speedball binge and was soon back to being a dopefiend full time. Throughout this process, he had been calling Tina at the detox center from the pay phone at the corner store to congratulate her and to express his love.

Jeff's Fieldnotes

The morning following Tina's release from detox, I head to Carter's camp at the abandoned factory, but it is fenced off. Workers in hardhats and orange reflector vests are gutting the premises.

The young foreman tells me that "the homeless were evicted earlier this morning." The ten-thousand-square-foot structure is scheduled to become a mini shopping mall and a food court.

This reminds me that shortly before Carter's arrest, Tina had told me eagerly that the owner of the factory had promised Carter a job in the renovation. Sifting through the junk still left at their old spot, I come upon a half-empty bottle of Trazedone, an antidepressant, with Tina's name on it.

I drive to Edgewater Boulevard and find Tina washing windshields in the parking lot of McDonald's.

Tina: "I'm sorry, Jeff, but that place they took me to wasn't nothin' but a nasty-ass shelter. When I walked in, they were serving some sloppy food. And I wasn't going out like that. So I said I could do it my own self. I could take care of myself. Thank God."

Jeff: "How come you started fixing again?"

Tina: [loudly] "… 'Cause I wanted to, Jeff. I'm a dopefiend. I wanted to make the program work, but I ain't fit to make like I'm ready… and get off this shit.… I still like this shit… because I'm a failure. I just felt confused, disorientated, overwhelmed."

Jeff: "But you were a success at the detox. Everyone loved you there."

Tina: "I'm a loveable person, but I'm a failure. I wanna be clean and sober and get off my ass and do what I need to do for me. But I don't know why everything changes when I'm on dope. I never complete a damn thing.

"I don't have no place to go right now, and I'm not fixin' to go and whine to my mother. I know that I'm gonna want some hop… some crack. I can't do that to her. So I just gotta stay out here and tough it out and get my ass together and just go on."

Tina took full responsibility for her relapse, despite her counselors' inability to locate post-detox housing and services. Twelve-step Narcotics Anonymous self-help meetings were the only free and accessible form of post-detox treatment in the United States in the 1990s and 2000s, and they rely on individual willpower and spiritual solidarity. Predictably, most long-term indigent heroin injectors and crack smokers relapse on multiple occasions before finally ceasing to engage in personally destructive patterns of drug use. Without substantial institutional resources, it is difficult for long-term chronic users to figure out how to pass the time of day. They have to construct a new personal sense of meaning and dignity. Instead, they often fall back on their more familiar and persuasive righteous dopefiend ways of being in the world, and they seek out old drug-using friends and acquaintances.

Six months after having been briefly "clean and employed," for example, Carter was back in jail for a "dirty urine" parole violation and Tina was reaching a new low. She had built a lean-to next to a dumpster in the empty lot by the Discount Grocery Outlet and, for protection, camouflaged it as a mound of garbage. She mourned her relapse, convinced of her own worthlessness, and this deepened her commitment to heroin and crack.

Tina: Look at me! I wake up dopesick every morning. It's my own damn fault. Carter, he blames hisself and says it's his fault. But it was my choice. I'm a stupid-ass fool.

You don't love me no more, Jeff. You don't come check on me. I know I hurt your feelings when I left the program—and broke your heart. [wiping tears from her eyes with a McDonald's napkin] I hurt my own feelings and I broke my heart, too. But I tried. That's all I can say, Jeff.

[voice cracking] I think about it every day that I have to keep hustling to live. Gotta get my high. Last month I got busted pushing a cart. I'm frightened now. I am praying to God they never catch me.

[whispering] I'm eatin' out of the garbage now, and I think I got food poisoning. I be so tired now. . . . I can't even eat. My bones achy. Maybe I got the flu. I been washing my clothes by hand and puttin' them on half-dry. [lighting her crack pipe]

Jeff: Why don't you just rest tonight instead of hustling for more crack?

Tina: No! No! No! [laughing while inhaling crack] I'm fit to smoke crack, Jeff. But the crack takes my dope away and makes my bones start hurtin'. [grabbing her syringe like a dagger and pretending to stab her arm] Take a picture, Jeff! I'm a dopefiend. I'm not gonna stop livin' till I die!

Once again finding herself alone on the street with no running partner, Tina drew on her charismatic performance of femininity and used her access to African-American street dealers to broker five- and ten-dollar crack deals for the white men. Normally excluded from performing masculinity in their interactions with women, the white men, under Tina's tutelage and with Carter locked up, deployed a version of chivalry that protected Tina from violence and benefited her in the balance of the moral economy.

Tina: I never do a whole sack of dope alone. I just sit in the car, and my mens come to me. They loves the hell outta me! All my mens stop by to make sure I'm okay.

When they on crack they come over here wanting a pipe. [imitating Felix's voice] "You know I love you, Tina. . . ." Frank has three pipes now: a big one, a medium one, and a small one. [notching the sizes along the side of the stem of her pipe] I bought him his first pipe, and now he smokes more crack than me.

And Petey comes by, too, for crack . . . but on the sneaks from Hank. And I tell Petey, "Get your ass on this bus with me." And we go to Third Street. And we smoke some crack together. I buy him beer 'cause I don't want him drinking that Cisco because of what he been through with his hep C. And he hasn't gave up on life. That means a lot.

Hank comes by sometimes too, on the sneaks from Petey, so we can fix some dope together. But I don't want to feel bad for Petey so I sneaks with him again later for dope. [laughing] Carter and I used to do that to each other, too.

Crossing the lines of intimate apartheid in her relations with men, Tina frequently encountered their routine expressions of racism. On one occasion, we walked up to Frank's camper to find Tina arguing furiously with him. He attempted to defuse the tension by apologizing to her for being "a white racist grouch." This made her even angrier: she was hurt and embarrassed that Frank had self-identified as a racist in front of us, even if he was apologizing for it. Later, in private, Tina felt compelled to save face by reassuring us that she never subordinated herself to her white male friends: "I don't kiss they ass at all. When I get mad, I cuss they ass out." At other times, Tina made statements that reflected the symbolic violence of internalized racism: "The white people is real nice and concerned about me and what I'm going through out here now. They the nicest ones, white people is." Moments later, she would criticize whites for their habitus-level deficiencies. For example, when a white couple, who were methamphetamine injectors and running partners, established themselves on Edgewater Boulevard for a few months, she complained:

That new bitch a copycatter—tryin' to wash windows at my gas station. I beat her ass. Nasty white bitch. . . . So filthy! Her and her husband, I even been keeping them from beating each other. But then he gonna watch me beat his woman's ass, and he ain't gonna say shit.

Both of them is nasty. [inhaling crack] They even got dirt on them. Yup! Nasty-ass bitch!

Methadone: Biopower in Action

Since the 1970s, the U.S. medical establishment has promoted methadone maintenance as the cure for heroin addiction (National Consensus Development Panel 1998). This has caused considerable political and popular controversy over methadone as a treatment modality. It has been at the center of what Foucauldians call an "intradiscursive conflict." Biomedical science declares methadone to be a medicine, but contrary discourses of law enforcement, health fitness, and moral and religious abstinence consider methadone to be a dangerous and immoral drug. The "birth of the methadone clinic" in the late twentieth century offers an interesting case study of the emergence of an expensive, conflictive, and humiliating apparatus of governmentality for regulating heroin addicts (Bourgois 2000).

Despite strong support for methadone maintenance by the federal government's National Institutes of Health, the treatment remained illegal in many Bible-Belt states; federal law required that methadone be distributed solely through specialized clinics and that it be dispensed daily through "directly observed therapy" to prevent its diversion for resale on the street. Furthermore, doses, cost, and accessibility varied across the country (D'Aunno and Pollack 2002), depending on the local influence of doctors, epidemiological researchers, evangelical ministers, for-profit treatment clinics, law and order advocates, and public health budgets. In San Francisco, for example, from the 1990s through the 2000s it was difficult for the homeless to access methadone maintenance because it was administered primarily though private for-profit clinics that charged approximately three hundred fifty dollars a month (Rosenbaum et al. 1996). The county hospital reserved its limited number of subsidized maintenance slots for indigent addicts with one or more potentially fatal medical diagnoses such as active tuberculosis, full-blown AIDS, metastatic cancer, or emphysema. Inexpensive methadone was more readily available through twenty-one-day detox programs, but they had negligible success rates. In contrast, in New York City during these same decades, long-term, high-dose methadone maintenance was easily available to everyone at low cost through large public health clinics.

Methadone and heroin stimulate the same neurotransmitters in the brain. The first time an individual consumes methadone, he or she often feels pleasure and falls into a deep nod. Within a few days, however, patients develop what doctors politely call "a tolerance" for the drug (and what users describe as a physical craving more powerful than that caused by daily heroin injection): the neurotransmitters that simulate a heroin high become saturated, but do not generate pleasurable sensations. Following the logic of biopower, methadone is a technology that is designed to block the euphoria produced by opiates at the molecular level in the brain's synapses. Critics denounce methadone for being more pharmacologically addictive than heroin: its withdrawal symptoms are notably more severe and prolonged than those caused by heroin. Debates over methadone in the 2000s resonate with those of the 1880s, when the medical establishment hailed both heroin and cocaine as cures for morphine addiction (Bourgois 2000). Nevertheless, for hundreds of thousands of former heroin addicts methadone has been a life-saving substance that dramatically reduces their suffering (Drug Policy Alliance 2007).

In 2002, the United States finally approved buprenorphine as a substitute treatment for heroin addiction, prompting new magic-bullet promises and new counter-polemics among treatment specialists. Whatever the merits of the debate, buprenorphine, in its first years of deployment in the United States, represented one more detox and treatment alternative that thousands of injectors used to stabilize their lives (see Lovell 2006). None of the Edgewater homeless tried buprenorphine treatment, but we met several younger injectors on the periphery of our scene who spoke positively about buprenorphine and who marveled at how much less painful it was to detox from it compared to heroin or methadone.

Most of the Edgewater homeless believed, at least to some degree, that methadone could potentially change their lives. When they obtained legal jobs, for example, and wanted to avoid the necessity of injecting heroin on their breaks, several of them sought admission to private methadone clinics, despite their fears of the drug's addictive properties and their resentment of the directly observed therapy rules that clinics imposed on their patients. Consistent with the broader ethnic pattern of unequal access to services, none of the African-Americans in our social network entered methadone treatment during our years of fieldwork, whereas almost all the whites and Latinos received methadone on multiple occasions—usually through the relatively cheap, for-profit, twenty-one-day detox venues. None of the Edgewater homeless lasted longer than two weeks in those short-term detox programs because the rapid tapering of the dose caused severe withdrawal symptoms. Although their relapses were pharmacologically predictable and represent an obvious institutional deficiency in the treatment modality, these failures became yet another forum for symbolic violence that encouraged vulnerable individuals to blame themselves for their lack of willpower.

Only one peripheral member of the Edgewater scene was consistently registered in a long-term methadone maintenance program during our time on the boulevard. Chester was legally blind and qualified for Supplemental Security Income. He still lived with his parents in the neighborhood up the hill, and his mother made sure that his treatment bill was paid on time every month through his disability check. Chester drank large quantities of Cisco Berry to boost the latent euphorigenic effects of his methadone. By midday, after his third or fourth bottle, he would burst into tears, calling out for his deceased Native American girlfriend, Carmen. They had met at the methadone clinic and had become inseparable lovers. Carmen was killed during our second year of fieldwork when she ran into rush hour freeway traffic during an argument with Chester. We were never able to interview her because, like Chester, she became incoherently monosyllabic when she combined alcohol with methadone. Years later, Chester would obsessively reenact the horror of her death during the evening rush hour, shouting across the freeway at the top of his lungs, "Carmen! Carmen! Stop!"

Halfway through our fieldwork, Chester's abdomen suddenly swelled to triple its normal size from cirrhosis of the liver. Six months later he was dead. The Edgewater homeless were convinced that methadone had killed him.

On one occasion, we gave Max, Frank, and Chester a ride to the for-profit methadone clinic where all three were enrolled at the time. Max was beginning the final week of his twenty-one-day detox arrangement. It had been prepaid by a social worker after Max spent three and a half weeks in the county hospital for a skin graft over a large abscess. Frank was self-paying for his twenty-one-day detox in order to finish a large sign-painting job without interruption. Chester was fetching his standard morning maintenance dose. Our conversation in front of the clinic highlights the dissonance between how methadone treatment is experienced by injectors on the street and how it is understood by scientists and clinicians.

Philippe: Explain how methadone works for you, Max.

Max: It sort of stops you from craving the heroin. But now I'm craving the methadone, 'cause I got so used to drinking it every day in the hospital that by the time I got out, I was hooked on it. That's why they sent me to detox.

Methadone has kept me off the heroin. . . .

Philippe: What are you talking about? You just fixed some heroin twenty minutes ago before we left for the clinic.

Max: Well, yeah. Today I broke down because I was sick. The last three days have been real hard because the dose they've been giving me is cut way down now. I mean, I was so sick I could hardly walk this morning. It's sort of the same as when you don't have heroin. You start throwing up. It comes out everywhere. Your eyes water; your nose runs. You can't sleep.

There is nothing they can do about the dose at the clinic unless I had the money to pay twelve dollars a day. But I don't like the whole idea of methadone. [shouts and curses coming from the clinic door behind us] But methadone works if you let it work for you. You just have to be a little bit stronger than I am.

Philippe: How many times have you been on methadone detox?

Max: Oh, gee whiz. I don't know, maybe twenty times over the past five years.

[turning toward the commotion at the clinic door] I'm gonna go see what Frank is upset about. Ask Chester about methadone.

Chester: Yeah, I've been staying clean. I'm on eighty milligrams. The stuff works. On methadone you're just like normal. You wake up, you're not sick at all. I mean, hey, you feel normal. I can get up, smile, brush my teeth and eat, go to work . . . if I worked. I can do things I'm supposed to do: I can shave, change clothes, wash clothes.

You know who invented methadone? I heard it used to be called "Adolphine," after Adolph Hitler.

Philippe: Not quite, man. It was invented during World War II by IG Farben, the same company that made Zyklon B, the poison gas the Nazis used to kill the Jews.

Frank: [running toward us] We gotta get out of here [pointing to an African-American security guard running toward us]. King Kong over there has a hair up his ass.

Philippe: [scrambling into the car] What happened, Frank?

Frank: They breathalyzed me. I had too much alcohol on my breath. . . . One fucking point over the limit, so they didn't serve me. I lost twelve dollars! They used to fucking give the money back, but now they say it's in the computer. Bullshit, man! That's another scam of theirs.

Chester: [furious] That happened to me, too, for a whole week—just for drinking.

Max: [whispering in awe] At eighty milligrams! You don't know how wrong that is. That stuff is strong, man. It's stronger than heroin.

Frank: [shouting] They got complete control of your fucking life.

That fucking bitch nurse! That's why I'd never get on maintenance again. It's like being in prison. I can't stand that. They got you scared all the time. They threaten you: "Do this" and "Do that." And they fuck with you all the time. You know, fuckin' following the rules. And then when they get a little hair up their ass about something, they gonna cut you down. And that shit is life and death, man.

Chester: Yeah . . . goin' into convulsions and seizures that could kill a person!

Frank: It does! It has. They're just legalized dope dealers. They could give a fuck less about people.

Mandating daily attendance at methadone clinics for directly observed therapy, a requirement imposed by law enforcement advocates, ironically promotes poly-drug use among methadone maintenance patients. For a few hours each morning, the corners surrounding clinics become open-air markets for the drugs that boost methadone's latent, euphoric effects—primarily crack and benzodiazepines such as Valium.

Coercive Treatment

In 2001, California implemented a voter-approved ballot initiative mandating the option of treatment instead of incarceration for nonviolent, drug-using criminals. Carter was already in jail at the time, but he was granted early release on the condition that he attend a residential treatment program and remain "clean and sober" for ten months. As a military veteran he was eligible for free job training in a program serving the dot-com industry.

Carter's "computer career" never materialized. He almost obtained a job as a garbage collector through "connections" his niece provided, but he was rejected "'cause I got a bunch of fucking felonies." Eventually, the Veterans Administration program managed to clear his driving record, and he obtained a license to operate heavy machinery. Soon he was bulldozing fruit and nut orchards south of San Francisco for a developer who was building a gated bedroom community in Silicon Valley's exurbs.

A month into his new job, Carter arranged to meet Jeff in the Mission District.

Jeff's Fieldnotes

Carter is late and I cannot stop myself from worrying. I am waiting on the same corner where I watched him buy heroin for the first time. It is a Latino scene, and after making the buy, he had walked right past me without making eye contact. Back on Edgewater, we had shared a pastry, and he had explained that he had not wanted to risk letting the dealers see him "talking to a white boy." Most undercover officers are young white men and if, by coincidence, the police had arrested someone later that day, or even later that week, he could have been banned or beaten up simply for having been seen talking to an unidentified thirty-year-old white male at the copping corner within the last few days.

Despite the ongoing War on Drugs over the past six years, this scene remains unchanged today. Dealers are out in full force.

Carter finally arrives, and he looks great. He is at least thirty-five pounds heavier than when I last saw him in court—"all neck," as Max describes him. We drive to a café in the neighborhood

where he grew up and find ourselves surrounded by the new boho residents who have gentrified it. He holds up his key chain, a series of color-coded Narcotics Anonymous milestones celebrating his sobriety—thirty days, three months, six months—and talks earnestly.

Carter: "This is a major, major stepping stone for me in my life, Jeff. At forty-two, being able to do this. Ain't nobody human out here could of did that. On giving me another chance. I stay ever mindful for that.

"I get tried a whole lot of times. Just last week, my car got hit; I got laid off from my first job in delivery; there was a death in my family. But I ain't using none of that as no excuse.

"Deep down in my heart and mind and soul I know that I shouldn't be here. I should have been dead or in the penitentiary for a long time, bro'. I done took a whole lot of people's stuff.

"I always tried to keep that protective macho image up. In treatment, people cried and hug in groups. Men supporting other men. . . . I never bonded with no men before. True love support. It made me take a hard look at my life. After a few weeks they made me a mentor and that was kinda cool. It wasn't like that other Choices Program I was in, where they do violence therapy in like, groups. There they do a lot of screamin' and yellin'. A lot of name callin', and they try to break you down. They have a sign that says WARM AND FLUFFY. It's how they want to make you.

"And this year I was bringing in the New Year's drinking apple cider in a clean and safe environment. Last New Year's I was drunk, loaded, laying up in the hospital. I had got hit by a car, and my head was bust open.

"And the guys out on Edgewater, when they see me, they talking, 'Hey, man, I got this bag. You want some of it?'

"I just tell 'em, 'I fittin' to go to the store and go get me some juice.' Right! 'I been thinking about this Sunny Delite.' Right! 'It's hot and I got a taste for orange juice.'

"Oh Jeff, why don't you and Philippe come to my graduation from the program on Saturday? My sister's comin'. My new girl, Clarice. My daughter, my niece, my grandson. Bill, my sister's husband, is coming. Smokey's wife is coming, but Smokey can't be there; he's in jail again."

Jeff: "Your grandson?!"

Carter: "Yeah. I'm a grandfather by both my daughter and my son. [taking baby pictures out of his wallet] And this past Christmas they gave me a pass from the program to go visit. I went to my daughter's house. And we put the little toys together . . . and the puzzles. And we played and wrestled on the bed. . . . Then, you know, we ate and stuff. That's one Christmas I never will forget.

"The only thing we didn't do was take no pictures, which was what I wanted to do, but at the time I didn't have no camera. But I got plenty of time for that.

"You know, Jeff, I drive by a lot of construction sites and see so much wood and opportunities . . . piles of money just sitting right there. [laughing] Contractors, here I come! It's like a natural reaction—like homing instinct—peoples, places, and things.

"But I just look and laugh. 'Oh Lord, please dismiss that thought. I'm just looking, Lord. I'm just looking.'"

Most of the forty-two graduates at Carter's drug rehab graduation ceremony were African-American, and most had been mandated to complete the program by the court. The staff members at the treatment program were all African-Americans, funded by the Alternative Programs Division of the sheriff's department. Evoking the slavery experience, their logo depicted chains "bursting asunder." Wearing suits and ties, many of the graduates burst into tears at the podium in front of the microphone when they were handed their diplomas. Several of them thanked the district attorney for arresting them. Carter punched the air to the audience's cheering and announced, "I wasn't arrested; I was saved." At the end of his speech, he raised his arms in the air like a boxing champion and shouted, "I did it!"

Following the rules of his Narcotics Anonymous program, Carter avoided seeing Tina, and she responded to news of his graduation from the program like a jilted lover:

> Don't talk to me about Carter. He just likes to stand on the street corner talking in his cell phone to make people look bad.
>
> I seen him last night. I said, "Help me out," and he gave me a dollar. I gave it back to him: "I don't want no dollar!"

Two months later, Carter's bulldozing job ended, and Philippe ran into him on Edgewater Boulevard. With a can of malt liquor in his hand, Carter was celebrating his forty-third birthday with a sex worker who was sitting in the beat-up Toyota belonging to his girlfriend, Clarice. He cut short Philippe's expression of concern with the quip, "What's the matter! Wanna turn? I'm just freakin' with this chick. . . . You can go next; she gives great head." He then tried to reassure Philippe that he had already found a new position in Silicon Valley, "movin' office equipment. I like meeting all the secretaries. They talk to me about stock options. In a year, I'll have enough money to buy a house in Vallejo." He then kicked the broken headlight on the Toyota and laughed about using the insurance company's reimbursement money from his accident earlier in the day to make a down payment on an SUV.

Two weeks later Carter died under the freeway in the hole. It was payday, and he had stopped by Edgewater Boulevard on his way home from work. His overdose generated the familiar spate of rumors and recriminations.

> *Tina:* Sonny came by just as I was fixing. He put out his outfit and said, "Sis, could I get a little?"
>
> I gave him some dope. And then he was crying and actin' all spooky and scary and shit and starts hollerin', "Tina, Tina!" He was on his knees. "Tina, let me talk to you. It's Carter. He's dead!"
>
> I'm like, "What? When? How?"
>
> "The paramedic said he swallowed his vomit."
>
> I'm like, "Oh, yeah, Sonny. I thought you wasn't shootin' dope with Carter? I knew you was. You don't have to lie to me. When did it happen?"
>
> "About an hour ago."
>
> At the time I was shockin'. . . . But that motherfucker Sonny was just waitin' to spend up some of Carter's money. They robbed him. I found all that out later, 'cause later, every time

Sonny came around here, I could see that he be tweakin'. Carter's pockets was full of money and Sonny probably pulled his coat, watch, and rings too. All I know is, Sonny let him die! Sonny didn't save his friend's life.

And if Carter was gonna die, at least he could have died in the hospital, or in the ambulance—not on that damn ground. [pointing to Hank] Hank's around crying too. He's crying, wantin' to kill everybody so I gave him some crack. Talk to him, Jeff. He feels bad too.

Jeff: What exactly happened?

Hank: Well, maybe Sonny and Carlos [a peripheral Latino in the scene] didn't really know that Carter was gonna die. But they robbed him. They took his money and his jewelry. It was over nine hundred bucks. 'Cause I'd seen Carter earlier that day and he'd had a eleven-hundred-dollar check.

The two guys, Sonny and Carlos, kept hanging around. They wouldn't leave Carter's side 'cause they knew he had the money on him.

When the coroner picked him up, he didn't have no money in his pocket. He had about seven cents, something like that. They couldn't even find the keys to the car. Sonny and Carlos had their hands in Carter's pockets. Carter was on his back.

And Jeff, I'm lookin' for Carter's brother—Lionel. I got a good idea of what I wanna do to them. . . .

Frank: [walking up with Spider-Bite Lou] I'd kill that motherfucker Carlos myself, if I knew I could get away with it.

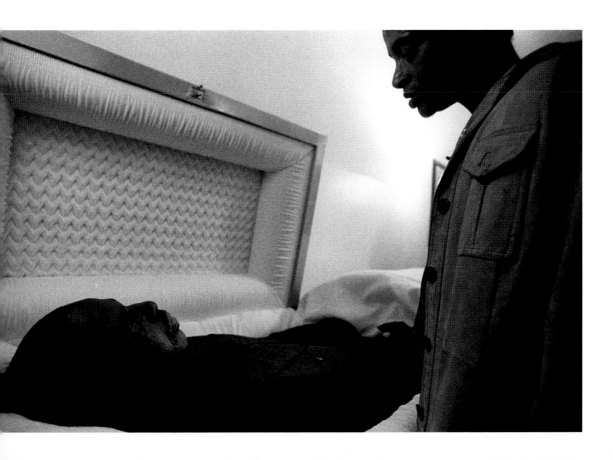

Hank: They should have sat Carter upright. They should never have left him laying down like that.

Frank: [softly] Yup. He's dead all right. [kicking the ground] I've had so many friends die in the last few years.

Spider-Bite Lou: [ruefully scratching the scab on the back of his neck] When the devil comes a callin', he comes screamin'.

Tina built a shrine to Carter in her lean-to by the Discount Grocery Outlet dumpster. The centerpiece was a plastic wedding cake decoration of a white bride and groom holding hands, bordered by a rose in plastic sheathing and a photo Jeff had taken of her with Carter at the beach. At the base of the shrine she taped three condolence cards addressed to Carter's sisters. She signed them, "Tina James," thereby formally taking Carter's surname. A homeless woman who lived down the boulevard and who had "buried three husbands to overdoses" sympathetically prepared French nails for Tina to make her "look like a lady for the funeral." As the woman painted Tina's nails, she gently chided her for not putting aloe on her tracks to hide them. Going in and out of a nod, Tina reported matter-of-factly that the doctors had given her a hysterectomy two weeks earlier. This explains why she had been bleeding, cramping, and urinating so much over the past year:

> Thank God it wasn't cancer. I'm blessed, but I got stitches inside me; and they gave me four pints of blood, two when I got there and two in surgery. They gave me thirty ccs methadone and morphine, and I was well. [smiling] They gave me a voucher for a cab to go to that same nasty-ass shelter the detox sent me to. I put the cab on another destination and went back to my camp next to Frank. The cabbie gave me three dollars from the voucher to get rid of me.

Tina's medical record confirms that she lost a great deal of blood and notes that she is homeless. Despite these complications, she was released from the hospital early, after only three days.

Jeff accompanied Tina to Carter's viewing at the funeral parlor.

Jeff's Fieldnotes

Tina introduces herself as "Carter's fiancée," and we are greeted warmly by Carter's thirty-two-year-old daughter and his thirty-year-old son. The daughter is petite and has Carter's same endearing smile. In contrast, Carter Jr. is well over six feet tall and weighs at least two hundred fifty pounds. Both children are very calm, soft-spoken, and friendly. Although they have different mothers, and hardly knew their father, they are clearly very close to each other.

Carter Jr. looks carefully at a recent portrait of Carter that I give him and notes that his beard grows exactly like his father's, reminding me that he is an abandoned son, only now in direct contact with his biological father.

In the parking lot, Lionel, Carter's oldest brother, walks up to Tina and hugs her. They have not talked since she snitched on Smokey. One of Carter's grand-nieces (Smokey's sister) calls Tina "auntie" and reassures her that she will "always have a home with me and my mother."

Patriotic Death

Tina did not attend the funeral the next day, nor did anyone from Edgewater Boulevard except for Vernon, who arrived with his wife, the nurse. The preacher made no direct mention of how Carter died or of how he lived his life, but he did blast the outlaw lives of many of the young men and women in the audience in a right-wing evangelical political idiom.

Jeff's Fieldnotes

The church is packed with close to one hundred people. Carter's head is propped up in the casket against a folded American flag. Looking around, I notice that I am the only white person in the room. Beverly, Carter's oldest sister, stands next to me and graciously introduces me to everybody, explaining that I am "writing a book about Carter's life." Several cousins request photographs to send to "family back in Louisiana."

About twenty members of Carter's immediate family file in and sit together in the front two rows. I recognize Smokey, who has recently been released from prison. All of Carter's grandnephews who sell crack for Smokey in the alley by the A&C corner store are also present in the seats of honor.

Carter's son reads the obituary, highlighting military experience and connections to neighborhood and family. He lists all of Carter's legal jobs, from "restaurant and food services" to "construction" to his very last position as a "commercial Class A truck driver."

The preacher begins with a patriotic reference to Carter's birthday, the Fourth of July, being the anniversary of the "birth of the nation." The preacher proceeds into a hellfire and brimstone sermon, condemning crack dealing and drug use. First, however, he establishes his credibility as an O.G. who ran the streets with Carter's oldest brother, Lionel, and was hospitalized twice for overdosing on heroin.

He proceeds to blast hip-hop clothing styles, claiming that homosexuals in prisons wear their pants low and baggy as an invitation to "come and get it. But I know we don't got no saggers here today." This prompts a murmured assent from most of the mourners. Smokey and his dealing crew—all of whom "sag"—sit attentive but expressionless in the front rows.

The pastor denounces crack dealers by impersonating a "toss up" [a woman who exchanges sex for crack]: "Mr. Dopester, here is my body; come and get it. And take my twelve-year-old daughter into the back room and do what you want with her, too."

Moments later, Smokey escorts his mother, Glenda, to the podium. He holds her shoulders throughout her tearful homily, embracing her affectionately when she finishes.

As we are leaving, the funeral director announces that the burial will not take place for another week because "the U.S. Army, by request of the family, is holding a military burial. There will be a twenty-one-gun salute." The audience cheers.

Jeff's Fieldnotes (one week later)

I drive 106 miles along the Blue Star Memorial Highway to the San Joaquin Valley National Cemetery, a designated national military shrine. At the entrance to the cemetery, five elderly white gentlemen wearing pointed hats and blue shirts sit in the shade of a gazebo shelter. They are the honor guard—all Veterans of Foreign Wars. A van pulls up with Carter's core family members: his sister Beverly, his brother Lionel, and their spouses; his new girlfriend, Clarice; his niece Glenda; his daughter, Charlotte; and his three grandchildren. Only his son, Carter Jr., is missing.

The funeral director drapes an American flag over the silver coffin and signals for Beverly's husband, Lionel, and me to lift the coffin onto a gurney. The veterans take turns reading a prepared statement from a three-ring notebook, while the family weeps.

In unison, the honor guard fires off three shots each, producing three echoless "pops." Charlotte chokes back tears as the veterans slowly fold the flag with soldierly formality. When they are done, they salute one another. The highest-ranking veteran gives the flag to Charlotte, leaning down to meet her eyes and express his remorse. The soldiers follow behind him in line to give their condolences to the family members individually. One of the shooters presents Charlotte with the spent bullet cartridges as "a symbol of patriotism."

From the cemetery's vista platform, we watch them bury the casket. Charlotte is now weeping quietly, with two children draping their arms around her. The hearse becomes a tiny speck among other tiny specks, a quarter of a mile away. When it finally drives off, we take this to be our cue to leave.

Carter's family was presented with a Presidential Memorial Certificate: "The United States of America honors the memory of Carter James. This certificate is awarded by a grateful nation in recognition of devoted and selfless consecration to the service of our country in the Armed Forces of the United States."

If we knew why we were out here, then something could be done. None of us going to say, "I want to be a dopefiend all my life." —*Sonny*

Conclusion **Critically Applied Public Anthropology**

As anthropologists studying people who live under conditions of extreme duress and distress, we feel it is imperative to link theory to practice. Otherwise, we would be merely intellectual voyeurs. It is politically and analytically gratifying to engage with critical theory, but we also need to operate at the level of immediate policy options and specific local interventions that can be implemented in both the short and long term to reduce the structurally imposed suffering of our research subjects.

Applied work is never straightforward politically, theoretically, or practically, and we enter the public health and social service policy debates with trepidation. As Foucauldians have argued, policy debates become part of the problem by shifting political issues into a technocratic register (Ferguson 1990). Policy choices are framed by the discursive logics of power that propel governmentality, shape subjectivities, reinforce habitus-based inequalities, and extend the reach of biopower. Furthermore, applying Bourdieu's concept of misrecognition and symbolic violence (Bourdieu 2000) to Foucault's insights into the power/knowledge nexus alerts us to the fact that policy debates and interventions often mystify large-scale structural power vectors and unwittingly reassign blame to the powerless for their individual failures and moral character deficiencies. More mundanely, policy is often an irrelevant bureaucratic sideshow and sometimes, despite good intentions, intensifies the deeper forces that distribute misery unequally.

Unfortunately, Foucault's critique of governmentality, combined with postmodernism's well-taken skepticism of "truth claims," paralyzed many academic researchers in the late twentieth century both politically and practically. In the United States, this academic withdrawal from critical public debate was exacerbated by an intellectual heritage shaped by the Cold War and McCarthyism. Foucault was a public intellectual and a leftist political activist. He argued, at least intermittently, for direct involvement in the details of everyday public policy debates (Foucault 1988:209).

In the introduction, we discussed the politics of representation inherent in a photo-ethnography of a population that is likely to be dismissed as unworthy by unsympathetic

297

audiences. Nevertheless, we called for a good-enough photo-ethnography to expose the distress of the socially vulnerable who remain invisible to the larger society. In the same vein, in this conclusion we call for a good-enough applied anthropology, rooted in critical theory and aimed at redressing the "useless suffering" that is imposed politically and institutionally on the socially vulnerable (Levinas 1998:91–102; see also discussion by Das 1994). By using the term *good-enough critically applied anthropology,* we want to emphasize the need for humility and self-reflection when building theory to inform urgent public debates. Our theory of lumpen abuse has informed our analysis and our presentation of ethnographic data. But how do theoretical and philosophical concepts drawn from the work of Marx, Foucault, Bourdieu, Mauss, Benjamin, and Levi (among others) translate into practical, useful, and effective services and policies that could benefit homeless heroin injectors and crack smokers?

What are the implications, for example, of linking habitus to intimate apartheid, or of exploring the dynamics of governmentality through an understanding of discursive discipline and physical punishment and self-punishment? How can our understanding of the moral economy translate into helpful public health interventions? What practical use is there for identifying symbolic violence and the misrecognition of power; for exploring the interface of everyday violence and structural violence; for defining suffering as politically and institutionally structured; for recognizing the phenomenon of the formation of lumpen subjectivities under globalized neoliberalism? What do we learn that is of concrete utility by placing the sphere of homelessness and chronic drug use in the gray zone continuum? Reciprocally, how have our applied practical research concerns informed our formulation of theory and sharpened our observational focus? Had we not been working on an applied HIV prevention project, would we have recognized that mechanisms of administering injections (skin-popping versus intravenous) are a technique of the body that inscribes ethnicity and propels symbolic violence?

Heroin Prescription

Opiate withdrawal symptoms are indisputably painful, and they merit medical treatment without stigma. A heroin prescription program delivered through pain clinics and treatment programs would immediately reduce the everyday torments of the Edgewater homeless. Arguably, a simple prescription constitutes the short-term, magic-bullet solution for much of the embodied suffering presented in these pages.

In the mid-1990s, Switzerland pioneered opiate prescription programs for long-term heroin addicts who had repeatedly failed attempts at conventional methadone maintenance and abstinence treatments (Uchtenhagen 1997). Soon after entering these programs, outlaw addicts with life histories of crime, violence, vagrancy, and ill health (at great cost to society) often begin to lead comparatively stable, pacific, and healthier lives through the simple, cheap medical intervention of prescribing heroin *and allowing them to experience the drug's pleasurable effects* (Marset 2005). Heroin injectors in the Swiss prescription programs have generally had better outcomes than those enrolled in other treatment modalities. They tend to stay in treatment more consistently, engage in less poly-substance abuse, reduce their participation in crime and violence, and score higher on quality of life indices. Most dramatic (and initially counterintuitive) was the finding that over time patients treated with heroin transitioned to complete abstinence more frequently than those on methadone maintenance. (For a report on the Swiss program, see Federal Office of Public Health, Confédération suisse n.d. For information on the Dutch program, see Central Committee on the Treatment of Heroin Addicts 2002. On the German program, see Center for Interdisciplinary Addiction Research, Hamburg University 2006. See also Dazord et al. 1998; Marset 2005; Perneger et al. 1998; van den Brink et al. 2003.)

Foucault's concept of governmentality allows us to construe the Swiss heroin prescription program as an example of biopower controlling and redefining pathologized individuals via medicalization rather than criminalization. This insight explains the increased docility of former outlaw addicts as they morph into therapy-seeking patients on the path to sobriety when provided with legal heroin. The bottom line is that, despite critiques of medicalization, the Swiss opiate prescription program reduces pain (Bourgois 2000). It also benefits the larger society by decreasing crime, violence, and family disruption, and it is less expensive than incarceration.

Righteous dopefiends like the Edgewater homeless are ideal candidates for heroin prescription. We caught a practical glimpse of how effective medical access to opiates might be when a sympathetic medical resident in training at the county hospital agreed to prescribe a high, stable dose of morphine pills for Hank. The law enforcement and morality concerns about potential drug diversion for resale on the street were secondary to the doctor's sense of professional responsibility to treat the acute pain Hank was experiencing from both heroin withdrawal symptoms and the decayed disk in his spinal column. She decided on these ethical priorities and this prescription regimen after presenting Hank's condition at a case conference seminar, which, by coincidence, Philippe was teaching. At the time, Hank was at the height of the multiple medical crises described in chapter 7. He had missed his last two outpatient appointments for triple-antibiotic chemotherapy, and his life-threatening spinal and brain fluid infection was flaring up yet again. On his previous visit to the outpatient clinic, Hank had stomped out of the resident's office, cursing because she refused to increase his morphine prescription. He also left behind the antibiotic medications she was giving him.

The medical residents attending the case conference seminar debated the ethics of prescribing opiate-based painkillers to a heroin addict who complains of back pain. Hank's spinal decay was visible on his X-rays, thereby justifying a morphine prescription. Several of the residents objected that Hank was probably selling some of his prescribed pills each month—as evidenced by his aggressive demand for an increased supply. Philippe noted that addicts sometimes did indeed sell some of their prescription pills for emergency cash. He added that indigent patients had to cover a new fifty-dollar prescription medication co-pay required by the county hospital pharmacy. The residents were unaware of the onerous co-pay regulation. Philippe told them that when homeless users obtain legal prescriptions, they tend to ration their supply of morphine pills. In Hank's case, to prolong his limited supply, he took the pills only when he could no longer bear his combined back pain and withdrawal symptoms. Philippe also described the inability of homeless users to jump through bureaucratic hoops even when they would qualify for SSI. The residents reached a consensus that if the goal was to treat Hank's life-threatening spinal fluid infection, they would have to address his central concern: his physical addiction to heroin.

After the seminar, Philippe went to Hank's camp and related what had happened in the case conference seminar. He told Hank, "You made your doctor cry!" and urged him to go to the doctor's outpatient clinic the next morning. Shamefacedly, Hank explained that he had not showered in over a month and was too ashamed to see his doctor, "especially since . . . you know . . . I think she is in love with me."

Hank made it to the clinic the next morning. Over the next year, the resident provided him with enough morphine to stabilize him, but only on the condition that he attend his outpatient chemotherapy appointments. He complied, and his regular visits to the outpatient clinic enabled the resident to oversee the successful processing of Hank's Medi-Cal and SSI disability paperwork. When he started receiving a $727 monthly disability check, Hank gave half of it to Paul, Hogan's benefactor, as rent, and moved into the garage with Hogan. Safely "housed," Hank gained weight, bathed regularly, wore clean clothes, and began repairing used cars for resale (although he was unable to regain his driver's license, which had been suspended after multiple tickets for "driving under the influence"). Petey was in jail at the time, and Hank started saving money to buy Petey a set of dentures, "to make him feel good on the inside." In addition, Hank helped to bathe and feed Hogan, who had become catatonically depressed.

Petey was also eventually stabilized and obtained precarious housing. His exit from homelessness, however, was precipitated by coercion and enforced abstinence rather than medication. Dressed in filthy rags, hunched over in obvious pain, and smelling foul, Petey was declared a "public nuisance" by the police at the insistence of the manager of the Taco Bell where he panhandled. This enabled the police to issue a warrant for his arrest (panhandling per se was not illegal in San Francisco at the time). It took them several weeks to catch Petey because Felix stood guard for him, whistling whenever a patrol car came in sight. At Felix's signal, Petey limped through the back of the Taco Bell parking lot into the bushes and hid under garbage. Petey became the personal nemesis of an officer in the local precinct. Even when he was off duty, driving home in his private car, the officer would screech to a stop at the Taco Bell exit sign and chase Petey to the edge of the parking lot, but he would not follow him into the muck and bushes. When the officer finally managed to catch Petey, he added a felony charge for possession of controlled paraphernalia with intent to sell to the original public nuisance misdemeanor.

Under California's new approach to drug-using offenders, Petey was remanded by the court to an inpatient treatment program. While waiting to appear before the judge, Petey detoxed "cold turkey" in the holding cell. His filth was his only protection from predatory cellmates. Ben, who happened to be cycling through county jail at the same time, described Petey as "a sitting duck, barely able to talk. He wasn't even wearing shoes—throwing up and shitting all over himself."

Petey qualified for a program funded by the Veterans Administration, and he responded well to its "tough love" regimen. Within six months, he was released to a halfway house and given a temporary job as a janitor in a VA facility. He also had to report weekly to the court for a witnessed urine test. Unfortunately, the program adhered to a "one-strike-you're-out" policy; one month before he was scheduled to graduate, Petey was evicted from his halfway house for smoking cigarettes in his room. He found a room for $350 a month in a subsidized SRO hotel, on a block in the Mission District where the Edgewater homeless often bought heroin. Despite the easy availability of drugs on the streets surrounding his hotel, Petey managed to pass the probationary period on his job at the VA and was hired as a full-time janitor with union and civil service benefits.

Good-Enough Treatment and Risk Reduction

The two paths out of homelessness taken by Hank and Petey offer an interesting contrast. Different modalities of treatment and services are effective for different people at different times in their careers of drug use and homelessness. Coercive treatment is emotionally and physically brutal and can have lethal consequences, as in Carter's relapse. Nevertheless, many street-based drug users respond obediently to coercion because of the pervasive logic of violence in their lives. Many of the homeless respond positively to the rigid limits set by punitive programs, as Petey did. It is important to remember that despite the inadequacies of treatment funding in the 2000s, almost half of the core members of our social network maintained several prolonged periods of sobriety, some lasting over a year. A wide diversity of treatment and social support models needs to be made available to drug users, ranging from one-strike-you're-out abstinence to harm reduction, methadone maintenance, buprenorphine detox, heroin prescription, and subsidized employment initiatives. Treatment programs also need to take advantage of the moments of life crisis that drive long-term injectors to seek treatment. Most of the spur of the moment, crisis-driven windows of opportunity for changing the lives of street addicts are missed because underfunding, exacerbated by neoliberal audit culture, forces treatment programs to exclude risky patients.

Furthermore, as Tina's relapse demonstrates, the post-detox stages of treatment services are not coordinated with detox, which sets up drug users for a predictable failure, condemning them to a cycle of self-blame and triumphant, self-destructive oppositionality. Even though physically painful, detox is a relatively straightforward and technical procedure compared to the complex psychological, social, economic, and institutional obstacles to maintaining long-term sobriety in the community context. Follow-up services that address structural problems after detox are the weakest link in drug treatment in the United States. Despite their obvious susceptibility to relapse, most addicts are left to find a job, housing, and a supportive social network on their own.

Unfortunately, in the early twenty-first century, at the height of the War on Drugs, the war on terror, and the war in Iraq, tolerant programs like heroin prescription were politically taboo in the United States despite their growing success in Europe, Australia, and Canada. In the mid-2000s, merely using the phrase *harm reduction* disqualified U.S. researchers from receiving federal funding, and most politicians publicly condemned harm reduction as immorally encouraging illegal drug use (Substance Abuse Research Center n.d.). Under President George W. Bush's administration, project officers at the National Institute on Drug Abuse routinely advised researchers to remove the words *condom, needle exchange, sex worker,* and *homosexual* from the titles and abstracts of their grant proposals (*New York*

Times 2003, April 18). The public health practice of harm reduction slipped under the radar of the evangelical organizations that monitored government-funded research and interventions only when it was referred to as *risk reduction*. Numerous harm reduction public health programs continued to thrive in large U.S. cities. Many of them simply dismantled or edited their Web sites to avoid harassment by right-wing religious ideologues.

In San Francisco, for example, needle exchange was the single most effective publicly funded program serving street-based injectors. The Edgewater homeless, unfortunately, were not able to utilize needle exchange services efficiently when "one-for-one" exchange rules were enforced. To increase their utility and cost-effectiveness, needle exchange programs should be organized around effective distribution, and all logistical and legal limits to accessing clean syringes should be removed (Bourgois and Bruneau 2000). Aggressive enforcement of paraphernalia laws promotes the reuse of dirty needles (Koester 1994). As we have shown, the routine practice of reincarcerating parolees for four to six months simply for needle possession is counterproductive from a public health perspective.

During the early years of our fieldwork, we volunteered at a streetcorner needle exchange site that was open once a week. We experimented with needle distribution to the Edgewater homeless by promising anyone in our network a box of one hundred needles if they attended the exchange. Felix took advantage of our offer and began selling syringes on the boulevard. Although some of the needle exchange activists were offended by the resale of free needles, from a public health perspective, Felix's opportunistic entrepreneurship revealed the potential of informal market forces when they are subsidized. In pursuit of personal profit, Felix flooded the encampments along Edgewater Boulevard with clean syringes at all hours of the night or day. He became such a regular patron of the mobile needle exchange that he was given a sanitary "sharps container" for the safe disposal of the large supply of used needles he collected each week. Unfortunately, convenient, inexpensive access to clean needles on Edgewater Boulevard ended when the police confiscated Felix's stash. This occurred during the white flight episode, and, predictably, Felix blamed the "niggers" for precipitating the police sweep. He did not criticize law enforcement for disrupting an effective public health initiative.

The San Francisco county hospital and the Department of Public Health supported several effective programs modeled on harm reduction during our years on Edgewater Boulevard, benefiting considerable numbers of homeless addicts:

- An outpatient abscess clinic for injectors, staffed by nonjudgmental clinicians who minimized incision size and prescribed adequate local analgesic (Harris and Young 2002)
- Two targeted case management initiatives for frequent users of the emergency department and inpatient services that used teams of social workers, nurses, psychiatrists, and internists to deliver intensive follow-up services intended to address the multiple and overlapping social, psychological, legal, and logistical problems of these vulnerable patients (Okin et al. 2000)

- A van-based mobile health clinic that made "house calls" to homeless encampments and included counselors to facilitate on-site treatment screening (San Francisco Community Clinic Consortium 2004)
- A mobile psychiatric clinic
- A "home visit" program to homeless encampments, staffed by nurses (Wlodarczyk and Wheeler 2006)
- A van service that took the homeless from their encampments to clinic appointments
- A mobile methadone treatment clinic for the homeless
- A new mandatory curriculum addressing socially vulnerable populations for medical residents in training at the county hospital
- A monthly service fair for the homeless sponsored by the mayor's office
- An SRO housing program earmarked for the homeless with integrated medical and social work services on site (Trotz 2005)

Most of these programs were cost-effective because they decreased utilization of both the hospital emergency room and the county jail (see Shumway et al. 2008 on the effectiveness of the Emergency Department High User Program). The county hospital outpatient abscess clinic alone saved almost $9 million during its first year of operation (Harris and Young 2002). Despite these successes, San Francisco's public health budget remained woefully underfunded, and these alternative pilot programs were constantly losing their support. Throughout our fieldwork, harm reduction volunteers at needle exchanges were forced to ration the nutritional supplements, vitamins, tampons, bus tokens, bandages, and food they distributed to indigent drug injectors. In contrast, law enforcement was overfunded. The city of San Francisco spent between three hundred and four hundred dollars per day to confine an inmate in jail-based medical and psychiatric facilities—more than one hundred thousand dollars per year per person (Hoenigman and SPUR Homelessness Task Force 2002:5, 14).

The problems of providing access to health care for the homeless cannot ultimately be solved through a technical tweaking of services. The inadvertent exacerbation of the physical pain and angst of the Edgewater homeless by the emergency health services mandated to help them reveals deep structural problems within biomedicine. The narrow "biological gaze" that emerged with the "birth of the clinic" in the 1800s (Foucault 1994) has discouraged healthcare providers from taking seriously the social, cultural, and economic dimensions of disease and healing. Medicine has consolidated itself since World War II as a high-tech discipline that seeks magic-bullet solutions for chronic human conditions (Brandt 1987; Kaufman 1993; Rhodes 1990; Taussig 1980). Medical technology is effective in curing many acute biological pathologies, but it is not designed to address the social structural problems that wreak havoc on the bodies of poor people.

All sick people, not just the homeless, would benefit if doctors were trained to engage practically with the social dimensions affecting the health of their patients. Piecemeal attempts to teach "cultural competence in medicine" as add-ons to scientific training exacerbate the problem (see Good et al. 2002 for a critique). Framing the problem as "cultural" also obscures the political-economic constraints that deform the provision of medical care (see Stonington and Holmes 2006, special issue of *PLoS Medicine* on social medicine).

It is remarkable that the medical residents in the case conference seminar discussing Hank's failure to take antibiotics for his spinal infection were unaware of the new institutional obstacle imposed by the pharmacy's fifty-dollar co-pay. Despite their genuine dedication to serving the homeless, they were unaware of the bureaucratic obstacles to qualifying for SSI and the importance of a monthly disability check in obtaining safe shelter and maintaining a stable mailing address.

We encountered many excellent, devoted doctors and administrators—especially at the county hospital and in community-based clinics—but they had to work against the logics of their training and bend the rules of their institutions in order to serve the homeless effectively. They were sometimes punished by their institutions for providing care to the noninsured. Despite a discourse of commitment to pursuing "best scientific practices," market-based principles dominate U.S. medical practice. One of the physicians at the methadone clinic was repeatedly reprimanded by hospital authorities for "diverting" urgently needed medication to his uninsured patients. His career at the medical school was hampered because of his dedication to serving indigent street injectors. Many students entering medical school are inspired by a sense of service and vocation. The economic incentives and ritualized hierarchies that pervade medical schools and hospitals convert most of these idealistic students into hierarchical and financially driven practitioners by the time they graduate from residencies.

Culturally sensitive styles of interaction in user-friendly clinics are a bonus for patients, but they do not address the root of the problem: access to care and medication. The Edgewater homeless were primarily concerned about obtaining more treatment and more resources, not friendlier, "culturally appropriate" treatment. Their biggest problem was the same one faced by most of the working poor and self-employed in the United States: the neoliberal distribution of health care through a market logic that is primarily driven by profit rather than by service and responsible oversight. A disproportional number of the homeless throughout the United States in the 2000s were middle-aged, and their lives of substance abuse, poverty, and homelessness had prematurely damaged their bodies (Golub and Johnson 1999; Hahn et al. 2006), leaving them in chronic need of medical services. With the exception of the iatrogenic pain and scarring caused by the abscess surgery protocol that was remedied in 2002, most of the Edgewater homeless appreciated the high-tech care they received at the county hospital, especially from the nurses. They needed that expensive medical care to be coordinated with and supplemented by nonemergency social and preventative services.

The work of the anthropologist-doctor Paul Farmer and his colleagues at Partners in Health reveals how the provision of medical care can become a political movement to redistribute resources from the rich to the poor. Farmer reminds us that the root of the problem is not the goodwill or cultural competency of doctors, but rather the historically reproduced structures of inequality that organize international relations and express themselves very concretely in preventable premature mortality. Most of the poor die young from treatable diseases (Farmer 2003). Farmer's organization represents a charismatic example of political dedication, humane charity, and institutional excellence (Kidder 2003) and is part of a growing social movement in the 2000s asserting that access to health care is a basic human right. This international solidarity movement has the potential to redistribute resources to the poor in the name of the efficient delivery of medical technology—as well as justice and human rights. Arguably, with the increased lumpenization of ever larger proportions of the population, who by definition have no productive relationship to the economy, class-based solidarity has been replaced by biosociality (such as being HIV positive) as a new mode of organizing for political rights (Biehl 2007; Comaroff 2007; Epstein 1996; Petryna 2002).

In chapter 3, we advocated a harm or risk reduction approach to drugs, but we also applied insights from theory to critique the blame-the-victim effects of public health campaigns that deliver hypersanitary scientific knowledge about infection risks to homeless addicts without providing material support. Harm reduction promotes knowledge that can be easily integrated into middle- and upper-class lifestyles to reduce risky practices. This positive manifestation of biopower, however, inadvertently has the effect of fueling symbolic violence against the lumpen, whose choices are shaped by institutional, structural, and political-economic forces that contradict the logics of safer injection practices. The moral economy, for example, forces the Edgewater homeless to share injection paraphernalia with each other in order to stave off heroin withdrawal symptoms. Given the way class and other social power categories (such as ethnicity, gender, sexuality, age) shape techniques of the body, self-help knowledge in the era of neoliberalism is *both* power and symbolic violence simultaneously because it persuades individuals to blame themselves for their politically and institutionally imposed vulnerability and embodied suffering.

The epidemiology that informs public health interventions needs to engage the local categories, logics, and appropriate technologies of street people and wean public health from its subordination to the narrow focus of high-tech medicine. Reframing the knowledge flow between science and street could facilitate the propagation of simpler, more realistic messages such as "water works, rinse twice" to reduce the spread of HIV from needle sharing (Ciccarone and Bourgois 2003). It would counter the dogmatic techno-scientific definition of methadone as "medicine" versus heroin as "drug," and it might prevent multimillion-dollar boondoggles such as the "condom and bleach" messages delivered to street injectors during the first two decades of the HIV epidemic in the United States.

From a science studies perspective, the bleach debacle reveals how the War on Drugs shaped, and continues to shape, the direction of epidemiological public health research. Epidemiologists supported by U.S. federal funds were not allowed to evaluate needle exchanges before 1992—let alone advocate for needle distribution or safe injection sites. In 1999 the *American Journal of Epidemiology*, the flagship public health journal, published an article that denounced the U.S. debate on needle exchange as "reminiscent of the McCarthy era" (Moss and Hahn 1999:216). Public health researchers, however, did not want to stand by uselessly, and they researched alternative HIV prevention interventions, such as rinsing with bleach. The leading U.S. public health journals published dozens of articles in the 1980s and early 1990s claiming that rinsing syringes with bleach could prevent HIV transmission. By the mid-1990s, these "statistically significant findings," based on self-report surveys, conveniently dropped out of the literature. Some laboratory-based scientists argued that bleach may actually propagate HIV infection because of its abrasive effects on tissue (Contoreggi et al. 2000; see Bourgois 2002:261–263 for a critique of the research that promoted bleach messages).

In contrast to the United States, public health departments in most of Europe and much of the industrialized world prioritized the distribution of clean needles to injectors relatively early in the HIV epidemic and wasted less time with bleach. By 1991, needle exchange programs in Montreal were already systematically cultivating relationships with managers of shooting galleries to create on-site outlets for distributing syringes where the riskiest practices were occurring. By the mid-1990s, public health departments in Switzerland and Germany were overseeing safe injection sites, and the city of Vancouver opened one in 2003 (Tyndall et al. 2006). Pharmacists in France were obligated by law to dispense a syringe for free when a customer did not have money to pay for it. Subsidized vending machines were placed at heavily transited locations in Paris in an effort to destigmatize and massify needle exchange by making it convenient and anonymous. Several cities in Europe as well as Canada and Australia opened "safe injection rooms." Street drug users also received free medical attention at these locations.

Despite the turn toward harm reduction policies among industrialized nations, even minimal needle exchange services continued to be illegal in most U.S. states in the late 2000s, and federally funded researchers kept the term *harm reduction* out of their grant proposals (see Substance Abuse Research Center n.d. for an interview with a former branch director at the National Institute on Drug Abuse who was disappointed that his institution regarded harm reduction as a "dirty word"). In 2002, the NIH was forced to conduct a "scientific audit" of 182 of its research projects (including ours) because of complaints lodged by politicians at the behest of the Traditional Values Coalition, a right-wing political lobby group representing forty-three thousand evangelical churches (*New York Times* 2004, July 11; *San Francisco Chronicle* 2003, October 30). Predictably, abstinence- and faith-based interventions became a more popular topic among NIH-funded HIV prevention researchers.

Cease Fire in the War on Drugs

During the last quarter of the twentieth century, incarceration rates exploded to historic levels in the United States, with a fourfold increase in the state and federal prison population (Lawrence and Travis 2004; Wacquant 2007, 2009). Throughout most of the 1990s and 2000s, the United States had the highest rate of incarceration among industrialized nations (Sentencing Project 2006); the U.S. rate was six to twelve times higher than that of any nation in the European Union (Public Safety Performance Project 2008:35; Wacquant 2009). The rise in the U.S. prison population was primarily driven by the War on Drugs, with a more than fivefold increase in the number of drug offenders admitted to state prisons in 1998 compared to 1984 (Gainsborough and Mauer 2000:17).

California was a leader in the U.S. War on Drugs, and, as we have documented, the state's revolving door parole system was particularly irrational, prompting Republican governor Arnold Schwarzenegger to declare a "state of emergency in the prison system" in 2006 (*New York Times* 2006, December 11). The War on Drugs has also been extremely expensive. In 2007, for example, it cost an average of $35,587 to house each one of California's 173,312 adult prisoners, and the state spent an additional $554,336,040 processing its 126,330 adult parolees, for a grand total of $6.72 billion. Per capita cost for each juvenile delinquent was $71,700 in the 2004 fiscal year. Between 1979 and 2000, the state built fifty-three new prisons (California Department of Corrections 2007, 2005; Lawrence and Travis 2004:20). In 2005, the operating cost for each prisoner in the United States was $23,876 (Public Safety Performance Project 2008:11).

The dynamics of intimate apartheid manifest themselves as formal apartheid in U.S. prisons as a result of the War on Drugs. African-Americans have been incarcerated at more than six times the per capita rate of whites, and two and a half times the per capita rate of Latinos (Bourgois 2004; Public Safety Performance Project 2008:6, 34). In 2003, blacks were over ten times more likely to be imprisoned for drug offenses than whites (Human Rights Watch 2008). Federal statutes passed in 1986 at the height of the moral panic over crack defined possession of five grams of crack as a felony, carrying an automatic five-year prison term. Until the disparity in the sentencing guidelines was reduced in 2007, an individual had to be caught with five hundred grams of powder cocaine (a 1:100 ratio) to receive a similarly long sentence, despite the fact that crack and powder cocaine contain exactly the same pharmacologically active ingredients. Crack is disproportionately found in poor African-American communities, and 89 percent of those arrested for violating federal crack laws from the late 1980s through the 1990s were African-American.

The macrostatistics documenting ethnic disparities in health and unemployment are equally dramatic. For example, compared to white men, African-American men were seven times more likely to be infected with HIV, six times more likely to be murdered, and more than twice as likely to be unemployed (Bureau of Justice Statistics 2004, 2005; Centers for Disease Control and Prevention [2005] 2007a; Parker and Pruitt 2000; Pettit and Western

2004; see also Krieger 2000; McCord and Freeman 1990; Wallace 1990). Examined in a vacuum, these numbers can exacerbate symbolic violence. An understanding of the ethnic dimensions of habitus, however, turns these macrostatistics into a documentation of the salience of racism and politically imposed suffering in the United States, by revealing how historically structured political-economic inequalities seep through to the capillary level of desire and identity (such as a predilection for crack or the pursuit of the sexualized masculine outlaw persona).

Ironically, by any measure, the United States had already lost the War on Drugs by the early 1990s. During the 2000s, it turned into a full-scale debacle. According to figures from the U.S. Drug Enforcement Agency and the White House Office of National Drug Control Policy, heroin and cocaine supplies on inner-city streets were of higher purity in the 2000s than in the early 1980s (*New York Times* 2005, November 18; see also Caulkins et al. 2005; Ciccarone, Kraus, and Unick 2007). Policy analysts have also documented that there was no clear relationship between incarceration rates and decreases in crime, drugs, and violence during the 1990s (Blumstein and Wallman 2000; Gainsborough and Mauer 2000). Draconian law enforcement relegates the homeless to interstitial no-man's-lands such as the highway embankments and back alleys along Edgewater Boulevard. The police can keep the homeless mobile and render them less visible in downtown business and tourist districts (Davis 1990; Dordick 1997; Marcus 2005; Wacquant 2009), but unless they die or are jailed, the homeless do not disappear until they are housed. In short, despite the neoliberal rhetoric of market efficiency, it was not pragmatic but rather ideological considerations that caused the safety net to be replaced by the carceral dragnet in the last quarter of the twentieth century (Wacquant 2001b:410).

Pragmatic Tolerance and Strategic Support

Specific public policies and structural economic shifts in the local and global economy produce homelessness. Mentally ill men and women flooded onto the street in the 1960s and 1970s when psychiatric facilities closed without providing former patients with adequate community-based services. The "able-bodied poor," however, were not yet a common sight on the streets. Deindustrialization, the gentrification of skid row neighborhoods, the loss of affordable housing, the increased criminalization of the poor (especially ethnic minorities), and the gutting of the welfare safety net created the phenomenon of homelessness in the late 1970s through the early 1980s, and the number of men living on the street increased dramatically in the 1990s (see Hopper 2003:60–65; Lyon-Callo 2004; Maharidge 1996; Marcus 2005:viii; Snow and Anderson 1993:17–20, 234–253). Homelessness is a crisis of housing, poverty, and social justice. By the late 1990s and mid-2000s, the homeless had become an urban phenomenon that was simply taken for granted as a regular feature of cityscapes (see Marcus on "American Thatcherism" [2005:138–154]).

There is no mystery about how to house the homeless. At the turn of the twentieth century, skid row neighborhoods provided inexpensive lodgings accessible to the transient poor, including alcoholics and drug users (DePastino 2003:71–81, 131–152; Groth 1994:8–25). Since the 1950s, however, most government urban renewal and inner-city revitalization programs resulted in a net expulsion of poor people from affordable rental apartments. The extraordinary wealth and income inequality of the San Francisco Bay Area further exacerbated homelessness by turning the city's housing market into one of the most expensive and profitable in the world and leaving little room for affordable housing (National Low Income Housing Coalition 2006; Quigley et al. 2001). Market forces and tax incentives devastated the already limited stock of low-income studio apartments and SRO hotels. In contrast to Europe, the United States failed to build sufficient public housing for the working poor to offset the market forces that promote homelessness. Furthermore, in the mid-1990s, the federal housing authority exacerbated the housing insecurity of the family members of drug users by instituting a national "one-strike-you're-out" law mandating the eviction of entire households when any single member was convicted of a drug felony while living on federally funded premises.

In the mid-2000s, progressive cities such as San Francisco and Seattle bypassed federal zero-tolerance regulations by building or rehabilitating SRO-style apartments for the homeless using only municipal funds. This allowed them to develop a flexible harm reduction approach to housing the homeless and to tolerate nondisruptive drug users and alcoholics. Cities that cannot afford to finance the building of public housing without federal aid can increase access to affordable housing for the homeless by enforcing laws that protect low-income SROs and providing incentives for the construction of new low-income rental units for transients. Public funds also need to be invested in community-based infrastructures that benefit the entire working class, such as public transportation, sanitation, entry-level employment opportunities, and social services. Systematic zoning and planning must decentralize these public-sector initiatives to promote class diversity and avoid the social isolation that occurs when poor people become ghettoized by the geographic concentration of subsidized housing in neighborhoods with inferior infrastructures (Vergara 1991a, 1991b).

Employment and income inequality represent a more complicated, long-term challenge for policy, but here too a harm reduction approach would be beneficial. In chapter 5, we analyzed the relationship of the Edgewater homeless to legal employment and noted that they had come of age at a time when the urban United States was deindustrializing, as multinational corporations sought cheaper production costs internationally. By any measure, they were undisciplined workers. They could not compete with younger and healthier undocumented Latino immigrant laborers for the dwindling number of jobs in their formerly industrial neighborhood. Nevertheless, most of them were ashamed of begging and valorized worker identities. They scrambled to find jobs, fighting among themselves for the few part-time, low-paid day labor opportunities still available to active drug users on the boulevard, such as moving furniture or selling Christmas trees for a few weeks each year. The African-

Americans expressed appreciation for legal employment as long as labor conditions were not exploitative or personally humiliating.

The employers on Edgewater Boulevard who were willing to hire the homeless had to have at least a minimally tolerant attitude toward alcohol and drug use. In fact, many of them profited by manipulating the physical addictions of their day laborers. Current social service rules inadvertently punish the homeless when they work legally. Their subsistence checks are docked, and they are forced to recertify complicated paperwork at central offices. Tax codes also discourage employers from formally hiring casual day laborers. It would be easy to eliminate these bureaucratically imposed disincentives and to expand the limited niche for low-cost, just-in-time manual labor. This precarious labor market requires some regulation and subsidies, however, to prevent the inordinate (abusive) levels of exploitation we documented at several businesses on Edgewater Boulevard. In short, regulatory and administrative adjustments to counterproductive social service entitlement rules and tax codes could attract larger proportions of the homeless into the legal economy, enabling them to reduce their reliance on crime and protecting them from the predatory practices of bosses like Bruce, who take advantage of the illegal status of their addicted employees.

Similarly, bureaucratic regulations and dysfunctional policies exacerbate the patterns of psychodynamic interpersonal abuse within families that we documented in the lives of most of the Edgewater homeless. An obvious minimal requisite is to invest adequate public funds in services for children whose families are in crisis. Social service workers in the field of child protection, adoption, and foster care routinely complain of overwhelming caseloads. Foster parents are often inadequately screened, trained, and supervised. Some foster parents are themselves desperately poor and accumulate children for the sake of the minimal state subsidies that accompany fostering (Bourgois 2003b:341). As the sexual molestation case of Tina's eldest son, Ricky, illustrates, foster care can be even more traumatic than an unstable natal home. More fundamentally, the patriarchal rhetoric of "family values" manipulated by politicians in the United States since at least World War II has been counterproductive for developing strategies to relieve the distress of poor families in crisis. Family services tend to prioritize maintaining children in stressed families or in dysfunctional extended families on the basis of bloodlines and kinship, which can hurt lumpenized children and mothers for whom patriarchal values frequently legitimize violence in the guise of romantic love.

The relationship of most of the Edgewater homeless to their children was physically violent and psychologically damaging. As we suggest in chapter 6, it was probably better for their families to have minimum contact with them. Tina was the most honest in recognizing her role in the cycle of drugs and violence engulfing her children, and she gave them up. She sometimes yearned for them, and they probably missed her, as evidenced by Ricky seeking her out every time he was released from prison. Nevertheless, her self-segregation from her children was protective.

Unlike our proposal for heroin prescription through pain clinics and treatment centers, our suggestions for housing, employment, and family policy are not quick-fix solutions. They are merely first steps. In absolute terms, it is impossible to know with certainty what an "improved quality of life" means for homeless heroin injectors. Addiction is a deeply embodied, contradictory social and pharmacological experience. Drug consumption on the street is often pleasurable, and running partners and passing acquaintances can provide companionship and sometimes even solidarity. Stabilization through housing and methadone can have unintended negative consequences, as the last two years of our fieldwork revealed.

Hogan's success in obtaining housing and treatment services ultimately proved fatal. He became even more isolated and depressed after he obtained permanent SRO shelter through the Housing First program instituted in 2004 by Mayor Gavin Newsom. Hogan's benefactor, Paul, had completed the complicated paperwork to qualify him for the mayor's housing program because Hogan had started, once again, to threaten suicide despite Paul and Hank's attempts to care for him. When Jeff last visited Hogan, he found him sprawled on the floor, naked, watching Spanish soap operas, surrounded by a half dozen empty Cisco bottles, several of which were half-full of urine. Hogan was too depressed to raise himself off the floor into his Medicare-funded wheelchair. Jeff tried to persuade him to seek immediate psychiatric help, but Hogan had already been released from the county's emergency psychiatric ward too many times as a frequent flyer (see Rhodes 1991), and he refused to budge.

A few weeks later, Hogan died of an overdose. The coroner found both opiate and methamphetamine metabolites in his bloodstream. Statistical data reveal that overdose deaths in San Francisco occur disproportionately in SROs, where individuals often inject alone (Davidson et al. 2003).

Felix, Nickie, and Frank finally obtained access to subsidized methadone maintenance after they were diagnosed with terminal medical conditions by the Department of Public Health's Homeless Outreach Team. Felix and Nickie qualified because of emphysema, and Frank because of cancer of the larynx. Ben also began to receive methadone, but at a for-profit clinic paid for by his mother, following a bout of necrotizing fasciitis that almost killed him. The stability of methadone enabled Ben to obtain short-term jobs through the painters union, but he continued to binge on crack and alcohol.

Nickie's outcome was not any better. Following an arrest for shoplifting, she benefited from priority access to subsidized methadone maintenance as a court-ordered treatment alternative to incarceration. She was thus able to retain her housing project apartment, which she would have lost had she been sentenced to several years in prison. Philippe visited Nickie to express his concern for her emphysema diagnosis. She was in good spirits because her son, Alexander, had just been hired permanently by the city's Park and Recreation Department. She kept repeating, between chain-smoked cigarettes and muffled coughs, "The one good thing I've done in my life is raise a good kid." At the end of the visit, however, she began cursing because the conversation with Philippe reminded her that she had forgotten to call Alexander on his nineteenth birthday. She could not remember where she had written down his telephone number.

A month later, Nickie died on the bathroom floor of her apartment, choked by phlegm. Her death precipitated the predictable cycle of gray zone accusations. A consensus emerged that "Hank killed Nickie" by having given her too many of his morphine pills. She had been combining the pills with Cisco Berry and Valium to boost the latent psychoactive effects of her daily methadone dose.

Frank, like Hogan, complained of loneliness and boredom after he became housed, and he increased his crack binging. His laryngeal cancer had been caught just in time. A doctor on the mobile van who was especially devoted to serving the homeless arranged for an emergency tracheotomy and fast-tracked him into subsidized methadone maintenance. A few days post-surgery, Frank was released to the streets with a brand-new hole in his throat. He had not yet learned how to use his speaking valve, and it hissed incomprehensibly when he tried to communicate. He did manage to inhale crack through the hole, and this further irritated the ill-fitting valve, causing it to leak pus and chewing tobacco juice.

Despite repeated probing and advocacy, it took us over a month to obtain a studio apartment for Frank in the mayor's SRO program. Three months later we had to intervene once again to prevent his eviction because of errors in the processing of his Social Security checks. Frank claimed that he was being sabotaged by "the niggers" who administered services in his building, and he was arguing with everyone. The other whites on Edgewater Boulevard

refused our repeated offers to broker access to the mayor's homeless housing program, complaining that there were "too many niggers" in the SROs. The African-Americans politely ignored our offers to help them obtain housing.

Felix, who had moved permanently into his mother's garage, also turned to alcohol and crack once he was on methadone maintenance. He began frequenting the violent young hangout scene in the housing project parking lot to sell crack on consignment. Soon he ran afoul of his suppliers for smoking too much of his product, and a teenage crack dealer shot him in the left eye at close range with a paint gun, permanently blinding him to enforce a twenty-dollar crack debt. Felix dismissed the event as "doin' a nigger deal with the niggers."

Petey's stabilization through VA services was arguably more positive. He successfully maintained his job as a custodian at the VA hospital and stayed away from Edgewater Boulevard. He invited us to a Mexican restaurant and insisted on paying the bill with his new Visa card. He was scheduled to move out of his subsidized SRO, however, and admitted, "The real

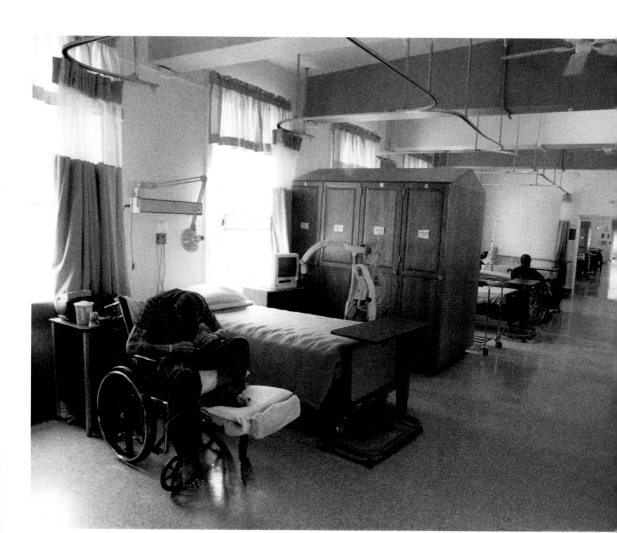

problems of my life are only just beginning." He felt lonely and consumed by guilt for breaking contact with Hank at the injunction of his treatment counselors and Narcotics Anonymous support group, adding "Hank is still very dear to me. He saved my life when I was dyin' of hep C. Now I'm all alone." Hank, meanwhile, safely sheltered in the garage that he had formerly shared with Hogan and sufficiently supplied with morphine pain-reliever pills, also felt lonely and abandoned.

Like Petey, Tina stayed away from Edgewater Boulevard after successfully completing a second court-mandated treatment program, following yet another arrest for shoplifting. Rumor had it that she was "fat," implying that she was healthy and staying off crack.

Max stopped using heroin when he was institutionalized in a city-funded hospice. He qualified for this safe medicalized shelter only after his health had deteriorated to such an extent that he could no longer take care of himself, or be taken care of by others on the street. He had lost the ability to walk and was easily disoriented. The curvature in his spine had become so accentuated that he was forced to stare at the ground when he stood up. The soles of his feet had become so swollen and his toes so mangled that he could not fit into his sneakers even after their tops were cut open. After his throat surgery, Frank could no longer look after Max. The same dedicated public health doctor who identified Frank's cancer diagnosed Max with dementia and arranged for him to be admitted to the city's long-term hospice for the indigent. Max's cognitive abilities deteriorated rapidly. Frank visited him regularly. Max was so hunched over that we had to get down on our knees to make eye contact so that he could see who was visiting him.

Within a few months he no longer appeared to understand who we were or where he was. Nevertheless, on each visit, Frank carefully combed Max's hair, kissed him on the back of his neck, and brought him news of what was happening on the boulevard. On Max's birthdays, Frank corralled anyone he could find on Edgewater Boulevard to come to the hospice and sing "Happy Birthday." Frank also brought cake and ice cream on these occasions, patiently helping Max lift the food into his mouth and blowing out the candles for him. It gave Frank pleasure to see him eating sweets with gusto, even though Max did not appear to know what the celebration was for or recognize the person feeding him.

Several of the other core members of our social network disappeared from Edgewater Boulevard, but not to access treatment or housing. Sonny changed scenes, allying himself with a primarily African-American crew of homeless recyclers ten blocks away. He continued to scavenge and hit licks, visiting his mother's home intermittently but refusing his family's repeated offers to shelter him and help him enter a treatment program. Likewise, he expressed no interest in our offer to broker access to the SRO housing program for the homeless. Stretch moved back to his aunt's apartment in a downtown housing project and visited the county hospital on a regular basis to receive HIV medication and to steal telephones, food, and medications to support his drug use. Spider-Bite Lou was forced to flee the boulevard after battering his girlfriend one time too many. She re-partnered with an old boyfriend, recently re-leased from jail, who publicly promised to avenge her mistreatment. Eventually Lou was arrested on domestic violence charges and sent to San Quentin as a recidivist.

Lumpen Abuse and Globalized Neoliberalism

If history teaches us anything, it is that distinguishing between the worthy and unworthy poor never withstands the test of time. One historical epoch's evil sinners are another's virtuous needy (see Katz 1986 for a critique). In the United States, the appearance of "tramps," "hobos," and other disreputable transient laborers during periods of economic retrenchment and rapid technological change repeatedly caused moral panics. These outcries dissipated when the visibly unemployed suddenly disappeared at the onset of the two world wars because of tight labor markets. The formerly unworthy poor found jobs in government-subsidized factories. The homeless reappeared on skid rows in the 1950s as "winos" and "alkies" when the factories that supplied U.S. armed forces during World War II closed and when the mechanization of agriculture reduced the demand for rural migrant labor (cf. De-Pastino 2003; Hopper 2003; Kusmer 2002; Snow and Anderson 1993:13–16).

The longer-term international historical record reveals even clearer connections between structural transformations in economic, political, and technological systems and the ebbs and flows of lumpen sectors of the population. For example, during the late Roman Empire, a demographic revolution flooded Rome with roving masses of desperately poor, unruly people (Brown and Lamont 2002). During the "fourteenth-century crisis" of the late Middle Ages, urban and rural vagrants died of hunger and disease in massive numbers throughout Europe, sparking complaints of a "plague of beggars" threatening public order (Geremek 1994:188). In the late eighteenth and early nineteenth centuries, the enclosures movement in England usurped common lands in rural villages, and soon "vagabonds" and "highwaymen" scoured the countryside (Defoe [1722] 2002). In the 1820s, Napoleonic war veterans (forerunners of the homeless Vietnam vets in the United States) tramped through England, spawning a moral panic against "rogues and vagabonds" (Rose 1988). Similarly, in the United States in the late nineteenth century, muckrakers bemoaned the vice-ridden lifestyles of immigrants in the overcrowded tenements of New York and condemned the vices of "street waifs" (Riis 1890:ch. 16; see Gilfoyle 2004 for a historical documentation of street children in New York).

The people living through epochs that produce large numbers of ungovernable indigents are usually unable to fathom the structural forces affecting them. Eyewitness accounts by journalists and well-intentioned advocates for policy reform often blame the character defects of the poor for their foul living conditions. During the industrial revolution in England, only a handful of critical public intellectuals recognized the larger transformations that were creating the patterns of class-based hardship engulfing most urban dwellers in their society (see Engels [1845] 1968). Instead, most chroniclers of the era engaged in righteous denunciations of the sinful behaviors of the intemperate and criminal poor of London (Mayhew and Others [1861] 2005; see also Stallybrass and White 1986:130–133 for a critique of Engels).

The U.S. neoliberal political-economic model of capitalism—free markets protected by law enforcement and military intervention, for the benefit of corporate monopolies with minimal redistribution of income and social services for the poor—has obviously exacerbated homelessness. Despite the neoliberal rhetoric of individual entrepreneurship, freedom of choice, and decreased government spending, the U.S. neoliberal model since 1980 has been accompanied by massive state expenditures on punitive forms of governmentality as well as massive corporate subsidies for the financial sector (Harvey 2005). The wars on drugs, crime, and terrorism tipped the balance of governmentality toward physical repression rather than strategic, population-level interventions. Biopower had become more abusive, and less productive and protective, for increasing numbers of people like the Edgewater homeless.

Arguably, in the post–Cold War era, this shift in governmentality was also occurring (unevenly) internationally (see De Giorgi 2006; Rose 1999; Wacquant 2009). Under advanced punitive neoliberalism, large sectors of the population were being lumpenized as working conditions in the legal labor market deteriorated with the acceleration of globalization, and as states intervened aggressively on behalf of the financial interests of multinational corporations and the very wealthy. Hundreds of millions, if not billions, of people were pushed out of unsustainable rural lifestyles at the same time that stable industrial jobs were disappearing (Davis 2006; Ferguson 2006). The destructive scale of lumpenization in the early twenty-first century parallels what occurred in the early stages of the industrial revolution in the mid-nineteenth century, when famished, displaced peasants swarmed into British factory towns and stifled their hunger with sugary tea, easing their physical pain and social dislocation with opium and gin (Courtwright 2001).

Wars also filled the vacuum in the 2000s. Armies have always consumed and produced lumpen populations. Under President George W. Bush, unilateral military invasion was reaffirmed as the cornerstone of U.S. international relations (Johnson 2004). Warlordism proliferated across the globe, side by side with an extractive form of capitalism.

Foucault developed his concepts of power in Europe at the height of social democracy in the late 1960s and 1970s, and he tended to deemphasize the active role of violence and carnal punishment in maintaining social control. His insights on how subjectivities are constituted through the "positive effects" of discursive power worked best for the Cold War era of welfare states and state socialism. To invert the bloody image of sovereign power from mid-1700s France with which Foucault opens his book *Discipline and Punish* (1995), the Edgewater homeless in the late 2000s were being drawn and quartered by a punitive version of neoliberalism in the public, inner-city no-man's-lands surrounding San Francisco's freeways and its decayed industrial districts.

Our theory of abuse is a product of these shifts in our historical epoch. It allows us to analyze, without falling prey to the facile moral judgments of character that dominate neoliberal discourse, the way structural forces operate at the individual everyday level. Recognition of the political-economic forces that impose patterns of suffering is the foundation for an applied critique of policy and services that persecute oppositional, marginalized populations in the name of morality (Duster 1970).

In chapter 7, we put class into the center of Foucault's understanding of subjectivity in order to explore the congruence of homosocial masculine love among homophobic men. Conversely, putting subjectivity, biopower, and governmentality into the center of a class analysis of the phenomenon of lumpenization under neoliberalism elucidates in greater detail the mechanisms through which structural inequality operates at the capillary level. Our reconceptualization of the category of lumpen as a subjectivity suggests that the phenomenon of class is not a bounded social entity (see Day, Papataxiarchis, and Stewart 1999:10 for an alternative discussion of "thoroughgoing marginality" and "the difficulties of reproducing through time"). There is no single "working class" or "bourgeoisie"; as historian E. P. Thompson (1966:10) argued, class is not a "thing." Instead, drawing on Foucault and Bourdieu, we can identify patterns of subjectivities and dimensions of habitus that can usefully be understood as being associated with working-class, bourgeois, or lumpen ways of being in the world attached to material and cultural exigencies. The same effects of biopower, governmentality, habitus, and the mode of production that give rise to homophobic male lovers explain the phenomenon of the righteous dopefiend.

The widespread misrecognition of class power by most people in the United States and their celebration of individual agency stem from a historically engrained cultural valorization of rugged individualism, which subjects the poor, the powerless, and especially those addicted to drugs to dismissive moralizing judgments. On Edgewater Boulevard, society's social pariahs have hit rock bottom. They are simultaneously fleeing and expelled from family, labor force, and government services. Like most of the U.S. public, the homeless tend to blame themselves for their fate. The logic of the gray zone makes their self-condemnation appear to be justified, because victims often desperately lash out against those closest to them. They frequently mistreat the only people over whom they still have a shred of power—usually their loved ones, often themselves. The ugly spectacle of everyday interpersonal violence and mutual betrayal often obscures the impact of larger long-term social forces. It also legitimizes purposefully hostile or dysfunctional governmental policies toward the poor.

In a country as wealthy as the United States, where upwardly mobile immigrants achieve the American dream in the midst of rampant homelessness, it is no accident that a punitive version of neoliberalism is enthusiastically celebrated by both the poor and the rich. Government priorities that unambiguously minimize the provision of social services to the poor, maximize profits for the rich and powerful, and punish the unruly were considered efficient, moral governance by most U.S. citizens in the 2000s. Popular misrecognition of class-based inequality is also consistent with the Calvinist puritanical heritage of the original British immigrants (Bellah 1985) who settled the American colonies in the seventeenth and eighteenth centuries.

The community of addicted bodies on Edgewater Boulevard ironically offers a refuge in a hostile world, even though its moral economy is set within a context that looks like the self-inflicted torture of sociopaths to many outside observers. In his autobiographical account of Auschwitz, Levi forbids us from shielding ourselves with righteous indignation over the mutual betrayals of concentration camp inmates. Condemning the actions of powerless victims colludes with and exonerates those who are directly responsible for creating gray zones (Levi 1988, 1996). Levi shows how inhuman constraints are capable of transforming people into evil agents with non-choices. Under these constraints, good, bad, love, betrayal, and solidarity are intertwined. The categories of victim and villain overlap and even produce one another. Binary moral categories misrepresent these abusive realities—especially when applied to the actions of indigent addicts.

Ethnographies of gray zones such as homeless encampments reveal the limits of anthropology's notion of cultural relativism. They require an ethical stance that recognizes the consequences of power and inequality. A well-intentioned, dignified representation that celebrates the unfolding of individual agency and creativity can be reassuring to readers, but it misrecognizes the effects of power. Nevertheless, from a practical perspective, on the street individuals are, and in some sense have to be, held "responsible" for their actions. A dramatic diversity of styles, personalities, and levels of cognitive engagement and moral integrity is immediately apparent to any street-based observer. Sonny and Max's easy gentleness, Hank's naive generosity, Frank's intelligent curmudgeonliness, Little Vic's angry violence, Sal's bully tactics and brutality, Stretch's smooth treachery, Tina's instrumental but affectionate charisma, and Carter's masculine sexualized bravado play an important part in the unfolding of events on Edgewater Boulevard.

We hope that this photo-ethnography of the everyday lives of the Edgewater homeless in San Francisco motivates readers to care about the phenomena of homelessness and income inequality in the United States. During the 1990s and the 2000s, the United States was the wealthiest and most militarily powerful nation in the world, yet a larger proportion of its population lived in abject destitution than that of any other industrialized nation. Globally, the United States promoted an ideological celebration of inequality and buttressed it with political-economic and military force. The United States rates poorly in international comparisons of the quality of life statistics that measure life expectancy, health, homicide, income inequality, incarceration, ethnic segregation, literacy, and homelessness (United Nations Development Programme 2006:295–296). It has consistently had the highest levels of income inequality of any wealthy nation in the world. Its economy benefited from global dominance, but social disparities worsened significantly during the 1990s and 2000s (Dreier

2004b; *New York Times* 2003, January 22; Reed 2004). This was part of the long-term trend that enabled the federal minimum wage to hit a fifty-year low in 2007 (*New York Times* 2006, October 25, October 15).

At the turn of the twenty-first century, most San Franciscans earned more money and lived in more expensive houses than the residents of almost any other metropolis in the world. The streets of their city, however, overflowed with people in visible physical distress who were incapable of paying for minimal shelter and food. The burden of lumpenization is even more extreme, painful, and violent in nonindustrialized poor countries that are transitioning into neoliberalism (Auyero 2000; Biehl 2007; Davis 2006; Ferguson 2006; Ferrandiz, forthcoming). Anthropology in the early twenty-first century cannot physically, ethically, or emotionally escape the hardship of the lives of its traditional research subjects. Ever larger proportions of the world's population survive precariously in refugee camps, rural wastelands, zones of ecological devastation, shantytowns, housing projects, tenements, prisons, and homeless encampments (Davis 2006). The Edgewater homeless represent the human cost of the American neoliberal model. Tina, Carter, Sonny, Al, Frank, Max, Felix, Victor, Sal, Scotty, Nickie, Spider-Bite Lou, Hogan, Ben, Stretch, Vernon, Reggie, Hank, and Petey are as all-American as the California dream.

Notes on the Photographs

page ii Hank raising the American flag at the new white camp

page iv Black tar heroin, rigs, and cooker

page vi Max in his camp under the freeway overpass

page viii Under the pedestrian ramp crossing the two freeways

page x Felix muscling in the abandoned shack in the alley behind the corner store

page xii Hank and Petey's clothesline

page xiv Hank backloading heroin into the syringe of a peripheral member of our network

page xvi Frank in a temporary camp under the freeway overpass

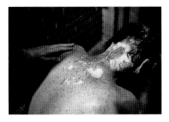

page xviii Philippe comforting Spider-Bite Lou while the doctor on our ethnographic team changes Lou's bandages on a street corner

page xx Carter helping Tina inject

page xxii Hank muscling in his camp following his early release from the hospital

page xxiv Hank preparing to leave his camp in the morning

page 2 Frank injecting in the hole

page 7 Hank helping Sonny inject

page 10 Nickie fixing with Petey inside Hank and Petey's compound

page 10 Nickie: "If you can't see the face, you can't see the misery."

page 20 Felix nodding by the A&C corner store

page 24 Carter, Spider-Bite Lou, and Vernon nodding in the shack

page 46 Tina and Carter inside the Chinook camper

page 49 Tina, after taking a hit from her crack pipe

page 61 Early morning at the I-beam camp

page 62 Cooking dinner

page 72 Tina at Twin Peaks, posing for a picture for her mother on Mother's Day

pages 74–75 The road crew lick

page 78 Hogan leaving camp

page 81 Hank, dopesick, by the freeway retaining wall

page 85 Sonny, Carter, and Tina smoking crack in the factory camp

page 86 Hank being treated to a hit of crack in his tent

page 86 Hank and Petey muscling in the foyer of their compound

page 89 Crazy Carl with Sonny nodding in the alley behind the corner store

page 89 Frank and Max nodding in their camp under the freeway

page 92 Frank, Tina, Felix, and Carter by the corner store

page 97 Max, halfway through an abscess surgery, waiting for a skin graft

page 101 Sonny's first and only abscess

page 104 Hogan during his hospitalization for necrotizing fasciitis

page 105 Hogan in the bus shelter by the corner store after muscling into his right shoulder, showing the skin graft on his left shoulder

page 110 Frank abandoning the white camp during the big Caltrans eviction with his sign painting tools and jacket

page 116 Tina at the beach

page 136 Felix keeping his leg elevated following two knee surgeries, after he was hit by the Pizza Hut delivery car

page 146 Max piling sandbags at Macon's construction supply depot

page 168 Christmas at Hank and Petey's camp

page 169 Hank preparing for a day of panhandling

page 176 Carter and Sonny sorting wood for sale after hitting a lick

page 182 Sonny looking for his son's gravestone with Jeff and Carter

page 208 Sonny comforting Hank: "Everyone's rooting for you. Lord, please protect our Petey."

page 211 Hank and Petey

page 216 Hank positioning the flag next to Jeff's Thanksgiving barbecue group portrait

page 220 Hank, Felix, and Carter cutting pockets of brush on the embankment for the Bayshore business owners

page 231 Petey in intensive care for liver failure

page 233 Hank having blood drawn during one of his hospitalizations

page 234 Hank AWOL from the hospital, attempting to trade a stolen bouquet of flowers for a bag of heroin

page 240 Carter and Tina

page 243 Al helping Tina inject

page 245 Tina demonstrating that she has learned to inject herself

page 250 Carter and Tina hitting a lick at a construction site

page 258 Carter and Tina receiving the Holy Ghost at Crystal's evangelical church

page 270 Tina preparing to enter the detox program's van

page 278 Persia visiting Tina in the detox program

page 283 Tina looking for food in a dumpster behind the Discount Grocery Outlet

page 288 Carter celebrating a full year of sobriety at the graduation ceremony of his court-mandated drug rehab

page 291 Carter's viewing in the funeral home

page 295 Carter's military burial

page 300 Hogan in Paul's garage

page 313 Frank inhaling crack through his tracheotomy hole

page 314 Max in the city's long-term hospice for the chronically ill and indigent

Africa Today. 2000. "Sexuality and Generational Identities in Sub-Saharan Africa." Special issue. Vol. 47, no. 3/4.

Agee, James, and William Evans. [1941] 1988. *Let Us Now Praise Famous Men: Three Tenant Families.* Boston: Houghton Mifflin.

Althusser, Louis. 1967. "Contradiction and Overdetermination." *New Left Review* 41:15–35.

American Psychiatric Association. 1994. *Diagnostic and Statistical Manual of Mental Disorders.* 4th ed. Washington, D.C.: American Psychiatric Association.

Anderson, Elijah. 1990. *Streetwise: Race, Class, and Change in an Urban Community.* Chicago: University of Chicago Press.

Ariëns, Ilva, and Ruud Strijp. 1989. "Anthropological Couples: In the Field and Beyond." *Focaal* 10:5–24.

Arthur D. Little Inc. 1975. *Commercial and Industrial Activity in San Francisco: Present Characteristics and Future Trends.* San Francisco: Department of City Planning.

Asad, Talal. 1973. *Anthropology and the Colonial Encounter.* London: Ithaca Press.

Ashforth, Adam. 2000. *Madumo: A Man Bewitched.* Chicago: University of Chicago Press.

Atlas, John, and Peter Dreier. 1994. "Decent Public Housing: What Went Wrong?" *Shelterforce,* no. 74, September/October. www.nhi.org/online/issues/77/pubhsg.html (accessed October 19, 2007).

Auyero, Javier. 2000. "The Hyper-Shantytown: Neo-Liberal Violence(s) in the Argentine Slum." *Ethnography* 1 (1): 93–116.

Barthes, Roland. 1981. *Camera Lucida: Reflections on Photography.* Translated by Richard Howard. New York: Hill and Wang.

Bay Area Social Planning Council. 1969. "Background Information for Use of the Study Committee, San Francisco Juvenile Court, Vol. 1968–1969: Oakland, California." San Francisco Council. Mimeographed report.

Beck, E. M., and Stewart Tolnay. 1990. "The Killing Fields of the Deep South: The Market for Cotton and the Lynching of Blacks, 1882–1930." *American Sociological Review* 55 (4): 526–539.

Bellah, Robert N. 1985. *Habits of the Heart: Individualism and Commitment in American Life.* Berkeley: University of California Press.

Belmonte, Thomas. 1989. *The Broken Fountain.* New York: Columbia University Press.

Benjamin, Walter. [1931] 1979. "A Small History of Photography." In *One-Way Street and Other Writings,* edited by Marcus Paul Bullock and Michael William Jennings, translated by Edmund Jephcott and Kingsley Shorter, 240–257. New York: Verso.

———. [1931] 1999. "Little History of Photography." In *Walter Benjamin: Selected Writings,* edited by Michael W. Jennings, Howard Eiland, and Gary Smith, 507–530. Cambridge, Mass.: Belknap, Harvard University Press.

———. [1936] 1968. "The Work of Art in the Age of Mechanical Reproduction." In *Illuminations: Essays and Reflections,* edited by Hannah Arendt, translated by Harry Zohn, 217–251. New York: Schocken Books.

———. [1940] 1968. *Illuminations: Essays and Reflections.* Edited by Hannah Arendt; translated by Harry Zohn. New York: Schocken Books.

Berger, John. 1972. *Ways of Seeing.* London: Penguin Books.

Biehl, João. 2007. *Will to Live: AIDS Therapies and the Politics of Survival.* Princeton, N.J.: Princeton University Press.

Bipartisan Millennial Housing Commission. 2002. *Meeting Our Nation's Housing Challenges: Report of the Bipartisan Millennial Housing Commission Appointed by the Congress of the United States.* Washington, D.C.: U.S. Government Printing Office.

Bletzer, Keith V. 1995. "Use of Ethnography in the Evaluation and Targeting of HIV/AIDS Education among Latino Farm Workers." *AIDS Education and Prevention* 7 (2): 178–191.

Blumstein, Alfred, and Joel Wallman, eds. 2000. *The Crime Drop in America.* New York: Cambridge University Press.

Bonham, Vence L. 2001. "Race, Ethnicity, and Pain Treatment: Striving to Understand the Causes and Solutions to the Disparities in Pain Treatment." *Journal of Law, Medicine, and Ethics* 29 (1): 52–68.

Bourdieu, Pierre. 1977. *Outline of a Theory of Practice.* Translated by Richard Nice. Cambridge: Cambridge University Press.

———. 1990. *The Logic of Practice.* Translated by Richard Nice. Cambridge: Polity Press.

———. 2000. *Pascalian Meditations.* Translated by Richard Nice. Stanford, Calif.: Stanford University Press.

———. 2001. *Masculine Domination.* Translated by Richard Nice. Stanford, Calif.: Stanford University Press.

———. 2002. *Le bal des célibataires: Crise de la société paysanne en Béarn.* Paris: Éditions du Seuil.

———. 2004. "The Peasant and His Body." *Ethnography* 5 (4): 579–600.

Bourdieu, Pierre, and Loïc Wacquant. 1992. *An Invitation to Reflexive Sociology.* Chicago: University of Chicago Press.

Bourgois, Philippe. 1989. *Ethnicity at Work: Divided Labor on a Central American Banana Plantation.* Baltimore: Johns Hopkins University Press.

———. 1995. *In Search of Respect: Selling Crack in El Barrio.* New York: Cambridge University Press.

———. 1996a. "Confronting Anthropology, Education, and Inner-City Apartheid." *American Anthropologist* 98 (2): 249–258.

———. 1996b. "In Search of Masculinity: Violence, Respect, and Sexuality among Puerto Rican Crack Dealers in East Harlem." *British Journal of Criminology* 36 (3): 412–427.

———. 1997. "Overachievement in the Underground Economy: The Life Story of a Puerto Rican Stick-Up Artist in East Harlem." *Free Inquiry for Creative Sociology* 25 (1): 23–32.

———. 1998a. "Just Another Night in the Shooting Gallery." *Theory, Culture, and Society* 15 (2): 37–66.

———. 1998b. "The Moral Economies of Homeless Heroin Addicts: Confronting Ethnography, HIV Risk, and Everyday Violence in San Francisco Shooting Encampments." *Substance Use and Misuse* 33 (11): 2323–2351.

———. 1999. "Theory, Method, and Power in Drug and HIV-Prevention Research: A Participant-Observer's Critique." *Substance Use and Misuse* 34 (14): 2155–2172.

———. 2000. "Disciplining Addictions: The Bio-Politics of Methadone and Heroin in the United States." *Culture, Medicine, and Psychiatry* 24 (2): 165–195.

———. 2001a. "Culture of Poverty." In *International Encyclopedia of the Social and Behavioral Sciences,* edited by Neil J. Smelser and Paul B. Baltes, 11904–11907. Oxford: Pergamon.

———. 2001b. "The Power of Violence in War and Peace: Post–Cold War Lessons from El Salvador." *Ethnography* 2 (1): 5–37.

———. 2002. "Anthropology and Epidemiology on Drugs: The Challenges of Cross-Methodological and Theoretical Dialogue." *International Journal of Drug Policy* 13 (4): 259–269.

———. 2003a. "Crack and the Political Economy of Social Suffering." *Addiction Research and Theory* 11 (1): 31–37.

———. 2003b. *In Search of Respect: Selling Crack in El Barrio.* 2nd ed. New York: Cambridge University Press.

———. 2004. "U.S. Inner-City Apartheid and the War on Drugs: Crack among Homeless Heroin Addicts." In *Unhealthy Health Policy: A Critical Anthropological Examination,* edited by Arachu Castro and Merrill Singer, 303–316. Walnut Creek, Calif.: Alta Mira.

———. 2005a. "Epilogo 2005." In *Cercando rispetto: Drug economy e cultura di strada,* edited by Philippe Bourgois, 339–349. Milan: Derive Approdi.

———. 2005b. "Missing the Holocaust: My Father's Account of Auschwitz from August 1943 to June 1944." *Anthropological Quarterly* 78 (1): 89–123.

———. 2008. "The Mystery of Marijuana: Science and the U.S. War on Drugs." *Substance Use and Misuse* 43 (3/4): 581–583.

Bourgois, Philippe, and Julie Bruneau. 2000. "Needle Exchange, HIV Infection, and the Politics of Science: Confronting Canada's Cocaine Injection Epidemic with Participant Observation." *Medical Anthropology* 18 (4): 325–350.

Bourgois, Philippe, Mark Lettiere, and James Quesada. 1997. "Social Misery and the Sanctions of Substance Abuse: Confronting HIV Risk among Homeless Heroin Addicts in San Francisco." *Social Problems* 44 (2): 155–173.

Bourgois, Philippe, Alexis Martinez, Alex Kral, Brian R. Edlin, Jeff Schonberg, and Dan Ciccarone. 2006. "Reinterpreting Ethnic Patterns among White and African American Men Who Inject Heroin: A Social Science of Medicine Approach." *PLoS Medicine* 3 (10): 1805–1815. http://medicine.plosjournals.org/perlserv/?request=get-document&doi=10.1371%2Fjournal.pmed.0030452 (accessed October 24, 2007).

Bourgois, Philippe, Bridget Prince, and Andrew Moss. 2004. "Everyday Violence and the Gender of Hepatitis C among Young Women Who Inject Drugs in San Francisco." *Human Organization* 63 (3): 253–264.

Bourgois, Philippe, and Jeff Schonberg. 2007. "Intimate Apartheid: Ethnic Dimensions of Habitus among Homeless Heroin Injectors." *Ethnography* 8 (1): 7–31.

Bovenkerk, Frank. 1984. "The Rehabilitation of the Rabble: How and Why Marx and Engels Wrongly Depicted the Lumpenproletariat as a Reactionary Force." *Netherlands Journal of Sociology* 20 (1): 13–41.

Brandes, Stanley H. 1980. *Metaphors of Masculinity: Sex and Status in Andalusian Folklore.* Philadelphia: University of Pennsylvania Press.

Brandt, Allan M. 1987. *No Magic Bullet: A Social History of Venereal Disease in the United States since 1880.* New York: Oxford University Press.

Broussard, Albert. 1993. *Black San Francisco: The Struggle for Racial Equality in the West, 1900–1954.* Lawrence: University Press of Kansas.

Brown, Peter, and Robert Lamont. 2002. *Poverty and Leadership in the Later Roman Empire.* Hanover, N.H.: University Press of New England.

Bureau of Justice Statistics. 2004. "Homicide Trends in the U.S.: Trends by Race." U.S. Department of Justice. www.ojp.usdoj.gov/bjs/homicide/race.htm (accessed August 11, 2005).

———. 2005. "Prison Statistics: Summary Findings on June 30, 2004." U.S. Department of Justice. www.ojp.usdoj.gov/bjs/prisons.htm (accessed August 11, 2005).

Bussard, Robert. 1987. "The 'Dangerous Class' of Marx and Engels: The Rise of the Idea of the *Lumpenproletariat.*" *History of European Ideas* 8 (6): 675–692.

Butler, Judith P. 1997. *The Psychic Life of Power: Theories in Subjection.* Stanford, Calif.: Stanford University Press.

Cáceres, Carlos F., and Ana Maria Rosasco. 2000. *Secreto a voces: Homoerotismo masculino en Lima: Culturas, identidades y salud sexual.* Lima: Universidad Peruana Cayetano Heredia/REDESS Jóvenes.

California Department of Corrections. 2005. "Ward per Capita Cost [Department of Juvenile Justice]." www.cdcr.ca.gov/Reports_Research/wardcost_0405.html (accessed December 6, 2007).

———. 2007. "First Quarter 2007 Facts and Figures." www.cdcr.ca.gov/Divisions_Boards/Adult_Operations/Facts_and_Figures.html (accessed December 5, 2007).

Caulkins, Jonathan P., Peter Reuter, Martin Y. Iguchi, and James Chiesa. 2005. *How Goes the "War on Drugs"? An Assessment of U.S. Drug Problems and Policy.* Occasional Paper. Drug Policy Research Center. Santa Monica, Calif.: RAND.

Center for Interdisciplinary Addiction Research, Hamburg University. 2006. "The German Model Project for Heroin Assisted Treatment of Opioid Dependent Patients." www.heroinstudie.de/english.html (accessed January 2, 2007).

Centers for Disease Control and Prevention. [2005] 2007a. "Fact Sheet: HIV/AIDS among African Americans." http://www.cdc.gov/hiv/topics/aa/resources/factsheets/aa.htm (accessed December 5, 2007).

———. 2007b. "Racial/Ethnic Disparities in Diagnoses of HIV/AIDS: 33 States, 2001–2005." *Morbidity and Mortality Weekly Report* 56 (9): 189–193.

Central Committee on the Treatment of Heroin Addicts. 2002. "Medical Co-Prescription of Heroin: Two Randomized Controlled Trials." www.ccbh.nl/ENG/indexN4.htm (accessed January 2, 2007).

Chauncey, George. 1994. *Gay New York: Gender, Urban Culture, and the Making of the Gay Male World, 1890–1940.* New York: Basic Books.

Ciccarone, Dan, Josh Bamberger, Alex Kral, Brian Edlin, Chris Hobart, A. Moon, E. L. Murphy, Philippe Bourgois, Hobart W. Harris, and D. M. Young. 2001. "Soft Tissue Infections among Injection Drug Users: San Francisco, California, 1996–2000." *Morbidity and Mortality Weekly Report* 50 (19): 381–384.

Ciccarone, Dan, and Philippe Bourgois. 2003. "Explaining the Geographic Variation of HIV among Injection Drug Users in the United States." *Substance Use and Misuse* 38 (14): 2049–2063.

Ciccarone, Dan, Ali Kraus, and George Unick. 2007. "Dope at Discount: Public Health Consequences of Historically Low-Cost and Pure Heroin in the United States, 1990–2004." Paper presented at annual meeting of the American Public Health Association, Washington D.C., November 3–7.

CNN. 1995. "Races Disagree on Impact of Simpson Trial—CNN/Time Magazine Poll." www.cnn.com/US/OJ/daily/9510/10-06/poll_race/oj_poll_txt.html (accessed February 15, 2005).

Collier, John, Jr., and Malcolm Collier. 1990. *Visual Anthropology: Photography as a Research Method.* Albuquerque: University of New Mexico Press.

Comaroff, Jean. 2007. "Beyond Bare Life: AIDS, (Bio)Politics, and the Neoliberal Order." *Public Culture* 19 (1): 197–219.

Connell, R. W. 1995. *Masculinities.* Berkeley: University of California Press.

Contoreggi, C., S. Jones, P. Simpson, W. R. Lange, and W. A. Meyer. 2000. "Effects of Varying Concentrations of Bleach on In Vitro HIV-1 Replication and the Relevance to Injection Drug Use." *Intervirology* 43 (1): 1–5.

Courtwright, David T. 2001. *Forces of Habit: Drugs and the Making of the Modern World.* Cambridge, Mass.: Harvard University Press.

Dallas Observer. 1994. November 17. Denise McVea, "Wine Punch: The Economics of Selling the 'Wine Fooler' to Dallas' Minority Community." www.dallasobserver.com/1994-11-17/news/wine-punch/1 (accessed December 4, 2007).

Das, Veena. 1994. "Moral Orientations to Suffering." In *Health and Social Change in International Perspective,* edited by Lincoln C. Chen, Arthur Kleinman, and Norma Ware, 139–167. Cambridge, Mass.: Harvard University Press.

D'Aunno, Thomas, and Harold A. Pollack. 2002. "Changes in Methadone Treatment Practices: Results from a National Panel Study, 1988–2000." *Journal of the American Medical Association* 288 (7): 850–856.

Davidson, Peter J., Rachel L. McLean, Alex H. Kral, Alice A. Gleghorn, Brian R. Edlin, and Andrew R. Moss. 2003. "Fatal Heroin-Related Overdose in San Francisco, 1997–2000: A Case for Targeted Intervention." *Journal of Urban Health* 80 (2): 261–273.

Davis, Mike. 1990. *City of Quartz: Excavating the Future in Los Angeles.* New York: Verso.

———. 2006. *Planet of Slums.* New York: Verso.

Day, Sophie, Evthymios Papataxiarchis, and Michael Stewart. 1999. "Consider the Lilies of the Field." In *Lilies of the Field: Marginal People Who Live for the Moment,* edited by Sophie Day, Evthymios Papataxiarchis, and Michael Stewart, 1–24. Boulder, Colo.: Westview Press.

Dazord, A., B. Broers, F. Giner, and A. Mino. 1998. "Qualité de la vie de patients toxicomanes ayant une prise en charge comportant une prescription contrôlée d'héroïne." *Annales médico-psychologiques* 156:681–693.

Defoe, Daniel. [1722] 2002. *Moll Flanders: The Fortunes and Misfortunes of the Famous Moll Flanders.* New York: Modern Library.

De Giorgi, Alessandro. 2006. *Re-Thinking the Political Economy of Punishment: Perspectives on Post-Fordism and Penal Politics.* Aldershot, England: Ashgate.

Deleuze, Gilles. 1995. *Negotiations, 1972–1990.* Translated by Martin Joughin. New York: Columbia University Press.

D'Emilio, John. 1983. "Capitalism and Gay Identity." In *Powers of Desire: The Politics of Sexuality,* edited by Ann Snitow, Christine Stansell, and Sharon Thompson, 100–113. New York: Monthly Review Press.

DePastino, Todd. 2003. *Citizen Hobo: How a Century of Homelessness Shaped America*. Chicago: University of Chicago Press.

Donaldson, Stephen. 2004. "Hooking Up: Protective Pairing for Punks." In *Violence in War and Peace: An Anthology*, edited by Nancy Scheper-Hughes and Philippe Bourgois, 348–353. Malden, Mass.: Blackwell.

Dordick, Gwendolyn. 1997. *Something Left to Lose: Personal Relations and Survival among New York's Homeless*. Philadelphia: Temple University Press.

Draper, Hal. 1972. "The Concept of the 'Lumpenproletariat' in Marx and Engels." *Économies et sociétés* 6 (12): 2285–2312.

Dreier, Peter. 2004a. "Reagan's Legacy: Homelessness in America." *Shelterforce*, no. 124, May/June, www.nhi.org/online/issues/135/reagan.html (accessed October 23, 2007).

————. 2004b. "Urban Neglect: George W. Bush and the Cities: The Damage Done and the Struggle Ahead." *Shelterforce*, no. 137, September/October, www.nhi.org/online/issues/137/urbanneglect.html (accessed October 23, 2007).

Drug Policy Alliance. 2007. *Methadone Maintenance Treatment*. www.drugpolicy.org/library/research/methadone.cfm (accessed January 9, 2007).

Duneier, Mitchell. 1999. *Sidewalk*. New York: Farrar, Straus and Giroux.

Duster, Troy. 1970. *The Legislation of Morality: Law, Drugs, and Moral Judgment*. New York: Free Press.

Earls, Felton, and Jacquelin Barnes. 1997. "Understanding and Preventing Child Abuse in Urban Settings." In *Violence and Childhood in the Inner City*, edited by Joan McCord, 207–255. Cambridge: Cambridge University Press.

Edlin, Brian. 2004. "Hepatitis C Prevention and Treatment for Substance Abusers in the United States: Acknowledging the Elephant in the Living Room." *International Journal of Drug Policy* 15:81–91.

Edwards, Elizabeth, and Janice Hart. 2004. *Photographs Objects Histories: On the Materiality of Images*. New York: Routledge.

Engels, Frederick. [1845] 1968. *The Condition of the Working Class in England*. Stanford, Calif.: Stanford University Press.

————. [1870] 2000. "Preface to the Second Edition." In *The Peasant War in Germany*, 2nd ed., vii–xiv. New York: International Publishers.

————. [1884] 1942. *The Origin of the Family, Private Property and the State, in the Light of the Researches of Lewis H. Morgan*. New York: International Publishers.

Epele, Maria Esther. 2002. "Scars, Harm, and Pain: About Being Injected among Drug Using Latina Women." *Journal of Ethnicity in Substance Abuse* 1 (1): 47–69.

Epps, Kevin. 2003. *Straight Outta Hunters Point*. 75 min. USA: Mastamind Productions.

Epstein, Steven. 1996. *Impure Science: AIDS, Activism, and the Politics of Knowledge*. Berkeley: University of California Press.

Evans-Pritchard, E. E. [1937] 1976. *Witchcraft, Oracles, and Magic among the Azande*. Oxford: Clarendon Press.

Farmer, Paul. 1992. *AIDS and Accusation: Haiti and the Geography of Blame*. Berkeley: University of California Press.

————. 2003. *Pathologies of Power: Health, Human Rights, and the New War on the Poor*. Berkeley: University of California Press.

Farmer, Paul, Margaret Connors, and Janie Simmons. 1996. *Women, Poverty, and AIDS: Sex, Drugs, and Structural Violence*. Monroe, Maine: Common Courage Press.

Faubion, James D. 1993. *Modern Greek Lessons: A Primer in Historical Constructivism*. Princeton, N.J.: Princeton University Press.

Federal Office of Public Health, Confédération suisse. n.d. "Heroin-Assisted Treatment (HAT)." www.bag.admin.ch/themen/drogen/00042/00629/00798/01191/index.html?lang=en (accessed March 13, 2008).

Ferguson, James. 1990. *The Anti-Politics Machine: "Development," Depoliticization, and Bureaucratic Power in Lesotho*. Cambridge: Cambridge University Press.

———. 2006. *Global Shadows: Africa in the Neoliberal World Order*. Durham, N.C.: Duke University Press.

Ferrandiz, Francisco. Forthcoming. "Open Veins: Spirits of Violence and Grief in Venezuela." *Ethnography* 9 (3).

50 Cent. 2003. "P.I.M.P." From *Get Rich or Die Tryin'*. Shady/Aftermath/Interscope, Universal Music and Video Distribution, Santa Monica, Calif.

Fischer, Benedict, Sarah Turnbull, Blake Poland, and Emma Haydon. 2004. "Drug Use, Risk, and Urban Order: Examining Supervised Injection Sites (SIS) as 'Governmentality.'" *International Journal of Drug Policy* 15 (5–6): 357–365.

Fordham, Signithia. 1996. *Blacked Out: Dilemmas of Race, Identity, and Success at Capital High*. Chicago: University of Chicago Press.

Foucault, Michel. 1975. "Entretien sur la prison: Le livre et sa methode." *Magazine littéraire* 101:27–33.

———. 1978. *The History of Sexuality*. Translated by Robert Hurley. New York: Pantheon.

———. 1981a. *Power/Knowledge: Selected Interviews and Other Writings, 1972–1977*. New York: Pantheon/Random House.

———. [1981b] 1991. *Remarks on Marx: Conversations with Duccio Trombadori*. Translated by R. J. Goldstein and J. Cascaito. New York: Semiotext(e).

———. 1988. "Confinement, Psychiatry, Prison." In *Politics, Philosophy, Culture: Interviews and Other Writings, 1977–1984*, by Michel Foucault, edited by Lawrence Kritzman, 178–210. London: Routledge.

———. 1994. *The Birth of the Clinic: An Archaeology of Medical Perception*. Translated by A. S. Smith. New York: Vintage Books.

———. 1995. *Discipline and Punish: The Birth of the Prison*. New York: Vintage Books.

Freud, Sigmund. [1900] 1965. *The Interpretation of Dreams*. Translated by James Strachey. New York: Avon.

Gainsborough, Jenni, and Marc Mauer. 2000. *Diminishing Returns: Crime and Incarceration in the 1990s*. Washington, D.C.: The Sentencing Project. www.sentencingproject.org/pdfs/9039.pdf.

Gang Research.net. 2006a. "Who Are the Vice Lords?" www.uic.edu/orgs/kbc/ganghistory/UrbanCrisis/ViceLords/VLDiscussion.html (accessed December 6, 2006).

———. 2006b. "Youth Organizations United." http://gangresearch.net/cvl/cvlhistoryfinal/you.html (accessed December 6, 2006).

Garland, David. 1997. "'Governmentality' and the Problem of Crime: Foucault, Criminology, Sociology." *Theoretical Criminology* 1 (2): 173–214.

Gates, Henry Louis. 1988. *The Signifying Monkey: A Theory of Afro-American Literary Criticism.* New York: Oxford University Press.

Geremek, Bronislaw. 1994. *Poverty: A History.* Translated by A. Kolakowska. Oxford: Blackwell.

Gfroerer, Joseph, Michael Penne, Michael Pemberton, and Ralph Folsom. 2003. "Substance Abuse Treatment Need among Older Adults in 2020: The Impact of the Aging Baby-Boom Cohort." *Drug and Alcohol Dependence* 69 (2): 127–135.

Gilfoyle, Timothy. 2004. "'Street-Rats and Gutter-Snipes': Child Pickpockets and Street Culture in New York City, 1850–1900." *Journal of Social History* 37: 853–882.

Goldberg, Jim. 1995. *Raised by Wolves.* New York: Scalo.

Goldman, Emma. [1911] 1969. "The Traffic in Women." In *Anarchism and Other Essays,* 177–194. New York: Dover.

Golub, Andrew, and Bruce D. Johnson. 1999. "Cohort Changes in Illegal Drug Use among Arrestees in Manhattan: From the Heroin Injection Generation to the Blunts Generation." *Substance Use and Misuse* 34 (13): 1733–1763.

———. 2001. "Variation in Youthful Risks of Progression from Alcohol and Tobacco to Marijuana and to Hard Drugs across Generations." *American Journal of Public Health* 91 (2): 225–232.

Good, Mary-Jo DelVecchio, Cara James, Anne Becker, and Byron Good. 2002. "The Culture of Medicine and Racial, Ethnic, and Class Disparities in Health Care." In *Unequal Treatment: Confronting Racial and Ethnic Disparities in Health Care,* edited by Brian D. Smedley, Adrienne Y. Stith, and Alan R. Nelson, 594–625. Committee on Understanding and Eliminating Racial and Ethnic Disparities in Health Care, Institute of Medicine. Washington, D.C.: National Academies Press.

Groth, Paul Erling. 1994. *Living Downtown: The History of Residential Hotels in the United States.* Berkeley: University of California Press.

Gupta, Akhil, and James Ferguson, eds. 1997. *Anthropological Locations: Boundaries and Grounds of a Field Science.* Berkeley: University of California Press.

Guterman, Stuart. 2000. *Putting Medicare in Context: How Does the Balanced Budget Act Affect Hospitals?* Washington, D.C.: Urban Institute. www.urban.org/publications/410247.html (accessed September 17, 2008).

Hahn, Judith, Margot Kushel, David Bangsberg, Elise Riley, and Andrew Moss. 2006. "The Aging of the Homeless Population: Fourteen-Year Trends in San Francisco." *Journal of General Internal Medicine* 21 (7): 775–778.

Harper, Douglas. 2002. "Talking about Pictures: A Case for Photo Elicitation." *Visual Studies* 17:13–16.

Harris, Hobart, and David Young. 2002. "Care of Injection Drug Users with Soft Tissue Infections in San Francisco, California." *Archives of Surgery* 137 (11): 1217–1222.

Harvey, David. 2005. *A Brief History of Neoliberalism.* Oxford: Oxford University Press.

Herman, Judith Lewis. 1992. *Trauma and Recovery.* New York: Basic Books.

Hirsch, Kenneth, and Teresa Wright. 2000. "'Silent Killer' or Benign Disease? The Dilemma of Hepatitis C Virus Outcomes." *Hepatology* 31 (2): 536–537.

Hoenigman, Vince, and SPUR Homelessness Task Force. 2002. "Homelessness in a Progressive City." *San Francisco Planning and Urban Research Association Newsletter,* no. 408, 1, 3–9, 14–15.

Holmes, Seth M. 2006. "'Parce qu'ils sont plus près du sol': L'invisibilisation de la souffrance sociale des cueilleurs de baies." *Actes de la Recherche en Sciences Sociales* 165:28–51.

Hopper, Kim. 2003. *Reckoning with Homelessness.* Ithaca, N.Y.: Cornell University Press.

Hughes Brothers. 2000. *American Pimp*. Seventh Art Releasing, MGM Home Entertainment.

Human Rights Watch. 2008. *Targeting Blacks: Drug Law Enforcement and Race in the United States*. New York: Human Rights Watch. http://hrw.org/reports/2008/us0508 (accessed June 14, 2008).

Jackson, John L., Jr. 2001. *Harlem World: Doing Race and Class in Contemporary Black America*. Chicago: University of Chicago Press.

Jarrett, Robin L., and Linda M. Burton. 1999. "Dynamic Dimensions of Family Structure in Low-Income African American Families: Emergent Themes in Qualitative Research." *Journal of Comparative Family Studies* 30:177–188.

Jay-Z. 2004. "Big Pimpin'." From *Collision Course*. Warner Bros. Records, Burbank, Calif.

Johnson, Chalmers. 2004. *The Sorrows of Empire: Militarism, Secrecy, and the End of the Republic*. New York: Metropolitan Books.

Juvenile Court Department. 1975. "Annual Report." San Francisco, Calif.

Katz, Jack. 1988. *Seductions of Crime: Moral and Sensual Attractions in Doing Evil*. New York: Basic Books.

Katz, Michael. 1986. *In the Shadow of the Poorhouse: A Social History of Welfare in America*. New York: Basic Books.

Kaufman, Sharon R. 1993. *The Healer's Tale: Transforming Medicine and Culture*. Madison: University of Wisconsin Press.

Kaye, Kerwin. 2003. "Male Prostitution in the Twentieth Century: Pseudohomosexuals, Hoodlum Homosexuals, and Exploited Teens." *Journal of Homosexuality* 46 (1/2): 1–77.

Keane, Helen. 2002. *What's Wrong with Addiction?* New York: New York University Press.

Kidder, Tracy. 2003. *Mountains beyond Mountains*. New York: Random House.

Kids Count. 2002. *Children at Risk: State Trends 1990–2000; A First Look at Census 2000 Supplementary Survey Data*. Baltimore, Md.: Annie E. Casey Foundation; Washington, D.C.: Population Reference Bureau. www.eric.ed.gov/ERICDocs/data/ericdocs2sql/content_storage_01/0000019b/80/1a/57/a0.pdf (accessed October 23, 2007).

King, Ryan S. 2008. *Disparity by Geography: The War on Drugs in America's Cities*. Washington, D.C.: Sentencing Project. www.sentencingproject.org/Admin/Documents/publications/dp_drugarrestreport.pdf (accessed June 14, 2008).

Kleinman, Arthur, Veena Das, and Margaret M. Lock. 1997. *Social Suffering*. Berkeley: University of California Press.

Kleinman, Arthur, and Joan Kleinman. 1991. "Suffering and Its Professional Transformation: Toward an Ethnography of Interpersonal Experience." *Culture, Medicine, and Psychiatry* 15 (3): 275–301.

Koester, Stephen K. 1994. "Copping, Running, and Paraphernalia Laws: Contextual Variables and Needle Risk Behavior among Injection Drug Users in Denver." *Human Organization* 53 (3): 286–295.

Krieger, Nancy. 2000. "Refiguring 'Race': Epidemiology, Racialized Biology, and Biological Expressions of Race Relations." *International Journal of Health Services* 30 (1): 211–216.

Kusmer, Kenneth L. 2002. *Down and Out, On the Road: The Homeless in American History*. Oxford: Oxford University Press.

Lancaster, Roger. 1992. *Life Is Hard: Machismo, Danger, and the Intimacy of Power in Nicaragua*. Berkeley: University of California Press.

Lander, J. 1990. "Fallacies and Phobias about Addiction and Pain." *British Journal of Addiction* 85:803–809.

Lawrence, Sarah, and Jeremy Travis. 2004. *The New Landscape of Imprisonment: Mapping America's Prison Expansion.* Washington, D.C.: Urban Institute Justice Policy Center. www.urban .org/url.cfm?ID=410994 (accessed October 23, 2007).

Leri, Francesco, Robert E. Sorge, Erin Cummins, David Woehrling, James G. Pfaus, and Jane Stewart. 2007. "High-Dose Methadone Maintenance in Rats: Effects on Cocaine Self-Administration and Behavioral Side Effects." *Neuropsychopharmacology* 32:2290–2300.

Levi, Primo. 1988. *The Drowned and the Saved.* Translated by Raymond Rosenthal. New York: Summit Books.

———. 1996. *If This Is a Man: Remembering Auschwitz. A 3-in-1 Volume (Survival in Auschwitz, The Reawakening, Moments of Reprieve).* Translated by Stuart Woolf. New York: Vintage.

Levinas, Emmanuel. 1998. *Entre Nous: On Thinking-of-the-Other.* Translated by Michael B. Smith and Barbara Harshav. New York: Columbia University Press.

Levine, Lawrence W. 1977. *Black Culture and Black Consciousness: Afro-American Folk Thought from Slavery to Freedom.* New York: Oxford University Press.

Litwack, Leon F. 2000. "Hellhounds." In *Without Sanctuary: Lynching Photography in America,* by Hilton Als, John Lewis, and Leon F. Litwack, edited by James Allen, 8–37. Santa Fe, N.M.: Twin Palms Publishers.

Lovell, Anne M. 2006. "Addiction Markets: The Case of High-Dose Buprenorphine in France." In *Global Pharmaceuticals: Ethics, Markets, Practices,* edited by Adriana Petryna, Andrew Lakoff, and Arthur Kleinman, 136–170. Durham, N.C.: Duke University Press.

Lupton, Deborah. 1995. *The Imperative of Health: Public Health and the Regulated Body.* London: Sage.

Lyon-Callo, Vincent. 2004. *Inequality, Poverty, and Neoliberal Governance: Activist Ethnography in the Homeless Sheltering Industry.* Peterborough, Ontario: Broadview Press.

MacLeod, Jay. 1987. *Ain't No Makin' It: Leveled Aspirations in a Low-Income Neighborhood.* Boulder, Colo.: Westview Press.

Maharidge, Dale. 1996. *Journey to Nowhere: The Saga of the New Underclass.* New York: Hyperion.

Marcus, Anthony. 2005. *Where Have All the Homeless Gone? The Making and Unmaking of a Crisis.* New York: Berghahn Books.

Marset, Miguel. 2005. "Le PEPS: 10 Ans Déjà." Paper presented at the "Portes ouvertes" conference, Geneva, September 26. Département de psychiatrie, Service d'abus de substances, Hôpitaux universitaires de Genève.

Martin, Thomas J., Michael Coller, Conchita Co, and James E. Smith. 2007. "Mu-Opioid Receptor Alkylation in the Ventral Pallidum and Ventral Tegmental Area, But Not in the Nucleus Accumbens, Attenuates the Effects of Heroin on Cocaine Self-Administration in Rats." *Neuropsychopharmacology,* advance online publication, June 20. http://dx.doi.org/10.1038/sj.npp .1301490 (accessed January 4, 2008).

Marx, Karl. [1852] 1963. *The Eighteenth Brumaire of Louis Bonaparte.* Translated by C. P. Dutt. New York: International Publishers.

Marx, Karl, and Friedrich Engels. [1848] 2002. *The Communist Manifesto.* London: Penguin Books.

Mauss, Marcel. [1924] 1990. *The Gift: The Form and Reason for Exchange in Archaic Societies.* Translated by W. Halls. London: Routledge.

———. 1936. "Les techniques du corps." *Journal de psychologie* 32 (3–4): 365–386.

Mayhew, Henry, and Others. [1861] 2005. *The London Underworld in the Victorian Period: Authentic First-Person Accounts by Beggars, Thieves and Prostitutes*. Mineola, N.Y.: Dover Publications.

McCord, C., and H. P. Freeman. 1990. "Excess Mortality in Harlem." *New England Journal of Medicine* 322 (3): 173–177.

Mead, Margaret. 1970. "Fieldwork in the Pacific Islands, 1925–1967." In *Women in the Field: Anthropological Experiences*, edited by P. Golde, 293–331. Chicago: Aldine.

Melhuus, Marit, and Kristi Anne Stolen. 1996. "Introduction." In *Machos, Mistresses, Madonnas: Contesting the Power of Latin American Gender Imagery*, edited by Marit Melhuus and Kristi Anne Stolen, 1–33. New York: Verso.

Messerschmidt, James W. 1993. *Masculinities and Crime: Critique and Reconceptualization of Theory*. Lanham, Md.: Rowman and Littlefield.

———. 1997. *Crime as Structured Action: Gender, Race, Class, and Crime in the Making*. Thousand Oaks, Calif.: Sage.

Military Analysis Network. 1998. "Hunters Point Naval Shipyard, San Francisco Naval Shipyard." Federation of American Scientists. www.fas.org/man/company/shipyard/hunters_point.htm (accessed July 25, 2005).

Mitchell, W. J. T. 1994. *Picture Theory*. Chicago: University of Chicago Press.

Moore, David. 2004. "Governing Street-Based Injecting Drug Users: A Critique of Heroin Overdose Prevention in Australia." *Social Science and Medicine* 59 (7): 1547–1557.

Moss, A. R., and J. A. Hahn. 1999. "Invited Commentary: Needle Exchange—No Help for Hepatitis?" *American Journal of Epidemiology* 149 (3): 214–216.

Nader, Laura. 1997. "The Phantom Factor: Impact of the Cold War on Anthropology." In *The Cold War and the University: Toward an Intellectual History of the Postwar Years*, by Noam Chomsky, Ira Katznelson, R. C. Lewontin, David Montgomery, Laura Nader, Richard Ohmann, Ray Siever, Immanuel Wallerstein, and Howard Zinn, 107–146. New York: New Press.

National Consensus Development Panel. 1998. "Effective Medical Treatment of Opiate Addiction." *Journal of the American Medical Association* 280 (22): 1936–1943.

National Institute of Diabetes and Digestive and Kidney Diseases. 2003. *Chronic Hepatitis C: Current Disease Management*. Bethesda, Md.: National Institutes of Health.

National Low Income Housing Coalition. 2006. *Out of Reach 2006*. www.nlihc.org/oor/oor2006/ ?CFID=21326798&CFTOKEN=73538490 (accessed December 5, 2007).

New York Times. 1983. June 2. "San Francisco Fire Raises Anxiety on Old Devices with PCBs," B9.

———. 2003. January 22. Edmund Andrews, "Economic Equality Grew in 90's Boom, Fed Reports," C1, C7.

———. 2003. April 18. Erica Goode, "Certain Words Can Trip Up AIDS Grants."

———. 2003. November 14. Fox Butterfield, "Study Calls California Parole System a $1 Billion Failure," A24.

———. 2004. July 11. Mireya Navarro, "Experts in Sex Field Say Conservatives Interfere with Health and Research," A16.

———. 2005. November 18. Juan Forero, "Cocaine Prices Rise and Quality Declines, White House Says," A14.

———. 2006. October 15. Eduardo Porter, "After Years of Growth, What about Workers' Share?" B3.

———. 2006. October 25. David Leonhardt, "Voters Weigh Plentiful Jobs vs. Scant Pay," B1, B5.

———. 2006. December 11. Jennifer Steinhauer, "Bulging, Troubled Prisons Push California Officials to Seek a New Approach," A18.

———. 2007. February 23. Randal Archibold, "'Dumping' of Homeless by Hospitals Stirs Debate," A12.

———. 2008. February 4. Thom Shanker, "Proposed Military Spending Is Highest since WWII," A10.

New York Times Magazine. 2003. August 3. Benoit Denizet-Lewis, "Double Lives on the Down Low." http://query.nytimes.com/gst/fullpage.html?res=9F0CE0D6IE3FF930A3575BC0A 9659C8B63 (accessed September 17, 2008).

Okin, Robert L., Alicia Boccellari, Francisca Azocar, Martha Shumway, Kathy O'Brien, Alan Gelb, Michael Kohn, Phyillis Harding, and Christine Wachsmuth. 2000. "The Effects of Clinical Case Management on Hospital Service Use among ED Frequent Users." *American Journal of Emergency Medicine* 18 (5): 603–608.

Orwell, George. [1937] 1972. *The Road to Wigan Pier.* San Diego: Harcourt Brace Jovanovich.

Padilla, Mark, Ernesto Vasquez del Aguila, and Richard Parker. 2006. "Globalization, Structural Violence, and LGBT Health: A Cross-Cultural Perspective." In *The Health of Sexual Minorities: Public Health Perspectives on Lesbian, Gay, Bisexual, and Transgender Populations,* edited by Ilan H. Meyer and Mary E. Northridge, 209–241. New York: Springer.

Paras, Eric. 2006. *Foucault 2.0: Beyond Power and Knowledge.* New York: Other Press.

Parker, Andrew. 1993. "Unthinking Sex: Marx, Engels, and the Scene of Writing." In *Fear of a Queer Planet: Queer Politics and Social Theory,* edited by Michael Warner, 19–41. Minneapolis: University of Minnesota Press.

Parker, Karen F., and Matthew V. Pruitt. 2000. "Poverty, Poverty Concentration, and Homicide." *Social Science Quarterly* 81 (2): 555–570.

Passaro, Joanne. 1996. *The Unequal Homeless: Men on the Streets, Women in Their Place.* New York: Routledge.

Pateman, Carole C. 1999. "What's Wrong with Prostitution?" *Women's Studies Quarterly* 27 (1–2): 53–64.

Patterson, Orlando. 1998. *Rituals of Blood: Consequences of Slavery in Two American Centuries.* Washington, D.C.: Civitas/CounterPoint.

Pearson, Charles, and Philippe Bourgois. 1995. "Hope to Die a Dope Fiend." *Cultural Anthropology* 10 (4): 1–7.

Perneger, Thomas V., Francisco Giner, Miguel del Rio, and Annie Mino. 1998. "Randomised Trial of Heroin Maintenance Programme for Addicts Who Fail in Conventional Drug Treatments." *British Medical Journal* 317:13–18.

Petersen, Alan. 1997. "Risk, Governance, and the New Public Health." In *Foucault, Health, and Medicine,* edited by Alan Petersen and Robin Bunton, 188–206. London: Routledge.

Petryna, Adriana. 2002. *Life Exposed: Biological Citizens after Chernobyl.* Princeton, N.J.: Princeton University Press.

Pettit, Becky, and Bruce Western. 2004. "Mass Imprisonment and the Life Course: Race and Class Inequality in U.S. Incarceration." *American Sociological Review* 69 (2): 151–169.

Pine, Adrienne. 2008. *Working Hard, Drinking Hard: On Violence and Survival in Honduras.* Berkeley: University of California Press.

Poole, Deborah. 2005. "An Excess of Description: Ethnography, Race, and Visual Technologies." *Annual Review of Anthropology* 34:159–179.

Price, David H. 2004. *Threatening Anthropology: McCarthyism and the FBI's Surveillance of Activist Anthropologists*. Durham, N.C.: Duke University Press.

Public Safety Performance Project. 2008. *One in 100: Behind Bars in America 2008*. Pew Center on the States, Washington, D.C. www.pewcenteronthestates.org/report_detail.aspx?id=35904.

Quigley, John, Steven Raphael, Eugene Smolensky, Erin Mansur, and Larry A. Rosenthal. 2001. *Homelessness in California*. San Francisco: Public Policy Institute of California.

Reed, Deborah. 2004. "Recent Trends in Income and Poverty." *California Counts: Population Trends and Profiles* 5 (3): 1–15.

Rhodes, Lorna A. 1990. "Studying Biomedicine as a Cultural System." In *Medical Anthropology: A Handbook of Theory and Method,* edited by Thomas M. Johnson and Carolyn F. Sargent, 159–173. New York: Greenwood Press.

———. 1991. *Emptying Beds: The Work of an Emergency Psychiatric Unit*. Berkeley: University of California Press.

Rich, Josiah D., Brian P. Dickinson, John M. Carney, Alvan Fisher, and Robert Heimer. 1998. "Detection of HIV-1 Nucleic Acid and HIV-1 Antibodies in Needles and Syringes Used for Non-Intravenous Injection." *AIDS* 12 (17): 2345–2350.

Richards, Eugene. 1994. *Cocaine True, Cocaine Blue*. New York: Aperture.

Riis, Jacob A. 1890. *How the Other Half Lives: Studies among the Tenements of New York*. New York: Charles Scribner's Sons.

Rose, Lionel. 1988. *"Rogues and Vagabonds": Vagrant Underworld in Britain, 1815–1985*. London: Routledge.

Rose, Nikolas. 1999. *Powers of Freedom: Reframing Political Thought*. Cambridge: Cambridge University Press.

Rosenbaum, Marsha, Allyson Washburn, Kelly Knight, Margaret Kelley, and Jeanette Irwin. 1996. "Treatment as Harm Reduction, Defunding as Harm Maximization: The Case of Methadone Maintenance." *Journal of Psychoactive Drugs* 28 (3): 241–249.

Roy, Élise, Éva Nonn, Nancy Haley, and Joseph Cox. 2007. "Hepatitis C Meanings and Preventive Strategies among Street-Involved Young Injection Drug Users in Montréal." *International Journal of Drug Policy* 18 (5): 397–405.

Rubin, Gayle. 1984. "Thinking Sex: Notes for a Radical Theory of the Politics of Sexuality." In *Pleasure and Danger: Exploring Female Sexuality,* edited by Carole S. Vance, 267–319. Boston: Routledge and Kegan Paul.

Sahlins, Peter D. 1987. "America's Permanent Housing Problem." In *Housing America's Poor,* edited by Peter D. Sahlins, 1–13. Chapel Hill: University of North Carolina Press.

Said, Edward. 1989. "Representing the Colonized: Anthropology's Interlocutors." *Critical Inquiry* 15 (2): 205–225.

Sandweiss, Martha. 2002. *Print the Legend: Photography and the American West*. New Haven: Yale University Press.

San Francisco Board of Supervisors. 2002. *San Francisco Housing Databook*. San Francisco: Bay Area Economics.

San Francisco Chronicle. 1983. May 16. Reginald Smith and Bill Soiffer, "Big PG&E Explosion; S.F. Highrise Shut," A1, A18.

———. 1996. April 17. Glen Martin, "Judge Dismisses More than 39,000 Matrix Charges; S.F. Trying for 'Kinder' Action on Homeless," A13.

———. 1997. November 8. Alex Barnum, "Police Chief Defends Helicopter Searches," A15.

———. 1999. May 5. William C. Brady, "Less Care for Sick Poor," A21.

———. 1999. September 21. John Wildermuth, "S.F. Voters Upset Most about the Homeless," A1.

———. 2000. April 28. Jonathan Curiel, "Slice of Heaven: Former 'Highrise from Hell' Residents Open New Door," A23.

———. 2003. October 30. Sabin Russell, "Controversial AIDS Grants under Review; Conservatives Accused of Providing 'Hit List,'" A4.

———. 2004. March 21. Kevin Fagan, "Shame of the City: The Missing Homeless; Desperate Search for Bridget—Sister, Mother, Addict," A1.

———. 2008. January 15. Cecilia M. Vega, "Guns, Crack Cocaine Fuel Homicides in S.F.; 98 Killings in 2007," B1.

San Francisco Community Clinic Consortium. 2004. "Street Outreach Services (SOS)." http://sfccc .org/sos/ (accessed January 6, 2006).

San Francisco Examiner. 1997. March 26. Gregory Lewis and Zachary Coile, "Mayor: Lease Homeless Camps," A1.

———. 1997. March 31. "Survey Results," A5.

San Francisco Independent. 1997. October 21. Johnny Brannon, "Mayor Signals New Get-Tough Policy," 1, 5.

Scheper-Hughes, Nancy. 1989. "Death without Weeping; Has Poverty Ravaged Mother Love in the Shantytowns of Brazil?" *Natural History,* 98 (10): 8–16.

———. 1992. *Death without Weeping: The Violence of Everyday Life in Brazil.* Berkeley: University of California Press.

———. 1996. "Small Wars and Invisible Genocides." *Social Science and Medicine* 43 (5): 889–900.

Scheper-Hughes, Nancy, and Philippe Bourgois. 2004. "Introduction: Making Sense of Violence." In *Violence in War and Peace: An Anthology,* edited by Nancy Scheper-Hughes and Philippe Bourgois, 1–27. Oxford: Blackwell.

Schifter, Jacobo. 1999. *Macho Love: Sex behind Bars in Central America.* Binghamton, N.Y.: Haworth Hispanic/Latino Press.

Schonberg, Jeff, and Philippe Bourgois. 2002. "The Politics of Photographic Aesthetics: Critically Documenting the HIV Epidemic among Heroin Injectors in Russia and the United States." *International Journal of Drug Policy* 13 (5): 387–392.

Seidman, Steven, ed. 1996. *Queer Theory/Sociology.* Oxford: Blackwell.

Sekula, Allan. 1989. "The Body and the Archive." In *The Contest of Meaning: Critical Histories of Photography,* edited by Richard Bolton, 342–389. Cambridge, Mass.: MIT Press.

Self, Robert O. 2003. "California's Industrial Garden: Oakland and the East Bay in the Age of Deindustrialization." In *Beyond the Ruins: The Meanings of Deindustrialization,* edited by Jefferson Cowie and Joseph Heathcott, 159–180. Ithaca, N.Y.: ILR Press.

———. 2005. *American Babylon: Race and the Struggle for Postwar Oakland.* Princeton, N.J.: Princeton University Press.

Sentencing Project. 2006. "New Incarceration Figures: Growth in Population Continues." www.sentencingproject.org/pdfs/1044.pdf (accessed March 13, 2008).

Shavelson, Lonny. 2001. *Hooked: Five Addicts Challenge Our Misguided Drug Rehab System*. New York: New Press.

Shumway, Martha, Alicia Boccellari, Kathy O'Brien, and Robert L. Okin. 2008. "Cost-Effectiveness of Clinical Case Management for ED Frequent Users: Results of a Randomized Trial?" *American Journal of Emergency Medicine* 26 (2): 155–164.

Snow, David, and Leon Anderson. 1993. *Down on Their Luck: A Study of Homeless Street People*. Berkeley: University of California Press.

Spargo, Tamsin. 1999. *Foucault and Queer Theory (Postmodern Encounters)*. New York: Totem Books.

Stack, Carol B. 1974. *All Our Kin: Strategies for Survival in a Black Community*. New York: Harper and Row.

Stallybrass, Peter. 1990. "Marx and Heterogeneity: Thinking the Lumpenproletariat." *Representations* 31:69–95.

Stallybrass, Peter, and Allon White. 1986. *The Politics and Poetics of Transgression*. Ithaca, N.Y.: Cornell University Press.

State of California, Little Hoover Commission. 2003. *Back to the Community: Safe & Sound Parole Policies*. www.lhc.ca.gov/lhcdir/report172.html (accessed March 8, 2004).

Steinberg, Paul. 2000. *Speak You Also: A Survivor's Reckoning*. Translated by Linda Coverdale. New York: Metropolitan Books/Henry Holt.

Sternlieb, George, and David Listokin. 1987. "A Review of National Housing Policy." In *Housing America's Poor*, edited by Peter D. Sahlins, 14–44. Chapel Hill: University of North Carolina Press.

Stevens, Evelyn P. 1973. "Marianismo: The Other Face of Machismo in Latin America." In *Female and Male in Latin America: Essays*, edited by Ann Pescatello, 89–102. Pittsburgh: University of Pittsburgh Press.

Stocking, George W. 1992. *The Ethnographer's Magic and Other Essays in the History of Anthropology*. Madison: University of Wisconsin Press.

Stonington, Scott, and Seth M. Holmes, eds. 2006. "Social Medicine in the Twenty-First Century." Special issue. *PLoS Medicine* 3 (10). http://medicine.plosjournals.org/perlserv/?request=get-toc&issn=1549-1676&volume=3&issue=10 (accessed October 24, 2007).

Strathern, Marilyn. 2000. *Audit Cultures: Anthropological Studies in Accountability, Ethics, and the Academy*. New York: Routledge.

Substance Abuse Research Center. n.d. "Oral History Interviews with Substance Abuse Researchers." University of Michigan. www.sitemaker.umich.edu/substance.abuse.history/oral_history_interviews&mode=single&recordID=1894364&nextMode=list (accessed March 13, 2008).

Tabet, Paola. 1987. "Du don au tarif: Les relations sexuelles impliquant une compensation." *Les temps modernes* 490: 1–53.

Tagg, John. 1988. *The Burden of Representation: Essays on Photographies and Histories*. Amherst: University of Massachusetts Press.

Taussig, Michael. 1980. "Reification and the Consciousness of the Patient." *Social Science and Medicine* 14B (1): 3–13.

———. 1984. "Culture of Terror–Space of Death: Roger Casement's Putumayo Report and the Explanation of Torture." *Comparative Studies in Society and History* 26 (3): 467–497.

———. 1992. *The Nervous System*. New York: Routledge.

Thompson, E. P. 1966. *The Making of the English Working Class*. New York: Vintage Books.

Thorne-Lyman, Abby, and Sarah Treuhaft. 2003. "Bay Area Neighborhood Commercial Districts: A Pilot Study." www-iurd.ced.berkeley.edu/cci/publications/Abby-Thorne-Lyman-NH-Retail-Findings-Spring2003.pdf (accessed October 24, 2007).

Todd, Knox H., Christi Deaton, Anne P. D'Adamo, and Leon Goe. 2000. "Ethnicity and Analgesic Practice." *Annals of Emergency Medicine* 35 (1): 11–16.

Trotz, Marc. 2005. "Direct Access to Housing: A Project of the San Francisco Department of Public Health." National Alliance to End Homelessness. http://naeh.org/content/article/detail/1116 (accessed June 11, 2008).

Turner, William. 2000. *A Genealogy of Queer Theory*. Philadelphia: Temple University Press.

Tyndall, Mark W., Evan Wood, Ruth Zhang, Calvin Lai, Julio S. G. Montaner, and Thomas Kerr. 2006. "HIV Seroprevalence among Participants at a Supervised Injection Facility in Vancouver, Canada: Implications for Prevention, Care, and Treatment." *Harm Reduction Journal* 3:36. doi:10.1186/1477-7517-3-36. www.harmreductionjournal.com/content/3/1/36 (accessed January 3, 2009).

Uchtenhagen, Ambros. 1997. *Essais de prescription médicale de stupéfiants*. Zürich: Institut für Suchtforschung, University of Zurich.

United Nations Development Programme. 2006. *Human Development Report*. New York: Palgrave Macmillan.

U.S. Bureau of the Census. 1991. *1990 Census of Population and Housing*. www.census.gov/main/www/cen1990.html (accessed January 19, 2007).

———. 2001. *Money Income in the United States, 2000*. Current Population Reports: Consumer Income, P60–213. By Carmen DeNavas-Walt, Robert W. Cleveland, and Marc I. Roemer. Washington, D.C.: U.S. Government Printing Office. www.census.gov/prod/2001pubs/p60-213.pdf (accessed December 7, 2007).

———. 2002. *2000 Census of Population and Housing*. Washington, D.C.: U.S. Government Printing Office. www.census.gov/prod/cen2000/index.html (accessed December 7, 2007).

van den Brink, Wim, Vincent M. Hendriks, Peter Blanken, Maarten W. Koeter, Barbara J. van Zwieten, and Jan M. van Ree. 2003. "Medical Prescription of Heroin to Treatment Resistant Heroin Addicts: Two Randomised Controlled Trials." *British Medical Journal* 327:310–315.

Vergara, Camilo. 1991a. "Lessons Learned, Lessons Forgotten: Rebuilding New York City's Poor Communities." *The Livable City* 15 (1): 3–9.

———. 1991b. "The View from the Shelters: New York's New Ghettos." *The Nation* 252 (23): 804–810.

———. n.d. *Invincible Cities*. Mid-Atlantic Regional Center for the Humanities at Rutgers-Camden. http://invinciblecities.camden.rutgers.edu/intro.html (accessed November 2, 2006).

Wacquant, Loïc. 1998. "Inside the Zone: The Social Art of the Hustler in the Black American Ghetto." *Theory, Culture, and Society* 15:1–36.

———. 2001a. "Deadly Symbiosis: When Prison and Ghetto Meet and Mesh." *Punishment and Society* 3 (1): 95–134.

———. 2001b. "The Penalisation of Poverty and the Rise of Neo-Liberalism." *European Journal on Criminal Policy and Research* 9:401–412.

———. 2005. "Habitus." In *International Encyclopedia of Economic Sociology*, edited by Jens Beckert and Milan Zafirovski, 315–319. London: Routledge.

———. 2007. *Deadly Symbiosis: Race and the Rise of Neoliberal Penalty.* Cambridge: Polity Press.

———. 2009. *Punishing the Poor: The Neoliberal Government of Social Inequality.* Durham, N.C.: Duke University Press.

Walker, David. 1990. "The Political Economy of the San Francisco Bay Area in the 1980s." In *Fire in the Hearth: The Radical Politics of Place in America,* edited by Mike Davis, Steven Hiatt, Marie Kennedy, Susan Ruddick, and Michael Sprinker, 3–82. New York: Verso.

Walker, Kara. 2007–2008. "My Complement, My Enemy, My Oppressor, My Love." Exhibit at the Whitney Museum of American Art. New York, October 11, 2007–February 3, 2008. www.whitney.org/www/exhibition/kara_walker/index.html (accessed February 9, 2008).

Wallace, Michele. 1979. *Black Macho and the Myth of the Superwoman.* London: John Calder.

Wallace, Rodrick. 1990. "Urban Desertification, Public Health, and Public Disorder. 'Planned Shrinkage,' Violent Death, Substance Abuse and AIDS in the Bronx." *Social Science and Medicine* 31 (7): 801–813.

Wardlow, Holly. 2004. "Anger, Economy, and Female Agency: Problematizing 'Prostitution' and 'Sex Work' among the Huli of Papua New Guinea." *Signs: Journal of Women in Culture and Society* 29 (4): 1017–1040.

Willis, Paul. 1981. *Learning to Labor: How Working Class Kids Get Working Class Jobs.* New York: Columbia University Press.

Wlodarczyk, Dan, and Margaret Wheeler. 2006. "The Home Visit/Mobile Outreach." In *Medical Management of Vulnerable and Underserved Patients: Principles, Practice and Populations,* edited by Talmadge E. King Jr., Margaret B. Wheeler, Andrew B. Bindman, Alicia Fernandez, Kevin Grumbach, Dean Schillinger, and Teresa Villela, 111–120. London: McGraw-Hill Medical.

Wojcicki, Janet Maia. 2002. "Commercial Sex Work or *Ukuphanda?* Sex-for-Money Exchange in Soweto and Hammanskraal Area, South Africa." *Culture, Medicine and Psychiatry* 26 (3): 339–370.

Wolf, Eric R. 1982. *Europe and the People without History.* Berkeley: University of California Press.

Wolf, Eric R., and Joseph Jorgensen. 1970. "Anthropology on the Warpath in Thailand." *New York Review of Books* 15, no. 9, 26–35. November 19.

Wollstonecraft, Mary. 1790. *A Vindication of the Rights of Men, in a Letter to the Right Honourable Edmund Burke, occasioned by his Reflections on the Revolution in France.* London: J. Johnson. http://oll.libertyfund.org/title/991 (accessed June 19, 2008).

Wooden, Wayne S., and Jay Parker. 1982. *Men behind Bars: Sexual Exploitation in Prison.* New York: Plenum Press.

Wright, Erik Olin. 2004. "Patterns of Job Expansion in Developed Capitalist Economies: Some Preliminary Descriptive Results." Paper presented at Network on the Effects of Inequality on Economic Performance, October 8, Cambridge, Mass.

Zelizer, Viviana A. Rotman. 2005. *The Purchase of Intimacy.* Princeton, N.J.: Princeton University Press.

Acknowledgments

Over the twelve years of our fieldwork, we were assisted by seven additional ethnographers: Maxwell Burton, Dan Ciccarone, Mark Lettiere, Ann Magruder, Joelle Morrow, Charles Pearson, and Jim Quesada. We did not include their names in the text so as not to confuse readers with too many characters; instead, we occasionally refer to "members of the ethnographic team" when drawing on events they documented.

Our collaboration with Charles and Mark was the most intensive. Charles first brought Philippe to a homeless encampment on Edgewater Boulevard in November 1994 and worked on the project until the spring of 1995. Excerpts from his fieldnotes and tape recordings were especially useful in the first chapter for detailing daily life before the white flight episode, as well as in several sections of the chapters on employment and families.

Mark worked on the project from spring 1996 to spring 1998. Excerpts from his tape recordings (and to a lesser extent from his fieldnotes) contributed to at least two dozen conversations and descriptions reported in the text. His material focused on constructions of gender, racial tensions, violence, illegal income-generating strategies, and life histories.

The materials collected by Joelle, Ann, and Jim contributed to some half dozen descriptions of events in the book. Maxwell shared with us his knowledge of San Francisco streets and corrected some of our interpretations of events and street terms. Dan Ciccarone's ethnographic contribution drew on his experience as a medical doctor working with heroin injectors. He not only treated the Edgewater homeless in their encampments and visited them in the hospital but also took a half dozen sets of fieldnotes and served as our consultant on medical issues and epidemiological and clinical methods throughout the second half of the project. We consulted with several additional quantitative research colleagues at the University of California, San Francisco, including Andrew Moss, Brian Edlin, Alex Kral, Judy Hahn, Paula Lum, Peter Davidson, and Jennifer Evans.

We thank the many clinicians at San Francisco General Hospital and in the Department of Public Health's community-based clinics who provide outstanding services to the homeless (especially the medical residents who work in the primary care program directed by Margaret Wheeler). Doctors Michelle Schneiderman and especially Daniel Wlodarczyk earned our admiration for saving the lives of several of the main characters in this book. During the final years of our fieldwork, Josh Bamberger, the medical director of Housing and Urban Health in the Department of Public Health, arranged for permanent housing for several of the homeless individuals who appear in these pages.

Rob Borofsky convinced us to sign a book contract before we thought we were ready, and we are grateful for that impetus. We thank Naomi Schneider at University of California Press for supporting this project since its inception as part of the public anthropology series. Mary Renaud indefatigably copyedited a challenging multivoiced manuscript, and Dore Brown graciously coordinated all aspects of production. We truly appreciate Nola Burger's dedication to creating the design and layout of the photographs and text. Javier Auyero and João Biehl provided useful detailed comments that helped reshape the book. Laurie Hart deserves to be a co-author; her edits and restructuring of our theoretical analysis were invaluable.

We are especially thankful to Ann Magruder, who coded, organized, and reviewed notes and transcripts and sat side by side with us to type the first drafts. Additional heavy lifting (typing, editing, formatting, and yet more editing) was performed by Emi Bretschneider, Xarene Eskandar, David Hess, Jesse Davies-Kessler, Joelle Morrow, Mary Katherine Sheena, Lisa Lisanti, and Mimi Kirk. Zoe Marquardt vetted final copy edits; Fernando Montero Castrillo incorporated the last set of edits, fact-checked, revamped the bibliography, and coordinated the preliminary submission of the photos and files with remarkable elegance, patience, clarity, and good cheer. Last-minute emergency help was provided by Emiliano Bourgois-Chacon, Nick Iacobelli, and Ross Lerner.

This project was primarily funded by National Institutes of Health (NIH) grant DA10164, which was initially shepherded by Richard Needle, Susan Coyle, Nick Kozel, and especially Mike Agar. The grant subsequently was expertly guided for ten years at the NIH by Elizabeth Lambert, with additional help from Jacques Normand and Angela Pattatucci Aragón. We also received funds from N01-DA-3-5201, DA-263-MD-519210, the California University AIDS Research Program (UARP) R99-SF-052, the Russell Sage Foundation 87–03–04, the National Endowment for the Humanities RA-20229, two NIH diversity supplements, the Wenner Gren Trustee Program, the President's Office at the University of Pennsylvania (through a Richard Perry University Professorship), and the Institute for Advanced Study in Princeton. The collection of comparative background and historical data was supported by California HIV/AIDS Research Program ID-06-SF194, UARP R99-SF-115, Center for Substance Abuse Treatment H79-TI12103, the Office of AIDS at the California Department of Health Services (SYNC Project 06–55787), the Social Science Research Council, the Ford Foundation, and the Harry Frank Guggenheim Foundation, as well as NIH grants DA06413, DA012803, DA010164, DA016165, DA09532, DA013245, DA016159, DA017389, DA021627, NR08324, MH054907, MH078743, and MH064388. The analysis presented in this book does not necessarily represent the views of the funders.

Above all, we thank the Edgewater homeless for allowing us into their lives.

Index

California Series in Public Anthropology

The California Series in Public Anthropology emphasizes the anthropologist's role as an engaged intellectual. It continues anthropology's commitment to being an ethnographic witness, to describing, in human terms, how life is lived beyond the borders of many readers' experiences. But it also adds a commitment, through ethnography, to reframing the terms of public debate—transforming received, accepted understandings of social issues with new insights, new framings.

Series Editor: Robert Borofsky (Hawaii Pacific University)　**Contributing Editors:** Philippe Bourgois (University of Pennsylvania), Paul Farmer (Partners in Health), Alex Hinton (Rutgers University), Carolyn Nordstrom (University of Notre Dame), and Nancy Scheper-Hughes (UC Berkeley)　**University of California Press Editor:** Naomi Schneider